Communication in the
Age of Trump

POLITICAL COMMUNICATION

FRONTIERS IN

Mitchell S. McKinney and Mary E. Stuckey
General Editors

Vol. 39

The Frontiers in Political Communication series
is part of the Peter Lang Media and Communication list.
Every volume is peer reviewed and meets
the highest quality standards for content and production.

PETER LANG
New York • Bern • Berlin
Brussels • Vienna • Oxford • Warsaw

Communication in the Age of Trump

Edited by Arthur S. Hayes

PETER LANG
New York • Bern • Berlin
Brussels • Vienna • Oxford • Warsaw

Library of Congress Cataloging-in-Publication Data

Names: Hayes, Arthur S., editor.
Title: Communication in the age of Trump / edited by Arthur S. Hayes.
Description: New York: Peter Lang, 2018.
Series: Frontiers in political communication; vol. 39 | ISSN 1525-9730
Includes bibliographical references and index.
Identifiers: LCCN 2018019043 | ISBN 978-1-4331-5030-2 (hardback: alk. paper)
ISBN 978-1-4331-5031-9 (paperback: alk. paper)
ISBN 978-1-4331-5032-6 (ebook pdf) | ISBN 978-1-4331-5033-3 (epub)
ISBN 978-1-4331-5034-0 (mobi)
Subjects: LCSH: Communication in politics—United States.
Press and politics—United States. | Mass media—Political aspects—United States.
Trump, Donald, 1946–.
Classification: LCC JA85.2.U6 C646 2018 | DDC 320.97301/4—dc23
LC record available at https://lccn.loc.gov/2018019043
DOI 10.3726/b12017

Bibliographic information published by **Die Deutsche Nationalbibliothek**.
Die Deutsche Nationalbibliothek lists this publication in the "Deutsche
Nationalbibliografie"; detailed bibliographic data are available
on the Internet at http://dnb.d-nb.de/.

The paper in this book meets the guidelines for permanence and durability
of the Committee on Production Guidelines for Book Longevity
of the Council of Library Resources.

© 2018 Peter Lang Publishing, Inc., New York
29 Broadway, 18th floor, New York, NY 10006
www.peterlang.com

Printed in the United States of America

Contents

Figures

Tables

Introduction

ARTHUR S. HAYES

Franklin Delano Roosevelt used radio fireside chats to connect with millions of Americans (Levin, 2008, p. 109). The highly articulate and telegenic John F. Kennedy was dubbed the first TV president (Walsh, 2013). Ronald Reagan, the so-called Great Communicator, had a conversational way of speaking to the common man (Nunberg, 2004) and the Federal Communication Commission (FCC) pursued a radical deregulation agenda under President Reagan's watch (Sterling, n.d.). Bill Clinton left his mark on media industries by championing and signing the landmark Telecommunication Act of 1996 into law (McCabe, 2016). Barack Obama was the first social media presidential campaigner and president (Eilperin, 2015). And now there is President Donald J. Trump.

Presidential candidates, particularly successful ones, and presidents can directly and indirectly alter the political communication landscape by reshaping the norms of voters' expectations, by their use of rhetoric and communication technologies, by the laws and policies they champion and the legal responses to their communicative practices and policies and by mainstream journalism's response to presidents and presidential hopefuls. Moreover, as Kevin Coe (2016) argued in summing up research on presidential rhetoric, the role of the president has "become less about being head of state and more about being a constant campaigner for public attention and support." *New York Times* media columnist David Carr's (2008) did not predict the rise of Trump, but his assessment about the social media's potential as a political communication tool when he wrote about Obama's capitalization of social media now seems prescient.

> The juxtaposition of a networked, open-source campaign and a historically imperial office will have profound implications and raise significant questions. Special-interest groups and lobbyists will now contend with an environment of

transparency and a president who owes them nothing. The news media will now contend with an administration that can take its case directly to its base without even booking time on the networks.

As a political campaigner and now as President, Trump has been a political communication phenomenon. Thus, one can argue that communication and media scholars are particularly well positioned to make sense of Trump's unconventional candidacy and presidency because so much of what has made him so dramatically different from his predecessors has been about communication—his experience in reality TV, what he has said to voters, how he has said it, how he has used Twitter to convey his political messages and how the news media and voters have interpreted and responded to his public words and persona. Concisely, that is the rationale behind this collection of studies and essays. Here, 21 communication and media scholars apply agenda setting, parasocial interaction relationship, and media representation of race, press criticism, political economy, and political rhetorical and ethical theories along with legal and textual analyses to assess the Trump phenomenon. Their works cover the presidential campaign and the first year of the Trump Administration.

Eighteen months into his presidency when this anthology went to press, we could not know for certain whether Trump's use of Twitter during the election campaign and into his presidency, his self-dubbed "fake news" campaign against the news media, his incivility and his status as the first reality TV president would have long-term effects on political campaigning, presidential rhetoric, democratic discourse, journalism practice and politicians' use of social media. The scholars here, however, tells us that his impact on political communication, journalism coverage and social media has been significant even when he was not the catalyst such as in the Russian-created disinformation fake news and ad campaign on Facebook and Twitter. Their works are presented in four parts: "I. Blurred Lines: When Reality TV becomes Political Reality," II. "Campaign and Presidential Rhetoric," III. "Assessing News Media Performance," and IV. "Why Twitter and Facebook May Never be the Same."

Trump, of course, was an unconventional presidential candidate and the 2016 campaign in which a candidate who never held political office squared off against the first female presidential candidate was singular in American history. Though a presidential campaign novice, Trump had the advantage of personal wealth to help him partially fund his campaign and to allow him to claim he wasn't beholden to big money (Carroll, 2016). But more to the point, Trump was an experienced public communicator in three kinds of media: books, television and Twitter. He had hands-on experience in self-promotion as a book author, reality TV star, and as a highly public casino owner and real estate developer, which he exploited on his way to the White House. In his bestseller, *The Art of the Deal*, he explained (Lozada, 2015):

> One thing I've learned about the press is that they're always hungry for a good story, and the more sensational the better. It's in the nature of the job, and I understand that. The point is that if you are a little different, or a little outrageous, or if you do things that are bold or controversial, the press is going to write about you. I've always done things a little differently, I don't mind controversy, and my deals tend to be somewhat ambitious.

During the campaign, he drew upon his 14 seasons as the host and executive producer of the reality TV shows *The Apprentice* and *Celebrity Apprentice* to develop "a blunt speaking style, a tendency to taunt his rivals and play them against one another, and a theatrical sense of timing—that have flustered rivals who at times can't seem to believe that they are losing to him" (Sellers, 2016). John H. Parmelee (2016), a contributor to this scholarly anthology, has suggested that Trump's reality TV presence translated into votes.

> The case for explaining much of Trump's support in terms of parasocial interaction is especially strong because parasocial relationships happen the most among those who also fit the demographic profile of Trump supporters. Research indicates that parasocial interaction is at its highest among the poorly educated and those heavily dependent on TV, of which the elderly make up the largest segment … Polling data suggest Trump found his greatest support among those with a high school diploma or less, as well as those ages 65 and over. … Finally, parasocial interaction is high when a TV personality's portrayal is consistent over many years. As mentioned before, "The Apprentice" spent more than a decade displaying the most favorable attributes of Trump.

In Part I. "Blurred Lines: When Reality TV Becomes Political Reality," June Deery and co-authors, Sara S. Hansen and Shu-Yueh Lee build on parasocial relationship theory to make a case for attributing a good deal of Trump's campaign success to the "illusion of intimacy" (Horton & Wohl, 1956) TV viewers developed with Trump from watching "The Apprentice" and "Celebrity Apprentice." In "American Idol: Trump's Administration and Reality TV," Deery compares the Trump Administration to two reality TV formats: the gamedoc and the docusoap because much of what the president practiced on *The Apprentice*—attracting sponsorship, maximizing attention, faking it, or winning at all costs—translated well into politics for Trump. "His rise," Deery maintains, "certifies that we are in an era of politainment, where politicians are marketed as entertainers, entertainers are injected into politics, and the commercial pressure to entertain creates a distortion field within which journalists must work."

Co-authors Hansen and Lee conducted an online survey in spring 2016 of 268 young voters, ages 18–25 years, to determine the parasocial effects of watching *The Apprentice* and *The Celebrity Apprentice* and attitudes toward Trump as a presidential candidate. The findings of their study show, among other things, a link between wishing to be like Trump as he was depicted on the reality TV shows—"a real, successful businessman in a reality show who not only demonstrated his business skills but also showed the way he was a powerful and decisive boss"—and voting for him. Their findings are reported in "Young Viewers Turned Voters—How 'Wishing to be Trump' and Other Parasocial Effects from Watching *The Apprentice* Predict Likeability, Trust, and Support for a Celebrity President."

Part II: Campaign and Presidential Rhetoric. "Popular or mass rhetoric, which Presidents once employed only rarely, now serves as one of their principle tools in attempting to govern the nation" wrote Ceaser, Thuerow, Tulis, and Bessette (1981, p. 159) when they introduced their theory of the rhetorical presidency. "More important even than the quantity of popular rhetoric is the fact that presidential speech and action increasingly reflect the opinion that speaking *is* governing."

Though Ceaser et al. (1981) were talking about radio and television, the role they assigned to broadcasting, as a facilitator of the rise of the rhetorical presidency, seems equally appropriate to the new mass media technology of Twitter. "[Broadcasting] has given the President the means by which to communicate directly and instantaneously with a large number national audience, thus tearing down the communications barrier on which the Founders had relied to insulate representative institutions from direct contact with the populace" (Ceaser et al., 1981, p. 164). In Trump's tweeting, we see the full incarnation of the rhetorical presidency theory. Trump decrees domestic and foreign policy in his tweets and engages in an almost daily campaign to shore up his standing with his political base.

"Dog Whistle politics" is a form of campaign and presidential rhetoric—coded language about race—that politicians, primarily white Republicans, have used to "win elections and also to win support for regressive policies that help corporations and the super-rich, and in the process wreck the middle class" (López, 2014, xii). In "Donald Trump 'Tells You What He Thinks,'" Mira Sotirovic and Christopher Benson identify "dog whistle" related words and phrases in transcripts of the three presidential debates and transcripts of the next day coverage on CNN and Fox News, CNN online stories, and CNN and Fox News Facebook page comments. Their psycho-linguistic approach and application of computerized text analyses methodology reveal (i) that news media discussions on race and ethnicity lacked positive emotion and cognitive processes that people use to understand their world; (ii) discussion among Facebook users about the debate, however, revealed emotional reactions and attempts to understand (iii) and coverage of race was strikingly different on CNN and Fox.

"The rhetorical signature that Donald Trump deployed as a presidential candidate, as president-elect, and during the first 100 days of his presidency includes seeming spontaneity laced with Manichean, evidence-flouting, accountability-dodging, and institution-disdaining claims" (Jamieson & Taussig, 2017, p. 620). In "'Enemies of the People': Elites, Attacks, and News Trust in the Era of Trump," Jason Turcotte assesses Trump's evidence-flouting and accountability-dodging as a strategy of deflection, "a rhetorical tactic that enables politicians to dodge questions and shift public focus onto news professionals in ways that seem to strain the relationship the news media has with their audiences." The result, derived from his online pilot study, show that Trump's news media bashing rhetoric has mixed effects. It reduces the levels of trust in truth in the news among those sharing Trump's ideological view, but increases trust in the news among those more critical of the Trump presidency. The strategy of deflection, Turcotte says, now a mainstream on the campaign trail, taps into growing public dissatisfaction with the news media and is normalized through Trump's rhetorical style.

In "The Commander in Tweets: President Trump's Use of Twitter to Defend," Jeffrey Delbert identifies rhetorical patterns in Trump's Twitter-produced messages from @realDonaldTrump and @POTUS that he used to defend himself from critics during the president's first 100 days in office and looks at how Trump's tweeting molds conversations in the United States. Delbert identifies a four-part rhetorical strategy in Trump's tweets: (i) dismantle traditional information sources; (ii) shift the blame; (iii) dismiss the significance of longstanding institutions and (iv) deny accusations via Twitter and not through the filters of most major mainstream news outlets. "With an indiscriminate tongue, Trump's words make us question all the ways we are able to communicate, especially those that foster trust in the processes that guarantee our rights," Delbert concludes.

Part III: Assessing News Media Performance. "Journalism scholars critique news in many ways, but a central thread involves questions around truth and accuracy" (Bird & Dardenne, 2009, p. 205). Another core component of journalism studies is the belief that journalism plays a critical role in liberal democracies, that it should operate in the interest of the public and not for government or powerful institutions and corporations and that journalists "may be expected or obligated to render an account of their activities to their constituents" (Pritchard, 2000, p. 2). Accordingly, the authors of this section assess news coverage here and abroad of the 2016 presidential election campaign, and fake news and mainstream media's response to it from a variety of theoretical perspectives.

In "American Media and the Rise of Trump" Victor Pickard looks through the lens of history and political economy of the media theory to reveal how corporate broadcast and cable news media's profit imperative gave ratings-magnet Trump an advantage over his political rivals and at the voters' expense. Pickard offers alternatives to profit-motivated news media, which, he argues, would better promote meaningful democratic discourse.

Mitchell T. Bard's "From Fox News to Fake News: An Anatomy of the Top 20 Fake News Stories on Facebook Before the 2016 Election" examines the content of the 20 most engaged fake news stories on Facebook before the election. Specifically, the study looks at how the fake news articles were crafted and the themes they covered. An analysis of the Fox News Channel program "The O'Reilly Factor" provides insight into why the authors of the fake news articles may have chosen the topics and approaches found in the pieces. Bard found that more than half of the articles made no attempt to mimic traditional news tone and structure and the vast majority were advocacy or persuasion pieces and many focused on the same themes—Hillary Clinton was corrupt or a criminal. Those themes were topics discussed on "The O'Reilly Factor" in July and August 2016, though the author makes no claim of proof of causality. "This mixing of mainstream and the fringe helps illustrate another takeaway from this study," Bard concludes, "namely the two factors that enabled and shaped the explosion of the 2016 version of fake news: the solidification of the role of partisan cable television—specifically, Fox News Channel—and the emergence of social media."

Laurel Leff offers a critique of *The New York Times* and *The Washington Post*'s coverage of Wikileaks disclosure of Hillary Clinton-related emails published from July 22, 2016 to November 8, 2016. In "We've Got Mail (But Probably Shouldn't): The Press, WikiLeaks and Democratic Disclosures in the 2016 Election," Leff contends that decisions to publish the stolen and private emails violated six traditional journalistic norms and that the mundane and gossipy content of the emails failed to rise to the level of newsworthiness in the public's interest when weighed against the concerns about publishing stolen private information.

In "The Media was the Message: Gendered Coverage of Hillary Clinton's Historic 2016 Campaign for U.S. President," Dianne Bystrom and Kimberly Nelson report the results of a computer-assisted content analysis designed to assess how *The New York Times, Wall Street Journal, Washington Post* and *USA Today* covered Hillary Clinton during the two-and-one half months leading up to the 2016 presidential election. Their study found that masculine issues were around three times more likely to be mentioned in newspaper articles about presidential candidate Clinton than feminine issues, "words associated with scandals comprised a large percentage of her newspaper coverage" and references to white or whites as her constituency was virtually on par with mentions of women as constituents. Consistent with the findings of previous studies of women in politics, Bystrom and Nelson found that Clinton received more coverage than Trump on words associated with personal appearance, health and family.

How did the Mexican news media cover the Trump presidency? Melissa A. Johnson and Héctor Rendón applied agenda-setting concepts to analyze Mexican news coverage by three Mexico-city based newspapers of Donald Trump's first 100 days in office, focusing primarily on the immigration issue in "Goodbye Neighbor: Mexican News Coverage of the Wall and U.S. Immigration Proposals." The newspapers, according to Johnson and Rendón, gave the most attention to the proposed wall, actions taken by Mexico related to U.S. proposals, effects of Trump proposals and U.S. immigration policies on Mexico, U.S. actions against Mexicans and U.S.-Mexico bilateral actions or statements and multi-lateral relations, all of which appeared to align with public opinion in Mexico. Not surprisingly, "the newspapers' sources and topics showed equal contempt for Trump's wall and the proposed immigration policies" with most articles expressing concern about Mexico's dignity or sovereignty.

Nataliya Roman and John H. Parmelee's "A 'Political Novice' vs. the 'Queen of War': How State-Sponsored Media Framed the 2016 U.S. Presidential Campaign" also assesses foreign news coverage, specifically how the Voice of America (U.S.) and *Sputnik* (Russia) covered the presidential candidates, Trump and Clinton, and their related policies. Some unanticipated findings: Clinton appeared in more Sputnik stories than Trump and Trump drew more attention from Voice of America. About half of Sputnik stories about Trump and Clinton were neutral though Trump looked like the lesser of two evils in Sputnik reports and opinion pieces. Not so surprisingly, a large number of Sputnik articles hinted that a Clinton president would lead to war with Russia. Sputnik, however, repeatedly mentioned Trump's character flaws and lack of political experience.

All politicians lie. But Trump has arguably lied more than any other president in American history, creating an unparalleled need for the media and politically oriented citizens to fact-check the words of the president. So says Beth Knobel, the author of "'Judicious Skepticism': Fact-Checking Trump." Knobel documents the efforts by new and traditional news outlets to verify

Trump's statements and applies the classical philosophies of René Descartes and Baruch Spinoza and psychological studies of Harvard psychologist Daniel Gilbert to assess whether the new fact-checking effort by news organization helps the public sort out the truth from Trump's lies. Does fact-checking work? In the age of post-truth politics that Trump has ushered in and when most Americans are consuming media that align with their ideological perspectives, fact checking has had a mixed impact, Knobel concludes.

As even a casual follower of the news knows, Trump is the Press Critic-In-Chief who rails against the mainstream news media. He accuses his primary targets—*CNN, The New York Times, NBC, ABC and the Washington Post*—of trying to undermine his presidency with false reports from unnamed sources and intentionally reporting inaccurate and biased stories that put him in a bad light. I argue, however, in "Trump, the Press Critic: Unethical and Ineffective," that gauged by the norms of press criticism theories, Trump engages in coercive speech that is incompatible with democratic discourse and, based on my own theory of press criticism introduced in 2008, he, unlike press critics such as liberal Jon Stewart or conservative Reed Irvine, has failed to persuade his targets or the bulk of the news audiences that his criticism has merit.

Part IV: Why Twitter and Facebook May Never be the Same. Diana Owen identifies three distinctive but overlapping phases of the evolution of campaign communication in the new media era: (i) "old media, new politics; (ii) new media, new politics 1.0 and new media, new politics 2.0 (Owen, 2017, pp. 824–825). In the first phrase political candidates sought to gain favorable coverage by appearing on entertainment media outlets such as television talk and comedy shows. In the second phase, "by the year 2000 election, all major and many minor candidates had basic websites that were heavily texted" (2017, p. 824). In the third phase, starting with the 2008 election the most notable development was "the use of social media, such as Facebook, and video sharing sites, like YouTube, for peer-to-peer exchange of election information, campaign organizing, and election participation (2017, p. 825).

Does Trump's use of Twitter fall into Owen's third phase? Owen has doubts. "Initially, I thought that Trump was taking 'new media, new politics 2.0' to an extreme," Owen explained in an email (D. Owens, personal communication, February 20, 2018). "But I am starting to reconsider this position, as his media strategy has upended conventional wisdom. It may be that phase IV is a period of 'digital media ascendancy.'"

Co-authors Flora Khoo and William Brown analyze framing and priming effects of Twitter messages from Clinton and Trump—239 for each tweets—during a critical period in the fall of 2016 coinciding with the presidential debates in "Tweeting the Election: Comparative Uses of Twitter by Trump and Clinton in the 2016 Election." How did the candidates use Twitter? To do what politicians have been doing to rivals for centuries—mostly, to sling mud and criticize: "At 37.7%, Clinton was more likely to criticize her opponent's character and highlight his scandals as compared to Trump (28.5%). Trump (23%) was more likely to criticize other people or organizations compared to Clinton (7.5%)." Khoo and Brown discussed these findings and others in the context of the election outcome and with an eye on future research on the use of Twitter for political campaigns.

Social media companies such as Twitter and Facebook insist that they are not media companies primarily because they do not produce original content and that their editorial gatekeeping decisions are not made by humans but by algorithms (Napoli & Caplan, 2016). Facebook, however, has caught flak from Congress for its role in allowing false and misleading news stories to be fed to its users during the presidential election campaign.

Facebook's algorithms are designed to determine what information and news each user wants, but they have done a poor job in separating fact from fiction and news from propaganda as evidenced by the indictments against Russian individuals and companies for conspiring in a scheme to subvert the 2016 election and support the Trump presidential campaign handed down by the U.S. Justice Department in mid-February 2018. Facebook and its Instagram were mentioned 41 times (Frenkel & Benner, 2018).

Would algorithm-editors have made better news decisions and weeded out fake news had they been programmed for ethics? In "Are Algorithms Media Ethics Watchdogs? An Examination of Social Media Data for News" Tao Fu and William A. Babcock apply W. D. Ross's ethical principles of non-maleficence, beneficence, and self-improvement and gatekeeping theory to examine emerging ethical issues in algorithm-driven results of social media. They argue that, "Algorithms are amoral, without moral sense or principles, and thus incapable of distinguishing between right and wrong." Therefore, Fu and Babcock call for a new algorithm model "especially for Facebook and social media—one that reconceptualizes the media ethics toolbox of the 21st century, which traditionally include ethics codes, ombudsmen, media critics, news councils, journalism reviews, and public/civic journalism initiatives."

Two major social media controversies of 2017—Trump's Twitter use and Russian-created fake news—have spurred two lawsuits filed against Trump and two proposed federal statutes, the merits of which I assess in "Emerging Free Speech and Social Media Law and Policy in the Age of Trump." The lawsuits—*Knight First Amendment Institute at Columbia University v. Trump* and *Citizens for Responsibility and Ethics in Washington v. Trump*—challenge the president's deletion of tweets from his personal Twitter account,

@realdonaldtrump, on First Amendment and federal statutory grounds. The goal of the proposed federal Honest Ads Act is to thwart foreigners from interfering in our elections with fake ads. It would require social media companies to keep publicly available records of the political ads they publish, their advertisers and the targets of the ads. I contend that success by the plaintiffs could significantly change how presidents and other elected and government officials use Twitter, but the Honest Ads Act's impact on protecting democratic discourse on social media would be modest. The proposed COVFEFE Act, designed to classify presidential social media posts and tweets as presidential records, has little or no chance of becoming law in a Republican dominated Congress.

Conclusion

Collectively, the chapters paint a portrait of turmoil and tension for traditional notions and practices of political campaigning, presidential rhetoric and communication with constituents, social media's role as a forum for democratic discourse and news distribution, and professional journalism norms and practice. Still, from these chapters we can draw the following observations about the state of communications in the age of Trump:

- Trump's victory is in part testimony to the image he crafted of himself as a champion of capitalistic opportunity and enterprise on the *Apprentice* and the *Celebrity Apprentice* television series. Consequently, he has paved the way to the White House for other celebrities with no political experience to capitalize on the bonds they have built with mass media audiences. Witness, for example, the overblown response to Oprah Winfrey's Golden Globe Award speech and the equally absurd amount of news coverage that ensued.
- Social media have the potential to allow citizens to engage in conversations with elected officials and hold them accountable. The 2016 presidential campaign and Trump's use of Twitter as president, however, have shown that politicians are likely to use the social media platform the way they used offline media—to engage in one-way communication.
- Similarly, notions and predictions that social media platforms would usher in a new era of increased dissemination of meaningful information, news and political discourse must be reassessed in the wake of the incivility, untruthfulness and pettiness of Trump's tweets and Facebook's unwillingness or inability to screen its newsfeeds for fake news.
- Trump's tweeting strategy shows how social media provides an elected official with the means to conduct a permanent re-election campaign

by micro-targeting a core constituency and largely ignoring or demonizing mainstream news media.

- Conservative cable news operations appeared to have played a role in legitimizing fake news.
- Mainstream news media's most troubling biases may have more to do with gender and profit than political ideology.
- In the era of post-truth politics, legacy news media's heightened commitment to fact-based reporting and truth telling exemplified in the new fact-checking efforts may not be enough to bolster their credibility among conservatives.

Certainly, those of us who consume traditional news media, use social media, or own them live in interesting times in the age of Trump. Aware that scholarship produced early during the throes of political, technological and social upheaval may be subject to substantial revision in years to come, I, nonetheless, hope that readers will find the chapters useful in understanding what appears to have been a unique two-and-a half year period in U.S. communication and media history and helpful in spurring more scholarly examination of the Trump Administration's impact on communication.

References

Bird, S. E., & Dardenne, R. (2009). Rethinking news and myth as storytelling. In T. Hanitzcsh & K. Wahl-Jorgensen (Eds.), *Handbook of journalism studies* (pp. 205–217, 205). New York, NY: Routledge. Retrieved from https://keralamediaacademy.org/wp-content/uploads/2015/02/Handbook-of-Journalism-Studies.pdf

Carr, D. (2008, November 8). How Obama tapped into social networks' power. *New York Times.* Retrieved from http://www.nytimes.com/2008/11/10/business/media/10carr.html

Carroll, L. (2016, February 10). Is Donald Trump self-funding his campaign? Sort of. *Politifact. com.* Retrieved from http://www.politifact.com/truth-o-meter/statements/2016/feb/10/donald-trump/donald-trump-self-funding-his-campaign-sort/

Ceaser, J. W., Thuerow, G. E, Tulis, J., & Bessette, J. M. (1981, Spring). The Rise of the rhetorical presidency. *Presidential Studies Quarterly, 11*(2), 158–171.

Coe, K. (2016). Political rhetoric. In G. Mazzoleni, K. Barnhurst, K. Ikeda, R. Maia, & H. Wessler (Eds.), *International encyclopedia of political communication* (p. 1428). Hoboken, NJ: John Wiley & Sons. Retrieved from http://www.academia.edu/20785033/Political_Rhetoric_The_International_Encyclopedia_of_Political_Communication_

Eilperin, J. (2015, May 26). Here's how the first president of the social media age has chosen to connect with Americans. *Washington Post.* Retrieved from https://www.

washingtonpost.com/news/politics/wp/2015/05/26/heres-how-the-first-president-of-the-social-media-age-has-chosen-to-connect-with-americans/?utm_term=.99cf95463bfb

Frenkel, S., & Benner, K. (2018, February 17). To stir discord in 2016, Russians turned most often to Facebook. *New York Times*. Retrieved from https://www.nytimes.com/2018/02/17/technology/indictment-russian-tech-facebook.html

Horton, D., & Wohl, R. (1956). Mass communication and para-social interaction: Observations on intimacy at a distance. *Psychiatry, 19*(3), 215–229, 217. Retrieved from http://visual-memory.co.uk/daniel/Documents/short/horton_and_wohl_1956.html

Jamieson, K. H., & Taussig, D. (2017, November). Disruption, demonization and norm destruction: The rhetorical signature of Donald J. Trump. *Political Science Quarterly, 132*(4), 619–650. Retrieved from http://onlinelibrary.wiley.com/doi/10.1002/polq.12699/epdf

Levin, L. L. (2008). *The making of FDR: The story of Stephen T. Early, America's first modern press secretary*. Amherst, NY: Prometheus Books.

López, I. H. (2014). *Dog whistle politics: How coded racial appeals have reinvented racism & wrecked the middle class*. New York, NY: Oxford University Press.

Lozada, C. (2015, June 17). How Donald Trump plays the press, in his own words. *Washington Post*. Retrieved from https://www.washingtonpost.com/news/book-party/wp/2015/06/17/how-donald-trump-plays-the-press-in-his-own-words/?utm_term=.87bf9d22d179

McCabe, D. (2016, February 7). Bill Clinton's telecom law: Twenty years later. *The Hill*. Retrieved from http://thehill.com/policy/technology/268459-bill-clintons-telecom-law-twenty-years-later

Napoli, P. M., & Caplan, R. (2016, March 18). When media companies insist they're not media companies and why it matters for communications policy. Retrieved from https://ssrn.com/abstract=2750148 or doi:10.2139/ssrn.2750148

Nunberg, G. (2004, June 13). And, yes, he was a great communicator. *New York Times*. Retrieved from http://www.nytimes.com/2004/06/13/weekinreview/and-yes-he-was-a-great-communicator.html

Owen, D. (2017). New media and political campaigns. In K. H. Jamieson & K. Kenski (Eds.), *The Oxford handbook of political communication* (pp. 823–835). New York, NY: Oxford University Press.

Parmelee, J. H. (2016). *Donald Trump, reality TV, and the political power of parasocial relationships*. Centre for the Study of Journalism, Culture & Community, Bournemouth University. Retrieved from http://www.electionanalysis2016.us/us-election-analysis-2016/section-7-pop-culture-and-populism/donald-trump-reality-tv-and-the-political-power-of-parasocial-relationships/

Pritchard, D. (2000). *Holding the media accountable citizens, ethics and the law*. Bloomington, IN: Indiana University Press.

Sellers, F. S. (2016, November 6). What Trump learned on "The Apprentice." *Washington Post*. Retrieved from https://www.washingtonpost.com/politics/what-trump-learned-on-the-apprentice/2015/11/06/8dd79928-67a8-11e5-9ef3-fde182507eac_story.html?utm_term=.48c0261a96bc

Sterling, C. H. (n.d.). Deregulation. *Museum of Broadcasting Communications*. Retrieved from http://www.museum.tv/eotv/deregulation.htm

Walsh, K. T. (2013, November 20). J.F.K: First TV President. *U.S. News & World Report*. Retrieved from https://www.usnews.com/news/blogs/ken-walshs-washington/2013/11/20/jfk-first-tv-president

Part I

Blurred Lines: When Reality TV Becomes Political Reality

1. American Idol: Trump's Administration and Reality TV

June Deery
Rensselaer Polytechnic Institute

A common remark among pundits is that Donald Trump has turned politics into a reality TV show, or that he operates as though it were one. Others declare that Reality TV "created" candidate Trump. In this chapter, I argue that these conclusions, despite being somewhat glib, do merit closer attention. Reality TV cannot take the credit for producing Trump, but it did likely increase his chances of getting to the White House. A better equivalence would be to say that the kind of person who is successful on reality TV is now apt to be successful in politics also. Regarding the popular sentiment that Trump is transforming politics into reality TV, it might be more accurate to say that the process of turning politics into entertainment has been going on for some time but that Trump's rise suggests it has increased exponentially.

Certainly, the campaign and presidency of ex-reality TV host Donald J. Trump has crystallized and benefitted from significant trends in the confluence of entertainment media and politics, among them: fragmentation and polarization—seen, not coincidentally, in both politics and media distribution; the diminution of professional journalism; ratings-driven politainment; and the rise of "fake news," "post-factual information," and, underlying it all, decades of subterranean public relations. In this chapter, I will explore how Trump's political persona reflects and capitalizes upon attitudes and behavior witnessed on reality television, the extent to which the characteristics he displayed while on reality TV (many of them life-long), in addition to what he may have learned from his experience as TV host and producer, are now evident in his roles as candidate and president (these roles at the time of writing still appear conflated). His success in media and in politics are, in other words, related; and this success draws attention to some contemporary desires and anxieties among politicians and their voters, since the current chief represents an extreme instance of contemporary political behavior.

Focusing on the epistemological and ontological skepticism that has brought the aforementioned post-facts, fake news,[1] and other forms of deception to the fore of US politics and expanding on my own work on reality TV and that of other media scholars who look at the relationship between politics and popular culture (e.g., Jones, 2005, 2010; Street, 1997), this chapter will compare Trump's administration to two primary reality TV formats: the gamedoc, of which *The Apprentice* was a prominent example, and the docu-soap, with its less overtly competitive interpersonal rivalries (e.g., *The Real Housewives*).[2] Both formats require the staging of real events with various configurations and ratios of deception and authenticity. More broadly, I will be drawing on the fact that reality TV has for over a decade encouraged millions to think about the authenticity of everyday performance—perhaps to the point of loosening expectations—and has both validated and exploited the "ordinary" person by tapping into lowest-common-denominator desires and impulses.

Even attaching the label of "reality" to TV programming has problematized the concept of the real and foregrounded the idea of fakeness as entertainment. Enter the as-seen-on-TV candidate, Donald Trump who maintained his media exposure, the lifeblood of politics, by being outrageous. His victory represents an escalation of the transformation of "public interest" into "what interests the public" (as interpreted by ratings) and underlines how the commercial pressure to entertain creates a distortion field within which journalists must work. Of course, some distinctions still exist: one being that in politics one's ratings as a spectacle can be high and one's ratings as a politician can be low. However, the question remains: does politainment strengthen or weaken democracy? Does it open up or close off access and engagement in the political sphere?

Mediating Politics and the Participant-Viewer

As a media operator but political ingénue, Trump's brand combines familiarity and novelty. And if he wasn't always a successful businessman in real life, he did play one on TV. Indeed, as is often speculated, it may be that the political run was intended simply to enhance Trump's media and brand exposure but that the means became an end and—in somewhat typical, unscripted reality TV fashion—the unpredictable happened. As with any successful reality show, huge audiences watched staged but partly spontaneous events and engaged in fan/ anti-fan activity on social media. The "ratings" were now being measured by Gallup, Marist, and Pew, but for TV producer Trump the transition from one metric to the other was easy since the same principles apply: in the attention economy, popularity equals influence equals commercial opportunity. Much of what the current president practiced on his popular TV show translated well into politics: e.g., attracting sponsorship, maximizing attention, faking it, or winning at all costs. Not surprising, given that in politics as in the media power depends upon commercial support (political donors) and brand recognition.

Whatever the eventual legislative record, clearly the Trump administration has already had a transformative effect on the media, not so much through policy as practice. Again, standing as an extreme of contemporary political behavior, Trump continues to make politics almost exclusively in and through commercial media and his media preferences have underlined that professional narrowcasting in conjunction with widespread social media use has serious political consequences. If citizens can now inhabit separate, hermetic mediaspheres, then media distribution drives politics even more radically than before. Reality TV was early to promote the twinning of broadcast and social platforms and Trump has brought second screening to the White House (an interesting development from the oldest person to be elected president). He appears, often, to occupy the position of a docusoap *participant-viewer* (Deery, 2012, p. 38) one who watches their own portrayal on TV and what others are saying behind their back. We know this because, in what could only be characterized as advanced media narcissism, the president compulsively tweets about his performance and reviews, sometimes within minutes of broadcast remarks. A devoted TV watcher and media-provocateur, he has made media-bashing into a popular form of entertainment—with the result that the media is increasingly turning inward and producing content about itself.

Trump as Former Reality TV Star

Before *The Apprentice*, Trump had occasionally played himself on TV: in cameo appearances on sitcoms or TV commercials, he invariably played the role of the rich tycoon (even when his businesses were actually failing). Acting as his own fake PR agent, for years he also assiduously courted the New York tabloids hoping to get some mention. With *The Apprentice* (2004–2010), a show created by uber-producer Mark Burnett, Trump went from New York City celebrity to national celebrity still by playing the tycoon. Burnett wanted a large personality who would provoke drama; Trump wanted media exposure and a chance to increase his brand equity and hence core business—which largely involves selling his name. Having a successful TV show became a big part of Trump's personal and commercial identity, affecting both how the public regarded him and how he regarded himself (his interest in his show's TV ratings was apparently obsessive).

Today, Trump has not left television and as a politician now employs many of the same techniques he utilized as TV producer, even bringing back some old reality TV contacts. Mark Burnett was his special guest at the Presidential Prayer Breakfast in 2017 and again in 2018 (at the Sept. 2016 Emmys, Jimmy Kimmel had humorously called out Burnett for producing Trump and turning reality into a reality TV show).[3] But more importantly, the most prominent *Apprentice* villain, Omarosa, was for a while the Director of Communications for the Office of Public Liaison. Trump credits her with helping to make him a star thanks to her Machiavellian role on his TV show: ironically, she was criticized on *The Apprentice* for inflating her credentials about her previous White House job but then went on to occupy a relatively important position—for a different political party. So, the fake became real, if not convincingly authentic.[4]

Reality, the TV Show

For most people, politics is a video. That is, their primary political engagement is in the form of viewing a screen. More particularly, Trump's campaign often resembled a reality TV competition: a live show with unpredictable, suspenseful, up-to-the-minute revelations and interwoven multiple plots involving alliances, conspiracies, and betrayal. These elements are certainly not new to politics but what is new, and what is more like the frankness and intimacy of reality TV, is the bluntness and personal nature of the competitive display. As on *The Apprentice*, Trump's campaign precipitated examples of aggression, mockery, name-calling, and unstable team affiliation, with strategies for openly appealing to the most basic fears, hatreds, ambitions, and greed. Much of this drama has persisted into the early administration. Indeed, some presidential communiqués have become uncomfortably close to the responses of a gamedoc contestant complaining about rivals or the inept player who doesn't realize they can be caught out when trying to deceive. Trump personalizes even global politics, creating headlines with his invective against individual world leaders. All of this has a distortive effect on professional journalism when (as is often the case) its members dwell on such outbursts, ignoring other consequential matters in favor of mirroring the president's ad hominem criticism: as in reality TV, it is the personal and the confrontational that attract immediate and repetitive attention.

Contrary to a traditional sense of presidential decorum, and more in line with the promise of *The Real World* (MTV, 1992-), we are now seeing in politics what happens "when people stop being polite ... and start getting real" (*The Real World* slogan). As on *The Apprentice*, Trump encourages rival alliances and intrigue, hence news coverage is of the drama of loyalty tests and jostling egos. Inner-circle politicians and staffers are now widely known by a larger public which keeps up with who is in or out in the White House as though it were a *Bachelor* mansion or exotic island. Cast members have sometimes implausible names: like "Trump" embodying the desire to trump others, "Mad Dog" Mattis as Secretary of Defense, spokespeople "Spicey" (Sean Spicer) and "the Mooch" (Anthony Scaramucci), Chief of Staff General John Kelly (known to some as "the church lady"), and even the improbable "Reality Winner" who leaked classified information about the Russians hacking the election (i.e., the foreign staging of events by rival producers). Reality programming is also known for profanity and bleeped-out expletives and it seems some Trump advisors have reduced the level of civic discourse to language that media companies and the FCC (Federal Communications Commission) have judged to be unacceptable. This was seen dramatically in the brief tenure of Anthony Scaramucci when the bleep quota in political reporting increased dramatically. Trying to process this change in politics, news anchor Anderson Cooper reached for analogies to reality TV. Reeling from Scaramucci's vulgar rant and the surrounding palace intrigue, Anderson said: "It's like an episode of *The Real Housewives*, only in Washington and with men. With harsh expletives and who said what to the press and who's upset about not being invited to dinner" (*Anderson Cooper 306*, CNN: July 27, 2017).

Staged Actuality

I have elsewhere suggested that reality TV is in essence a "staged actuality" (Deery, 2012), drawing on both meanings of staged as planned and as performed, and actuality as referring to real-life, empirical occurrences. Similarly, some staging of the actual has always been necessary in politics, a profession that has accrued multiple rituals and scripts. American presidents have long employed professional writers and media experts to orchestrate their conventions and props, with some props like the Oval Office and Air Force One having an essential and metonymic status.[5] To some extent, Trump reveals more presidential conventions by his breaking of them, by his going off script. But like any good reality TV producer, he is also a serendipitous manipulator of the reality that media presence can produce. An impresario who first thought of a career as a filmmaker, he already knew how to stage reality in the past for commercial gain: e.g., staging work on a construction site to fool potential investors (Trump & Schwartz, 1987). And on reality TV, he and his producers again manipulated physical reality for rhetorical purposes, whether it be the fake boardroom or fake elevator ride. Even his pivotal role, his ability to say "you're fired," was also a form of dramatic pretense since the "employees" were not losing a job but being asked to leave a gameshow, with a common phrase Trump nevertheless tried to copyright due to its entertainment value. When he was contemplating becoming a presidential candidate he did trademark "Make America Great Again," a phrase and sentiment he took from Reagan's playbook. From there, he kicked off his campaign with a group of actors paid to cheer him on and held a press conference to display Trump Steaks as a going concern, which it wasn't (and the steaks curiously were from the label "Bush Brothers"). After his inauguration, he went on to defy facts about crowd sizes, the weather, and so on. Trump, in other words, has always been a stage manager who is entrepreneurial with both physical and social reality.

As with reality TV, the staging works best in conjunction with spontaneity and unpredictability. Trump has trained a nation (or world) to check Twitter throughout the day for the latest in a live show that creates suspense about nominees for office, or trade deals, or possibly an apocalyptic war. The president says he will make a decision or announcement in one or two weeks and one suspects this delay tactic is used to frame a lack of policy or knowledge as masterful suspense. Part of the populist drama is that the president can and does change his mind suddenly and seemingly on a whim about major policy issues or personnel. Even when reading prepared remarks he is notorious for going off script. Like reality TV, his is at most a *lightly* scripted performance with a good deal of improvisation based on what will get a strong, immediate reaction. But while television producers can exercise some control over such characters, if only in the editing bay, the same is not true of Trump's staff, especially if he insists on going live. As noted, Trump's personal mode of address is more like the ordinary reality TV participant than a president. Eschewing prepared oratory, he resorts to live tweets with sentence fragments and unfinished thoughts that appear to be aimed directly at his readers-as-fans. We see him leveraging the intimate (but parasocial) acquaintanceship seen in reality TV production, where viewers can bond with participants in a more immediate and lasting way than with fictional characters. The resultant *close distance* in a *mass* relationship is very valuable in both business and politics.

More crafted and episodic, but still improvised, are the daily White House briefings. These have become a popular afternoon series, a sort of docusoap starring beleaguered and aggressive spokespeople who scramble to put up a convincing front and impose some kind of coherent script on a chaotic and inconsistent reality spontaneously being created behind them by their boss. Indeed, on some days, regular soap operas have been pre-empted to carry the White House briefings live, an acknowledgement of reality TV's dominance over legacy forms. Indeed, the briefing's audience of journalists and viewers at home resembles reality TV fans who have to speculate about who is being manipulative and why. This is not lost on a president who knows from experience that deceptive and combative performances drive up ratings. Still viewing democratic institutions through the eyes of a TV producer, he forecast when he threatened to cancel the briefings that the networks would be "very unhappy, because ratings are so high. I don't know what these networks would do, they're going to start to cry."[6] Certainly, it seems that evasion or deception by Trump's professional obfuscators is now a performance art. These often controversial figures produce dilemmas for news organizations: they generate great ratings but only because they are either regarded as successful fact-defying cheerleaders or as macabre theater, depending on the viewer and network framing.

Fact and Fake

A central strain of reality TV makes entertainment out of deception or self-deception and ambiguities within the concept of truth. Over a decade of gamedocs and docusoaps have featured people who are not performing fictional and scripted characters whose ontological status would be clear, but are interacting with and manipulating each other while "playing themselves": except that they also attempt to perform other roles, usually not very successfully. Hence, much confusion and drama occur within the gap between the authentic and the fake, categories which viewers must sort out for themselves. Indeed, all reality TV shows—since they employ so-called "real people" in actual situations but are also TV shows produced by someone else—open up questions about who is honest or deceptive, who is authentic or fake. Viewers puzzle over what is known, what is being hidden, what the motives for deception could be. Switching between suspicion and trust seems to be part of the viewing experience (Andrejevic, 2004; Hill, 2005; Skeggs & Wood, 2009).

Many trends in the last few decades have helped de-stabilize truth or even fact in news making: a shrinking of investigative journalism; increased commercial pressure on news divisions; multiple news outlets and 24/7 coverage; the removal of the fairness doctrine; the establishment of news organization with a definite political slant; and ratings-attracting shouting matches and confrontation. Also crucial is the rise of public relations, the professional distribution of the selective and spun, something I have elsewhere likened to a cultural "dark matter": powerful, pervasive, and largely undetected (Deery, 2012). These are all significant factors. But it could be argued that another contribution to the problematizing of truth is millions of people watching hundreds of hours of representations of "reality" where what is real or fake is up for grabs and a matter of some dispute.

While truth in politics has always been more instrumental than absolute, in Trump's rhetoric we see a consistent elision of the distinction between truth and falsity and instead the promotion of opinion, false accusation, and willful ignorance so often seen in the dramas of reality TV. In both reality TV and Trumpian politics there is radical subjectivism where "if I feel it, it is true." A longtime proponent of "hyping," or what his co-writer Tony Schwartz charitably dubbed "truthful hyperbole," Trump appears to have a casual relationship with fact (Trump & Schwartz, 1987). Given this, one Trump spokesperson seized on the idea of offering "alternative facts."[7] Orwell, whose dystopia immediately became a best-seller after these remarks, warned us in the wake of European totalitarianism that the ultimate power in politics is epistemological skepticism, and it seems Trump and his staff have tried to deflect criticism by characterizing any negative reporting as "fake news"—at the cost of further alienating large populations from professional journalism. Using this pre-emptive skepticism encourages supporters to believe that if the president is criticized this only "proves" that the media are biased and untrustworthy, a maneuver that short-circuits getting at truth and makes "fact-checking" pejorative. So we are now, indeed, in the realm of post-facts and pseudo-facts—i.e., beyond non-verifiable claims to the *rejection of the whole idea of verification*. The establishment Right, many of whom are now looking on with dismay, prepared the ground for this skepticism by insisting for decades that the "mainstream" (i.e., professional) media can't be trusted because they have a liberal bias (Alterman, 2003). And while untruth has long been a political weapon, it has now become democratized thanks to social media and a massive and strategic use of rumor and lies, some motivated by political agendas and others for purely commercial reasons (domestic or foreign individuals trying to attract viewers and advertisers). It seems the implosion of fact into an impenetrable core of belief and desire—what comedian Stephen Colbert termed "truthiness" in the Bush era—has now gone supernova and it is not clear what impact the resultant energy will have.

Selling Reality

For decades, the enormous industry of public relations has been developing techniques for obfuscation and persuasion, drawing from those trained in journalism to invisibly influence and re-direct journalism on behalf of its clients. As an individual, Trump was an amateur enthusiast in this regard: posing as a PR agent called John Barron, he learned the basics of how to shape news content. But, beyond this, what his presidency illustrates is that the social and economic model of public relations and politics are similar to that of media productions like reality TV: *they are all selling a version of reality for commercial purposes.* The confusion of fact and fiction is profitable not just on reality TV but also, in a myriad of ways, in politics (a topic beyond the scope of this chapter). For media companies, the advantages of selling different versions of reality are more straightforward: confusion, deception, and polarized truth generate exciting news stories every day and so whether anchors applaud or roll their eyes industry profits accumulate.[8] As with reality TV, part of the attraction is schadenfreude and being able to look down on other people: which isn't traditionally how the population is supposed to regard its leaders. Les Moonves, CEO of CBS, acknowledged this when discussing coverage of Trump's controversial campaign: "It may not be good for America, but it's damn good for CBS" (Bond, 2016).

Of course, presidents have always deceived voters to some extent (Alterman, 2004); ironically, the notion that the first president wasn't able to lie about the cherry tree was, in fact, a fake story developed by early public relations. But such is the comingling of politics and entertainment that presidential proclamations are now part of an expanding politainment. Satiric formats like *The Daily Show* (Comedy Central), *Real Time with Bill Maher* (HBO) or *Saturday Night Live* (NBC), which for some time have taken on the role of investigating truth in politics—some, ironically, by posing as fake news shows—have found in Trump's presidency plenty of material. As the political impact of satire grows, as late-night monologues are relied on to provide political correctives, it is perhaps not surprising that parodies and impersonations have sometimes superseded the original and real (e.g., Alec Baldwin over Trump).[9]

Self-Branding

As mentioned earlier, Trump has for some time been a prominent example of the neoliberal push to self-brand. Early on, he found he was more successful at selling his image than selling real estate and so, as well as using his name as leverage in business deals, he began to license his brand to others; for example, selling others the right to put the name Trump on the facade of a building he doesn't own. In *No Logo* (2000), Naomi Klein identifies this as part of a broader capitalist evolution from companies manufacturing a product to companies establishing a brand: image therefore supersedes product or *is* the product. We see this focus on image and surface extend into Trump's political life. Like any good postmodern marketer, he appears comfortable in the third order of simulation where the image has supplanted the real (Baudrillard, 1983), where the façade is (literally) his business and identity.

Very pragmatically, we know that Trump saw *The Apprentice* primarily as an opportunity to enhance his brand presence: holistically, by being the star, and specifically, by embedding his products in the programming. Indeed, his series had one of the highest ratios of product placement on TV. More specifically, this show featured *performative placement* (Deery, 2014) when competitors were asked to create a campaign to sell a product for Trump or for others. By featuring this task they did, in fact, advertise the product on national TV, a deliberately prolonged placement that elevated a product's status from object to event. There was also a good deal of *location placement* (Deery, 2015), as when competitors visited a Trump's golf resort or casino and heard him extol its virtues in superlative terms. After winning the ultimate competition, Trump has continued to use some of the same advertising techniques as in his TV show. Location placement continues when the president travels to his resorts (this time at the tax payers' expense) or when he lures journalists to a location with promises of a political announcement but instead merely advertises one of his businesses. In addition, while a resident of the White House he is also an innkeeper on the same street (Trump International Hotel). It could be, therefore, that in making a presidential run Trump wasn't so much intending to use his celebrity to enhance his political standing as he was hoping to use his political status (as candidate) to enhance his celebrity and therefore brand equity.

Trump: The Game

Trump's rise also illustrates the gamification of real life and the promotion of extreme neoliberal individualism, a favorite scenario of reality TV.[10] For some time, the media have framed political campaigns as games or races, focusing on polls rather than policy. Candidate Trump seemed very conscious of being in the ultimate gamedoc whose prize (winning the presidency) was not a political *means* but an *end*. Entering office without a coherent political agenda, it seems he now wants to "win" the legislative competition and, like any good reality TV player, makes and switches alliances and lends or removes support as it benefits his own personal chance of success. While not new in politics, the extent and frequency of these shifting alliances more closely resembles reality TV and, as much as it alarms professional administrators, it also increases viewer interest. The interpersonal drama began with the pre-inaugural interviews in Trump Tower—the same location as *The Apprentice*—when a national audience was kept in suspense about who would win which job. Many months into the administration, and after a series of "resignations," viewers (and staff) are often left speculating about who will be eliminated next and who is in alliance with whom within the White House. As is often noted, both in business and on *The Apprentice* Trump seems to prefer that those under him battle it out for his approval. On the TV show, he had license to say highly critical and frank things about other people's worth while himself remaining immune to criticism, and he now continues to make such criticisms of top-level politicians or major institutions.

The Apprentice gave Trump a simple and ideal role: the ego at the center of it all, the undisputed authority and judge who took the opportunity to promote himself to a captive audience. Participants who were competing to be his employees were at all times deferential to "Mr. Trump" and the boardroom set visually positioned him as the central power. But in his new role as president, Trump has found it difficult to command widespread automatic respect. Perhaps to reconstruct some of that TV deference, he at one point had news cameras film his cabinet sitting around a table (in what Trump apparently calls "the boardroom") with each member professing how much they admired their boss. The resemblance to *The Apprentice* set was not lost on commentators who saw the imitation of a reality show as dishonoring the office of the president (Nussbaum, 2017; Poniewozik, 2017). However, I would argue that Trump is apt to adopt an even more worrisome role when he morphs from a reasonably disciplined TV host into a rogue cast member whom producers can't rein in.

One important lesson that Trump learned from reality TV is how to get media attention and therefore win by being the most outrageous person in the room. The environment of gamedocs and docusoaps encourages extroversion, vanity, self-regard, bullying, meanness, impetuosity, and false accusation. It often features bombastic personalities who speak their mind, can't take criticism, and enjoy getting into a fight. They are generally rewarded, with fame and future employment, for being unfiltered, for being offensive, or for espousing the politically incorrect. Trump, too (as they say on docusoaps) likes to stir the pot. He resembles the reality TV provocateur who viewers and producers keep on the show because they are exciting and unpredictable and larger-than-life. Instead of being a bland, middle-of-the road, family production, his 2016 campaign became a scandalous, unpredictable, and opinionated drama. The formal debates began to resemble docusoap reunions where Trump jostled for position by trying to shame or humiliate other "contestants"—when he wasn't claiming to be their friends. Now in office, his unfiltered and pugilistic behavior continues, as when he indulges in personal insults or appoints people to head up departments they seek to eviscerate. This provocative casting and planting of the seeds of conflict would be applauded by reality TV producers who use the same techniques to convert the actual into the dramatic.

The Amateur and the Extra-ordinary

It is perhaps ironic that the star of *The Apprentice* has not apprenticed himself to the job and sees little value in doing so. Like reality TV participants, Trump is selling the authenticity of being a non-professional and non-actor. Related to the erosion of the distinction between true and false is the distrust in some circles of the informed, the educated, and the expert. Indeed, it is generally thought that Trump's victory is partly due to the revenge and anger of what Trump (in a typically unfiltered fashion) called the "poorly educated." The populist idea that it is better to be an amateur and political outsider was ground prepared both by conservative talk radio and then to some extent by liberal comedians like Bill Maher or John Stewart (Jones, 2005, p. 87). Although a privileged oligarch whose sometimes lavish (and nouveau rich) display satisfies the "wealth voyeurism" that is also a draw on some reality programing (Deery, 2012, p. 142), Trump managed to market himself as someone who identifies with and represents ordinary people. He presents himself as the *extra*-ordinary so popular on reality TV: someone who is a regular person in extraordinary circumstances. And as with the phenomenon of reality TV, Trump promises the ordinary person more recognition—*as* ordinary people. However, the lack of real agency among reality TV participants is a warning here; for both the promises of reality TV and of Trump's presidency could be described as more *demotic* than *democratic*, a distinction cultural critic Graeme Turner (2010) uses to differentiate between giving ordinary people more visibility and giving ordinary people more power.

Conclusion

If Trump's rise was a political stress test, it revealed serious fissures and fatigue in a commercially supported media system whose drive for ratings clearly compromises its role as the Fourth Estate. Trump's attacks on the media have been relentless, but much damage has also been self-inflicted. When journalists first treated his candidacy as a lucrative sideshow, it turned out to be a serious miscalculation. More than a strategic upset, Trump's victory demonstrated how treating politics as another form of entertainment can have serious consequences. Since Frankfurt and Birmingham, critical scholars have worried about media entertainment being a political distraction and hence a form of hegemonic control. I would argue instead that now *what passes for politics* is the distraction from politics.

Notes

1. According to Google trends, the term "fake news" spiked at the time of the Trump election and has been strong since.
2. A gamedoc is a reality TV competition format and a docusoap is the reality TV version of a soap opera.
3. On February 8, 2018 Trump tweeted: "Will be heading over shortly to make remarks at The National Prayer Breakfast in Washington. Great religious and political leaders, and many friends, including T.V. producer Mark Burnett of our wonderful 14 season Apprentice triumph, will be there. Looking forward to seeing all!"
4. After being fired by Trump again, this time as President, Omarosa showed up within a few months on *Celebrity Big Brother* where her revelations about her time in the White House helped market the show.
5. Apparently, Ronald Reagan even had theatrical spikes marking where he should stand.
6. Trump said this in an interview on Fox News (May 13, 2017).
7. "Alternative facts" is a phrase used by Kellyanne Conway during a *Meet the Press* interview on January 22, 2017, in which she defended White House false statements about the inauguration crowd. Many commentators subsequently compared the usage to Orwell's "doublespeak."
8. Daniel Boorstin (1992) foresaw the trend toward news having to be entertaining and the blurring of the distinction between fiction and fact.
9. Baldwin's photo was mistakenly used to represent Trump in the Dominican newspaper *El Nacional* on February 10, 2017.
10. There is, in fact, a board game called *Trump: The Game* issued in 1989.

References

Alterman, E. (2003). *What liberal media? The truth about bias and the news.* New York, NY: Basic Books.

Alterman, E. (2004). *When presidents lie: A history of official deception and its consequences.* New York, NY: Viking Penguin.

Andrejevic, M. (2004). *Reality TV: The work of being watched.* Lanham, MD: Rowan & Littlefield.

Baudrillard, J. (1983). *Simulacra and simulation.* (P. Foss, P. Patton, & P. Beitchman, Trans.) New York, NY: Semiotext(e). (Original work published 1981).

Bond, P. (2016, February 29). Leslie Moonves on Donald Trump: 'It May Not Be Good for America, but It's Damn Good for CBS.' *Hollywood Reporter*. Retrieved from https://www.hollywoodreporter.com/news/leslie-moonves-donald-trump-may-871464

Boorstin, D. (1992). *The image: A guide to pseudo-events in America*. New York, NY: Vintage Books. (Original work published in 1962).

Deery, J. (2012). *Consuming reality: The commercialization of factual entertainment*. New York, NY: Palgrave Macmillan.

Deery, J. (2014). Mapping commercialization in reality television. In L. Ouellette (Ed.), *A companion to reality television* (pp. 11–28). Malden, MA: Wiley-Blackwell.

Deery, J. (2015). *Reality TV*. Cambridge: Polity Press.

Hill, A. (2005). *Reality TV: Audiences and popular factual television*. London: Routledge.

Jones, J. P. (2005). *Entertaining politics: New political television and civic culture*. Lanham, MD: Rowman & Littlefield.

Jones, J. P. (2010). *Entertaining politics: Satiric television and political engagement* (2nd ed.). Lanham, MD: Rowman & Littlefield.

Klein, N. (2000). *No logo*. New York, NY: Picador.

Nussbaum, E. (2017, July 31). The TV that created Donald Trump. *The New Yorker*. Retrieved from https://www.newyorker.com/magazine/2017/07/31/the-tv-that-created-donald-trump

Poniewozik, J. (2017, June 12). Vanity cabinet: Trump throws himself a TV pep talk. *New York Times*. Retrieved from https://www.nytimes.com/2017/06/12/arts/television/donald-trump-cabinet.html

Skeggs, B. & Wood, H. (2009). The labor of transformation and circuits of value "around" reality television. In T. Lewis (Ed.), *TV transformations: Revealing the makeover show* (pp. 119–132). New York, NY: Routledge.

Street, J. (1997). *Politics and popular culture*. Cambridge: Polity Press.

Trump, D., & Schwartz, T. (1987). *Trump: The art of the deal*. New York, NY: Ballantine Books.

Turner, G. (2010). *Ordinary people and the media: The demotic turn*. London: Sage.

2. Young Viewers Turned Voters—How "Wishing to Be Trump" and Other Parasocial Effects From Watching The Apprentice Predict Likeability, Trust, and Support for a Celebrity President

SARA S. HANSEN AND SHU-YUEH LEE
University of Wisconsin Oshkosh

Populist support for a new type of presidential candidate—a rich reality TV star who never held public office—carried Donald Trump to the White House in 2016. Trump won broad appeal across voter demographics and beliefs (Bowman, 2017) while making a series of controversial campaign statements that typically would lessen a candidate's appeal (McCammon, 2016). His direct communication, at times combative and controversial, through his campaign, White House, and Twitter channels has been cast as reality TV politics in *Fox News* to *The New York Times*, for the "showman who has made a career of keeping the audience engaged and coming back for more" (Baker, 2017, p. 1).

Many Americans first became familiar with Trump as the showman hosting the reality TV series *The Apprentice* and *The Celebrity Apprentice*, which ran for 14 seasons since 2004. NBC parted ways with the host in 2015 after he made inflammatory campaign comments about Mexicans. Arnold Schwarzenegger, a former movie star and two-term governor of California, served as new host for one season (Keveney, 2017). Trump's role as politician conflicted with his *Apprentice* role on NBC. Yet, could the way Americans related to Trump from watching his reality show have influenced their attitudes and behavior toward his presidency?

Intersections of celebrity and politics, evident in the multiple roles of Trump and Schwarzenegger, have been evolving for years. The celebrity politician develops when traditional politicians adopt marketing techniques and appearances related to popular culture, or an entertainment or sports star takes up politics (Street, 2004). Like other celebrities, these politicians produce desired personas through visibility in mass media and convergent media environments (Turner, 2013). However, the connection of "reality-based" program consumption with viewer attitudes and behaviors related to celebrities in roles beyond the show, such as running for president, has been less studied.

This work examines viewers' parasocial experiences—the illusion of interpersonal social interaction with a TV character or star (Horton & Wohl, 1956) that feels like a social relationship (Cohen, 2004)—underway with Trump on *The Apprentice*, and potentially impacting voter attitudes and actions toward his presidential run. Viewers feel identity connections with a TV personality for shared identity, goals, and perspective (Cohen, 2001). These relationships may further take shape in conversations with others in person or on social networks (Eyal & Dailey, 2012). Further, viewers in parasocial relationships may feel wishful identification of wanting to be the personality or character from the show (Hoffner, 1996). This study extends this line of research with reality TV and politics to see impacts of parasocial relationships on how viewers liked and trusted Trump as president, and whether they intended to vote for him. It focuses on young people, who use popular culture in political decision-making (Scott, Street, & Inthorn, 2011). As well, young adults take in the "authenticity" of reality TV as they work through identity development in this life stage (Allen & Mendick, 2012).

An online survey was conducted in spring 2016 of 268 young voters, 18–25 years of age, about parasocial effects of watching *The Apprentice* and *The Celebrity Apprentice* and attitudes toward Trump as a presidential candidate. Results were examined with regression analysis to study parasocial factors and wishful identification impacts on voting attitudes and intentions. Outcomes add insight about Trump's appeal, and relatable aspects as candidate, and potentially as president, that influence his relationship with viewers turned voters.

Literature Review

Trends and mechanisms of media visibility and celebrity politics are explored related to ways popular culture offers mediated political communication, and connects to voter experiences, attitudes, and behaviors. Aspects of parasocial relationships that viewers experience through media exposure, specifically reality TV, add dimension to popular culture influences beyond program consumption. Parasocial feelings viewers may have toward identifying with a TV personality or wishing to be like that personality are discussed.

Media Visibility and Celebrity Politics

Increasingly, intersections exist between celebrity and politics due to political systems and governments, as well as politicians, evolving with the technological, social, and political changes of late modernity (Marsh, 't Hart, & Tindall, 2010). Celebrities of popular culture may use their status and media visibility toward politics, or traditional politicians may adopt celebrity associations for image making or communication to the public (Street, 2004). Schwarzenegger and Trump exemplify what Driessens (2013) described as gaining celebrity capital through accumulated media visibility in popular culture that is leveraged as political capital. Similarly, President Obama used the draw of media spectacle to sway public opinion for votes and to promote his agenda (Kellner, 2009).

Street (2004) explores how media depictions of image, noting Brennan and Hamlin's (2000) application of rational choice theory, are legitimate to help voters identify with candidates. Image, appearances, and techniques aligned with popular culture impact relationships to politics and civic participation. Young voters use various media—television, music video games—to understand and relate to politics, offering "salient points of identification with the national and international arena in a way that news media do not" (Scott et al., 2011, p. 15). Recent work from Street (2017) explores the analysis of the kind of celebrity that makes up the celebrity politician and aligns Trump with "rock stars" that act out politics with authenticity. Street argues this celebrity was aided by media coverage through narratives (how media reported on him), performance styles (his political style to convey authenticity), and audience reactions (ways crowds reacted as fans).

In his presidential campaign Trump arguably could use his celebrity gained from media visibility on a reality TV show. In the series, he played the part of a successful and rich businessman who decided which contestants famously heard "You're Fired!" on episodes until *The Apprentice* candidate won money and a job or *The Celebrity Apprentice* candidate won money for charity. Reality TV is scripted for dramatization, and Trump in *The Apprentice* is the ideological center displaying capitalist principles, authoritative leadership, individualism, and the belief that winning is everything (Franko, 2006). Critics may question what is real or dramatized, and what storylines are aimed to show business principles or spectacle for ratings. Reality TV has varying levels of authenticity with audiences as content can be scripted or emphasized for entertainment (Allen & Mendick, 2012).

Trump's media visibility may have supported political coverage of him as a candidate. The media is an essential agent in political communication to disseminate messages to the public (McNair, 2011). Political media coverage has associated positively with the turnout in elections (Banducci & Semetko, 2003). Several studies show a positive relationship between a positive tone in media visibility and a winning election or support (Mendelsohn, 1993; Vliegenthart, Oegema, & Klandermans, 2005). Even though media visibility does not guarantee winning an election, the lack of visibility may result in disadvantages for support or recognition (Blais, Gidengil, Fournier, & Nevitte, 2009). Ragsdale's (1981) study also supports the lack of media visibility for challengers that contributed to the House incumbent victories. Thus, gaining media visibility is the first critical step toward winning an election and obtaining support.

Trump gained recognition and popularity from more than a decade of media visibility as a reality TV star. This visibility related to the show, but was not limited to the television broadcast. Images and information related to Trump could be circulated through a variety of communication platforms, including shared content on social media platforms. Thus, more or less, the majority of the public knew Trump or gained a certain amount of knowledge about him before he even started to campaign. In recent years, entertainment media has played an important role in election cycles, especially for the presidential election. First, it can reach voters who rarely are exposed to traditional news media. Second, it can have positive effects on candidates. Chaffee, Zhao, and Leshner (1992) found that interviews or talk shows contributed to voters learning about candidates. Moy, Xenos, and Hess (2005) found late-night comedy shows could aid candidates in highlighting certain facets of their personas to give a positive image to voters. Thus, it is rational to hypothesize that Trump on *The Apprentice* not only increased his media visibility and popularity, but also contributed to voters' positive attitudes toward him.

> H1a: *Media visibility of Trump in* The Apprentice *will positively influence liking Trump.*

> H1b: *Media visibility of Trump in* The Apprentice *will positively influence trusting Trump.*

> H1c: *Media visibility of Trump in* The Apprentice *will positively influence voting for Trump.*

Parasocial Interaction and Relationships

Horton and Wohl (1956) described parasocial interaction (PSI) as the audience's interaction with actors viewed on screen as similar to interpersonal social interaction. An illusion of face-to-face experience with an actor—who may be performing in a real or fictional way—is facilitated through a crafted experience intentionally designed to engage the viewer. As the actor adjusts in a figurative give and take with the audience, a parasocial relationship develops. Levy (1979) described the parasocial relationship (PSR) that ensues in this interaction, using newscasters in his work, which through illusion creates a false feeling of intimacy for the viewer. Parasocial measures have evaluated how these perceived relationships with characters or personas form in newscasts to situational comedies and reality TV.

PSRs hold potential for depth similar to in-person social relationships. Cohen's (2004) study of parasocial attachment styles and relationship intensity for viewers questioned about favorite TV characters found PSRs operate as extensions of viewers' social relationships and "depend on the same psychological processes that influence close relationships" (p. 198). Several studies have attempted to clearly define PSI and PSR in terms of research and measures (e.g. Giles, 2002; Schramm & Hartmann, 2008). PSR is distinguished from PSI through duration of and processes within the experience. PSI entails interpersonal processes between viewer and persona confined to the time during a show or other media exposure, while PSR "stands for the cross-situational relationship a viewer or user holds with a persona, which may include specific cognitive, affective, and behavioral components ... like a friendship that exists between two persons beyond their face-to-face communication sequences" (p. 386).

Identification and Reality TV

When a viewer aligns his or her sense of identity and social action with a media character, a process of identification occurs. Cohen (2001) defined identification with media characters as one in which the viewer assumes the character's identity, goals, and perspective. This work considered how technical production and attributes of characters and audiences influence the process, and furthers the concept as more than an attitude toward a character, but an engagement during reception of the broadcast (Cohen, 2001). Identification, along with commitment and integration with a viewer's social network, contributes to parasocial relationships of favorite media personalities (Eyal & Dailey, 2012). Auter and Palmgreen (2000) formed a multidimensional measure of parasocial interaction with identification at its base. Sub-groups of the measure included audience identification with a favorite TV character, interest in the character, identification with the character's group, and the character's problem-solving ability.

Within reality TV studies, Ebersole and Woods (2007) found viewers were motivated to watch reality TV for personal identification with actors, leading to an interaction experience in which they could examine their own self-identities in comparison. Drawing on Davis (1983), they argue that the viewer's empathy or emotional contagion serves as a component of personal identification to extend it beyond momentarily stepping into the actor's shoes. "Personal identification thus goes well beyond 'pretending I am a contestant' to include 'pretending I am like, similar to or identifiable with one of the contestants actually performing' " (Ebersole & Woods, 2007, p. 34).

Similar studies reinforce ways audiences become cognitively and emotionally drawn to reality programming (Godlewski & Perse, 2010; Hall, 2006; Nabi, Biely, Morgan, & Stitt, 2003; Nabi, Stitt, Halford, & Finnerty, 2006; Papacharissi & Mendelson, 2007). Reality shows draw viewer interest to observe situations that are unpredictable and evoke feelings of being in the shoes of regular people experiencing unique circumstances. Just as the novelty of reality content serves as a motivator (Papacharissi & Mendelson, 2007), it ties in with enjoyment that varies with the type of reality program (Nabi et al., 2006).

In turn, the PSR may influence attitudes and behaviors of viewers. PSRs may aid the function of opinion leadership of celebrities to influence attitudes and behaviors of followers. Influence is felt when a follower feels a PSR with an opinion leader who also makes complex topics comprehensible and orients information and views to certain values or political attitudes, or arouses interest to be involved in new or previously unnoticed topics (Stehr, Rossler, Schonhardt, & Leissner, 2015). A key aspect of authenticity in reality TV viewing is feeling identification with characters (Rose & Wood, 2005). As young viewers negotiate their own identities, reality TV shows can affect their self-development and understanding. Behaviors of young people can connect to these attitudes and experiences with reality TV. For example, young viewers have identified with reality TV characters in PSRs that led to behaviors. In the case of sexual relationships in reality TV, they were more likely to engage in risky sexual behavior (Fogel & Kovalenko, 2013), and in the case of beauty in reality TV, they were more likely to engage in use of tanning (Fogel & Krausz, 2013).

Based on the literature, viewers may experience PSR feelings toward Trump from watching *The Apprentice*. They tune in for enjoyment, and through repeated exposure may develop identification feelings for the situations in which Trump engages. Trump is the boss on *The Apprentice*, offering challenges to regular people who star in his show for a chance at a job, money, and fame. Viewers may feel personal identification with contestants or Trump. Parasocial feelings may lead to attitudes and behaviors that extend the relationship beyond viewing the show and impact views of Trump as a candidate. Feelings of liking Trump, trusting him as the U.S. president, and voting for him in the election may result from parasocial predictors. As such, the following hypotheses are proposed:

H2a: Identification with Trump in The Apprentice *will positively influence liking Trump.*

H2b: Identification with Trump in The Apprentice *will positively influence trusting Trump.*

H2c: Identification with Trump in The Apprentice *will positively influence voting for Trump.*

H3a: Interest in Trump in The Apprentice *will positively influence liking Trump.*

H3b: Interest in Trump in The Apprentice *will positively influence trusting Trump.*

H3c: Interest in Trump in The Apprentice *will positively influence voting for Trump.*

H4a: Group identification with Trump in The Apprentice *will positively influence liking Trump.*

H4b: Group identification with Trump in The Apprentice *will positively influence trusting Trump.*

H4c: Group identification with Trump in The Apprentice *will positively influence voting for Trump.*

H5a: Problem-solving abilities seen with Trump in The Apprentice *will positively influence liking Trump.*

H5b: Problem-solving abilities seen with Trump in The Apprentice *will positively influence trusting Trump.*

H5c: Problem-solving abilities seen with Trump in The Apprentice *will positively influence voting for Trump.*

Wishful Identification

Related studies have extended the identification and parasocial literature to explain viewer feelings of a more developed relationship with TV characters in which viewers wish to be like a character in real life. In the study of viewer relationships with TV characters for children (Hoffner, 1996) and young adults (Hoffner & Buchanan, 2005) parasocial connections to characters showed viewer desire to become like a character. Termed wishful identification, the concept explains how identification lasts beyond the viewing experience as the viewer feels a desire or attempts to be like a character (Hoffner, 1996; Hoffner & Buchanan, 2005). Wishful identification originates in earlier studies (Rosengren, Windahl, Hakansson, & Johnsson-Smaragdi, 1976) that explored ways identification lasts beyond the viewing experience. For example, viewers of reality TV programs like *Jersey Shore* demonstrated wishful identification and PSRs that impacted emerging adults' sexual attitudes and behaviors (Bond & Drogos, 2014). Given the impact of wishful identification on attitudes and behaviors, the following hypotheses are posed:

> *H6a: Wishful identification with Trump in* The Apprentice *will positively influence liking Trump.*
>
> *H6b: Wishful identification with Trump in* The Apprentice *will positively influence trusting Trump.*
>
> *H6c: Wishful identification with Trump in* The Apprentice *will positively influence voting for Trump.*

Method

Based on the literature, a questionnaire using 7-point Likert scales was developed to assess young voters' responses to Trump, including likeability, trust, and voting intention. Several existing seven-point Likert scales were used to assess the level of parasocial audience involvement, wishful identification, and responses to Trump. The questionnaire was finalized as an online survey following Institutional Review Board approval in March 2016. The survey was administered during March and April 2016 to a convenience sample of students and recent graduates at a Midwestern university. A total of 268 valid responses was gathered. Of them, 171 (63.8%) were female and 97 (36.2%) were male. The majority of respondents were 18–25 years old (89.6%) and white (90.9%). The median family income was $50,001 to $75,000 (25.4%).

Demographic and Independent Variables

Besides identifying gender, age, family income, and race, respondents were asked to rate their political leaning (1 = very conservative and 7 = very liberal). Media visibility for Trump through *The Apprentice* or *The Celebrity Apprentice* was measured with three items (Cronbach's α = .84, M = 3.24) such as, "I frequently have watched one or both of these shows" and "I frequently have seen information on social media related to one or both of these shows."

Auter and Palmgreen's (2000) scale with four dimensions of parasocial interaction measured the degree to which the audience felt parasocial involvement with Trump. The respondents were asked to rate their feelings about Trump on the series. The four dimensions included identification, interest, group, and problem-solving ability. Six items were adjusted to measure identification (Cronbach's α = .94, M = 2.08), such as "Trump on the shows reminds me of myself" and "I have the same qualities as Trump on the shows." The dimension of interest was measured by four items (Cronbach's α = .89, M = 2.66), such as "I would watch Trump on another program" and "I enjoy trying to predict what Trump will do." The measure of group included six items (Cronbach's α = .93, M = 2.22), such as "Trump's interactions are similar to mine with my friends" and "While watching the shows, I felt included in the group." For problem-solving ability, four items were included (Cronbach's α = .93, M = 2.37) such as "I wish I could handle problems as well as Trump" and "I like the way Trump handles problems." Additionally, wishful identification was measured with five items (Cronbach's α = .91, M = 2.29) such as "I'd like to do the kinds of things Trump does on the shows" and "Trump is the sort of person I want to be like myself" (Hoffner, 1996).

Dependent Measures

The affective attitude or likeability felt toward Trump was assessed by three semantic items, adjusted from Homer and Batra (1994), including dislike/like, unfavorable/favorable, and bad/good (Cronbach's α = .98, M = 2.01). For the measure of trust, respondents were asked to rate, "I trust Trump to do the job of president right" and "I trust Trump" (Cronbach's α = .95, M = 1.90), which was modified from Gefen (2000). Voting intention was measured by asking respondents about the degree to which they would be unlikely/likely, very improbable/very probable, and very impossible/very possible to vote for Trump in the 2016 president election (Cronbach's α = .99, M = 1.85).

Results

A series of hierarchical regressions was performed with control for gender, age, family income, race, and political leaning in the first block of the regression models. The variable entered in the second block was media visibility. The third block focused on parasocial effects, including the factors of identification, interest, group, problem-solving ability, and wishful identification.

H1a–H1c examined the influence of *The Apprentice* and/or *The Celebrity Apprentice* on viewers' likeability, trust, and voting intention for Trump. Table 2.1 shows that after controlling for gender, age, family income, race, and political leaning, Trump's media visibility via *The Apprentice* and/or *The Celebrity Apprentice* was a positive factor to predict likeability (β = .28, p < .00), trust (β = .30, p < .00), and voting intention (β = .29, p < .00) for Trump. H1a–H1c were supported in this study. The more that respondents watched the shows or were made aware of them through social media, the more likely they were to like, trust, and vote for Trump.

H2a–H6c examined whether the level of parasocial interaction affected feelings of likeability, trust, and intention to vote for Trump. Table 1.1 shows that identification with Trump in *The Apprentice* did not affect liking, trusting, or voting for Trump. H2a, H2b, and H2c were not supported. The factors of feeling in the group and problem-solving skills were not significant. Thus, H4a–H4c and H5a–H5c were not supported. For H3a–H3c, the parasocial effect of feeling interest was not significant at a 0.5 level but the β values of interest in the liking (β = .21, p = .06) and voting models (β = .20, p = .09) were not small and both were at the margin of statistical significance.

Wishful identification appeared to be the most important parasocial factor to predict likability, trust, and voting intention. Wishful identification with Trump had a positive effect on liking (β = .26, p = .05) and voting for Trump (β = .27, p = .05). H6a and H6c were supported. Additionally, consistent with the results of liking and voting Trump, the effect of wishful identification on trusting Trump showed significance (β = .25, p = .08) even though it was not significant at a .05 level. To summarize, wishful identification was strongly significant for liking and voting for Trump and moderately significant for trusting Trump. The parasocial factor of interest was moderately significant for liking and voting for Trump. Of note, in the final model, media visibility remained significant for voters to like (β = .15, p = .03), trust (β = .18, p = .02), and vote (β = .18, p = .02) for Trump.

Discussion

Findings point to a parasocial relationship viewers developed with Trump through watching *The Apprentice* that leads to positive feelings toward Trump in a new role as a political candidate. Supported hypotheses indicate media visibility related to Trump on the series supported voter likeability, trust, and intention to vote for him, and was part of the final model with parasocial measures. A feeling of wishing to be like Trump, aligned with the PSR, positively influenced likeability and intention to vote for him. Wishful identification also

Table 2.1: Hierarchical Regression of Demographics, Political Leaning, Media Visibility, and Parasocial Interaction on Liking, Trusting, and Voting for Trump.

	β								
	Liking			Trusting			Voting		
Model	1	2	3	1	2	3	1	2	3
Block									
Step 1: Demographics and Political Leaning									
Gender	-.07	-.15	-.04	.00	-.08	.04	-.00	-.08	.02
Age	.03	.04	.01	-.00	.02	-.01	-.00	.01	-.01
Family Income	.06	.07	.00	.09	.10	.02	.03	.04	-.03
Race	-.02	-.07	-.08	-.02	-.07	-.10	-.05	-.09	-.11
Political Leaning	-.53***	-.44***	-.22**	-.46***	-.38***	-.14†	-.55***	-.46***	-.25**
Step 2: Media Visibility		.28***	.15*		.30***	.18**		.29***	.17**
Step 3: Parasocial Interaction									
Identification			.04			.20			.16
Interest			.21†			.11			.20†
Group			-.06			-.04			-.13
Problem-Solving Ability			.17			.13			.06
Wishful Identification			.26*			.25†			.27*

Note: (1) Liking model: $R^2 = .28$ for Step 1, $\Delta R^2 = .06$ for Step 2, $\Delta R^2 = .23$ for Step 3. (2) Trusting model: $R^2 = .20$ for Step 1, $\Delta R^2 = .07$ for Step 2, $\Delta R^2 = .23$ for Step 3. (3) Voting model: $R^2 = .29$ for Step 1, $\Delta R^2 = .07$ for Step 2, $\Delta R^2 = .18$ for Step 3. $†p ≤ .10$, $*p ≤ .05$, $**p ≤ .01$, $***p ≤ .001$.

was of moderate significance in voter trust of Trump. Interest in Trump on the show, as part of the PSR, was moderately significant in positively influencing likeability for Trump, and intention to vote for him.

Parasocial Relationships & Populist Support

Media coverage of populist support for Trump during the primary run-up to the Republican National Convention and national election suggested that middle-class conservative voters were angry—they expressed mistrust for government and the political system, while feeling like the U.S. is not as great as it use to be (Frum, 2016). And broad support for Trump beyond this group included other demographics (Bowman, 2017). This trend indicated a desire for change from the traditional political candidate as large numbers of voters chose Trump. He offered simple, understandable messages directly to voters in a complicated environment, and despite controversial statements, maintained strong appeal.

Trump's appeal is at the center of these findings. There is marginal statistical support for *The Apprentice* viewers to turn into Trump voters through interest in him on the show. Viewers enjoy Trump's character and entertaining or unpredictable performance, which prompted them to tune in to the reality show (Nabi et al., 2006; Papacharissi & Mendelson, 2007) and then carries over potentially into how they view his character and performance as a candidate. Perhaps Trump's controversial statements are more tolerated as exaggerated performance because viewers believe they already know him through a perceived parasocial relationship. Or, perhaps they are used to the unexpected and outlandish nature of his reality show persona as showman—dramatized through the scripted spectacle of reality TV—and find enjoyment (likeable) backed by the success demonstrated in his business, wealth, and lifestyle that leads to support (voting intention).

The strong influence of media visibility directly and with parasocial factors suggests that Trump entered the Republican primary with an advantage through widespread knowledge of his reality TV persona among the U.S. public. Trump accumulated media visibility to leverage his celebrity capital into political capital (Driessens, 2013). His persona as a successful, decisive businessman was a positive portrayal in that media visibility that gained populist support (Mendelsohn, 1993; Vliegenthart et al., 2005).

Further, the impact of media visibility in directly affecting voter attitudes and within parasocial relationships supports the idea that parasocial relationships can extend through social media content in addition to watching the show. Colliander and Dahlen (2011) found people responding with parasocial interaction to feel more trust and purchase intention toward blog content compared to traditional media. Parasocial interaction was among relationship factors that influenced engagement with corporate social media content (Men & Tsai, 2013). For Trump, extended media visibility in his reality TV persona may have aided his candidacy.

In celebrity culture studies, Turner (2006) explored ways reality TV in popular culture suggests democratic qualities—such as ordinary people attaining celebrity—and influences on cultural identity, particularly among the young. He argues that the media industries use reality TV for profit-making purposes with the illusion of ordinariness that the public may relate to while maintaining power in control of the symbolic economy. He questioned the impact on societal culture as these companies "represent forms of behaviour and identity that are motivated simply by their viability as commercial enterprise or spectacle" (Turner, 2006, p. 161). Trump's effective media visibility through reality TV may exemplify the entertainment focus that dominates mass media and aligns the public toward spectacle even regarding the presidential election. His ability to back his slogan of "making America great again" as a presidential candidate may resonate with voters who see him as *The Apprentice* leader who made positive outcomes on the show among ordinary Americans.

"Wishing to be Trump" Supports Attitudes and Behaviors

While identification of the self and group identification were not influential in the outcomes, wishful identification was significant. Young adults viewed Trump on *The Apprentice* as an example to emulate. While viewers may wishfully identify with ordinary people who vary in the reality show setting (Nabi & Clark, 2008), their experience with Trump was persistent in each episode and always within the dynamic of his leadership and authority. So rather than identify with him as a person like the self, identification appears to take on more of a model to which they aspire. This framework is constructed through the reality TV show format with him as the host and star throughout the episodes. Yet, as young people seek reality TV to help compare and examine their self-identities with ordinary cast members or Trump as the boss (Ebersole & Woods, 2007), their feelings may be more wishful for the star boss who is of higher aspiration and less attainable.

The strength of wishful identification on voter attitudes and behaviors is innovative and contributes to the body of knowledge on modeling influences. In terms of social cognitive theory, people learn information, values, and behaviors from symbolic modeling and the modeled characters could serve in various roles to boost persuasive messages (Bandura, 2002). Particularly when the modeled characters whom people developed identification with were popular celebrities, they could effectively influence viewers' cognitions, attitudes, and behaviors (Brown & Fraser, 2004; Cummings, 1988; Kamins, Brand, Hoeke, & Moe, 1989). It is reasonable to argue that people who liked to watch Trump in *The Apprentice* formed their impression of him and when the impression was ideal, people developed wishful identification. Further, the formation of wishful identification led people to not only like him but also vote for him.

At a moderately significant level, wishful identification supported trusting Trump to serve as the U.S. president. Viewers transferred their impressions of Trump and perceived relationship with him to the real world. It is reasonable to connect this phenomenon with representations of Trump in *The Apprentice*—a real, successful businessman in a reality show who not only demonstrated his business skills but also showed the way he was a powerful and decisive boss. This study showed a modeled character could not only directly influence viewers' cognitions, attitudes, and behaviors that the modeled character lived out, but also could possibly be more powerful, persuading viewers to vote for him as the president through the phenomenon of wishful identification in the show.

The lack of influence for group identification and problem-solving ability may relate to the type of TV genre examined in this study. Schramm and Hartmann (2008) note how group identification and problem-solving measures from Auter and Palmgreen (2000) are more of a fit for PSI measurement of fictional characters. With PSI connected to feelings at the time of exposure to media, these measures may lack influence in the reality TV genre.

Limitations and Future Study

This study examined media visibility and parasocial predictors for connections to voter attitudes and behaviors. Limitations of this work include its use of a convenience sample, which did not have a diverse race component. The online survey relied on self-reported information. More specific measures of media exposure to *The Apprentice*, and content related to *The Apprentice*, could offer further insight.

The focus of this study was limited to young voters, but other demographics would also be informative regarding differences in parasocial measures and in reflecting the wide appeal of Trump for president. Exposure to additional reality show content, via social network sites and news or entertainment coverage, could be factors that are measured in future work. And, finally, findings in this study were gathered during one timeframe within the presidential campaign season. Other points in time could add insight to the populism of Trump, and other celebrity politics influences such as through endorsements or political marketing techniques. Theoretically, content analysis of *The Apprentice* could help better delineate media effects that align or differ among viewers of the show. For example, identifying personality traits in Trump's reality show persona and ways voters understand and act upon those traits could be insightful toward effects. Further, this insight could better outline parasocial factors for possible effects that appeared as less impactful in this self-reported survey. Perspective on voter attitudes and behaviors for celebrity politicians could relate to particular social and economic policies, such as gun control, terrorism, immigration, and financial reform.

References

Allen, K., & Mendick, H. (2013). Keeping it real? Social class, young people and "authenticity" in reality TV. *Sociology, 47*(3), 460–476.

Auter, P. J., & Palmgreen, P. (2000). Development and validation of a parasocial interaction measure: The audience–persona interaction scale. *Communication Research Reports, 17*(1), 79–89.

Baker, P. (2017, October 10). For Trump, the reality show has never ended. *The New York Times.* Retrieved from https://www.nytimes.com/2017/10/10/us/politics/trump-corker-feud-tweet-liddle-bob.html

Banducci, S. A., & Semetko, H. A. (2003). Media and mobilization in the 1999 European parliamentary election. In M. Bond (Ed.), *Europe, parliament and the media* (pp. 189–204). London: Federal Trust.

Bandura, A. (2002). Social cognitive theory of mass communication. In J. Bryant & D. Zillmann (Eds.), *Media effects: Advances in theory and research* (pp. 121–153). Hillsdale, NJ: Lawrence Erlbaum.

Blais, A., Gidengil, E., Fournier, P., & Nevitte, N. (2009). Information, visibility and elections: Why electoral outcomes differ when voters are better informed. *European Journal of Political Research, 48*(2), 256–280.

Bond, B. J., & Drogos, K. L. (2014). Sex on the shore: Wishful identification and parasocial relationships as mediators in the relationship between Jersey Shore exposure and emerging adults' sexual attitudes and behaviors. *Media Psychology, 17*(1), 102–126.

Bowman, K. (2017, June 23). Who were Donald Trump's voters? Now we know. *Forbes.* Retrieved from https://www.forbes.com/sites/bowmanmarsico/2017/06/23/who-were-donald-trumps-voters-now-we-know/#31b5556d3894

Brennan, G., & Hamlin, A. (2000). *Democratic devices and desires.* Cambridge: Cambridge University Press.

Brown, W. J., & Fraser, B. P. (2004). Celebrity identification in entertainment-education. In A. Singhal, M. Cody, E. Rogers, & M. Sabido (Eds.), *Entertainment-education and social change: History, research, and practice* (pp. 97–115). Mahwah, NJ: Lawrence Erlbaum.

Chaffee, S. H., Zhao, X., & Leshner, G. (1994). Political knowledge and the campaign media of 1992. *Communication Research, 21*(3), 305–324.

Cohen, J. (2001). Defining identification: A theoretical look at the identification of audiences with media characters. *Mass Communication & Society, 4*(3), 245–264.

Cohen, J. (2004). Parasocial break-up from favorite television characters: The role of attachment styles and relationship intensity. *Journal of Social and Personal Relationships, 21*(2), 187–202.

Colliander, J., & Dahlén, M. (2011). Following the fashionable friend: The power of social media. *Journal of Advertising Research, 51*(1), 313–320.

Cummings, M. S. (1988). The changing image of the Black family on television. *The Journal of Popular Culture, 22*(2), 75–85.

Davis, M. H. (1983). Measuring individual differences in empathy: Evidence for a multidimensional approach. *Journal of Personality and Social Psychology, 44*(1), 113.

Driessens, O. (2013). Celebrity capital: Redefining celebrity using field theory. *Theory and Society, 42*(5), 543–560.

Ebersole, S., & Woods, R. (2007). Motivations for viewing reality television: A uses and gratifications analysis. *Southwestern Mass Communication Journal, 23*(1), 23–42.

Eyal, K., & Dailey, R. M. (2012). Examining relational maintenance in parasocial relationships. *Mass Communication and Society, 15*(5), 758–781.

Fogel, J., & Kovalenko, L. (2013). Reality television shows focusing on sexual relationships are associated with college students engaging in one-night stands. *Journal of Cognitive & Behavioral Psychotherapies, 13*(2), 321–331.

Fogel, J., & Krausz, F. (2013). Watching reality television beauty shows is associated with tanning lamp use and outdoor tanning among college students. *Journal of the American Academy of Dermatology, 68*(5), 784–789.

Franko, E. (2006). Democracy at work? The lessons of Donald Trump and The Apprentice. In D. S. Escoffery (Ed.), *How real is reality TV?: Essays on representation and truth* (pp. 247–258). Jefferson, NC: McFarland & Company.

Frum, D. (2016, January/February). The great Republican revolt. *The Atlantic.* Retrieved from http://www.theatlantic.com/magazine/archive/2016/01/the-great-republican-revolt/419118/

Gefen, D. (2000). E-commerce: The role of familiarity and trust. *Omega, 28*(6), 725–737.

Giles, D. C. (2002). Parasocial interaction: A review of the literature and a model for future research. *Media Psychology, 4*(3), 279–305.

Godlewski, L. R., & Perse, E. M. (2010). Audience activity and reality television: Identification, online activity, and satisfaction. *Communication Quarterly, 58*(2), 148–169.

Hall, A. (2006). Viewers' perceptions of reality programs. *Communication Quarterly, 54*(2), 191–211.

Hoffner, C. (1996). Children's wishful identification and parasocial interaction with favorite television characters. *Journal of Broadcasting & Electronic Media, 40*(3), 389–402.

Hoffner, C., & Buchanan, M. (2005). Young adults' wishful identification with television characters: The role of perceived similarity and character attributes. *Media Psychology, 7*(4), 325–351.

Homer, P. M., & Batra, R. (1994). Attitudinal effects of character-based versus competence-based negative political communications. *Journal of Consumer Psychology, 3*(2), 163–185.

Horton, D., & Wohl, R. (1956). Mass communication and para-social interaction: Observations on intimacy at a distance. *Psychiatry, 19*(3), 215–229.

Kamins, M. A., Brand, M. J., Hoeke, S. A., & Moe, J. C. (1989). Two-sided versus one-sided celebrity endorsements: The impact on advertising effectiveness and credibility. *Journal of Advertising, 18*(2), 4–10.

Kellner, D. (2009). Barack Obama and celebrity spectacle. *International Journal of Communication, 3*(2009), 715–741.

Keveney, B. (2017, March 3). Arnold Schwarzenegger leaves "Apprentice," Trump says he was fired. *USA Today.* Retrieved from https://www.usatoday.com/story/life/tv/2017/03/03/arnold-quits-apprentice-before-he-can-fired/98700892/

Levy, M. R. (1979). Watching TV news as para-social interaction. *Journal of Broadcasting & Electronic Media, 23*(1), 69–80.

Marsh, D., 't Hart, P., & Tindall, K. (2010). Celebrity politics: The politics of the late modernity? *Political Studies Review, 8*(3), 322–340.

McCammon, S. (2016, March 29). Donald Trump's word choices parsed by fans and critics. *National Public Radio.* Retrieved from http://www.npr.org/2016/03/29/472232836/donald-trump-s-word-choices-parsed-by-fans-and-critics

McNair, B. (2011). *An introduction to political communication.* New York, NY: Routledge.

Men, L. R., & Tsai, W. H. S. (2013). Beyond liking or following: Understanding public engagement on social networking sites in China. *Public Relations Review, 39*(1), 13–22.

Mendelsohn, M. (1993). Television's frames in the 1988 Canadian election. *Canadian Journal of Communication, 18*(2), 149–171.

Moy, P., Xenos, M. A., & Hess, V. K. (2005). Communication and citizenship: Mapping the political effects of infotainment. *Mass Communication & Society, 8*(2), 111–131.

Nabi, R. L., Biely, E. N., Morgan, S. J., & Stitt, C. R. (2003). Reality-based television programming and the psychology of its appeal. *Media Psychology, 5*(4), 303–330.

Nabi, R. L., & Clark, S. (2008). Exploring the limits of social cognitive theory: Why negatively reinforced behaviors on TV may be modeled anyway. *Journal of Communication, 58*(3), 407–427.

Nabi, R. L., Stitt, C. R., Halford, J., & Finnerty, K. L. (2006). Emotional and cognitive predictors of the enjoyment of reality-based and fictional television programming: An elaboration of the uses and gratifications perspective. *Media Psychology, 8*(4), 421–447.

Papacharissi, Z., & Mendelson, A. L. (2007). An exploratory study of reality appeal: Uses and gratifications of reality TV shows. *Journal of Broadcasting & Electronic Media, 51*(2), 355–370.

Ragsdale, L. (1981). Incumbent popularity, challenger invisibility, and congressional voters. *Legislative Studies Quarterly, 6*(2), 201–218.

Rose, R. L., & Wood, S. L. (2005). Paradox and the consumption of authenticity through reality television. *Journal of Consumer Research, 32*(2), 284–296.

Rosengren, K. E., Windahl, S., Hakansson, P. A., & Johnsson-Smaragdi, U. (1976). Adolescents' TV relations: Three scales. *Communication Research, 3*(4), 347–366.

Schramm, H., & Hartmann, T. (2008). The PSI-Process Scales. A new measure to assess the intensity and breadth of parasocial processes. *Communications, 33*(4), 385–401.

Scott, M., Street, J., & Inthorn, S. (2011). From entertainment to citizenship: A comparative study of the political uses of popular culture by first-time voters. *International Journal of Cultural Studies, 14*(5), 499–514.

Stehr, P., Rössler, P., Schönhardt, F., & Leissner, L. (2015). Parasocial opinion leadership media personalities' influence within parasocial relations: Theoretical conceptualization and preliminary results. *International Journal of Communication, 9*(2015), 982–1001.

Street, J. (2004). Celebrity politicians: Popular culture and political representation. *The British Journal of Politics & International Relations, 6*(4), 435–452.

Street, J. (2017, April). *What is Trump? Forms of "celebrity" in celebrity politics.* Paper presented at Political Studies Association Conference, Glasgow, Scotland.

Turner, G. (2006). The mass production of celebrity "Celetoids", reality TV and the "demotic turn". *International Journal of Cultural Studies, 9*(2), 153–165.

Turner, G. (2013). *Understanding celebrity.* London: Sage.

Vliegenthart, R., Oegema, D., & Klandermans, B. (2005). Media coverage and organizational support in the Dutch environmental movement. *Mobilization: An International Quarterly, 10*(3), 365–381.

Part II

Campaign and Presidential Rhetoric

3. Donald Trump "Tells You What He Thinks"

MIRA SOTIROVIC
University of Illinois at Urbana-Champaign

CHRISTOPHER BENSON
Northwestern University

Almost immediately after Barack Obama's 2008 election as the first African-American president of the United States, the media proclaimed we had entered a bright new period in our nation's history: a "post-racial America." Events that have transpired since that historic moment have shown that proclamation to have been more hopeful than real. Not only did the Obama presidency serve as something of a social astringent for racial hostility, but, ironically, the media have played a role, however unwittingly, by validating a darkly coded racialized message, if only through their uncritical transmission of it.

Nowhere can this be seen as clearly as it has been in the presidential campaign of Donald Trump in 2016. It was a year of racial conflicts triggered by a series of high-profile shootings of unarmed Black men by police and marked by the increased visibility of the Black Lives Matter protest movement in response to the tragic shooting deaths. The intensity of protests and confrontations over police abuse of force, unseen for decades, provided a backdrop for the presidential election campaign during which candidate Trump made a number of racially charged statements and earned the endorsement of White supremacist groups.

Wide media coverage brought the racial unrest to the attention of the American public. As a result, concerns over race and racial relationships were reflected in polls in which a record 18% of Americans mentioned them as the single most important problem facing the country. Since 2000, mentions of race have only once previously been in double digits—in December 2014, when 13% mentioned race as the top problem facing the nation. Race was infrequently mentioned as the top problem facing the nation from 1970 through 2000, with the exception of May 1992, a week after the Rodney King verdicts in Los Angeles, when 15% mentioned race as the top problem (Gallup News, 2016). Since then, the percentage of Americans who name race and racial relations as a top problem reverted to its historically more typical, relatively low, level of about 6%, however, race and racial relations remain one of the top four noneconomic problems (Gallup News, 2017a).

Trump's populist campaign message expressed in tough talk was among many reasons for his electoral victory, creating an impression that Trump "tells you what he thinks," even when those messages had racist and sexist overtones. Trump called for the end of political correctness and trashed the rules of civic decorum by insulting hundreds of people in his tweets, including the rivals of his own party. The television news media fed on every juicy bite Trump threw them, repeated them incessantly to their audiences, even when treating them as a bad joke. The very coverage by mainstream media lent an odd sort of validation to the message, if only because it was deemed worthy of coverage in the public mind. In part, Trump rode a wave of White working class discontent with Democratic policies many believed had not addressed their needs. But, in a closely related way, he also appealed to the groups that blamed traditionally marginalized groups in a racist and sexist zero-sum game in which Obama was not only the most visible representation of the Democratic policies, but also the embodiment of a demographic—and cultural—shift many felt would leave them out. In such a context, the words people use to convey their thought and emotions do not have only literal meanings, but they reflect their attitudes and perceptions and reveal the psychological processes involved in constructions of their narratives (Pennebaker, Mehl, & Nienderhoffer, 2003). As linguistic markers of those psychological processes, words can have "yuge" consequences.

This chapter examines the political discourses of the 2016 presidential election with the focus on how two presidential candidates, Donald Trump and Hillary Clinton, talked about race, racial issues and minorities (African Americans and Hispanics) in their three presidential debates. Then, it examines how two leading cable news media (CNN and FOX) reported on debates which together drew a record 259 million TV viewers, and how their audiences reacted to cable channels' coverage on Facebook sites. We tracked the progression of the discourse on race in the debates, through the news media coverage, to public reactions in the social media. How was the discourse in debates interpreted and explained in the news coverage and translated in the Facebook comments? How did social media complement the news media in construction of racial images, and what understandings of race and racial issues emerged among the public on the social networks?

We update and extend the seminal study on media representation of race in America by Entman and Rojecki (2000, p. 208) who found that Blacks were portrayed in the media mostly through "turmoil and inadequacy," often in the context of "social pathology" (crime, cheating, violence, low self-discipline) and unpopular social policies (welfare, affirmative action) (Entman & Rojecki, 2000, p. 208). These portrayals resulted in the images of Blacks that fuel the vicious cycle of majority ambivalence and opposition to progressive racial policies in the public sphere and animosity and separation in private lives (Entman & Rojecki, 2000, p. 209). Racism of the 21st century has moved significantly beyond old-fashioned expressions through physical violence and slurs, to symbolic and systemic racism, often encoded in the language of politics that comes with a wink and disingenuous condemnation of racism.

Politicians have long exploited double talk to trigger racial sentiments, such as Barry Goldwater's "law and order," Ronald Reagan's "welfare queen" and "war on drugs," George H. W. Bush's "tough on crime," Bill Clinton's ending of "welfare as we know it" and Newt Gingrich's labeling of Obama as a "food stamp president," without mentioning race. There is a built-in assumption, for example, that crime is a bigger problem than it really is, and that the face of crime is a face of color (Dixon & Linz, 2000). Similarly, poverty and federal assistance programs are associated with people of color and seen as costly to White working class and middle class families. Ian Haney López (2014) in his book "Dog Whistle Politics" asserts that racist codes are evolving and becoming more veiled. Loaded phrases such as "forced busing" and "states' rights," are supplanted by "abstract" calls for "tax cuts," with an implicit understanding that they will stop giveaways and starve programs that help undeserving groups. Deeper encoding within general social policies leaves room for plausible denial of associations with racial images. General anti-government attitudes that crystallized in the Tea Party movement are underwritten by explicit opposition of Whites for government aiding Blacks, and for preferential hiring and promotion of Blacks. Whites are also significantly less likely than Blacks to believe that differences between African-Americans and Whites in jobs, income and housing are due to discrimination and more likely to believe that Black people should overcome prejudice without favors (General Social Survey, 2014).

When former Ku Klux Klan grand wizard David Duke explained his support for Donald Trump, he did not mention race. He praised Trump's immigration stands, and hoped for ending the era of political correctness, for "breaking up 'Jewish dominated lobbies and super PACS that are corrupting and controlling American politics,' preventing war with Russia, exposing media 'lies' and ensuring 'that White-Americans are allowed to preserve and promote their heritage and interests just as all other groups are allowed to do.'" (Bradner, 2016, para. 10)

Since becoming President, Trump's executive orders, policy initiatives, and comments mirror significant elements of Duke's stated support. By March 2017, 69% of Americans said that they personally worry about race relations (Gallup News, 2017b). The percentage of Americans who worried about racial relations doubled since 2014 and they remain at the highest level in Gallup's 17-year poll results trend.

The goal of this chapter is to describe public talk about race and to identify the 21st century coded language that can give rise to racial sentiments. We trace racial appeals from the presidential candidates' statements during the debates, through interpretations of those statements in the news media coverage of debates, and into public understanding of those appeals as expressed in the Facebook comments. The three presidential debates serve as the starting point of our research. The first, third, and second presidential debates were respectively the second, third and fifth most watched TV broadcasts in the U.S. in 2016, topped only by the Super Bowl and its post-game show. With 84 million people watching the first debate, its audience was almost two and a-half times larger than the Academy Awards show—the only other non-sport event in the top ten (Nielsen, 2016). Debates traditionally attract large audiences because of the conflict and unpredictability of a face-off in which the true character of a candidate is revealed. Despite some spontaneous exchanges, candidates mostly deliver their carefully prepared and rehearsed remarks and try to drill in several essential points unfiltered by reporters' interpretations (Jamieson & Gottfield, 2010). Almost one third of debate viewers say that presidential debates are more helpful in deciding how to vote than news coverage of the campaign, political talk shows, campaign rallies, campaign ads and televised interviews with the candidates (Holz, Akin & Jamieson, 2016). However, the most important effect of debates might be on reporters and commentators who cover them. Their perception of candidates and their performance illustrated by few quotes and soundbites will find their way into next day stories and can define candidates for much larger audiences (Brubaker & Hanson, 2009). The first debate is considered the most important because it is typically seen by the largest number of people among whom are many who form their first unmediated impressions of candidates and their stands on issues.

The two cable news channels (CNN and FOX) were the top sources for election news in the 2016 presidential campaign. About one third of American voters in the Pew Research Center survey named them as their main news sources, followed at the distance by Facebook and Local TV, each with about 8% of voters. The news media performance in their roles to provide citizens with relevant information that will engage them in interpretations that will challenge assumptions and stereotypes is crucial for a society that values freedom, justice and equality. Their performance in this role is even more important in these times when partisan talk radio, web and social media fuel outrage and sectarianism, and spread conspiracies and lies. The expectation that the news media will save democracy is blunted by research consistently showing that the main and most enduring characteristics of election campaign coverage are "horse race" reporting and relentless, equal opportunity, criticism and negativity (Capella & Jamieson, 1997). The upward trend started in 1984 when about half of stories about presidential nominees were negative and culminated in 2016 with about two thirds. The negative tone also dominated coverage of Muslims, immigration, health policy and economy (Patterson, 2016). One of the consequences of increasing negativity is the public's cynicism and mistrust of politicians, government, and the news media (Jones, 2004).

The negative political climate in the traditional news media may be mirrored or even surpassed in the social media. Compared to other places where political issues are discussed, many social media users perceive the tone of political discussions on social media to be even more negative (Duggan & Smith, 2016). About half of social media users feel that the political discussions they see on social media are less respectful, less likely to come to a resolution, less civil and more angry than those they see elsewhere. Most users of social media (84%) think that social media encourage people to say things about politics that they never would say in person (Duggan & Smith, 2016).

Following Entman and Rojecki (2000, p. 66) we identified text relevant to race by searching for the word "black" and term "African-American" and their equivalents or associated words and terms (inner city, ghetto, race, racial, racist, racism, underclass, minority).[1] We added to the list words "Hispanic" as a more specific reference to "minority" and "Obama" as an exemplar representing all "Black" and "African Americans." The name "Obama" is also a racially charged referent for issues and policy preferences and it represents a symbolic trigger for racial sentiments. We searched Lexis-Nexis transcripts of all three presidential debates, transcripts of CNN and Fox news stories published during the day following each of the debates, and extracted comments

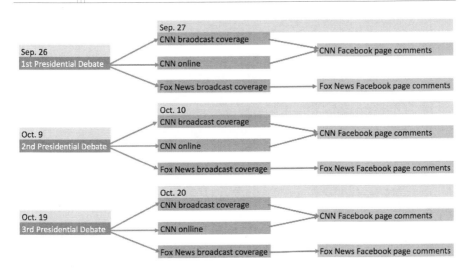

Figure 3.1: Transcripts of Documents Comprising the Analytical Corpus.

posted on the CNN and Fox Facebook pages during the same period.[2] Our collection or "corpus" of documents consists of transcripts of three debates, transcripts of the coverage on CNN and Fox News one day after each debate, CNN online stories one day after each debate, and CNN and Fox News Facebook page comments one day after each debate—in total, 18 documents.

Frequencies of the racial words used in three presidential debates adjusted for their length show that race was a much more prominent issue in 2016 than in two previous presidential elections (Figure 3.2). Only three "racial" words appear in the previous two election debates. The word "African" appears only six times per 10,000 words in 2008 presidential debates, and words "Hispanic" and "minority" appear five and 15 times per 10,000 words in 2012 presidential debates.

Most of the racial words in 2016 were used in the first debate that contained the segment about "America's direction" starting by "talking about race" (Presidential Debate at Hofstra University in Hempstead, New York, 2016).[3]

Clinton responded to the first question "How do you heal the (racial) divide?" by saying: "Unfortunately, race still determines too much, often determines where people live, determines what kind of education in their public schools they can get, and, yes, it determines how they're treated in the criminal justice system."

Clinton talked about "restoring trust between communities and *the police*," "*criminal justice* reform," "*gun* epidemic," and "the plague of *gun*

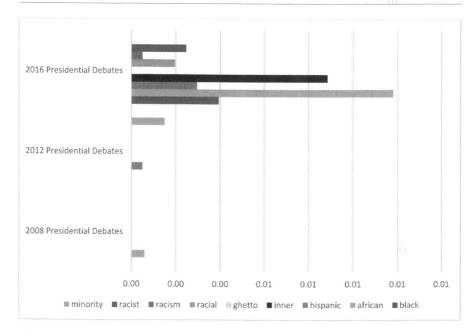

Figure 3.2: Frequencies or Racial Words in Presidential Debates 2008–2016.

violence, which is a big contributor to a lot of the problems that we're seeing today."

Trump responded: "Well, first of all, Secretary Clinton doesn't want to use a couple of words, and that's *law and order*. And we need *law and order*. If we don't have it, we're not going to have a country."

He said that his campaign has been endorsed by "almost every *police* group," and he praised the success of "*stop and frisk*" policy. He described places like Chicago where "gangs roaming the street," "and in many cases, they're *illegally* here, *illegal immigrants*" who have *guns*, and African-American communities "being decimated by *crime*." He also pointed out that it was Clinton who used the term "*super-predators*" to describe some of "young Black youth."

When asked about his perpetuating a false claim that the nation's first Black president was not a natural-born citizen, Trump tried to blame Clinton, suggesting falsely that she, too, had questioned the president's birthplace and boasted that he did a "great service not only for the country, but even for the president in getting (Obama) to produce his *birth certificate*." Clinton responded that Trump started his political activity based on the racist lie and persisted with it, because some of his supporters believed or wanted to believe it. Clinton also mentioned that Trump's early career as a real-estate developer was marked by a lawsuit by the Justice Department for racial discrimination. Trump responded that he opened a "tremendously successful club" in Palm Beach, Florida, where there is "no discrimination against African-Americans, against Muslims, against anybody."

The first debate typically sets the agenda and the tone for all the following discussion during the campaign. The candidates' carefully crafted slogans and phrases are quoted and their meaning dissected in the news, and they are commented on in the Facebook discussions. In this connection, it is important to note the framing of the race issue by Trump as the issue of crime, with the implication that people of color are responsible for the crime problem. Resurrecting Hillary Clinton's 1996 use of the term "super predator" in a racially inflected reference, Trump suggested agreement between them on the nature of the crime problem as a race problem, despite Clinton's expressed regret for use of the term. And, while Trump was determined to prevent Clinton from walking away from her past, his unchallenged and unverified assertion of non-discrimination at his private club, suggested a measure of reform of past racist actions. Of course, there was no discussion of the excessively high initiation fees and annual membership dues along with the reported personal approval of all new memberships by Trump, that create the possibility for quiet discrimination.

In the second debate, Clinton described herself as starting off as a young lawyer working against discrimination against African-American children in schools and in the criminal justice system, and demanded an apology to the president and our country for the "racist lie that President Obama was not born in the United States of America" (Presidential Debate at Washington University in St. Louis, Missouri, 2016). Trump responded that Clinton owes him (Obama) an apology for using pictures in her campaign with President Obama "in a certain garb." Clinton was also asked about her comment that half of Donald Trump's supporters are *deplorables*, racist, sexist, homophobic, xenophobic, Islamophobic.

Trump described "*inner cities* of our country" as a "disaster education-wise, job-wise, safety-wise, in every way possible." He said it's "devastating" what is happening in our "*inner cities*," the poverty rate of 45%, "the *violence* that's taking place," and claimed the biggest increase in murder in 45 years while Clinton merely has been talking about *inner cities* for 25 years and nothing happens; "she doesn't get it done." "She's done a terrible job for the African-Americans. She wants their vote, and she does nothing, and then she comes back four years later." He asked, "What do you have to lose?" "It can't get any worse." He promised he was going to help African-Americans, Latinos, Hispanics, and the *inner cities*. He said, "I will be a president for all of our people. And I'll be a president that will turn our *inner cities* around and will give strength to people and will give economics to people and will bring jobs back."

Alternatively, the gist of discussion on race during two debates could be described by a few evocative words and phrases such as: "law and order," "stop and frisk," "birth certificate," "criminal justice," "guns," "police," "illegal," "crime/violence." Apart from the use of Obama and the birther issue as symbols of inherent un-Americanism and unbridgeable differences between Blacks and Whites, the racial discourse of the 2016 presidential debates had familiar overtones. Entman and Rojecki (2000) found that the network news stories tend to present Blacks in the context of crime and victimization that requires intervention from government. Hispanics are portrayed in a similarly negative way. Those portrayals raise racial anxieties and stimulate negative feelings.

Our central analyses employ a computerized text analysis method to tap into psychological meanings of news media representations of Blacks and manifestations of those meanings in the public's reactions. Research on language as an "index of meaning" (Osgood, Suci & Tannenbaum, 1957) has a long tradition. Language signs, or words, that people use to express their ideas are consistently associated with certain representational processes that make all communication possible. The contention that words we use reflect "what we are paying attention to, what we are thinking about, what we are trying to avoid, how we are feeling, and how we are organizing and analyzing our worlds" (Tausczik & Pennebaker, 2010, p. 30) provided impetus for development of a computer program named Linguistic Inquiry and Word Count (LIWC) that categorizes words into psychologically relevant linguistic categories. LIWC categories capture over 86% of English words people use in writing and speech. Pennebaker, Booth, Boyd & Francis (2015) demonstrated that those language categories accurately identify psychological processes and states such as affective processes, cognitive processes and drives. Affective processes are indicated by expressions of positive and negative emotions, anxiety anger and sadness. Cognitive processes are indicated by expressions of insight, causation, discrepancy, tentativeness, certainty and differentiation. Drives are indicated by expressions of affiliation, achievement, power, reward and risk (Pennebaker, Boyd, Jordan & Blackburn, 2015).

In addition to validating the categories, research using LIWC showed that they differ significantly between contexts in which people use language. For example, the language of *The New York Times* is the least affective whereas Twitter contains the largest number of words that indicate affective processes.

We conducted LIWC analyses on the whole corpus of documents and also only on extracted passages that contained "racial" words and 140 characters—the former Twitter word limit—on each side of the word. We used AntConc software (Anthony, 2014), a concordance program for text analyses, to generate and extract passages. Those passages, consisting of 40 words on average, provide contextual basis for determining the psychological meanings of the "racial" words.

Figure 3.3 shows differences between language categories used in the whole and "race" corpuses. The race corpus contains fewer of the words that indicate cognitive processes such as insight (e.g. knowing, thinking, believing),

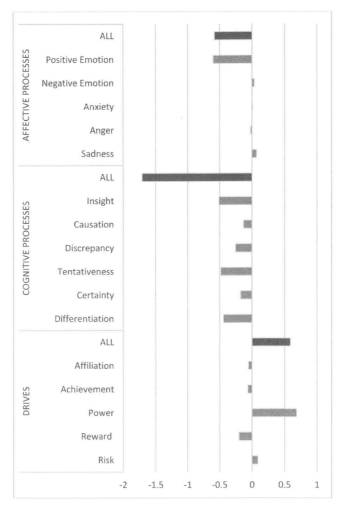

Figure 3.3: Differences in Psychological Processes Between Race and Whole Corpus (Negative Differences Indicate Smaller Values in Race Corpus).

tentativeness (e.g. somebody trying to do something, posing questions, and expressing hope) and differentiation (e.g. pointing and stating differences between views, events, people). Racial discourses also contain fewer words that express positive emotions (e.g. characterization as "good," expressing caring, love, support), and more of the words that indicate power (references relevant to status, dominance and social hierarchies such as law, order, justice, government, administration, help).

In addition to overall differences between racial and presidential campaign discourses, there are also pronounced differences in the use of language categories across different media sources in the context of race. To discern the pattern in the way the racial discourse is different in the debates from their cable coverage and Facebook comments we performed cluster analyses.[4] The simplest two-cluster solution revealed a striking mirror image of processes in Facebook comments and all other racial discourses in our analysis.[5]

Figure 3.4 shows that the Facebook discourse on race is driven by affective processes with the exception of expressions of "sadness," for which there was no reason before the election results were tallied. It is also rich with cognitive processes, as people try to understand what happened, except for the lack of "insight." The lower level of references to "power" suggest more

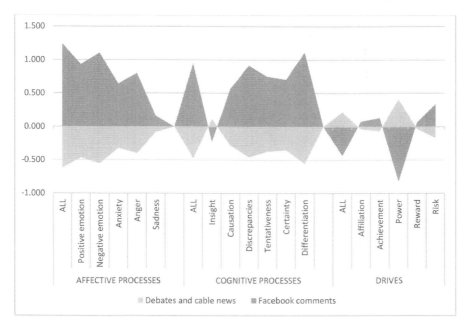

Figure 3.4: Psychological Processes Across Platform.

egalitarian and inclusive talk on the social medium platform. The results identified the CNN Facebook page comments on first debate as the prototype, or the "centroid,"[6] for all Facebook comments in our analysis.

The following are excerpts from some of the CNN Facebook page comments that were most repeated, shared or propagated by bots. They illustrate the language underlying the psychological processes captured by LIWC categories. These comments were found in the racial corpus of all six Facebook documents we analyzed. The numbers at the end of paragraphs indicate how many times they appeared in the corpus.

> **If** you are Black, **why** are you voting for Hillary when she admires Margaret Sanger and *defends* *Planned Parenthood* when they **want** to abort as many Black babies as **possible**. Exterminate the Black race **because** they are like "weeds". **Most** of those clinics are in Black *neighborhoods*. 651 (4% of total number of comments in our analysis)

> I lock my doors at night and I've own homes with walls and so do a **lot** of *us* for many **different reasons**. That doesn't **make** *us* racists! So listen to me, Millions of Trump supporters feel this way about Donald J. Trump. ...""" *We* don't care if the guy swears ... **or how** many times he's been *married* ... **or** who he voted for, **or** what his income tax return shows. *We* **want** the *problems* fixed. Yes he's an egomaniac, **but** *we* don't care. *We* **know** he's **not** a racist, **or** *bad* to women, **or all** the **other** things the liberal media is *trying* to label him with. *We* **know** he's raised a *good family*, and that says a **lot** about him. 178

> The hatred of this liberal media **against** DONALD TRUMP is so endemic to the extent that the can fabricate **something** and claim TRUMP said it, **but** they will turn around to call TRUMP a racist and **all sort** of *bad* name. **May** *GOD* have mercy on you people, one thing I **know** which I **believe** is **if** *GOD* has destined **someone** for *greatness*, no amount of propaganda and hateful *campaign* **against** the person can *stop* it. 161

> Hillary is CORRUPT! Hillary is a LIAR! Hillary is EVIL! The debate **didn't change any** of those **FACTS**! The birth certificate issue is a place of birth issue and not a racial one, mainstream media *trying* to spin people's head *over.* 110

> Call *us* deplorable, call *us* uneducated, call *us* racist, *we* don't care! **If** honest is deplorable, *we take* that name *proudly.* **If** honest is racist, then your **perception** is your *problem.* **If** honest is uneducated, *we* are thankful *we* **didn't** *get* your indoctrination. #VoteTrump be deplorable, it's fun being right and *winning* easily. 144

> Trump did not double African American unemployment. Trump did not increase welfare to a record level for eight years. Trump did not sign a *law* **making** it legal to execute, and imprison Americans. 160

> Why did the *first* African American *president* have to release his birth certificate? That wasn't a public service that was a way to smear the *president.* ... The African

American *community!*" (the phrase "birth certificate" appears 251 times across nine corpus documents)

Hillary Clinton's past runs contrary to the stated *goals* of Black Lives Matter. Hillary Clinton was against gay *marriage*, used a *campaign* ad accused of having racist undertones, waited a calculating 19 days to address Ferguson, and utilized racial prejudices against Barack Obama. (the phrase "black lives matter" appears 163 times across 10 corpus documents)

When talking about inner cities he was more concerned for his properties **than** what's happening to people. To **want** to revive *Stop* & Frisk that legalizes racial profiling is contemptible. No **wonder** he has the support of **All** White Supremacist Organizations. They *campaign* for him while recruiting for their racist organizations. He speaks for them! 144[7]

Distinctive patterns of differences also emerged between the debates and their cable news media coverage by the two channels analyzed. The cable news media coverage appeared to provide more insight and power references, but point somewhat less toward discrepancies possibly in an attempt to avoid alienating their core audiences and keep in line with their preferences. Conversely, more references to affiliations and reward were made in debates than in their coverage.

Most interesting, the two cable news channels covered the same events by using different language (Figure 3.5). The language of CNN was affective whereas Fox News was more cognitive, expressing more insight and causation. Words expressing drives, needs and motivations also portrayed two opposite worlds—the CNN world that is driven by affiliations and achievements and the Fox News world that emphasized the need for power (authority) and reward.

The CNN racial language does not only consist of more words expressing affect but also their range is much wider. Many of the emotionally charged words such as alarmed, anxiety, criticized, concerned, hurts, insulted, lie, problems, protests, shocking, supremacy, threatened, or violence, do not appear in the Fox News language used to cover the first and second debate. The main reason for more emotional language of CNN discussions compared to Fox News is CNN's much more diverse makeup of anchors, hosts, reporters, commentators and contributors, among whom was a significant number of African-Americans and Hispanics. Every hour of CNN programing featured at least one African-American guest, and there were several among them who were identified as Republicans or Trump supporters. Most of the CNN shows also included both Clinton and Trump surrogates, and by doing that captured the intensity and enthusiasm of voters on both sides. The CNN anchors and hosts actively encouraged the conflict between guests that played

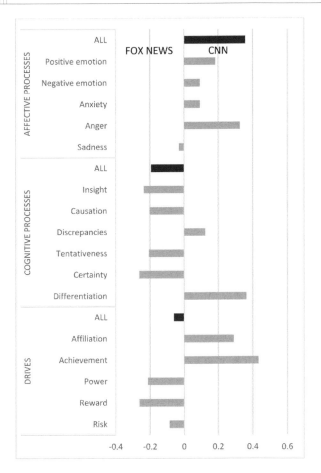

Figure 3.5: Differences Between CNN and Fox News.

out in many heated exchanges. The following excerpts from CNN show transcripts and web publications illustrate the emotional tone of racial discussions.

> Then stop—stop right now. Stop insulting Mexicans and stop insulting Muslims and stop insulting women and stop insulting Black people. Stop it. And insulting —MCCAUGHEY: You—your—and Hillary Clinton should stop insulting all the Americans she calls deplorables and unredeemables if they disagree (CNN, 2016a).[8]

> … when people who previously told us character matters are now just waving away really serious and shocking character issues as though they don't matter at all. We have had issues where for, over a year ago now, African-American and Hispanic evangelicals have been alarmed and concerned about, why are our leaders not taking these things seriously? (CNN, 2016b)

Trump reiterated his <u>support</u> for "law and order," once again characterizing America's inner-cities as forgotten places filled with <u>murder</u>, poverty and <u>miserable</u> Blacks who have been <u>abandoned</u> by politicians. <u>But</u> his description of the Black <u>community</u> sidestepped the way in which his own political rhetoric has contributed to the nation's growing racial divide. Its <u>promotion</u> of a brand of racial <u>anxiety</u>, <u>fear</u> and <u>anger</u> have turned his campaign into a galvanizing movement for racial intolerance. In fact, his Janus-faced stance on racial justice has helped normalize the notion of White <u>supremacy</u> in contemporary American politics … She also turned back his apocalyptic description of Black <u>communities</u> by discussing the <u>hopes</u> and dreams of ordinary Black <u>families</u>, the <u>strength</u> of the Black <u>church</u> and aspects of racial <u>progress</u> that Trump's rhetoric conveniently <u>ignores</u> (Joseph, 2016).

"My ancestors could not get papers simply because they were brought here as slaves. It took centuries before <u>we could</u> finally get papers," she said. "To bring this up over and over again and to smear the <u>first</u> Black president of the United States, Donald Trump <u>should</u> be ashamed of himself. And he should apologize. I get <u>emotional</u>. I've got a birth certificate <u>but</u> my grandparents did not. My <u>great</u> grandparents did not," she added (Scott, 2016).

He rose to the <u>top</u> because <u>not</u> enough of <u>us</u> spoke out when <u>we</u> had the chance. His daughter had an incredible <u>opportunity</u> to stand up to racism and <u>hate</u> when her father announced his candidacy, yet she has <u>failed to</u> disavow the <u>hateful</u> rhetoric that <u>we</u> have heard time and again (Arce, 2016).

Kaepernick's decision this NFL season to kneel during the national anthem to raise awareness about racial issues landed him on the cover of TIME Magazine last week. His <u>protest</u> has <u>inspired</u> a growing number of <u>other</u> athletes to join him. The <u>protests</u>, and a new series of police shootings of Black men, have helped reignite a <u>national conversation</u> on race. (Moshtaghian & Simon, 2016).

I <u>defend</u> Chicago because of what it does for me, <u>not</u> what it does—<u>or</u> doesn't do—for the 1.5 million Black and Hispanic people that may see it a <u>different</u> way. The <u>problems</u> in Chicago are rooted in history—a city more segregated <u>than</u> New York and Los Angeles that allows for economic disparity to fall along racial lines. <u>Gangs</u> and gun <u>violence</u> flourish in this economic void. I don't know <u>if</u> it's all the <u>fault</u> of city government (Kravarik, 2016).

In contrast to CNN, the Fox News coverage of debates was typically a discussion of the like-minded who mostly engaged in reaffirmations, rationalizations, and justifications of Trump's statements interlaced with sarcasm toward Clinton. Below are sample paragraphs from the Fox News coverage of the first debate.

Trump again held firm when asked <u>if</u> he has <u>anything</u> to say to those who <u>felt</u> it was racist to <u>question</u> the first Black <u>president's</u> birth certificate. (Fox News Network, 2016a)[9]

And I <u>think</u> for Donald Trump, what I <u>think</u> he needs to <u>learn</u> is what I call <u>trigger</u> words. If Hillary Clinton calls you a racist, <u>how</u> should Donald Trump respond? Sean, "basket of deplorables." If she says Donald Trump is hiding something, he needs to be automatically thinking, well, wait a second Hillary Clinton. You've been hiding your emails. You hid your private server. So I think that that is going to be key. (FNN, 2016b)

Donald Trump rightly brings up that in Chicago this year alone, over 3,000 people have been shot! And of course, 3,676 people have been killed since Obama became president just in the Windy City! And somehow, Hillary Clinton says, Well, everything's just fine. Now, we have failed the African-American community and also we're failing the country. They're failing schools, crime, poverty, drugs, and as you know, the list goes on and on. (FNN, 2016b)

And what you have basically illustrated—and I'll get to your question in a minute— is that when America has a cold, Black America has pneumonia. Thank you for saying it. And here's why. Many Black voices won't tell the truth to the Black community. You just did. Donald Trump is telling the truth to the Black community. (FNN, 2016b)

Or when birtherism came up. He could have said, "Who cares." (FNN, 2016c)

I guess we're all deplorable now. Before it was just half of Trump's supporters we're racist, now apparently, we're all racists. That's the, [sic] Hillary Clinton's ever-expanding world of deplorable. I mean look, the reality is she was asked on a nationally televised broadcast the question, do you believe police are implicitly biased against Black people. The proper answer to that is of course not. The vast majority of American police officers are good, decent, honorable people who risk their lives to protect us and they are not racists. (FNN, 2016d)

And you know what they found? Zero police zero race bias in police shootings. In fact, they found police more likely to fire their weapon when they weren't attacked when the suspect was white. So, this idea that somehow the police are out there shooting Black people willy-nilly is simply false and she should have said so ... And there are many people who believe that, who believe we all have some inherent fear of other whatever the other may be. (FNN, 2016d)

Yeah, there's a big difference between being biased and racist and let's make that clear right away. You know, everybody is inherently biased. There is 88 percent of Americans—there's a project called The Bias Project, the inherent bias project and it measured 88 percent of Americans have some form of implicit bias. But that doesn't mean racism. And that also includes law enforcement. And that's a danger zone for her politically because she's trying to appeal to the moderates. (FNN, 2016d)

During the whole day of coverage of the first debate Fox News featured only five Black commentators, comprised of two primary race presidential candidates, Ben Carson and Herman Cain, two conservative show hosts, Larry Elder and Charles Payne, and the chairman of The Tea Party Forward organization Niger Innis. The lack of diversity in Fox News coverage was further amplified by the one-sided viewpoints. When talking about the issue of race and race relations the Fox News coverage was all about Black people and communities that suffered many problems, among which racism was not included. The Fox News coverage systematically denied racism on both a social level and in Trump's attitudes. The language of power in the Fox News suggests its unique approach to the problems of Blacks. The Fox News coverage contains 20% more unique power words compared to CNN, and those unique words suggest that Blacks are the victims of failing policies, and the loci of power and agencies that can solve the problems of Blacks are revealed by the use of words "ownership," "manager" and "wealth."

Conclusion

In our study, we examined how politicians, cable news media and ordinary people talked about race and racial relations in the context of presidential elections. We focused on the psychological underpinnings of what they said under the assumption that affective, cognitive and motivational psychological processes give rise to the use of particular words that function as their linguistic markers. Those words portray attitudes and perceptions of the speaker, reveal non-literal meanings of what is said, and may lead to audiences' implicit understandings of the messages that may be the key to their effectiveness.

The psycho-linguistic approach and the application of computerized text analyses methodology resulted in three notable findings. First, media discourses about race and racial relations are psychologically distinct from the overall discussions that took place during the presidential debates and their coverage. The racial discourses were lacking in both positive emotion and cognitive processes that people employ to make sense of their world and analyze its problems. In contrast, they were more concerned with power, status, and authority. Second, the Facebook comments could be considered a medium in their own right given the striking contrast to race discussions in both debates and their coverage in all three psychological domains. The social media always have been viewed as a more inclusive and expressive or emotional complement to the public sphere, but our study shows that they also provided more opportunities than cable news coverage for reasoning and attempts to understand the positions of candidates on racial issues. Third, the media coverage of race is strikingly different on two cable channels, with CNN performing as journalism, however flawed, and FOX as propaganda for the Republican candidate and his party's ideology. CNN prioritized conflict and the emotional displays it engendered at the expense of explaining and analyzing, and FOX provided uncritical rationalization of Trump's statements. Unfortunately, each of those approaches may have been amplified in the Facebook comments without compensating for their deficiencies.

During the campaign, Trump repeatedly insisted that he was the "least racist person," and his supporters denied many times that he is racist. When Trump was asked in a June 2016 interview with CNN reporter Jake Tapper whether his comment that the U.S. District Judge Gonzalo Curiel was incapable of judging the Trump University lawsuits because of his Mexican heritage, was the "definition or racism," Trump denied it. "No, I don't think so at all," he replied (Borchers, 2016). After the election, in response to the August 2017 "Unite the Right" rally in Charlottesville, which resulted in one person's death, Trump issued conflicting, equivocal messages, virtually neutralizing his proclamation on the one hand that "racism is evil," by blaming "many sides" for the violent protest, and never strongly denouncing the White supremacist organizers. Many of his supporters—including administration officials—defended him against charges that he was giving tacit cover to racists. Despite his overt denials, Trump's dog whistle message is getting through. On Jan. 31, former Klan leader David Duke tweeted: "everything I've been talking about for decades is coming true and the ideas I've fought for have won" (Lenz & Gunter, 2017). According to the Southern Poverty Law Center, the effectiveness of Trump's messages of apparent support of a radical right—the so-called "Alt-right"—agenda is manifesting in an increased number of hate groups and in their emboldened activities since the election (Potok, 2017).

Rachel Pendergraft, a national organizer for the Knights Party, the successor to David Duke's Knights of the Ku Klux Klan, told *Mother Jones* magazine that, "The success of the Trump campaign just proves that our views resonate with millions. They may not be ready for the Ku Klux Klan yet, but as anti-white hatred escalates, they will" (Posner & Neiwert, 2016). During the campaign, it appears that the news media failed to do enough to instill a deeper appreciation of the continued existence of racial animus and its enduring impact, and, as a result, the public was denied vital information necessary for enlightened choice making in the democratic process. Moreover, by providing a platform for the dissemination of misinformation on race and negative racially coded messages without effective challenge, the legacy media arguably may have appeared to validate these messages and aided in their long-lasting impact on public consciousness.

Notes

1. We excluded the word "underclass" because of its absence from the text corpus.
2. Cable channel transcripts of stories and Facebook comments are first filtered to include only those that contained words "debate," "Trump," and "Clinton."

3. The following summary and all direct quotes are based on transcripts of debates.
4. Cluster analysis is a procedure for detecting groupings in the data. We used the k-means clustering method which allows the numbers of clusters to be specified based on theoretical considerations.
5. Figure 3 shows distances from cluster centers defined by the means for each cluster.
6. The centroid is the cluster center determined by the smallest distances from the mean of the cluster.
7. Affective words are underlined, cognitive are in bold, and drives are in italics. Some words belong to more than one category.
8. Affective words are underlined, discrepancies and differentiations are underlined in **bold**, and affiliation and achievement are underlined in dots.
9. Power and reward words are double underlined and insight, causation, tentativeness and certainty are wavy underlined.

References

Anthony, L. (2014). *AntConc (Version 3.4.3)* [Computer Software]. Tokyo, Japan: Waseda University. Retrieved from http://www.laurenceanthony.net/

Arce, J. (2016, September 27). Ivanka Trump once loved the story of an undocumented immigrant [Web publication]. *CNN.com*. Retrieved from Lexis Nexis database.

Borchers, C. (2016, June 3). Jake Tapper asked Donald Trump if his judge attack was racist, then followed up 23 times. *Washington Post*. Retrieved from https://www.washingtonpost.com/news/the-fix/wp/2016/06/03/jake-tapper-asked-donald-trump-if-his-judge-attack-was-racist-then-followed-up-23-times/?utm_term=.8d-2b2578a8b3

Bradner, E. (2016, February 29). Donald Trump Stumbles on David Duke, KKK. *CNN.com*. Retrieved from http://www.cnn.com/2016/02/28/politics/donald-trump-white-supremacists/index.html

Brubaker, J., & Hanson, G. (2009). The effect of Fox News and CNN's post-debate commentator analysis on viewers' perceptions of presidential candidate performance. *Southern Communication Journal, 74*(4), 339–351.

Cable News Network. (2016a, October 10). *CNN Newsroom* [Show transcript]. Retrieved from Lexis Nexis database.

Cable News Network. (2016b, October 10). *The lead with Jake Tapper* [Show transcript]. Retrieved from Lexis Nexis database.

Capella, J. N., & Jamieson, K. H. (1997). *Spiral of cynicism: The press and the public good.* New York, NY: Oxford University Press.

Dixon, T. L., & Linz, D. G. (2000). Overrepresentation and underrepresentation of African Americans and Latinos as lawbreakers on television news. *Journal of Communication, 50*(2), 131–154.

Duggan, M., & Smith, A. (2016). The political environment on social media. *Pew Research Center*. Retrieved from http://www.pewinternet.org/2016/10/25/the-political-environment-on-social-media/

Entman, R., & Rojecki, A. (2000). *Black image in the white mind: Media and race in America*. Chicago, IL: University of Chicago Press.

Fox News Network. (2016a, September 27). *Fox special report with Bret Baier* [Show transcript]. Retrieved from Lexis Nexis database.

Fox News Network. (2016b, September 27). *Fox Hannity* [Show transcript]. Retrieved from Lexis Nexis database.

Fox News Network. (2016c, September 27). *The five* [Show transcript]. Retrieved from Lexis Nexis database.

Fox News Network. (2016d, September 27). *The Kelly file* [Show transcript]. Retrieved from Lexis Nexis database.

Gallup News. (2016, July 21). *Americans' satisfaction drops sharply*. Retrieved from http://news.gallup.com/poll/193832/americans-satisfaction-drops-sharply.aspx

Gallup News. (2017a, August 10). *Government, healthcare most important issues*. Retrieved from http://news.gallup.com/poll/215645/government-healthcare-important-problems.aspx

Gallup News. (2017b, March 15). *Americans' worries about race relations at record high*. Retrieved from http://news.gallup.com/poll/206057/americans-worry-race-relations-record-high.aspx

Holz, J., Akin, H., & Jamieson, K. H. (2016). *Presidential debates: What's behind the numbers?* White paper of the Annenberg Public Policy Center of the University of Pennsylvania. Retrieved from https://cdn.annenbergpublicpolicycenter.org/wp-content/uploads/Presidential_Debates_white_paper_Sept2016.pdf

Jamieson, K. H., & Gottfried, J. A. (2010). Are there lessons for the future of news from the 2008 presidential campaign? *Daedalus, 139* (2) 18–25.

Jones, D. A. (2004). Why Americans don't trust the media: A preliminary analysis. *International Journal of Press and Politics, 9*(2), 60–75.

Joseph, P. (2016, September 27). Trump has normalized our worst racial impulses [Web publication]. *CNN.com*. Retrieved from Lexis Nexis database.

Kravarik, J. (2016, September 27). *A Chicago (tough) love letter* [Web publication]. *CNN.com*. Retrieved from Lexis Nexis database.

Lenz, R., & Gunter, B. (2017). *100 days in Trump's America. Southern poverty law center*. Retrieved from https://www.splcenter.org/20170427/100-days-trumps-america

López, I. H. (2014). *Dog whistle politics: How coded racial appeals have reinvented racism & wrecked the middle class*. New York, NY: Oxford University Press.

Moshtaghian, A., & Simon, D. (2016, September 27). Kaepernick: 'Let's make America great again, for the first time' [Web publication]. *CNN.com*. Retrieved from Lexis Nexis database.

Nielsen (2016, December 13). *Tops of 2016: TV*. Retrieved from http://www.nielsen.com/us/en/insights/news/2016/tops-of-2016-tv.html

Osgood, C. E., Suci, G. J., & Tannenbaum, P. H. (1957). *The measurement of meaning*. Urbana and Chicago, IL: The University of Illinois Press.

Patterson, T. E. (2016, December 7). *News coverage of the 2016 General election: How the press failed the voters.* Shorenstein Center on Media, Politics and Public Policy, Kennedy School of Government, Harvard University. Retrieved from https://shorensteincenter.org/news-coverage-2016-general-election/

Pennebaker, J. W., Booth, R. J., Boyd, R. L., & Francis, M. E. (2015). *Linguistic inquiry and word count: LIWC2015.* Austin, TX: Pennebaker Conglomerates (www.LIWC.net).

Pennebaker, J. W., Boyd, R. L., Jordan, K., & Blackburn, K. (2015). *The development and psychometric properties of LIWC2015.* Austin, TX: University of Texas at Austin.

Pennebaker, J. W., Mehl, M. R., & Niederhoffer, K. G. (2003). Psychological aspects of natural language use: Our words, our selves. *Annual Review of Psychology, 54,* 547–577.

Posner, S., & Neiwert, D. (2016, October 14). How Trump took hate groups mainstream. *Mother Jones.* Retrieved from http://www.motherjones.com/politics/2016/10/donald-trump-hate-groups-neo-nazi-white-supremacist-racism/.

Potok, M. (2017, February 15). The year in hate and extremism. *Intelligence Report.* Retrieved from https://www.splcenter.org/fighting-hate/intelligence-report/2017/year-hate-and-extremism

Presidential Candidates Debates: "Presidential Debate at Hofstra University in Hempstead, New York" (2016, September 26). Online by Gerhard Peters and John T. Woolley, The American Presidency Project. Retrieved from http://www.presidency.ucsb.edu/ws/?pid=118971.

Presidential Candidates Debates: "Presidential Debate at Washington University in St. Louis, Missouri" (2016, October 9). Online by Gerhard Peters and John T. Woolley, The American Presidency Project. Retrieved from http://www.presidency.ucsb.edu/ws/?pid=119038.

Scott, E. (2016, September 27). Donna Brazile to Donald Trump on Russia: "Don't tweet. Call me, boo" [Web publication]. *CNN.com.* Retrieved from Lexis Nexis database

Smith, T. W., Marsden, P., Hout, M., & Kim, J. (2014). *General Social Surveys, 1972–2016* [machine-readable data file]. NORC ed., Chicago: NORC at the University of Chicago [producer and distributor]. Data accessed from the GSS Data Explorer website at gssdataexplorer.norc.org.

Tausczik, Y. R., & Pennebaker, J. W. (2010). The psychological meaning of words: LIWC and computerized text analysis methods. *Journal of Language and Social Psychology, 29*(1), 24–54.

4. "Enemies of the people": Elites, Attacks, and News Trust in the Era of Trump

JASON TURCOTTE
California State Polytechnic University, Pomona

In a 2012 primary debate, CNN's John King questioned presidential candidate Newt Gingrich on allegations of an open marriage. In an attempt to undermine his integrity as a journalist, Gingrich flatly refused to answer the question and swiftly attacked King (Streitfeld & Steinhauser, 2012). When VP candidate Sarah Palin could not name a single news publication in a 2008 interview with Katie Couric, she was quick to accuse Couric of "gotcha" journalism (Rovzar, 2008). When asked to comment on Hillary Clinton's email scandal in a primary debate, Bernie Sanders waged a forceful critique on the media (Levine, 2015). No contemporary political figure has applied this strategic deflection as routinely and forcefully as President Trump. On the campaign trail Trump attacked journalist Hugh Hewitt after stumbling in an on-air interview (Barbaro, 2015). He routinely depicted the news media as a biased institution, using terms like "lame-stream" and "failing" to characterize the news media. Since taking office, President Trump has been unequivocally antagonizing toward the White House press corps. In addition to Twitter rants, he's engaged in a diatribe of CNN that labeled the network as "fake" news and referred to journalists as "enemies of the American people" (Trump, 2017).

Political elites have routinely dodged press questions by using rhetorical strategies that include overt refusals or more subtle topical shifts (Clementson & Eveland, 2016), including attacks on the journalists. Elite attacks on the news media delegitimize the press by questioning journalistic integrity in ways that implicitly or explicitly deride reporters for alleged sensational or biased journalism. The rhetorical tactic is now a mainstay on the campaign trail and taps into growing public dissatisfaction with the news media. Furthermore, the rhetorical tactic is normalized through Donald Trump's communication style both as candidate and president. Aside from an uneasy relationship between public officials and news outlets, there is also reason to suspect that elite attacks on the press come at a democratic cost.

The hostile media effect (HME), or the perception among partisans that the news media is biased against one's own political predispositions was first identified in the 1980s (Vallone, Less, & Lepper, 1985); however, much has changed in the media environment since then. Voters face vast media choice, and news coverage has adopted a more interpretive tone that caters to niche, partisan audiences. It is during this time that scholars observed declining levels of trust in the news media (Gronke & Cook, 2007). The prolific attacks on the press suggest that political elites exploit low levels of trust in the media to deflect attention from unwanted scrutiny. When elites attack the media, the rhetoric resonates with a public that increasingly views news professionals as untrustworthy and biased (Crawford, 2006; Ladd, 2010). Moreover, attacks from elites act as cues to the public to perceive the news media more negatively (Smith, 2010). What is unclear is whether this rhetorical strategy compounds the problem of declining trust in the news, and what role such attacks play in fostering the HME.

With the elevation of elite attacks on the press and their resonance with the public, we should expect these claims to strengthen the HME and reduce levels of news trust. Given that these effects heavily influence attention to news and motivation to meaningfully engage in a democracy (Tsfati & Cappella, 2003; Tsfati & Cohen, 2005; Williams, 2012), these are critical and timely research questions. As news organizations grapple with eroding and increasingly cynical news audiences (Gronke & Cook, 2007; Ladd, 2010), this chapter identifies a new cause of the growing hostility between the public and the press: the rhetoric of political elites. Studies on news trust and perceptions of bias have identified increasing media choice, news negativity, interpretive pundits, types of news sources, issue topics, and selective exposure as antecedents of negative attitudes toward the media (see Arceneaux, Johnson, & Murphy, 2012; Arpan & Raney, 2003; Eveland & Shah, 2003; Giner-Sorolla & Chaiken, 1994; Williams & Delli Carpini, 2002). The studies, however, overlook the role political elites play in facilitating negative perceptions of news.

This chapter will examine the real world consequences of elite rhetoric that attacks the media, and introduce experimental data examining the relationship between President Trump's attacks on the press and public attitudes.

The intent of this study is to explore the democratic cost of elite attacks on the press—a rhetorical tactic that enables politicians to dodge questions and shift public focus onto news professionals in ways that seem to strain the relationship the news media has with their audiences. To what extent is the news media's credibility affected by attacks manufactured by political elites? What is the democratic cost of these attacks, meaning to what extent do they compound negative attitudes toward the news media? These research questions will be explored within the context of Trump and his tenuous relationship with the press. This research addresses how elites may, perhaps unintentionally, disengage the public from the democratic process using rhetorical strategies that seek to undermine the Fourth Estate. Should attacks on the news media drive distrust among news audiences, the public is likely to be less attentive to credible and objective sources of information. In an era where market-driven models of news production prevail, elite attacks may also create a chilling effect, influencing how journalists interact with elites and the agendas set by news outlets. Thus, implications for the practice of journalism are also present. This research should improve our understanding of news trust and the phenomenon of the HME. Specifically, this study explores how President Trump's rhetoric influences public assessments of the news media and offers a preliminary framework for examining how news audiences are affected by elite attacks on the press.

Elite Attacks

Elite attacks on the press are not unique to today's political climate; however, the regularity of such attacks and the heightened level of vitriol not only undermine the press, but weaken U.S. democracy. McLeod, Wise, and Perryman (2017) suggest that when elites repeatedly attack the press, the public perceives these attacks as valid or truthful. Even use of the singular noun "the media" is problematic insofar that partisan and biased outlets are being lumped under a singular entity inclusive of objective, credible sources of news. According to scholars (Crawford, 2006; Smith, 2010; Watts, Domke, Shah, & Fan, 1999), elite attacks act as cues to the public to perceive not just a particular outlet, but the entire media industry as biased according to the direction of the attack or claim. Public assessments of the media are affected regardless of whether there is actual bias in the outlet or journalist under attack, and effects are especially strong among individuals whose party identification is congruent with the elite lodging the attack (Smith, 2010).

Studies have demonstrated a relationship between elite rhetoric that attacks the media and public negativity toward the news (Ladd, 2010). In examining the effects of talk radio on the public, Cappella and Jamieson

(1997) found that as elites criticize the media, public trust in news declines. Although this area of research remains under-developed, today's digital news environment may enhance the effects of elite attacks due to the ease in which selective perception and confirmation bias mold political attitudes. The effectiveness of elite attacks is partly attributed to such narratives fitting existing public perceptions of the news media (McLeod et al., 2017). In other words, elite attacks exploit people's prejudices of the news media. Given that public trust in the news is closely connected to levels of perceived media bias (Jones, 2004), scholars must fully examine the HME in today's polarized political climate and partisan information environment.

Hostile Media Effects

The HME, or the perception among partisans that the news media is biased against one's own political predispositions, was first identified in the 1980s (Vallone et al., 1985). Subsequent research discovered that hostile media effects are strongest among those who are highly partisan, regardless of whether the news bias is real or imagined (D'Alessio, 2003; Dalton, Beck, & Huckfeldt, 1998; Giner-Sorolla & Chaiken, 1994). Although the HME increases when people are more engaged with a particular issue, effects are nonetheless observed among those with lower issue involvement (Hansen & Kim, 2011). What is more, the hostile media perception creates new obstacles for democracy.

Research has shown that the HME fosters selective exposure: as perceptions of media bias increase, people actively avoid news sources they perceive—sometimes wrongly—of bias (McLeod et al., 2017). This influence over information seeking behaviors may create a more polarized electorate; such behavior also strains one's ability to stay objectively informed about politics. Other scholars have found that the HME hinders perceptions of news credibility for partisans, and suggest that the HME holds a negative relationship with news trust (See Choi, Watt, & Lynch, 2006; Dalton et al., 1998; Tsfati & Cohen, 2005). Although the HME was initially isolated to strong partisans, elite attacks and claims of media bias are being normalized in the Trump presidency. The increasingly hostile rhetoric of political elites may also enhance the HME. Given that the news media is an important democratic institution, the potential effects of elite attacks demand our attention.

News Trust

It is not news that trust in the media has steadily declined in the post-broadcast era (Gronke & Cook, 2007). Increasing competition in the industry ushered in an era of soft news and more interpretive content, and financially challenged newsrooms now have fewer resources to support investigative watchdog journalism. The percentage of those reporting having little confidence in the press climbed from 14% (as measured by the General Social Survey in 1973) to 46% in 2012 (McLeod et al., 2017). The perception of media bias is widespread among both political elites and the public (Lee, 2005). Today, news audiences are more likely to trust news shared by peers on social media compared to when identical content is shared directly from the news source (Turcotte, York, Irving, Scholl, & Pingree, 2015). Lack of public trust is rooted in many factors including news negativity, anonymous sources, the horserace, high profile cases of plagiarism and, perhaps most importantly, perceptions of media bias.

Jones (2004) found that low levels of news trust is attributed to perceptions of media bias and that declining public trust in the media is influenced more by this widespread perception of bias than journalistic standards or news quality. Other research indicates that the HME influences public trust in mainstream news (Tsfati & Cohen, 2005). In other words, the HME presents a great threat to news trust, and in politically polarized climates as the U.S. experiences today, the HME is heightened (Eveland & Shah, 2003). The relationship between the HME and news trust holds numerous problematic implications for democracy.

Low levels of trust in the news are a predictor of low levels of trust in democracy, which affects one's desire to participate in the political process (Tsfati & Cohen, 2005). In fact, declining news trust is also associated with declining trust in other democratic institutions such as government and public opinion polls (see Kim, 2015). Low levels of news trust impede on our ability to remain informed and rational in our political decision-making: news trust affects one's attention to news, perceptions of news credibility, media diets, and support for watchdog journalism (McLeod et al., 2017; Williams, 2012). Crawford (2006) also cautions that lack of trust in the media may have a chilling effect on the news agenda. He suggests that declining trust makes news professionals and outlets vulnerable to elite attacks and elite spin; news outlets may be less motivated to tackle stories unpopular with elites knowing that their credibility (and bottom lines) cannot sustain enduring attacks from elites. This research leads me to the following hypotheses:

H1: Exposure to an elite attack on the press will negatively correlate with news trust.
H2: Exposure to an elite attack on the press will positively correlate with perceived news bias.

Given that elite attacks are becoming normalized by President Trump and other public officials, it is important that research consider the possibility of repeated exposure to elite attacks on the press increasing the effects such attacks have on the public's assessment of the news media. Therefore, I also ask the following:

RQ1: Does additional exposure to attacks on the press (press release + political ad) strengthen the effects on news trust and perceived bias?

I explore the possibility of elite attacks as a key antecedent of the HME and declining news trust in a 2017 pilot study. The experiment not only examines the normative consequences of elite attacks but also extends HME research by testing effects using stimuli from elite political communication (e.g. press release and advertisement) rather than testing the HME using stimuli from news content. Importantly, this timely study is executed in the context of a presidential administration that has created a highly adversarial relationship with the press.

Method

To test these hypotheses, I administered an online pilot study utilizing a posttest experimental design. Although survey method is often used to examine news trust and the HME, a meta-analysis found that the HME is consistently observed for both survey research and experimental designs (Hansen & Kim, 2011). Given that issue topics have historically been used to test the HME (see Giner-Sorolla & Chaiken, 1994; Vallone et al., 1985), immigration was selected due to the timelessness of the issue, its emphasis in Trump's campaign rhetoric and policy responses, and the polarizing nature of the issue. Moreover, researchers have observed the HME in the context of the immigration issue prior (see Watson & Riffe, 2013).

Although the HME is not moderated by the medium of the news outlet (Hansen & Kim, 2011), medium can affect news trust; therefore, incorporating print and video communications allows me to address *RQ1* by including a double exposure to an attack on the media. Participants were assigned to one of three treatment groups. Group A (*n* = 35) was exposed to a Trump press release on immigration inclusive of two attacks on the media. The press statement was released by the White House on January 29, 2017 and appears verbatim in the questionnaire (see Appendix). Group B (*n* = 33) was exposed to the release verbatim, but also Trump's "100 Days" ad (released May 1, 2017) in which he touts policy achievements and attacks the media with a "fake news" claim. Thus, this group received a double exposure of elite attacks through text and video. Lastly, the control group, Group C (*n* = 34) was exposed only to the Trump release on immigration with both attacks on the media removed from the text. All participants were randomly assigned to the groups using the randomization function in Qualtrics. Once viewing their assigned stimuli, participants completed a questionnaire measuring their perceptions of news bias and attitudes toward the news media.

Sample

Online labor markets such as Amazon's MTurk are emerging tools for social science research; they are considered effective, low-cost methods for recruiting study participants (Berinsky, Huber, & Lenz, 2012). Scholars find that MTurk samples are not as generalizable as a national probability samples but far more generalizable than student convenience samples, and what key differences exist between MTurk users and the U.S. population are controlled in experimental research (Berinsky et al., 2012; Levay, Freese, & Druckman, 2016). Thus, a pilot study sample was generated using Amazon's MTurk Prime Lab. The volunteer sample (n = 102) included the following sample parameters: participants had to be adult U.S. citizens of voting age (18) and older who identify as conservative leaning.[1] Data were collected October 26–28, 2017.

The sampled consisted of 46.1% women and 53.9% men. The sample was 84.3% white, 5.9% Hispanic or Latino, 2.9% Black or African American, 2.0% Asian and 4.9% identifying as another racial group. Although few nonwhites participated in the experiment, demographics are unsurprising given that the study excluded those who did not identify as conservative. The sample skewed middle aged (M = 40.73, SD = 13.75). Approximately 40.2% of the sample holds a degree from a four-year college or university. Annual income levels reflected more participants in middle to lower socioeconomic classes: 20.6% earn less than $20,000 annually; 27.5% earn between $21,000 and 40,000; 19.6% earn between $41,000 and 60,000; 14.7% earn between $61,000 and 80,000; 7.8% earn between $81,000 and 100,000; and 9.9% earn more than $100,000. Using 1–7 Likert scale—one being very conservative, seven being very liberal—to measure political ideology (M = 3.06, SD = 1.32), the sample leans just right of center. Lastly, 54.9% identified themselves as Republicans, 44.2% as independents, and 2.9% as Democrats.

Measures

The dependent variable of general news trust is measured using Meyer's (1988) five-item scale adapted from his news believability index. Individual items are measured using a seven-point Likert type scale (1 = strongly disagree, 7 = strongly agree). They assess whether the news media is: (1) fair (M = 2.73, SD = 1.64), (2) accurate (M = 2.88, SD = 1.58), (3) unbiased

(M = 2.05, SD = 1.34), (4) tells the whole story (M = 2.36, SD = 1.50), and 5) trustworthy (M = 2.52, SD = 1.52). The News Trust Scale (M = 2.51, SD = 1.42) shows strong inter-item reliability, α = .96.

The HME is tested using a dependent variable that measures the perception of liberal news bias (liberal news bias is measured in lieu of non-directional bias given that participants represent those with a conservative-leaning ideology). The three items are measured with a 7-point Likert type scale (1 = strongly disagree, 7 = strongly agree), and assess whether the news media: (1) has a liberal bias (M = 5.30, SD = 1.62), (2) has an anti-Trump bias (M = 5.35, SD = 1.75), and (3) has a pro-immigration bias (M = 4.80, SD = 1.61). The Liberal Bias Scale (M = 5.15, SD = 1.54) shows strong inter-item reliability, α = .92.

The models also include a number of controls believed to affect assessments of news. For example, political knowledge is controlled for using a battery of six standard knowledge questions from Delli Carpini and Keeter's (1993) index. Given that political knowledge is often representative of engagement levels, a knowledge index (M = 5.43, SD = .92) variable is included in the OLS models. Prior research shows that strength of an attitude on specific issues affects news trust (Gunther, 1988); therefore, a variable measuring issue salience (M = 5.54, SD = 1.48) on immigration using a Likert type (1–7) scale is included, as perceived importance of the issue could influence the effects of elite attacks. The work of Lee (2005) finds that political cynicism is a predictor of distrust in the news media. Although a precise measure for cynicism is not accounted for, the model includes a broad scale for institutional trust (M = 2.01, SD = .49). Adopted from Gallup's Confidence in Institutions poll, the scale combines and averages attitudes measured on a five-point Likert scale of 14 democratic and social institutions. This controls for broad trust in various institutions and could be considered a proxy for political cynicism.[2]

Lastly, a number of demographic variables are included as controls. The research shows that whites, males, education level, age, and conservative ideology are predictors of distrust in the news (see Lee, 2005; McLeod et al., 2017). Therefore, gender, education, political ideology, age, and income are included. And given that President Trump is a polarizing political figure even among Republicans, I control for dissatisfaction with Trump (M = 4.01, SD = 2.03) using a Likert type scale (1 = most satisfied; 7 = most unsatisfied) combining three measures: satisfaction with his performance in office, whether the country is moving in the right direction, and his trustworthiness.

Findings

After running OLS regression, I find support for the news trust hypothesis: exposure to an elite attack on the press is negatively related to news trust. For the model testing the HME, I do not observe a relationship between exposure to an elite attack on the press and perceptions of liberal bias. Lastly, an additional exposure level—a video attack combined with a text-based attack on the press—does not seem to strengthen the negative relationship between attacks and news trust.

News Trust

After controlling for demographic variables and attitudinal constructs such as issue salience, satisfaction with Trump and broad institutional trust, the regression model shows support for *H1*. I find that exposure to an attack on the press held a negative relationship with news trust (β = -.266, p < .01). Those exposed to a White House press release that attacks the media demonstrated lower levels of news trust relative to the control group, or those who were exposed to the same press release with attacks removed from the text (see Table 4.1). In respect to *RQ1*, I find that an additional visual attack on the media coupled with the text-based attack in the release does not strengthen the effect. Participants in this treatment group also experienced lower levels of news trust relative to the control group (β = -.223, p < .05), however, the strength of the effect was comparable to those only exposed to an attack in a press release. Therefore, the negative effects elite attacks have on news trust is not necessarily intensified by a second, broadcast-based attack.

The model also reveals a number of control variables holding a relationship with news trust. Political knowledge held a negative relationship with news trust (β = -.203, p < .05), suggesting that perhaps those most engaged in politics harbor more unfavorable attitudes toward the news media. As expected, higher levels of broad institutional trust (β = .495, p < .01), liberal leaning ideology (β = .195, p < .05) and dissatisfaction with President Trump (β = .493, p < .01) held a positive relationship with news trust. These relationships suggest that those with more favorable attitudes toward other democratic institutions and those with more liberal political views are more trusting of the news media. Moreover, the dissatisfaction with Trump finding suggests an interesting dichotomy relating to the tension between the White House and press corps. The more critical people are of Trump's presidency, the more trust in the news media they have.

Hostile Media Effects

Despite observing negative effects on news trust, exposure to elite attacks on the press did not increase the perception of liberal news bias. Thus, *H2* was not supported. The relationship moved in the expected direction—exposure to elite attacks on the press held a positive relationship with perception of liberal media bias—but was not statistically significant. In other words, elite attacks on the media were not a predictor of the HME. As expected, liberal-leaning ideology ($\beta = -.337$, $p < .01$) and dissatisfaction with President Trump ($\beta = -.412$, $p < .01$) held a negative relationship with the perception of liberal media bias; however, these findings are not particularly novel.

Discussion

This project expands the mass communication literature by aiming to identify an overlooked antecedent of negative attitudes toward the news media. This research delves into the fragility of our democracy and unpacks the ways in which elites disengage the public from the democratic process. Research on news trust and hostile media effects explores public attitudes of the press without accounting for the role that political elites play in facilitating those attitudes. This research improves our understanding of the underlying causes of declining levels of news trust and the phenomenon of the HME.

The results show that exposure to elite attacks on the media reduces levels of trust in the news, at least among those with political ideology in line with the politician lodging the attack. This finding not only suggests that elites play a role in facilitating public distrust of the news media, but also holds implications for increasing polarization in U.S. politics. When partisans hold disdain for mainstream media, they are more likely to reject objective information and instead engage in selective exposure, seeking fringe sources that are more likely to reflect their political predispositions. Such behavior skews political realities for those seeking partisan news (see Morris, 2007), an especially troubling pattern in a political climate that is increasingly polarized and partisan. Thus, scholars must devote new attention to the relationship between elite attacks and news trust.

Unfortunately, this study does not yield any significant findings regarding elite attacks and the HME (as measured by perceived bias). A few factors may explain this. The first possibility is that conservative-leaning participants already hold exceptionally strong perceptions of liberal media bias. In fact, research suggests that the HME is stronger among Republicans than Democrats (Eveland & Shah, 2003). Another possibility for the null finding is that attacks from an untraditional Republican like Trump are less effective in establishing a greater perception of liberal bias because conservatives are not uniformly trusting of him or buy into the authenticity of his conservatism. Future studies should test this relationship in a pretest-posttest design, and with attacks from elites who more solidly represent the Republican Party. The HME may be observed with elite attacks that are more forceful and less subtle than those used as stimuli in this study, and future research could test effects using variance in strength of the attack (or tone). This preliminary study is not without some additional constraints.

First, the measure selected for media trust is general news trust and not specific to a particular type of news product or medium. Research suggests that news trust is more nuanced and may vary across mediums (Hansen & Kim, 2011; McLeod et al., 2017). Moving forward, researchers should test news trust and the HME across platforms. It is important to note that a relationship between exposure to an elite attack on the press and news trust was observed; however, those effects were found among those with party congruency of the political elite lodging the attack. Results may not be generalizable to moderate or liberal-leaning participants. Future studies should replicate the experiment using press attacks from a Democrat, and liberal-leaning participants. On the other hand, effects observed in this study may be understated in the sense that the cumulative effects of elite attacks should be stronger than those observed for a single exposure.

Bottom line pressures and competition from digital media have presented challenges for struggling newsrooms, but perhaps no challenge has been more paramount to the vitality of the news business than public trust in news. As Crawford (2006) has argued, declining trust in news is likely to have a chilling effect on the news agenda. The Fourth Estate is weakened when political elites attack its credibility. Despite the aggressive reporting of President Trump from many national reporters, journalists—particularly those working in small or mid-sized outlets—may have less motivation to engage in quality watchdog journalism when they and their news organizations face unfair scrutiny from political elites. What is more, a decline in investigative and watchdog journalism may further sully the reputation of the press and enhance the ease in which elites can effectively spin information. Thus, the role that political elites play in facilitating this distrust mustn't be understated. Although this study did not reveal that elite attacks facilitate the HME, the public's continued reliance on social media and algorithms for news and information suggest scholars should continue exploring this research agenda given that the echo chambers born from these digital spaces are increasing the frequency with which people engage with like-minded news content and like-mined people. The more engagement we have with views reflecting our preexisting political dispositions, the greater our perception of media bias (Eveland & Shah, 2003).

In summary, this study offers some preliminary evidence that elite attacks on the media are exacerbating the trust problem news outlets are grappling with. Elite attacks—which not only serve as a rhetorical device for dodging questions and appealing to populism—do more than simply undermine the credibility of news outlets; they undermine an institution necessary for holding power accountable and sustaining U.S. democracy. Only with continued research can we fully understand the extent elite attacks on the press harm the institution of news and U.S. democracy.

Notes

1. Given the stimuli are from the communications of a sitting Republican president and that research shows that shared party identity strengthens hostile media effects (see Reid, 2012), the study is limited to a conservative-leaning sample.
2. Research has shown that media diets also affect news trust (Jones, 2004; McLeod et al., 2017). Although I collected data on information seeking behavior (relative to entertainment seeking) and a categorical news diet variable, neither held a relationship with either dependent variable and they were excluded from the models.

References

Arceneaux, K., Johnson, M., & Murphy, C. (2012). Polarized political communication, oppositional media hostility, and selective exposure. *Journal of Politics, 74*(1), 174–186.

Arpan, L. M., & Raney, A. A. (2003). An experimental investigation of news source and the hostile media effect. *Journalism & Mass Communication Quarterly, 80*(2), 265–281.

Barbaro, M. (2015, September 3). Donald Trump stumbles and bristles during foreign policy interview. *The New York Times*. Retrieved from http://newyorktimes.com

Berinsky, A. J., Huber, G. A., & Lenz, G. S. (2012). Evaluating online labor markets for experimental research: Amazon.com's Mechanical Turk. *Political Analysis, 20*, 351–368.

Cappella, J N., & Jamieson, K. H. (1997). *Spiral of cynicism: The press and the public good.* New York, NY: Oxford University Press.

Choi, J., Watt, J. H., & Lynch, M. (2006). Perceptions of news credibility about the war in Iraq: Why war opponents perceived the internet as the most credible medium. *Journal of Computer-Mediated Communication, 12*(1), 209–229.

Clementson, D., & Eveland, W. P. (2016). When politicians dodge questions: An analysis of presidential press conferences and debates. *Mass Communication & Society, 19*(4), 411–429.

Crawford, C. (2006). *Attack the messenger: How politicians turn you against the media.* Lanham, MD: Rowman & Littlefield.

D'Alessio, D. (2003). An experimental explanation of readers' perception of media bias. *Journalism & Mass Communication Quarterly, 80*(2), 282–294.

Dalton, R. J., Beck, P. A., & Huckfeldt, R. (1988). Partisan cues and the media: Information flows in the 1992 presidential election. *American Political Science Review, 92*(1), 111–126.

Delli Carpini, M. X., & Keeter, S. (1993). Measuring political knowledge: Putting first things first. *American Journal of Political Science, 37*(4), 1179–1206.

Eveland, W. P., & Shah, D. V. (2003). The impact of individual and interpersonal factors on perceived news media bias. *Political Psychology, 24*(1), 101–117.

Giner-Sorolla, R., & Chaiken, S. (1994). The causes of hostile media judgements. *Journal of Experimental Social Psychology, 30,* 165–180.

Gronke, P., & Cook, T. E. (2007). Disdaining the media: The American public's changing attitudes toward the news. *Political Communication, 24*(3), 259–281.

Gunther, A. (1988). Attitude extremity and trust in media. *Journalism & Mass Communication Quarterly, 65*(2), 279–287.

Hansen, G. J., & Kim, H. (2011). Is the media biased against me? A meta-analysis of the hostile media effect research. *Communication Research Reports, 28*(2), 169–179.

Jones, D. A. (2004). Why Americans don't trust the media: A preliminary analysis. *International Journal of Press/Politics, 9*(2), 60–75.

Kim, H. (2015). Perception and emotion: The indirect effect of reported election poll results on political participation intention and support for restrictions. *Mass Communication & Society, 18,* 303–324.

Ladd, J. M. (2010). The neglected power of elite opinion leadership to produce antipathy toward the news media: Evidence from a survey experiment. *Political Behavior, 32*(1), 29–50.

Levay, K. E., Freese, J., & Druckman, J. N. (2016). The demographics and political composition of Mechanical Turk samples. *Sage Open, 6*(1): 1–17.

Levine, S. (2015, October 13). Bernie Sanders: Americans are sick of hearing about Hillary Clinton's 'damn emails.' *The Huffington Post.* Retrieved from http://huffingtonpost.com

McLeod, D. M., Wise, D., & Perryman, M. (2017). Thinking about the media: A review of theory and research on media perceptions, media effects perceptions, and their consequences. *Review of Communication Research, 5,* 35–83.

Meyer, P. (1988). Defining and measuring credibility of newspapers: Developing an index. *Journalism Quarterly, 65*(3), 567–588.

Morris, J. S. (2007). Slanted objectivity? Perceived media bias, cable news exposure, and political attitudes. *Social Science Quarterly, 88*(3), 707–728.

Reid, S. A. (2012). A self-categorization explanation for the hostile media effect. *Journal of Communication, 62*(3), 381–399.

Rovzar, C. (2008, September 30). McCain, Palin attack Couric for 'gotcha journalism.' *New York Magazine.* Retrieved from http://nymag.com/daily/intelligencer/2008/09/mccain_palin_attack_couric_for.html

Smith, G. R. (2010). Politicians and the news media: How elite attacks influence perceptions of media bias. *The International Journal of Press/Politics, 15*(3), 319–343.

Streitfeld, R., & Steinhauser, P. (2012, January 20). Gingrich delivers show-stopper at beginning of South Carolina debate. *CNN Politics.* Retrieved from http://cnn.com

Trump, D. [Donald J. Trump]. (2017, February 17). The FAKE NEWS media (failing @nytimes, @NBCNews, @ABC, @CBS, @CNN) is not my enemy, it is the enemy of the

American People! [tweeted]. Retrieved from https://twitter.com/realdonaldtrump/status/832708293516632065?lang=en

Tsfati, Y., & Cappella, J. N. (2003). Do people watch what they do not trust? Exploring the association between news media skepticism and exposure. *Communication Research, 30*(5), 504–529.

Tsfati, Y., & Cohen, J. (2005). Democratic consequences of hostile media perceptions: The case of Gaza settlers. *The International Journal of Press/Politics, 10*(4), 28–51.

Turcotte, J., York, C., Irving, J., Scholl, R., & Pingree, R. (2015). News recommendations from social media opinion leaders: Effects on media trust and information seeking. *Journal of Computer-Mediated Communication, 20*(5), 520–535.

Vallone, R., Less, R., & Lepper, M. (1985). The hostile media phenomenon: Biased perception and perceptions of media bias in coverage of the Beirut massacre. *Journal of Personality and Social Psychology, 49*, 577–588.

Watson, B. R., & Riffe, D. (2013). Perceived threat, immigration policy support, and media coverage: Hostile media and presumed influence. *International Journal of Public Opinion Research, 25*, 459–479.

Watts, M. D., Domke, D., Shah, D. V., & Fan, D. P. (1999). Elite cues and media bias in presidential campaigns: Explaining public perceptions of a liberal press. *Communication Research, 26*(2), 144–175.

Williams, A. E. (2012). Trust or bust? Questioning the relationship between media trust and news attention. *Journal of Broadcasting & Electronic Media, 56*(1), 116–131.

Williams, B. A., & Delli Carpini, M. X. (2000). Let us entertain you: The politics of popular media. In L. Bennett & R. Entman (Eds.), *Mediated Politics: The future of political communication*. Cambridge: Cambridge University Press.

Appendix

Table 4.1: OLS Regression: Effects on News Trust.

Variable	B	SE B	B
(constant)	−.007	1.214	
Text-based Attack	−.794	.276	−.266**
Text + Video Attack	−.676	.291	−.223*
Political Knowledge	−.312	.137	−.203*
Institutional Trust	1.431	.268	.495**
Trump Dissatisfaction	.345	.069	.493**
Issue Salience	−.081	.086	−.085
Ideology (liberal)	.210	.105	.195*
Education	.022	.112	.018
Income	.040	.064	.054

Table 4.1: (Continued)

Variable	B	SE B	B
Age	.004	.009	.041
Gender (female)	−.219	.239	−.077
Adjusted R²	.368		
F	6.354		

Note: *n* = 102; * *p* < .05; ** = *p* < .01

Table 4.2: OLS Regression: Hostile Media Effects (Perception of Liberal Bias)

Variable	B	SE B	B
(constant)	7.195	1.365	
Text-based Attack	.152	.310	.047
Text + Video Attack	.258	.327	.078
Political Knowledge	.283	.155	.169
Institutional Trust	−.553	.301	−.176
Trump Dissatisfaction	−.314	.078	−.412**
Issue Salience	.051	.097	.049
Ideology (liberal)	−.394	.118	−.337**
Education	−.002	.126	−.002
Income	−.034	.072	−.042
Age	−.004	.010	−.039
Gender (female)	−.238	.268	−.077
Adjusted R²	.325		
F	5.423		

Note: *n* = 102; * *p* < .05; ** = *p* < .01.

President Trump Statement Regarding Recent Executive Order Concerning Extreme Vetting:

America is a proud nation of immigrants and we will continue to show compassion to those fleeing oppression, but we will do so while protecting our own citizens and border. America has always been the land of the free and home of the brave. We will keep it free and keep it safe, *as the media knows, but refuses to say.*

My policy is similar to what President Obama did in 2011 when he banned visas for refugees from Iraq for six months. The seven countries named in the Executive Order are the same countries previously identified by the Obama administration as sources of terror.

To be clear, this is not a Muslim ban, *as the media is falsely reporting*. This is not about religion—this is about terror and keeping our country safe. There are over 40 different countries worldwide that are majority Muslim that are not affected by this order.

We will again be issuing visas to all countries once we are sure we have reviewed and implemented the most secure policies over the next 90 days. I have tremendous feeling for the people involved in this horrific humanitarian crisis in Syria. My first priority will always be to protect and serve our country, but as President I will find ways to help all those who are suffering.

(*Bolded text omitted from control group*).

Part III

Assessing News Media Performance

5. American Media and the Rise of Trump

VICTOR PICKARD

Annenberg School for Communication, University of Pennsylvania

The factors contributing to Donald Trump's election are many.[1] They include varying degrees of racism, misogyny, nativism, and xenophobia among sections of the American public. Trump, adopting a fake populism, also benefitted from economic conditions resulting from Republican and Democratic administrations' trade policies. In addition to these factors is the role of media, whether misinformation amplified through social media, or various failures in the more traditional news media (Pickard, 2017b). The latter institutions in particular deserve special scrutiny for their role in accelerating Trump's candidacy, most obviously because they help set agendas and frame political debates each election cycle (Confessore, 2016; Frank, 2016; Tufekci, 2016). News media's constant coverage has boosted Trump's visibility and helped popularize him, even in aggressive confrontations with the candidate. The benefit, however, is mutual.

As Trump attacked the press—mocking and feuding with journalists, threatening to change libel laws, holding campaign events where reporters are corralled and roughed up—he still served the media well (Becker, 2016; Hampson, 2016). Indeed, the news organizations covering Trump, particularly television news, accumulated vast amounts of money from their election coverage (Poggi, 2015). Cable news organizations, for example, made billions of dollars during the election season (Gold & Weprin, 2016).

This profit motive helps explain Trump's constant media exposure, which greatly advantaged his campaign over his competitors', especially in the primary season's early days. A study on newsworthiness calculated that, during 2015,

Trump received 327 minutes of nightly broadcast network news coverage, compared with Hillary Clinton's 121 minutes and Bernie Sanders' 20 minutes (Tyndall, 2015). The *New York Times* reported that Trump received nearly $2 billion in free media coverage during his primary campaign (Confessore & Yourish, 2016). As the Republican nominee for president, he became even more ubiquitous.

The news media's obsession with Trump is symptomatic of a highly commercialized system. Profit-seeking is in the media's very DNA and the always controversial Trump is money in the bank for ratings-driven news media. This economic relationship was summed up by the now-infamous statement by Les Moonves, CEO of CBS, when discussing Trump's candidacy: "It may not be good for America, but it's damn good for CBS" (quoted in Fang, 2016).

Such brazen disregard for the role of the press in a democratic society lays bare structural problems in the U.S. media system. Compared to other countries' media systems, America's is extremely commercialized and our weakly supported public media is unusual when compared to other nations (Benson & Powers, 2011). In fact, other democracies have developed strikingly different media systems, which aren't simply reflections of taste, culture, and style. This raises a number of troubling questions. How did Americans inherit such a system—one that, in many sectors, is dominated by a few corporations, is only lightly regulated by public interest mandates, and is predominantly commercial, with only weak public alternatives? Is this really the system—one so beholden to brute market forces—Americans chose?

These are, of course, historical questions. A look at modern media history, particularly the 1940s, shows that the American system did not emerge from entirely democratic decisions. It arose instead from a history of commercial interests winning out over others (Pickard, 2015). This history is marked by pronounced conflict, in which activists, industries, and regulators all fought over the fundamental nature and democratic role of the American media system.

The Historical Roots of American Media Exceptionalism

Profit-driven media in the United States began on a wide scale in the mid-19th century when technological changes and a growing readership produced the "penny press." As these cheap, mass-circulation newspapers commercialized and began to rely heavily on advertising revenue, sensationalistic reporting became more pronounced. What came to be called "yellow journalism" in the late 19th century featured salaciousness, dishonest reporting, and sensationalism as a way to sell papers. In the face of public criticism, professional norms based on objective and fact-based reporting began to crystallize in the early 20th century to prevent unfettered commercialism from completely debasing the news. Nonetheless, American journalism typically relied on advertising for roughly 80% of its revenues, much higher than its counterparts around the world.

The rise of commercial radio developed in the 1920s. It offered an alternative to print journalism, but also paralleled its development in important ways. The rules of this new media were officially codified by the 1934 Communications Act, which established the main regulatory agency for broadcast media, the Federal Communications Commission (FCC). The FCC was preceded by the Federal Radio Commission (FRC), a temporary agency founded in 1927 to provide regulatory stability, particularly around technical issues, for the increasingly contested airwaves. Like the FRC, the FCC was tasked with granting licenses and ensuring that broadcasting stations served the public interest. But programming regulation was thorny terrain because the FCC was forbidden by law to practice censorship. Moreover, the standards by which licensees were judged remained ill-defined, thereby inviting charges of arbitrariness. Any FCC attempt to establish public interest standards invited conflict with the commercial broadcast industry, drawing accusations of paternalism and attacks on free speech. Profit and public service were set at odds.

Through the Communications Act, Congress largely sanctioned commercial broadcasting at the expense of non-profit alternatives pushed by educators and reformers (McChesney, 1993). As a result, a strong public broadcasting system did not take root during American radio's early days as it did in many other democratic nations. American radio was quickly subsumed by the oligopoly of large networks. By the mid-1940s, the broadcast industry was dominated by four networks: the National Broadcasting Company (NBC), the Columbia Broadcasting System (CBS), the Mutual Broadcasting System (MBS), and the American Broadcasting Company (ABC, which had been NBC's "Blue Network" until 1943). Whenever the social mission of public broadcast systems in other countries—like the United Kingdom's BBC (British Broadcasting Corporation)—was questioned, the U.S. model served as a cautionary tale of what not to do.

Although these pre-television years are celebrated as radio's golden age, the medium's public service responsibilities remained vague. Most broadcasters viewed their primary role as selling airtime to advertisers who developed programs and promoted their products (Stole, 2012). Advertisers—usually called sponsors—would buy entire time segments of programming from a commercial broadcaster, usually an affiliate of one of the major networks. Shows like soap operas, the term given to 1940s radio serials due to their frequent soap company sponsorship, gave sponsors free rein to air numerous commercials and even to influence actual programming.

The FCC at this time was reactive rather than proactive. Despite its New Deal origins, the agency did not pursue a reformist or public agenda, and its early years saw few policy challenges to American radio's increasing commercialization. Although the 1934 Communications Act gave the FCC a mandate to serve the always-contested "public interest, convenience and necessity," the commission was largely non-confrontational toward commercial broadcasters. President Franklin D. Roosevelt's cozy relationship with broadcasters may have further encouraged complacency. The inveterate media reformer Everett Parker, recalling how the FCC's genesis was characterized by close ties to media corporations, quipped that prior to its formation, "four commissioners were vetted by AT&T and three by broadcasters" (Quoted in Pickard, 2015, p. 38).

But this all began to change by the late 1930s when newspapers rapidly bought up radio stations and, in some cases, exerted editorial authority over programming. FDR saw this media consolidation as a threat to democracy and a political challenge to his New Deal agenda. He needed a proxy to make an intervention. This proxy would come in the form of James Lawrence (Larry) Fly.

The New Deal's Last Gasp

Larry Fly's appointment to the FCC chairmanship in July 1939 marked a turning point for the commission (Edwardson, 2002). Fly initiated a nearly decade-long progressive regulatory orientation for American media policy. A strong-willed New Dealer from Texas, Fly had a deep-seated suspicion of monopoly power, believing that capitalism foundered without competition. Having cut his teeth on progressive policy battles during the mid- to late 1930s while heading the Tennessee Valley Authority's legal department, Fly developed a reputation as a tough liberal who relished a good fight and did not fear provoking powerful industries. Corporate attorney and Republican presidential candidate Wendell Willkie called Fly "the most dangerous man in America—to have on the other side" (Quoted in Pickard, 2015, p. 40).

Under Fly, the New Deal arrived late and stayed longer at the FCC compared to other areas of government. As the New Deal foundered elsewhere, Fly and the FCC represented social democracy's last stand. In this way, Fly helped transform the FCC from being a mere "traffic cop" concerned only with technical requirements into an institution that disciplined broadcasters for failing to fulfill their public-service responsibility. He believed that

such programming objectives required government-driven structural interventions. In the early 1940s, Fly would lead the FCC to confront media
corporations and aggressively defended public interest principles while facing
considerable political opposition (Stamm, 2011). Its mission aligned with the
objectives of various social movements and was buoyed by growing public
criticism, especially distaste for radio commercials. While the commercial system was fairly well established by the 1940s, during and immediately after
World War II, a three-pronged assault against commercial media arose from
above and below, led by grassroots activists, progressive policy makers, and
everyday American listeners and readers who were upset with specific aspects
of their media system.

Much of their criticism sounds familiar to us today: concerns about excessive commercialism, misrepresentations of marginalized people and ideas, lack
of minority-owned media, media concentration and a loss of local journalism.
These critiques gave rise to a nascent media reform movement as coalitions
composed of labor unions, civil rights organizers, civil libertarians, disaffected
intellectuals, progressive groups, educators, and religious organizations
sought to reform the media system (Fones-wolf, 2006; Pickard, 2015).

The 1940s witnessed a critical juncture for American media. In 1943, the
FCC took anti-monopoly measures against chain broadcasters, which forced
NBC to divest itself of a major network (which became ABC). Two years
later, the Supreme Court issued an antitrust ruling affirming the need for
"diverse and antagonistic sources" against the Associated Press (Associated
Press v. United States, 1945). In 1946 the FCC published its "Blue Book,"
which mandated broadcasters' public service responsibilities. The Hutchins
Commission on Freedom of the Press established journalism's democratic
benchmarks in 1947 (Pickard, 2010). And finally, in 1949, the FCC issued its
Fairness Doctrine outlining key public interest obligations for broadcasters.
Not all of these initiatives were successful, but they all sought to reorient the
balance between profit and public service in the American news media.

Taken together, these media policy debates and decisions all addressed
a key question: What did commercial media institutions owe the public in
return for their many benefits? For example, what would broadcasters give
back to society in return for their free and monopolistic use of the public
airwaves? They also all shared an expansive view of the First Amendment
that protected the audience's positive right to information as much as broadcasters and publishers' negative rights protecting their speech and property
from government intrusion. These policy interventions composed a broader
impulse, one defined by a social democratic vision of media that emphasized
its public service mission instead of treating it as only a business commodity.

Privileging social benefits over property rights, this perspective assesses a media system's value by how it benefits *all* of society rather than how it serves individual freedoms, private property rights, and profits for a relative few.

A prime example of this social democratic project was the Blue Book (so named because of its blue cover). Officially titled the "Public Service Responsibility of Broadcast Licensees," it defined substantive programming guidelines for judging radio broadcasters' performance at license renewal time and was the FCC's first significant effort to clarify its public interest standard. Its purpose was to mandate that broadcasters devote time to local, noncommercial, and experimental programming, and cut down on excessive advertising. But broadcasters fought it as if it posed an existential threat, and the Blue Book gradually fell into obscurity (Pickard, 2011).

Ultimately, reformers failed in their attempts to break up media monopolies while creating a more education-oriented broadcast system. This was largely due to anti-communist hysteria and Cold War anxieties, which became a favorite political tool used by corporate interests to beat back regulatory interventions. Reformers were accused of trying to "BBC-ize" American radio, and were denounced for being socialistic. Nonetheless, there were at least a few partial victories. For example, news media began to embrace a notion of social responsibility, and some alternative media institutions like Pacifica radio were established. Public interest policies like the Fairness Doctrine—the rule that broadcasters had to present contrasting views on issues important to local communities—created some potential for advocating public interest programming. While these reforms represented meaningful progress, they fell far short of the structural interventions reformers had initially sought (Pickard, 2015).

The Postwar Settlement for American News Media

The outcomes of these debates resulted in a kind of social contract between the state, the public, and media institutions. This postwar settlement was defined by three features: self-regulation, industry-defined social responsibility, and a negative understanding of the First Amendment. This kept in place a commercial media system with little public or governmental oversight or challenges from noncommercial media. This framework continues to shape much of the media Americans interact with today. The ideological formation that keeps this arrangement intact is what I refer to as corporate libertarianism (Pickard, 2014). Based on the assumption that government has little legitimate role in intervening in media markets, corporate libertarianism attaches individual freedoms to corporate entities, often elevating these rights over the rights of other groups, local communities, and society as a whole. That government has no role in media is, in reality, a libertarian fantasy: from spectrum management to copyright protections to the enforcement of ownership regulations, government is always involved. The real question is *how* the government should be involved.

These corporate-friendly policies for radio transferred seamlessly to television, where the same networks (CBS, NBC, and ABC) dominated for a generation. To be sure, public service exceptions persisted within this media landscape, with Edward R. Murrow's reporting being a prime example of journalism pushing the commercial constraints of the medium. And there is some evidence that the 1940s reform movement left a lasting cultural imprint on commercial news media that encouraged them to pay at least some attention to public service principles (Ehrlich, 2011). But this ethic certainly did not come to largely define American news media as it had in other public media systems established by democracies across the globe.

Challenges to an unregulated, heavily commercialized media system nonetheless continued, especially outside the FCC's purview. For example, the 1967 Public Broadcasting Act and the Supreme Court's 1969 *Red Lion* case, respectively, led to the formation of NPR and PBS, and upheld the Fairness Doctrine. In the latter decision, the court unabashedly articulated strong support for a positive First Amendment, determining that it is "the right of the viewers and listeners, not the right of the broadcasters, which is paramount." Another historic case was decided in 1969 when WLBT-TV's license was revoked because of racist programming—one of the few times a broadcast license was ever revoked (Office of the Communication of United Church of Christ, 1969). This case was made possible after the D.C. Circuit Court forced the FCC to allow citizen groups to challenge a license renewal, thus granting citizen groups legal standing for the first time (Horwitz, 1997).

The FCC made other attempts at progressive content regulation during the 1960s and 1970s, like the 1960 Programming Policy Statement, which maintained that government could mandate public interest obligations, and the 1971 Primer on Ascertainment of Community Problems, which mandated broadcasters' commitment to localism. Many of these policies, like the Fairness Doctrine and Ascertainment, were thrown out under President Ronald Reagan's deregulatory push in the 1980s. The Reagan-appointed FCC chair, Mark Fowler, who became infamous for saying that television was nothing more than "a toaster with pictures," helped reorient media policy according to a market-based understanding of the public interest (Boyer, 1987). While removing the Fairness Doctrine helped usher in a wave of rightwing cable television and talk-radio shows, potential alternatives like cable and satellite became dominated by a small number of lightly regulated corporations.

The deregulatory zeal that characterized media policy in the 1980s culminated with the 1996 Telecommunications Act, the first major overhaul of the landmark 1934 Communications Act (Aufderheide, 1999). An attempt to reform U.S. media policy for the digital era, the bill passed Congress with significant bipartisan support and was signed into law by President Bill Clinton. Going beyond just telecom legislation, the bill's broad sweep also deregulated cable rates and removed broadcast ownership limits. This latter provision led to a rapid and unprecedented merger mania resulting in media conglomerates and massive consolidation, especially in national radio station ownership. After the telecom act eliminated the 40-station national ownership cap, a series of acquisitions allowed the largest radio chain, Clear Channel, to own more than 1,200 stations nationwide, dominating most major markets and limiting the diversity of voices on the public airwaves.

The Rise of a Profit-Obsessed Media System

In understanding why media systems operate in particular ways, we rarely link patterns in news coverage to a media system's structural components. Much popular media criticism singles out specific journalists or news organizations' individual failures. But this suggests that the problem lies with just a few bad apples. Of course there is not a cabal of media owners who meet in smoky backrooms to plot their manipulation of the masses. But shoddy news coverage is a systemic problem—one that stems from the commercial pressures and profit imperatives that privilege particular types of news coverage over others.

Critiques of campaign coverage are well known. Election-related news typically focuses on the horse-race aspects of politics, with an emphasis on who is ahead and what the polls are saying with each changing minute. Campaign strategies, the most recent embarrassing gaffes, and outrageous insults that one candidate hurled at another, are the stuff of standard election news commentary—not historical context or information about substantive policy differences that may affect voters' daily lives. Typical news coverage often treats the election like a dramatic football game to be consumed by passive audiences instead of a democracy-sustaining act of citizenship.

While it is tempting to blame the audience for lapping up this coverage, it is actually more of a supply-side problem. Media do not simply give people what they want. They are also produced to satisfy advertisers' and media owners' needs. Screen-to-screen coverage of Trump does not just reflect audience desires; rather, it serves as bait for their attention. Because the audience's attention is the coveted product that media deliver to advertisers. And to keep our attention, media must entertain us.

Trump performs this role wonderfully by keeping ratings high and ad sales strong. He is pure gold for commercial media outlets' bottom line. Conflict and controversy attract eyeballs, and our hyper-commercialized media system cares most about what sells advertising, not what informs or enriches our democratic discourse. Most commercial media organizations—cable news, broadcast news, newspapers, and digital news outlets—profit most by serving up audiences to advertisers who pay handsomely. Desensitized over the span of generations, American audiences are conditioned to accept this relationship as normal and it is difficult to even imagine alternative scenarios.

Is There an Alternative?

Trump's election exposed the structural rot at the core of the American media system. What Stephen Cushion (2016) referred to as the "Trumpification of the media" captures the extreme commercialism driving these anti-democratic tendencies in the press, and reminds us that the news media are first and foremost profit-driven businesses. However, critical historical analyses also remind us that the current system was not inevitable—that there were other roads not taken—and we can begin to imagine that a very different media system was, and still is, possible.

In the 1940s there was an alternative vision to the corporate libertarian model, and recovering this forgotten reform movement may help show the way forward. For the past 100-plus years, the U.S. has tried to sustain its experiment in commercialized journalism by treating news as both a commodity and a public service. Although a perfect division never existed, the news industry (often out of fear of public backlash and government intervention) has long sought to prevent commercial imperatives from completely overwhelming democratic necessities.

Today any vestiges of that always-porous divide are quickly eroding. While television news media demonstrate this most blatantly, we are seeing similar trends with the rise of "clickbait" and other forms of digital journalism that expose readers to invasive and deceptive advertising (Colhoun, 2015; Libert & Pickard, 2015). With ever-diminishing revenues for hard journalism, this trajectory of increasingly degraded journalism is troubling.

What these problems actually call for is a structural overhaul of our media system where it is no longer rational to serve up fluff in place of actual news.

Alternative models, both from the American past and from other countries, show us that different systems are indeed viable. However, they require policy interventions to establish structural safeguards and incentives for responsible and informative media. For example, the United States could follow other democracies' leads and create a stronger public media system that actually behaves differently from its commercial counterparts (Pickard, 2017a). Research has shown that commercialized media correlates with low political knowledge (Curran, Iyengar, Lund, & Salovaara-Moring, 2009). The required public subsidies for such an expansion could be generated through any number of creative means, including revenues generated from spectrum sales or merger conditions.

We could also experiment with nonprofit news models, especially as print news media are rendered increasingly unprofitable by the market. While nonprofit experiments are beginning to take root (Embler, 2016), we could encourage proliferation via reforms geared toward expanding public service journalism that might involve tax incentives for struggling media institutions to transition into low- and nonprofit initiatives. Government-sponsored research and development efforts for new digital models and public/private hybrids could provide other opportunities for experimentation.

Another area for potential reform is to leverage already-existing public infrastructure to help support the production of local news content. Specifically, the U.S. could transform post offices and public libraries into local community media centers. These would not only provide news and internet access but also enable the actual production of local reporting through various media that adhered to meaningful public service obligations and high journalistic standards.

Combined with a revitalized antitrust program that would prevent or even break up media oligopolies, these initiatives could reduce market pressures and help restore journalism's public service mission. In essence, they could help prevent commercialism from trumping democracy (Pickard, 2018). But these reforms cannot happen until counter-narratives, with substantial grassroots support for policy interventions, can help bring about actual structural alternatives to profit-obsessed media.

The Fourth Estate's democratic purpose affords it special protections and responsibilities. But the irresponsible news coverage that now surrounds us does not comport with basic democratic ideals. Even if it is "damn good for CBS," the news media should not be permitted to recklessly pursue commercial interests to everyone's detriment. History shows that this was not the media system that many Americans wanted. History also shows that we can fight for—and sometimes even win—alternatives.

Note

1. This essay is adapted from an earlier article, Victor Pickard (2016). Media and Politics in the Age of Trump, *Origins: Current Events in Historical Perspective*, vol. 10, issue 2, November. https://origins.osu.edu/article/media-and-politics-age-trump/page/0/0

References

Associated Press v. United States (1945). 326 US 1. Retrieved from https://supreme.justia.com/cases/federal/us/326/1/case.html

Aufderheide, P. (1999). *Communications policy and the public interest: The telecommunications act of 1996*. New York, NY: Guilford Press.

Becker, O. (2016, February 29). Why it's no surprise a journalist got choked at a Donald Trump rally. *Vice News*. Retrieved from https://news.vice.com/article/why-its-no-surprise-a-journalist-got-choked-at-a-donald-trump-rally

Benson, R., & Powers, M. (2011). Public media and political independence: Lessons for the future of journalism from around the world. *Free Press* [report]. Retrieved from http://www.freepress.net/sites/default/files/stn-legacy/public-media-and-political-independence.pdf

Boyer, P. (1987, January 19). Under Fowler, F.C.C. treated TV as commerce. *New York Times*. Retrieved from http://www.nytimes.com/1987/01/19/arts/under-fowler-fcc-treated-tv-as-commerce.html

Colhoun, D. (2015, February 27). Victor Pickard on native ads and the new journalism economy. *Columbia Journalism Review*. Retrieved from http://archives.cjr.org/behind_the_news/qa_victor_pickard.php

Confessore, N. (2016, March 28). How the GOP elite lost its voters to Donald Trump. *New York Times*. Retrieved from https://www.nytimes.com/2016/03/28/us/politics/donald-trump-republican-voters.html

Confessore, N., & Yourish, K. (2016, March 15). $2 billion worth of free media for Donald Trump. *New York Times*. Retrieved from http://www.nytimes.com/2016/03/16/upshot/measuring-donald-trumpsmammoth-advantage-in-free-media.html

Curran, J., Iyengar, S., Lund, A. B., & Salovaara-Moring, I. (2009). Media system, public knowledge, and democracy: A comparative study. *European Journal of Communication*, 24, 5–26.

Cushion, S. (2016, March 10). The trumpification of the US media: Why chasing news values distorts politics. *The Conversation*. Retrieved from https://theconversation.com/the-trumpification-of-the-us-media-why-chasing-news-values-distorts-politics-56033

Edwardson, M. (2002). James Lawrence Fly's report on chain broadcasting (1941) and the regulation of monopoly in America. *Historical Journal of Film, Radio and Television*, 22(4), 397–423.

Ehrlich, M. (2011). *Radio Utopia: Postwar audio documentary in the public interest*. Urbana, IL: University of Illinois Press.

Embler, S. (2016, January 12). 3 Philadelphia publications are donated to a non-profit journalism institute. *New York Times.* Retrieved from https://www.nytimes.com/2016/01/13/business/media/3-philadelphia-publications-are-donated-to-a-nonprofit-journalism-institute.html

Fang, L. (2016, February 29). CBS CEO: For us, economically, Donald's place in this election is a good thing. *The Intercept.* Retrieved from https://theintercept.com/2016/02/29/cbs-donald-trump/

Fones-Wolf, E. (2006). *Waves of opposition: Labor, business, and the struggle for democratic radio.* Urbana IL: University of Illinois Press.

Frank, T. (2016, March 7). Millions of ordinary Americans support Donald Trump. Here's why. *The Guardian.* Retrieved from https://www.theguardian.com/commentisfree/2016/mar/07/donald-trump-why-americans-support

Gold, H., & Weprin, A. (2016, September 27). Cable news' election-year haul could reach $2.5 billion. *Politico.* Retrieved from http://www.politico.com/media/story/2016/09/media-tv-numbers- 004783

Hampson, R. (2016, March 10). Donald Trump blasts the news media that's helped him to dominate GOP field. *USA Today.* Retrieved from http://www.usatoday.com/story/news/politics/elections/2016/03/10/donald-trump-blasts-news-media-republican-new-york-times-des-moine-register/81576826/

Horwitz, R. (1997). Broadcast reform revisited: Reverend Everett C. Parker and the 'Standing' Case," *Communication Review,* 2(3), 311–348.

Libert, T., & Pickard, V. (2015, November 6). Think you're reading the news for free? New research shows you're likely paying with your privacy. *The Conversation.* Retrieved from https://theconversation.com/think-youre-reading-the-news-for-free-new-research-shows-youre-likely-paying-with-your-privacy-49694

McChesney, R. (1993). *Telecommunications, mass media & democracy: The battle for the control of U.S. broadcasting, 1928–1935.* New York, NY: The Oxford University Press.

Office of the Communication of United Church of Christ, 425 F.2d 543. (1969). Retrieved from https://law.justia.com/cases/federal/appellate-courts/F2/465/519/290119/

Pickard, V. (2010). "Whether the giants should be slain or persuaded to be good": Revisiting the Hutchins commission and the role of media in a democratic society. *Critical Studies in Media Communication, 27*(4), 391–411.

Pickard, V. (2011). The battle over the FCC blue book: Determining the role of broadcast media in a democratic society, 1945–1948. *Media, Culture & Society, 33*(2), 171–191.

Pickard, V. (2016). Media and politics in the age of Trump. *Origins: Current Events in*

Pickard, V. (2015). *America's battle for media democracy: The triumph of corporate libertarianism and the future of media reform.* New York, NY: Cambridge University Press.

Historical Perspective, 10(2), November. Retrieved from https://origins.osu.edu/article/ media-and-politics-age-trump/page/0/0 Republished on *Common Dreams:* http:// www.commondreams.org/views/2016/10/21/media-and-politics-age-trump

Pickard, V. (2017a). A social democratic vision of media: Toward a radical pre-history of public broadcasting. *Journal of Radio and Audio Media,* 24(2), 200–212.

Pickard, V. (2017b). The big picture: Misinformation society. *Public Books,* November 28. Retrieved from http://www.publicbooks.org/the-big-picture-misinformation-society/

Pickard, V. (2018). When commercialism Trumps democracy: Media pathologies and the rise of the misinformation society. In Pablo Boczkowski and Zizi Papacharissi (Eds.), *Trump and the Media,* Boston, MA: The MIT Press, 195–201.

Poggi, J. (2015, September 2). CNN charging 40 times its usual price for spots in Republican debate. *Advertising Age.* Retrieved from http://adage.com/article/media/ cnn-charging-40-times-usual-price-commercials-republican-debate/300185/

Public Broadcasting Act of 1967, Sec. 496 [47 U.S.C. 396]. Retrieved from http://www. cpb.org/ aboutcpb

Red Lion Broadcasting Co. v. FCC, 395 U.S. 367 (1969). Retrieved from https:// supreme.justia.com/cases/federal/us/395/367/

Stamm, M. (2011). *Sound business: Newspapers, radio, and the politics of new media.* Philadelphia, PA: University of Pennsylvania Press.

Stole, I. (2012). *Advertising at war: Business, consumers, and government in the 1940s.* Urbana, IL: University of Illinois Press.

Tufekci, Z. (2016, March 31). Adventures in the Trump twittersphere. *New York Times.* Retrieved from https://www.nytimes.com/2016/03/31/opinion/campaign-stops/ adventures-in-the-trump-twittersphere.html

Tyndall, A. (2015, December 21). Campaign 2016 coverage: Annual totals for 2015. *Tyndall Report.* Retrieved from http://tyndallreport.com/comment/20/5773/

6. From Fox News to Fake News: An Anatomy of the Top 20 Fake News Stories on Facebook Before the 2016 Election[1]

MITCHELL T. BARD
Iona College

A week after Donald Trump's surprising presidential election win in November 2016, Craig Silverman (2016) published a study that thrust the idea of fake news firmly into post-election analyses of the election. Silverman found that the 20 fake news stories that received the most engagement on Facebook—that is, the stories that were liked and shared the most—received more online interactions than the top actual news articles on the social media site did during that time period (see Table 6.1 for the list of articles).

Major news outlets not only quickly reported the findings but also asked questions about how the proliferation of fake news before the election might have affected the outcome. Both the *Washington Post* (e.g. Dewey, 2016; Timberg, 2016) and the *New York Times* (e.g. Higgins, McIntire, & Dance, 2016; Maheshwari, 2016; Mozur & Scott, 2016;) ran multiple pieces in the next week on fake news, from a profile of a producer who thinks he tipped the election to Trump (Dewey, 2016) to a step-by-step look at how one story went viral (Maheshwari, 2016).

Not surprisingly, with fake news becoming a discussion point as the presidential election campaigns began, academic researchers quickly started looking into the fake news phenomenon. A study conducted immediately after the election by Allcott and Gentzkow (2017) found that fake news stories favoring Donald Trump were shared on Facebook 30 million times, compared to only 8

Table 6.1: 20 Most Engaged Fake News Stories on Facebook (Silverman, 2016).

Rank	Article	Publication	URL Read by Researcher
1	Pope Francis Shocks World, Endorses Donald Trump for President, Releases Statement	Ending the Fed	https://web.archive.org/web/20161115024211/http://wtoe5news.com/us-election/pope-francis-shocks-world-endorses-donald-trump-for-president-releases-statement/
2	WikiLeaks CONFIRMS Hillary Sold Weapons to ISIS… Then Drops Another BOMBSHELL! Breaking News	The Political Insider	http://www.thepoliticalinsider.com/wikileaks-confirms-hillary-sold-weapons-isis-drops-another-bombshell-breaking-news/
3	IT'S OVER: Hillary's ISIS Email Just Leaked & It's Worse Than Anyone Could Have Imagined	Ending The Fed	http://endingthefed.com/its-over-hillarys-isis-email-just-leaked-its-worse-than-anyone-could-have-imagined.html
4	Just Read the Law: Hillary is Disqualified from Holding Any Federal Office	Ending The Fed	http://www.truthandaction.org/just-read-law-hillary-disqualified-holding-federal-office/2/
5	FBI Agent Suspected in Hillary Email Leaks Found Dead in Apparent Murder-Suicide	Denver Guardian	http://alexanderhiggins.com/fbi-agent-behind-hillary-email-leaks-found-dead-murder-suicide/
6	FBI director received millions from Clinton Foundation, his brother's law firm does Clinton's taxes	Ending The Fed	http://endingthefed.com/fbi-director-received-millions-from-clinton-foundation-his-brothers-law-firm-does-clintons-taxes.html
7	ISIS Leader Calls for American Muslim Voters to Support Hillary Clinton	World News Daily Report	http://theduran.com/hillary-clinton-picks-huge-endorsement-isis-number-two-leader-call-trump-satire/
8	Hillary Clinton In 2013: "I Would Like To See People Like Donald Trump Run For Office; They're Honest And Can't Be Bought"	Conservative State	http://therightists.com/hillary-clinton-in-2013-i-would-like-to-see-people-like-donald-trump-run-for-office-theyre-honest-and-cant-be-bought/

9	BREAKING: Fraudulent Clinton Votes Discovered By The "Tens Of Thousands"	Ending The Fed	http://endingthefed.com/breaking-fraudulent-clinton-votes-discovered-by-the-tens-of-thou-sands.html
10	President Obama Confirms He Will Refuse To Leave Office If Trump Is Elected	Burrard Street Journal	http://www.burrardstreetjournal.com/obama-refusing-to-leave-if-trump-elected/
11	Donald Trump Protester Speaks Out: "I Was Paid $3,500 To Protest Trump's Rally"—ABC News	abcnews.com.co	http://abcnews.com.co/donald-trump-protester-speaks-out-i-was-paid-to-protest/
12	Pentagon Officials Furious After Clinton Announces US Response Time for Nuclear Launch During Debate	Liberty News	http://libertynews.com/2016/10/pentagon-of-ficials-furious-after-clinton-announces-us-re-sponse-time-for-nuclear-launch-during-debate/
13	Hillary's Email Case Got Reopened And James Comey Asked For Immunity. Trey Gowdy Says Hell No.	Yes I'm Right	http://www.yesimright.com/hillarys-email-case-got-reopened-and-james-comey-asked-for-immu-nity-trey-gowdy-says-hell-no/
14	Hey Hillary, thanks for telling the world America's response time for a nuclear launch	Twitchy	http://twitchy.com/brettt-3136/2016/10/19/hey-hillary-thanks-for-telling-the-world-americas-response-time-for-a-nuclear-launch/
15	Rupaul claims Trump touched him inappropriately in the 1990s	World News Daily Report	http://worldnewsdailyreport.com/rupaul-claims-trump-touched-him-inappropriately-in-the-1990s/
16	Billy Graham Issues STUNNING Statement on Donald Trump .... No One Expected THIS!—World Politicus	World Politic US	http://worldpoliticus.com/2016/10/17/billy-graham-issues-stunning-statement-don-ald-trumpno-one-expected/

(Continued)

Table 6.1: (Continued)

17	Pence: "Michelle Obama Is The Most Vulgar First Lady We've Ever Had"	USA Newsflash	https://web.archive.org/web/20161018113500/http://usanewsflash.com/pence-michelle-obama-vulgar-first-lady-weve-ever/
18	Clinton Cash: Khizr Khan's Deep Legal, Financial Connections to Saudi Arabia, Hillary's Clinton Foundation Tie Terror, Immigration, Email Scandals Together	Breitbart	http://www.breitbart.com/2016-presidential-race/2016/08/01/clinton-cash-khizr-khans-deep-legal-financial-connections-saudi-arabia-hillarys-clinton-foundation-connect-terror-immigration-email-scandals/
19	Thousands Of Fake Ballot Slips Found Marked For Hillary Clinton! TRUMP WAS RIGHT!!	Donald Trump News	https://web.archive.org/web/20161019081605/http://donaldtrumpnews.co/news/thousands-fake-ballot-slips-found-marked-hillary-clinton-trump-right/
20	BREAKING: Hillary Clinton To Be Indicted … Your Prayers Have Been Answered	World Politic US	http://www.trendolizer.com/2016/11/breaking-hillary-clinton-to-be-indicted-your-prayers-have-been-answered—world politicus.html

million shares of pro-Hillary Clinton fake news articles, with 14% of Americans calling social media their most important source of political news. Jin, Cao, Zhang, and Luo (2016) proposed a process that uses crowd-sourcing and viewpoint identification as a way to verify Twitter content and identify fake news. Khaldarova and Pantti (2016) examined how fake news on Twitter drove strategic narratives in Ukraine.

But with fake news—at least the current, social-media-based incarnation—a relatively new topic for academic study, many questions remain unanswered about the phenomenon. This chapter focuses on the content of the 20 most engaged fake news stories on Facebook before the election. Specifically, the study looks at how the fake news articles are crafted—are they written to fool readers into thinking they are journalistic news stories?—and the themes they covered. An analysis of the Fox News Channel program "The O'Reilly Factor" provides insight into why the authors of the fake news articles may have chosen the topics and approaches found in the pieces.

Fake News

Silverman (2016) early on in his piece says that in classifying fake news he is looking at "false election stories from hoax sites and hyperpartisan blogs," which he distinguishes from "election stories from ... major news websites." Essentially, fake news, then, has two components. First, the content itself has to be nonfactual. Second, the source of the content has to be a website set up solely to disseminate false stories or a website that specializes in displaying strictly partisan information regardless of the veracity of the report.

While the term "fake news" may be relatively new to public and academic discourse, the idea of writers fabricating narratives and trying to pass them off to the public as accurate to further a cause is far from new. In 1475 an Italian preacher told his congregation a false story that a 2-year-old child had been murdered by the Jewish community for the purpose of drinking the child's blood during Passover, all in the service of beginning a purge against the Jewish residents of his city (Soll, 2016). Despite the fact that the founders of the United States included freedom of the press in the First Amendment and actively supported the growth of newspapers through, among other things, the Postal Act of 1792, the early American press was notoriously prone to false stories meant to promote political interests (Starr, 2004). Thomas Jefferson wrote to James Madison about Alexander Hamilton: "For god's (sic) sake, my dear Sir (sic), take up your pen, select the most striking heresies (sic), and cut him to peices (sic) in the face of the public" (Jefferson, 1793). William Randolph Hearst famously invented the story of Spanish authorities strip-searching women on an American ship in Cuba in 1897 because he wanted the United States to go to war with Spain (Schudson, 1978). It wasn't until the emergence of *The New York Times* under Adolph Ochs in the late 19th century and the move to objectivity in the American press after World War I that the press was expected to be strictly, consistently factual (Schudson, 1978).

Before the popularization of the Internet, tabloids like the *National Enquirer* were a source for fake news, especially about celebrities (McCartha & Strauman, 2009) and crime stories (Grochowski, 2002). The rise of the Internet brought with it hoaxes carried on websites and spread via emails that reported wild stories, so much so that a website, snopes.com, emerged as a clearinghouse to check the veracity of these viral claims (Degroot, 2011). At the same time, websites—some journalistic operations, others independent—emerged to check the veracity of statements by public officials, usually as they were reported in the news media (Graves, 2016).

Fake News or Something Else?

Beyond the metrics, we are left with little information about the fake news articles Silverman (2016) identified as the ones most widely shared on Facebook in the three months before the election, including their content and style. Were these posts written like journalistic news articles with the intention of fooling readers into thinking they were reading news reporting? Or, rather, were the articles supposed to feel more like content generated from like-minded compatriots, resembling what might arrive in an American's email inbox from a friend or relative or appear on a website whose ideological leanings match those of the reader? Put another way, do these fake news articles follow in the tradition of Hearst or a chain email debunked by snopes.com?

To answer these questions, I textually analyzed the 20 pieces Silverman (2016) identified to see if they were, in fact, meant to mimic journalistic news articles. That begs the question: What does a journalistic news article look like? Objectivity is regularly recognized as a central indicator of news in the United States. Michael Schudson (2001) argued, "'Objectivity' is the chief occupational value of American journalism" (p. 149). Similarly, David T.Z. Mindich posited, "If American journalism were a religion … its supreme deity would be 'objectivity'" (p. 1). But what is objectivity? Mindich (1998) points out that there is no one definition of the concept, but the same qualities—e.g. neutrality, fairness, balance, accuracy—come up again and again in offered definitions. Denis McQuail (1996) cited neutrality, balance and an allegiance to accuracy and the facts as the three keys to objectivity. Clearly, the fake news articles would not actually be neutral, fair and factual. However, if the perception of readers is meant to be that these are works of news, then there would at least seem to need to be an attempt at appearing fair and unbiased—accuracy is, of course, implied. Further, to look like a true piece of objective news, a byline would be needed, as part of the idea behind objectivity is allowing the audience to evaluate the content of a report, including its author (Schudson, 1978).

Objectivity only goes so far, though, as a barometer of journalistic writing. Obviously, the writers of fake news stories are not actually concerned with neutrality, balance, and accuracy in writing their pieces. But if the fake news articles are, in fact, meant to fool readers into thinking they are reading actual news articles, the reports at the least would have to appear to follow the rules of objectivity. But what does a writer have to do to allow readers to perceive that they are reading a news article? Mindich (1998) is helpful here, as he notes that one of the characteristics of objectivity is that an article is written in the inverted pyramid format with the information reported from most important to least important. The inverted pyramid structure has been at the center of American journalism since the late 19th century (Pottker, 2003). A summary news lead—an opening sentence that generally summarizes the who, what, where, when, why, and how of the article—which is generally used by journalists working in the inverted pyramid structure, is another common element of a journalistic news article (Schudson, 1995). And even as some news outlets are moving away from the inverted pyramid structure and summary news leads when possible—for example, many sports editors recognize that most fans know the outcome of sporting events long before a game story is published thanks to the ubiquity of live coverage on the internet and social media—nonetheless these traditional building blocks remain in place for most news outlets reporting on breaking news events.

So in analyzing the fake news articles, I noted if the piece was written in the inverted pyramid structure with a summary news lead, while taking on a tone that could fool a reader into thinking the writer was neutral, balanced and accurate. The textual analysis found that the pieces were all either almost wholly works of fiction or fictional spins on existing sets of facts, but beyond this link, the articles varied wildly in their fidelity to journalistic style. For nine of the articles, the writers, at least to some extent, seemed to make an attempt to adhere to journalistic style, attempting to use a summary news lead and the inverted pyramid structure while writing in a way that tried to appear neutral, fair and accurate, rather than taking a side or trying to persuade the reader (See Table 6.2). It should be noted, however, that these nine articles varied widely as to the success with which the writers worked within journalistic style. Some wrote like journalists better than others did where errors of style, punctuation, and grammar were common.

Table 6.2: Journalistic Styles Employed in Fake News Articles.

Top 20 Fake News Articles on Facebook August-November 2016, per Silverman (2016)	Byline	Summary News Lead	Inverted Pyramid	Large Block Quote(s)	Objective/ Neutral Style
Pope Francis Shocks World, Endorses Donald Trump for President, Releases Statement	None	Yes	No	Yes	No
WikiLeaks CONFIRMS Hillary Sold Weapons to ISIS ... Then Drops Another BOMBSHELL! Breaking News	Alias	No	No	Yes	No
IT'S OVER: Hillary's ISIS Email Just Leaked & It's Worse Than Anyone Could Have Imagined	None	No	No	No	No
Just Read the Law: Hillary is Disqualified from Holding Any Federal Office	None	No	No	Yes	No
FBI Agent Suspected in Hillary Email Leaks Found Dead in Apparent Murder-Suicide	None	Yes	Yes	No	Yes
FBI director received millions from Clinton Foundation, his brother's law firm does Clinton's taxes	None	No	No	No	No
ISIS Leader Calls for American Muslim Voters to Support Hillary Clinton	Yes	In part	In part	Yes	Yes

Hillary Clinton In 2013: "I Would Like To See People Like Donald Trump Run For Office; They're Honest And Can't Be Bought"	Alias	Yes	Yes	No	Yes
BREAKING: Fraudulent Clinton Votes Discovered By The "Tens Of Thousands"	None	Yes	Yes	No	Yes
President Obama Confirms He Will Refuse To Leave Office If Trump Is Elected	Site	Yes	Yes	No	Yes
Donald Trump Protester Speaks Out: "I Was Paid $3,500 To Protest Trump's Rally"—ABC News	Yes	In part	In Part	No	Yes
Pentagon Officials Furious After Clinton Announces US Response Time for Nuclear Launch During Debate	Yes	No	No	Yes	Yes
Hillary's Email Case Got Reopened And James Comey Asked For Immunity. Trey Gowdy Says Hell No.	Yes	No	No	No	No
Hey Hillary, thanks for telling the world America's response time for a nuclear launch	Alias	No	No	No	No
Rupaul claims Trump touched him inappropriately in the 1990s	None	Yes	Yes	Yes	Yes

(Continued)

Table 6.2: (Continue)

Billy Graham Issues STUNNING Statement on Donald Trump … No One Expected THIS!—World Politicus	None	No	No	No	No
Pence: "Michelle Obama Is The Most Vulgar First Lady We've Ever Had"	None	No	No	Yes	No
Clinton Cash: Khizr Khan's Deep Legal, Financial Connections to Saudi Arabia, Hillary's Clinton Foundation Tie Terror, Immigration, Email Scandals Together	Yes	Yes	No	Yes	No
Thousands Of Fake Ballot Slips Found Marked For Hillary Clinton! TRUMP WAS RIGHT!!	None	Yes	Yes	No	Yes
BREAKING: Hillary Clinton To Be Indicted … Your Prayers Have Been Answered	No	No	No	No	No

For example, an article from the *Denver Guardian* claiming that an FBI agent involved in the investigation into Hillary Clinton's email server killed his wife and then killed himself begins with a sentence that follows the style of the classic summary news lead, reporting the who, what, where, when, why, and how of the story:

> Walkerville, MD—An FBI agent believed to be responsible for the latest email leaks 'pertinent to the investigation' into Hillary Clinton's private email server while she was Secretary of State, was found dead in an apparent murder-suicide early Saturday morning, according to police.

The lead also has a dateline at the beginning and attribution at the end, which is a common approach in summary news leads. Of course, there is a misplaced comma, incorrect capitalization and the state abbreviation in the dateline does not follow AP style, but, in most respects, to the average reader, this piece begins much like real news articles, and then, like genuine news stories, proceeds to report the news using the inverted pyramid structure.

Less successfully, the site *Conservative State* attempted to write a news-like article alleging that Hillary Clinton said in 2013 that Donald Trump should run for office, with an effort to keep the tone neutral throughout. However, the lead is written more like an essay opening than a summary news lead:

> Before running against billionaire real estate mogul Donald Trump for the pres-idency, Secretary of State Hillary Clinton told an audience at a private, paid speech she wanted to see more successful businessmen and women run for office because they can't be bought.

Some readers may not notice the differing style, but others would pick up that the article doesn't read like a traditional newspaper story.

Other elements that add or subtract from the journalistic feel of a piece varied among the nine fake news articles that seemed to make an effort to portray themselves as legitimate news stories. Only three of the nine stories included a person's name in the byline. Four provided no byline, one featured an alias, and one used the name of the site. Also, two of the nine articles featured large block quotes—highlighted or otherwise designed to set the quote off from the content written by the author—in the text, with limited original writing around them. This style is more reminiscent of a blog than a news article. For example, the *World News Daily Report* piece saying that ISIS endorsed Clinton is made up of five short paragraphs arranged around two larger block quotes. The article looks like a partisan blog, not a news report.

Only two of the websites on which the nine more journalistic fake news stories appeared had names that a reader might take for a mainstream news organization. One site tried to fool readers into thinking the story was from ABC News, as the site uses the web address abcnews.com.co. In fact, after the election, the site added a message to the top of the article saying the story was made up and berating Trump supporters for believing the content to be true. Another fake news site, the *Denver Guardian*, took a name that sounded like a newspaper.

On the other side of the spectrum, 11 of the 20 articles did not use a neutral approach to the reporting. Instead they read as a work of persuasion or advocacy. In all 11 pieces, it is clear the writer prefers one of the candidates, and this group included the four most engaged fake news articles on Facebook during the period under study. Several of the articles openly revealed their partisanship right in the headline. For example, a *World Politic US* headline read: "BREAKING: Hillary Clinton To Be Indicted ... Your Prayers Have Been Answered." The first half of the headline reads like the reporting of news, but the second half has a clear point of view, something that wouldn't appear in a traditional news article. It seems unlikely that readers clicking on a link with that headline would do so thinking they were being brought to a neutral, journalistic piece.

The *Ending the Fed* story accusing Clinton of supporting ISIS is a good example of the approach taken by articles that did not try to maintain a neutral and balanced tone. The second and third paragraphs read like a political blog more than a news article:

> Even though when Trump called Hillary the 'founder' of ISIS he was telling the truth and 100% accurate, the media has never stopped ripping him apart over it. Today the media is forced to eat their hats because the newest batch of leaked emails show Hillary, in her own words, admitting to doing just that, funding and running ISIS.

The article explicitly takes Trump's side ("he was telling the truth and 100% accurate") while accusing the news media of dishonesty, using colloquial terms ("the media is forced to eat their hats"). It seems unlikely anyone reading this article would believe it was a genuine objective news story, and it does not appear that the writer of the story had such a reaction as a goal.

Avoiding the appearance of being a mainstream news source may have been a strategic choice of some of the fake news writers, given Trump's constant attacks on the traditional news media during the campaign (Shafer, 2016). As such, it is likely that many of the Trump supporters who engaged with these fake news articles may have been more likely to believe information coming from a site that didn't sound like a traditional journalistic source and wasn't written like a news article. It may well be that a website with a partisan name like *Conservative State* or *Liberty News* would be more credible to someone likely to read a partisan fake news article, making the need to match the journalistic style of legitimate news reports unnecessary. This lack of trust in mainstream news may explain why more than half of the fake news articles in Silverman's top 20 list did not attempt to mimic the form of genuine news, nor did most of them provide purported attributions to mainstream news sources in the text.

The Themes of the Fake News Articles

All but one of the top 20 fake news articles on Facebook before the election either supported Donald Trump or attacked Hillary Clinton and/or Barack or Michelle Obama. So the fake news stories were not, for the most part, aimed at both sides of the presidential race. Rather, collectively, the articles were an effort to aid Trump and hurt Clinton. A textual analysis of the fake news stories revealed that seven somewhat specific claims appeared in at least two of the 20 fake news stories (see Table 6.3). Of the 19 articles that favored Trump and/or attacked Clinton and/or her allies, 14 of them were built on the theme that Clinton was a criminal and/or corrupt. *Ending the Fed*, which was responsible for five of the top 20 articles on Facebook, including three of the top four, built all of its pieces around this theme. For example, in the most engaged fake news article of the period, the site claimed to quote Pope Francis as saying he was endorsing Trump because of the FBI's failure to prosecute Clinton despite the fact she had broken the law "on multiple occasions," so that the pope felt "voting against the powerful political forces that have corrupted the entire American federal government is the only option." Other *Ending the Fed* articles accused Clinton of "funding and running ISIS," being

Table 6.3: Themes.

Theme	Number of Occurrences
Hillary Clinton is a criminal/corrupt	14
Hillary Clinton's email investigation	7
Hillary Clinton and FBI investigations	5
Hillary Clinton linked to ISIS	3
Hillary Clinton weak on defense	3
Hillary Clinton and the Clinton Foundation	2
Hillary Clinton and voter fraud	2

ineligible to run for public office because of her law-breaking behavior, using her position as secretary of state to benefit herself financially, and engaging in voter fraud.

Four of the six other themes were, essentially, subsets of the claim that Clinton was criminal or corrupt. Seven articles made claims related to Clinton's email investigation, including the *Ending the Fed* reports of Pope Francis' endorsement of Trump, Clinton's disqualification from holding public office, and Clinton's self-dealing as secretary of state. A *World Politic US* article was direct on this point, reporting that Clinton was to be indicted due to the investigation into her email server. Relatedly, five articles made charges about the FBI's role in protecting Clinton, including the *Yes I'm Right* piece that claimed FBI Director James Comey was seeking immunity for his actions in failing to bring charges against Clinton and the *Denver Guardian* report that an FBI agent who had worked on the Clinton case had murdered his wife before killing himself. Two articles specifically linked Clinton's corruption to connections between her family's foundation and her work as secretary of state, while two others accused her of voter fraud, including an *Ending the Fed* claim that "tens of thousands" of ballots were found already marked for Clinton.

Claims of Clinton's weakness on national security made up a second, smaller general trend in the fake news articles. Three pieces accused Clinton of being weak on defense, including two that claimed Clinton had threatened U.S. security by revealing the response time for a nuclear launch. *Liberty News* reported that, "Pentagon officials found themselves completely dumbfounded as to why former Secretary of State Hillary Clinton would feel it appropriate to announce U.S. Special Access Program intel on national television," and that "[a]ccording to sources within the Department of Defense speaking under anonymity, Clinton likely violated at least two Dept. [sic] of Defense SAP protocols during the debate by announcing on *live television* the United States Government's response time for a nuclear launch" (emphasis in original). Similarly, the *Twitchy* story on the topic began, "There's no telling how many times during the campaign Hillary Clinton has brought up America's nuclear codes, and how important it is that someone who's riled by a tweet never be allowed anywhere near them."

Three other articles went a step further, accusing Clinton of allying herself with ISIS. *Political Insider* and *Ending the Fed* reported that Clinton sold arms to, supported, and/or helped run ISIS, while *World News Daily Report* said that ISIS had endorsed Clinton because "the ISIS leader was able to recognize that Hillary is aligned with ISIS." Given how increasing defense spending was one of Trump's prominent campaign promises (Diamond,

2016), this vein of fake news articles would seem to be an effective way to tap into the values of the readers to induce action.

Several clear themes ran through the top 20 fake news stories on Facebook before the election, even as the content came from 15 different publishers. This begs the question: How do 15 separate content producers coalesce around several topics? Since 19 of the 20 stories favored Trump over Clinton, and since the producers, regardless of motive, were seeking to get as many clicks on their articles as possible, it would seem that their task would be to figure out what issues and claims would generate the most interest among Trump's supporters. It's likely these authors were watching American traditional and social media to ascertain what values, beliefs, fears, concerns, and interests discreet groups of Americans held, and then attempting to produce content that would get a reaction from the group based on activating those values. In this way, the authors are not acting as individual agents, but rather they are iteratively creating and taking part in themes circulating on social media. In effect, these writers are part of a network of writers searching for and jumping onto themes that will stir interest in specific American communities.

Fox News and the Fake News Themes

Tracing and analyzing the sources of the themes that appeared in the fake news stories is a task too vast for this chapter, as it's likely that the producers were influenced by sources big and small, from cable news networks down to partisan blogs. Given the traditional role of Fox News Channel as a voice for conservative positions (Jamieson & Capella, 2008), with the highest ratings in cable news (Fox News Channel, 2017), a good place to start an inquiry would be to ask if the themes present in the fake news stories were also circulated on the cable network, especially during Fox News' most watched part of the schedule: prime time.

Fox News emerged early in Donald Trump's campaign as a supporter of his run. After Megan Kelly's tough questioning of Trump at a Republican presidential debate, Trump attacked Kelly over the next two days, insulting her by saying, "you could see there was blood coming out of her eyes, blood coming out of her wherever" (Peters & Victor, 2015). Trump reportedly told Fox News host Sean Hannity he was "never doing Fox again" (Sherman, 2015). When faced with Trump's threats, along with emails and other correspondence from Fox News viewers who supported Trump and criticized Kelly, then Fox News Chairman Roger Ailes chose to support Trump, giving him a platform on the network to defend himself and softening the network's defense of Kelly (Sherman, 2015). As president, Trump has often cited Fox News as a key source of his information, and the network has regularly defended his policies (Koblin & Korasaniti, 2017).

Bill O'Reilly's "The O'Reilly Factor" was the top-rated prime time program on Fox News during the period under study, averaging approximately four million viewers each show (Fox News, 2017). O'Reilly has also been a focus of scholarly work. Earlier studies have showed that O'Reilly heavily employed seven 1930s propaganda devices in his "Talking Points Memo" segment (Conway, Grabe, & Grieve, 2007), practiced an emotion-based approach to his topics in an effort to lower expectations for journalistic practice (Peters, 2010), and helped further the Fox News themes opposing health care reform in 2009 and 2014 even as he avoided explicitly endorsing some of the more patently false claims, like the existence of death panels (Bard, 2016). If established conservative news sources were circulating the same themes as the fake news writers, it seems as though O'Reilly's program should be involved in the discussions of the themes. A textual analysis of the transcripts of "The O'Reilly Factor" episodes between July 1, 2016—a month before the three-month period covered by Silverman (2016) began—and August 31, 2016—a month after Silverman's period began—sought to determine if the program trafficked in the themes found in the top fake news stories on Facebook. The transcripts were accessed via LexisNexis. Two main lines of attack were present across the top fake news articles before the election: First, Clinton was corrupt and engaged in criminal activity, with specific attention focused on the FBI investigation into her use of a private email server. Second, some fake news articles targeted Clinton's unfitness to defend the United States, with specific attention on her relationship with ISIS and revealing the country's nuclear response time.

Hillary Clinton's email investigation—one of the primary bases for claims that Clinton was corrupt—was mentioned 21 times on "The O'Reilly Factor," with most of the discussions of the issue occurring in the context of statements from then-candidate Donald Trump. The program served as a conduit for Trump's claims to reach this largely sympathetic audience. For example, O'Reilly began his August 23 program with the following:

> Hi, I am Bill O'Reilly, thanks for watching us tonight. New strategy from the Trump campaign and that is the subject of this evening's Talking Points Memo. To take the heat off their candidate, the Trump campaign is now focusing on Hillary Clinton's continuing email and foundation controversies. The plan is this. To demonize Mrs. Clinton with the corruption label. To demand an independent prosecutor be assigned to look at her behavior and to tell voters that ongoing scandal will not benefit the country. Yesterday, Mr. Trump made things clear.

O'Reilly himself does not take a position in this passage, but a viewer is exposed to Trump's message. With 21 mentions in two months, the Clinton email investigation was regularly conveyed to viewers during July and August 2016.

Sometimes, though, the host talked about the issue outside of the context of Trump. In the opening segment of his July 5 program, O'Reilly said: "The FBI saying no charges will be brought against Hillary Clinton but scorching the former secretary of state for her behavior regarding national security." He then showed a clip of FBI Director James Comey saying, "What I can assure the American people is that this investigation was done honestly, confidently and independently." O'Reilly responded, "Billions of Americans do not believe that. Are they being fair?" O'Reilly begins by saying that no charges would be brought against Clinton, but he immediately followed by including that the FBI director was "scorching" Clinton. Similarly, after showing Comey's claim of a fair investigation, O'Reilly said that "billions" of people don't believe the FBI director. The introduction to the story makes it clear to a viewer what the conservative take is on the issue: Clinton may not have been charged, but she is a threat to national security, and many question the fairness of the investigation. It's easy to see how an opportunist in Russia or Macedonia who is looking to get as many people as possible to read a fake news story would see that the FBI's investigation of Clinton's email server would resonate with conservative readers.

On nine occasions during the period of study, "The O'Reilly Factor" discussed the FBI's investigation of Clinton, including both her email server and actions of the Clinton Foundation. Eric Bolling, substituting for O'Reilly on August 10, said, "New revelations in the Hillary Clinton email scandal about 300 pages of emails released Tuesday are raising questions about quid pro quo relationships between Clinton Foundation staffers and Hillary Clinton's State Department." Bolling refers to the investigation as a "scandal." Further, he highlights charges of untoward dealings between Clinton and the Clinton Foundation, offering up the conspiracy theory to the audience. "The O'Reilly Factor" was able to deliver pro-Trump/anti-Clinton messaging to its audience, whether or not the host explicitly endorsed the message. In fact, the Clinton Foundation was a subject of "The O'Reilly Factor" seven times during July and August.

While "The O'Reilly Factor" did not explicitly claim that Clinton supported ISIS, the topic did come up five times during the period in language that was generally conditional. For example, Bolling, substituting for O'Reilly on August 11, said, "Senator Rand Paul said, if Julian Assange releases the emails that he says he has that tie Hillary Clinton to knowledge of weapons and arms going to ISIS, she should go to jail." Bolling is not saying Clinton sold arms to ISIS. He is two levels removed from the claim. Bolling is repeating Paul, and Paul references a third person, Assange. But, again, the message is getting through to viewers. The Clinton-ISIS story is given credence as a legitimate possibility. "The O'Reilly Factor" is part of the discussion on the issue, just like the three fake news articles on Silverman's (2016) list that claimed an alliance between Clinton and ISIS. The program was part of the circulation of themes the fake news article writers were tapping into.

Fake News, Fox News, and the 2016 Election

The writers of the fake news stories that appeared on Facebook before the 2016 election were seeking one action on the part of readers: a click. Whether the fake news articles were produced for financial gain (Higgins et al., 2016) or to upend American politics (Shane, 2017), the goal was the same: to get as many Americans as possible to read their content. This chapter provides some insight into what the writers were doing to get the clicks they sought.

First, while the 20 articles all purported to convey information to a reader, and the information was not, in fact, factual, the similarities between the articles end there. Even the name "fake news article" is not entirely accurate, as more than half of the pieces made little effort to maintain a journalistic tone or use a summary news lead and inverted pyramid structure that makes news articles feel like works of journalism. Such an approach is understandable, given Donald Trump's attacks on the press (Shafer, 2016). The writers likely calculated that appeals to his supporters might be more effective if not contained in a traditional news format. In fact, the finding that more of the fake news articles chose not to use a journalistic style says a lot about what kind of content Trump supporters would want most, assuming the fake news writers were doing all they could to make their work attractive to that group. Nevertheless, the vast majority of the fake news articles were written more as works of advocacy or persuasion than of purported journalism. They more resembled partisan blog posts than original news articles. Also, only two of the 20 articles came from sources trying to look like traditional news outlets: the *Denver Guardian*, which while not a real news site sounds like a traditional newspaper, and a site masquerading as ABC News. So, in the end, the fake news articles mostly were not trying to induce in viewers a reaction that the article itself was a work of journalism, but rather solely that the content itself was factual and newsworthy, even if it was coming from a fellow partisan rather than coming from an objective news outlet.

Second, despite the fact that the articles came from an array of sources (aside from *Ending the Fed*, which provided five of the top 20 fake news articles, two sites placed two articles on the list, and 11 outlets were responsible for one each), many of the pieces focused on the same themes. Nearly three-quarters of the fake news articles were based on a premise that Hillary Clinton was corrupt and/or a criminal. Within that claim, seven articles addressed her private email server and five involved claims about the FBI's handling of the investigation. It seems clear than in an effort to induce readers to click on the article, the writers calculated that claiming Clinton was corrupt or a criminal would successfully tap into the values of Trump supporters. Some writers based works on claims that Clinton was allied with ISIS and/or was inept at national security, which would tap into the traditional Republican view that Democrats are weak on defense. The fake news writers seemed to have clear ideas on which values, when activated, would elicit clicks in pro-Trump readers.

Finally, those two themes—Clinton as corrupt and a criminal and Clinton as a danger to national security—were reflected on "The O'Reilly Factor" in July and August 2016. This study cannot inform us about causation in this area. Was Fox News reflecting what the fringe was circulating online, or was the right wing fringe picking up and using messages it heard in mainstream conservative media? Reading the articles and transcripts alone can't answer this question. However, we do know that the issues were in play in both places. It may be more useful to think of these ideas as iteratively circling in the conversations of Trump supporters in a variety of media, both in mainstream outlets like Fox News and on partisan websites, until the ideas are distilled down to their essence—Clinton is a criminal, Clinton is dangerous, etc.—and taken as a given in the community and on traditional and social media, where they continue to be circulated.

Similarly, it should be noted that this iterative distilling of themes represents messaging more identified with mainstream partisan media as well as conspiracy theories bubbling up from the fringe. Claims of voter fraud, which have served as the rationale for states under Republican leadership to pass voter identification legislation (Schultz, 2008; Wilson & Brewer, 2013), are standard fare in traditional conservative media. However, more outlandish claims, like those linking Clinton to ISIS or involvement in murder-suicides, come from the fringe.

This mixing of mainstream and the fringe helps illustrate another takeaway from this study, namely the two factors that enabled and shaped the explosion of the 2016 version of fake news: the solidification of the role of partisan cable television—specifically, Fox News Channel—and the emergence of social media. By 2016 Fox News had been furthering the conservative strategy in arguing issue positions (Jamieson & Cappella, 2008), with the prime time programs eschewing an allegiance to facts in making these kinds of claims (Bard, 2017), for 20 years. The emergence of social media, including the ability of content producers to target and promote fake news articles on Facebook, allowed the fringe conspiracy theories that long existed but were confined to being spread by minor publications and, later, via emails to friends and family, to reach larger audiences. Fake news authors were able to distribute their content to tens of millions of readers in the three months before the 2016 election (Silverman, 2016).

This chapter only looked at 20 articles and one prime time *Fox News* program, so further research will be needed to understand the breadth and depth of fake news stories and their themes. Nonetheless, looking at those 20 articles and how their themes often appeared on Bill O'Reilly's program during the period provides a profile of the fake news articles that reached the most readers prior to the 2016 election. The findings will, it is hoped, provide some guidance to those engaging in research as to the form, content and role of fake news.

Note

1. This chapter is based on a paper presented at the AEJMC national conference in Chicago in August 2017.

References

Allcott, H., & Gentzkow, M. (2017). Social media and fake news in the 2016 election. Retrieved from https://web.stanford.edu/~gentzkow/research/fakenews.pdf

Bard, M. T. (2016). The role of differing host styles in Fox News' prime time coverage of health care reform in August 2009. *Journalism & Mass Communication Quarterly, 93*(3), 659–676.

Bard, M. T. (2017). Propaganda, persuasion or journalism? Fox News' prime-time coverage of health care reform in 2009 and 2014. *Electronic News, 11*(2), 100–118.

Conway, M., Grabe, M. E., & Grieves, K. (2007). Villains, victims and the virtuous in Bill O'Reilly's "No-Spin Zone": Revisiting world war propaganda techniques. *Journalism Studies, 8*(2), 197–223.

Degroot, J. M. (2011). Truth in urban legends? Using snopes.com to teach source evaluation. *Communication Teacher, 2*. Retrieved from http://dx.doi.org/10.1080/17404622.2010.527298

Dewey, C. (2016, November 17). Facebook fake-news writer: "I think Donald Trump is in the White House because of me." *Washington Post*. Retrieved from https://www.washingtonpost.com/news/the-intersect/wp/2016/11/17/facebook-fake-news-writer-i-think-donald-trump-is-in-the-white-house-because-of-me/

Diamond, J. (2016, September 7). Trump calls for military spending increase. *CNN*. Retrieved from http://www.cnn.com/2016/09/06/politics/donald-trump-defense-spending-sequester/

Fox News (2017, January 31). FOX News Channel marks ratings milestone. *Fox News Entertainment*. Retrieved from http://www.foxnews.com/entertainment/2017/01/31/fox-news-channel-marks-ratings-milestone.html

Graves, L. (2016). *Deciding what's true: The rise of political fact-checking in American journalism*. New York, NY: Columbia University Press.

Grochowski, T. (2002). The "tabloid effect" in the O. J. Simpson case: The National Enquirer and the production of crime knowledge. *International Journal of Cultural Studies, 5*(3), 336–356.

Higgins, A., McIntire, M., & Dance, G. J. X. (2016, November 25). Inside a fake news sausage factory: "This is all about income." *New York Times*. Retrieved from https://www.nytimes.com/2016/11/25/world/europe/fake-news-donald-trump-hillary-clinton-georgia.html

Jamieson, K. H., & Cappella, J. N. (2008). *Echo chamber: Rush Limbaugh and the Conservative Media Establishment*. Oxford: Oxford University Press.

Jefferson, T. (1793). To James Madison from Thomas Jefferson, 7 July 1793. *National Archives*. Retrieved from http://founders.archives.gov/documents/Madison/01-15-02-0037

Jin, Z., Cao, J., Zhang, Y., & Luo, J. (2016). News verification by exploiting conflicting social viewpoints in microblogs. Proceedings of the Thirtieth AAAI Conference on Artificial Intelligence, 2972–2978.

Khaldarova, I., & Pantti, M. (2016). The narrative battle over the Ukrainian conflict. *Journalism Practice, 10*(7), 891–901.

Koblin, J., & Korasaniti, N. (2017, March 25). One nation, under Fox: 18 hours with a network that shapes America. *New York Times*. Retrieved from https://www.nytimes.com/2017/03/25/business/media/fox-news.html

Maheshwari, S. (2016, November 20). How fake news goes viral: A case study. *New York Times*. Retrieved from https://www.nytimes.com/2016/11/20/business/media/how-fake-news-spreads.html

McCartha, M., & Strauman, E. C. (2009). Fallen stars and strategic redemption: A narrative analysis of the National Enquirer. *Florida Communication Journal, 37*(2), 71–82.

McQuail, D. (1996). Mass media in the public interest: Towards a framework of norms for media performance. In J. Curran & M. Gurevitch (Eds.), *Mass media and society* (2nd ed.). New York, NY: St. Martin's Press.

Mindich, D. T. Z. (1998). *Just the facts: How "objectivity" came to define American journalism*. New York, NY: New York University Press.

Mozur, P., & Scott, M. (2016, November 17). Fake news in the U.S. election? Elsewhere, that's nothing new. *New York Times*. Retrieved from https://www.nytimes.com/2016/11/18/technology/fake-news-on-facebook-in foreign-elections-thats-not-new.html

Peters, C. (2010). No-spin zones: The rise of the American cable news magazine and Bill O'Reilly. *Journalism Studies, 11*(6), 832–851.

Peters, J. W., & Victor, D. (2015, August 10). Megyn Kelly says she won't be cowed by Donald Trump. *New York Times.* Retrieved from http://www.nytimes.com/2015/08/11/us/megyn-kelly-says-she-wont-be-cowed-by-donald-trump.html

Pottker, H. (2003). News and its communicative quality: The inverted pyramid—When and why did it appear? *Journalism Studies, 4*(4), 501–511.

Schudson, M. (1978). *Discovering the news.* New York, NY: Basic Books.

Schudson, M. (1995). *The power of news.* Cambridge, MA: Harvard University Press.

Schudson, M. (2001). The objectivity norm in American journalism. *Journalism, 2*(2), 149–170.

Schultz, D. T. (2008). Less than fundamental: The myth of voter fraud and the coming of the second great disenfranchisement. *William Mitchell Law Review, 34*(2), 482–532.

Shafer, J. (2016, November 5). How Trump took over the media by fighting it. *Politico.* Retrieved from http://www.politico.com/magazine/story/2016/11/2016-election-trump-media-takeover-coverage-214419

Shane, S. (2017, September 7). The fake Americans Russia created to influence the election. *The New York Times.* Retrieved from https://www.nytimes.com/2017/09/07/us/politics/russia-facebook-twitter-election.html?_r=0

Sherman, G. (2015, August 11). How Roger Ailes picked Trump, and Fox News' audience, over Megyn Kelly. *New York Magazine.* Retrieved from http://nymag.com/daily/intelligencer/2015/08/fox-news-picked-trump-over-megyn-kelly.html

Silverman, C. (2016, November 16). This analysis shows how viral fake election news stories outperformed real news on Facebook. *BuzzFeed.* Retrieved from https://www.buzzfeed.com/craigsilverman/viral-fake-election-news-outperformed-real-news-on-facebook

Soll, J. (2016, December 18). The long and brutal history of fake news. *Politico.* Retrieved from http://www.politico.com/magazine/story/2016/12/fake-news-history-long-violent-214535

Starr, P. (2004). *The creation of the media: Political origins of modern communications.* New York, NY: Basic Books.

Timberg, C. (2016, November 24). Russian propaganda effort helped spread "fake news" during election, experts say. *Washington Post.* Retrieved from https://www.washingtonpost.com/business/economy/russian-propaganda-effort-helped-spread-fake-news-during-election-experts-say/2016/11/24/793903b6 8a40-4ca9-b712-716af66098fe_story.html

Wilson, D. C., & Brewer, P. R. (2013). The foundations of public opinion on voter ID: Political predispositions, racial resentment, and information effects. *Public Opinion Quarterly, 77*(4), 962–984.

7. We've Got Mail (But Probably Shouldn't): The Press, WikiLeaks, and Democratic Disclosures in the 2016 Election

LAUREL LEFF
Northeastern University

There is no longer any question that the Russians used the mainstream media to weaponize hacked Democratic emails in order to interfere with the 2016 presidential election. The remaining question is why the media abrogated their own standards and allowed themselves to be used as missiles in the Russians' campaign.[1]

During the final 15 weeks of the 2016 presidential campaign, *The New York Times* and *The Washington Post* ran over 50 articles each focused on the hacked emails: 57 in *The Times* and 53 in *The Post*. The articles clustered around the first Democratic National Committee emails disclosed during the party's convention at the end of July and Clinton campaign chair John Podesta's personal emails disclosed during the campaign's last four weeks.

What makes the extensive coverage in the nation's two most important news organizations so remarkable is that the decision to publish information from the hacked accounts violates six traditional journalistic norms.

- First, the emails were stolen and journalists rightly hesitate to use stolen information.
- Second, they were stolen by a foreign adversary to influence the outcome of an election.
- Third, they were disclosed by a source who declared he had bad motives, and were timed to inflict maximum damage.

- Fourth, they were published without any consideration of balance, in that they were harmful to one side, and no attempt was made to counter them with similar information from the other side.
- Fifth, they were published during a political campaign when concerns about balance are supposed to be at their height.
- Sixth, they contained conversations, primarily among private citizens (almost none of the emails were from Clinton herself) who had high expectations of privacy in their communications.

Although the second and third violations were not known with certainty at the time, the likelihood that Russia stole the emails and WikiLeaks published them out of animosity toward Clinton was great enough to raise serious questions at least. Combined with the other four and weighed together, these transgressions should have given *The Times* and *The Post* pause about how, and even whether, to use the emails. They never did. Of course, none of these norms are sacrosanct; journalists violate them all the time. *The Times'* and *The Post'*s publication of the stolen, classified documents known as the Pentagon Papers is rightly considered an important and heroic chapter in American journalism. Usually the test is whether the information is of such importance that the public interest in knowing it overcomes legitimate objections to how and why it was obtained. That test seemingly was never applied to the disclosure of the hacked Democratic emails.

This chapter argues that had a searching inquiry into relative importance been done *The Times* and *The Post* would not have found a publication rationale. As will be discussed in depth, the email disclosures revealed party insiders doing what party insiders do: complaining about candidates, sucking up to donors and the media, fretting about operations and optics. Because the correspondents thought they were speaking in private, they spoke more candidly and sometimes callously than they would have in public, which is what made their revelations seem at all unusual. Should that very difference—their more freewheeling expression—have become the justification for disclosing their private communications? To be clear: the argument is not that the press should never publish the contents of stolen documents. In fact, the greatest long run danger that arises from publishing information that is *not* in the public interest is that it will make it harder to publish information that is. That lesson becomes ever more important as the Trump Administration attacks the press and threatens to jail journalists.

This chapter explores news stories and opinion pieces about the WikiLeaks leaks published from July 22, 2016 to November 8, 2016 in *The New York Times* and *The Washington Post*, organizations that were chosen as most reflective of traditional news values. The chapter will first describe what was reported as news and assess its value to the public. Second, it will examine how the press handled questions of the information's origins and the motives of those who provided it. Finally, the chapter will discuss why the WikiLeaks 2016 disclosures matter going forward. The analysis is based on the information that would have been available to journalists at the time, not subsequent revelations about the role of the Russians, WikiLeaks and the Trump campaign.[2]

A June 21 article published inside *The Washington Post* provided the first sign of what was to come: independent researchers concluded the DNC had been "compromised by Russian government hackers" (Nakashima, 2016c). The hackers' haul wasn't revealed for a month, until the eve of the Democratic National Convention. On Friday July 22, WikiLeaks posted 19,252 emails and 8,034 attachments from the accounts of seven DNC staffers covering a 16-month period ending in May 2016. The timing was deliberate. WikiLeaks knew news organizations could easily incorporate the DNC disclosures into their already planned convention coverage (Savage, 2016). The disclosures also were likely to roil the convention, thus increasing their news value.

The Times and *The Post* agreed on the news out of the DNC emails. DNC officials "criticized and mocked" Clinton's primary opponent, Sen. Bernie Sanders, the *Times* said, while insisting publicly the committee was "neutral in the race" (Shear & Rosenberg, 2016).[3] DNC emails included "discussions about how to undermine" Sanders, *The Post* wrote (Hamburger & Tumulty, 2016).[4]

Yet, the news organizations' characterizations seemed to go beyond what was justified. "[A] trove of leaked emails showed party officials *conspiring to sabotage*" Sanders' campaign, *The Times* said (Martin & Rappeport, 2016) (emphasis added).[5] *The Post* declared that the emails "*undercut claims by the party* and the Clinton campaign that the process was open and fair for Sanders." The evidence to support the "sabotage" or "undercut" theory, however, was weak. *The Post* cited a Clinton campaign lawyer advising the DNC on how to respond to a Sanders' complaint and "a DNC official apparently discussing how to use Sanders's religion against him to help Clinton before the Kentucky and West Virginia primaries" (Gearan & Phillip, 2016). Lawyerly advice may suggest inappropriate chumminess, but it's unlikely to derail a campaign. And the Clinton campaign never did attack Sanders' religion, or more accurately his lack of religion.[6] (Indeed, the emails in general mostly show DNC officials musing, rather than acting.[7]) In addition, by the time of the West Virginia primary on May 10 and the Kentucky primary on May 17 Clinton had already sewn up the nomination. It's difficult to "sabotage" a race that has already been decided. The emails may have shown DNC officials favoring Clinton—perhaps a defensible position if she was already guaranteed to be the nominee—but that's a far cry from sabotaging Sanders.

Still, the emails, and particularly the way they were portrayed, had demonstrable effects on the Democratic Party. They led to the firing of DNC chairwoman Debbie Wasserman Schultz, which became front-page news (Martin & Rappeport, 2016), and to protests outside the convention and discord within. Both newspapers covered the protests. *The Times* described a "large, impassioned crowd of Bernie Sanders supporters," noting the hacked emails "reinforced a widespread view among marchers that party leaders had stacked the deck against him" (Gabriel, 2016). *The Post* ran a similar story, quoting a protestor saying "'We believe the primary was rigged against [Sanders]. The WikiLeaks emails prove that'" (Lowery, Loveluck, & Achenbach, 2016).

The Times and *The Post* also framed their initial convention stories around divisions within the Democratic Party, a narrative the Trump campaign embraced. "The Wikileaks[sic] e-mail release today was so bad to Sanders that it will make it impossible for him to support her, unless he is a fraud," Trump tweeted the Saturday before the convention (Weigel, 2016d). Trump mentioned the emails often at rallies, as on the day Wasserman Shultz resigned. "Republicans, led by Trump, seized on the episode," *The Post* reported (Gearan & Phillip, 2016). As the week progressed, dramatic speeches by Barack and Michelle Obama, and the parents of a Muslim soldier killed in Iraq, seemingly dampened the divisions and stories about them (Balz, 2016b; Gearan & Phillip, 2016; Horowitz, 2016b; Martin & Rappeport, 2016; Weigel, 2016c).

The Times and *The Post* glommed onto another story line that emerged from the DNC emails—that the party catered to wealthy donors. "The emails capture a world where seating charts are arranged with dollar totals in mind, where a White House celebration of gay pride is a thinly disguised occasion for rewarding wealthy donors and where physical proximity to the president is the most precious of currencies," *The Times* explained. Both newspapers named donors[8] and described them behaving in embarrassing ways. One extremely persistent donor, eager to meet with President Obama, mentioned that he had had cancer. Party officials considered that crass and one party fundraiser noted, "'I … don't understand why everyone seems to hate [him] so much'" (Confessore & Eder, 2016). Another story mentioned the cash flow problems of a named donor who couldn't sell her old house (Shear & Rosenberg, 2016). None of the stories suggested that the Party violated any laws in its fundraising, though a *Post* story implied language used in donor pitches might not comply with White House policy (Gold, 2016). Neither organization went as far as WikiLeaks and other news sites in including Democratic donors' credit card, Social Security and passport numbers. (Several individuals filed a privacy suit in 2017 against the Trump campaign based on these disclosures (*Cockrum, Comer and Schoenberg v. Donald J. Trump for President Inc.*, 2017).

The Times also saw a story in DNC staffers' relations with the media, which was sometimes fawning—trying to get tickets to an exclusive NBC party—and sometimes disdainful—dismissing one MSNBC host as a "hipster pit bull." The emails "feature the sort of snarky and un-self-conscious exchanges that are common between reporters and politicos in their day-to-day discussions," the story acknowledged. So what made those emails newsworthy? "[I]nsight into journalistic and political sausage-making" and "an unusual and evocative glimpse of ... an elbows-out reality of Washington life that is usually hidden from public view," the story explained (Grynbaum, 2016b). Presumably, similar stories could have been written about the Republican party's wooing of donors and the media. But they weren't because the press didn't have the Republicans' emails.

In weighing the newsworthiness of the DNC emails, journalists knew two things. First, Russian intelligence hacked DNC computers to obtain the emails and most likely provided the information to WikiLeaks. Second, WikiLeaks, which both news organizations routinely described as "the anti-secrecy organization" or a "transparency group," disclosed the information to harm the Clinton campaign. WikiLeaks head Julian Assange explained his reasons for posting the DNC emails in a June interview with a British broadcaster that *The Times* wrote about as the DNC email stories appeared. Assange's remarks "made it clear that he hoped to harm Hillary Clinton's chances of winning the presidency," *The Times'* lead declared, a formulation echoed in subsequent stories (Lichtblau & Schmitt, 2016). In the interview, Assange said he opposed Clinton on policy grounds ("a vote for Mrs. Clinton to become president is 'a vote for endless, stupid war'") and as a personal foe who had tried to indict him for his earlier leak of State Department diplomatic cables (Savage, 2016).[9]

It's true that for a month and a half after the disclosure, *The Post*, and to a lesser extent *The Times*, hadn't verified that the Russians provided the emails to WikiLeaks. Assange wouldn't say how WikiLeaks obtained the DNC emails and in a July 25 interview insisted there was no proof "that Russia was behind the original hacking." *The Post* didn't go as far as Assange in denying Russian involvement, but it trod carefully (Gearan & Phillip, 2016). *Post* stories said government officials hadn't determined whether Russia provided the information to WikiLeaks and cast doubt on the possibility that Russia would have done it to help Trump (Nakashima, 2016b, 2016e). *The Post* then basically dropped the Russian angle for the next month, except for an inside article on the animosity between Putin and Clinton that insisted, "no one has been able to suggest how the material got into the hands of WikiLeaks" (Englund, 2016). It also ran a story on WikiLeaks' having offered a $20,000 reward for information leading to the conviction of the killer of Seth Rich, a young DNC staffer murdered in Washington, D.C. *The Post* described Internet speculation that Rich might have been WikiLeaks' source for the DNC document (Hermann & Williams, 2016).[10]

The Times took a different tack. Within a few days of the WikiLeaks disclosure, *The Times* was treating seriously the possibility of Russian interference in the election. By the end of July, it had published four front-page stories and three inside stories. The first front-page story was speculative, yet it cited evidence that pointed to Russian intelligence agencies and suggested that the information might be being used to influence the election. The subsequent three front-page stories explained Putin's admiration for Trump and disdain for Clinton; described American intelligence agencies growing conviction that the Russian government was behind the DNC hacks, though they still didn't know whether it was done to affect the election; and described Russian intelligence services' hacking the Clinton campaign, as well as the DNC (Lichtblau, 2016; Myers & Macfarquhar, 2016; Sanger, 2016b; Sanger & Perlroth, 2016; Sanger & Schmitt, 2016; Savage, 2016; Savage & Perlroth, 2016).

Neither *The Times* nor *The Post* gave much credence to Clinton claims that the Trump campaign might have been involved, treating them as to-be-expected responses from a political opponent. Such responses usually appeared far down in a story (Martin & Rappeport, 2016). If anything, the news organizations seemed more alarmed that Clinton would raise the possibility. Claims of Russian interference were "emerging as a theme of Mrs. Clinton's campaign," a *Times* front page story stated, noting it was remarkable that a "presidential campaign would charge its rival" with "secretly doing the bidding of a key American adversary" (Myers & Macfarquhar, 2016; Sullivan, 2016). *The Times'* next-day, front-page story quoted Clinton campaign officials suggesting, "Putin could be trying to tilt the election," and yet insisted the officials "have no evidence." The article captured the Trump campaign's response through a Trump tweet: To deflect from "'the horror and stupidity of the Wikileakes[sic] disaster,' Democrats were saying: 'Russia is dealing with Trump. Crazy!'" (Sanger & Schmitt, 2016).

Unlike *The Post*, *The Times* didn't drop the story in August and early September. A front-page story reported that a broadened FBI investigation indicated additional Russian cyberattacks on Democratic politicians. A *Times* interview with Assange generated a lengthy September 1 front-page story, suggesting he didn't have direct ties to Russian intelligence but indicating Moscow "knew it had a sympathetic outlet in WikiLeaks." The story made Assange's attitude clear. "'He views everything through the prism of how he's treated,'" said a WikiLeaks associate. "'America and Hillary Clinton have caused him trouble, and Russia never has'" (Becker, Erlanger, & Schmitt, 2016; Lichtblau & Schmitt, 2016).

Given it was known that the Russians hacked the DNC and that WikiLeaks posted the hacked emails, the unwillingness to connect the two is a bit mystifying. (Both news organizations' editorial boards did (Editorial Board, 2016a, 2016b, 2016c, 2016d, 2016e). The hesitation seemed to be that connecting the Russians and WikiLeaks explicitly would transform the Russians' actions from standard espionage—seeking private information on adversaries—to an actual attempt to subvert a U.S. election. The press' reluctance matched that of American officials, who said privately the Russians supplied WikiLeaks but wouldn't say so publicly (Schmitt, 2016). A *Post* story pointed to growing frustration among lawmakers and national security officials. A former U.S. ambassador to Russia is quoted saying: "There's no other explanation out there that is credible'" (Nakashima, 2016f). Refusing to identify the Russians' role explicitly in news stories is one thing; ignoring that knowledge when judging the newsworthiness of the information is another. Knowing that WikiLeaks (for sure) and the Russians (highly likely) released the emails to hurt one presidential campaign should have set a high bar for their publication. It didn't.

It would take another month and another WikiLeaks dump before the government and thus the press officially identified Russia as the source of the DNC leaks. On October 8, both news organizations reported that the Obama administration had accused Russia of stealing and disclosing DNC emails and having done so to interfere with the U.S. election (Nakashima, 2016d; Sanger & Savage, 2016). Two new disclosures, however, overtook that news. That very same day, the Access Hollywood video in which Trump makes sexually predatory comments appeared (a sign that all leaks of private communications are not equal), as did the first of another round of WikiLeaks disclosures of hacked emails. WikiLeaks began posting the first of 50,000 documents stolen from Clinton campaign chair Podesta's personal Gmail account, with Assange promising periodic releases until the election. (Eddy, 2016).

News organizations agreed on what was news in the first batch from Podesta—comments Clinton made in private speeches to Wall Street bankers. Transcripts of the speeches, which Clinton had refused to disclose after

Sanders challenged her to, were among the 2,050 Podesta emails released October 8. "Hillary Clinton's paid closed-door speeches to Wall Street banks apparently included her dreams of 'open trade and open borders' and a suggestion that bankers are best positioned to know how the industry should be regulated," *The Post* declared (Helderman & Hamburger, 2016a). *The Times* struck a similar tone. "In lucrative paid speeches that Hillary Clinton delivered to elite financial firms but refused to disclose to the public, she displayed an easy comfort with titans of business, embraced unfettered international trade and praised a budget-balancing plan that would have required cuts to Social Security" (Chozick, Confessore, & Barbaro, 2016). These summaries miss the careful nuance in many of Clinton's comments and provide no examples of Clinton promising to pursue any particular industry-friendly positions.[11] *Times* business columnist Andrew Ross Sorkin in fact thought the emails hinted that Clinton "may be inclined to impose heavier regulations on the financial industry than is fully understood" (Sorkin, 2016).

That was one of the few times the two organizations agreed on the news in the 2,000 or so Podesta emails released every few days over the next four weeks. The disparity in itself suggests there wasn't much newsworthy about the emails. Reporters seemed to be hunting for news and finding relatively mundane campaign practices. *The Times* first front-page article, distilled from 2,086 emails released October 10, led with a despondent Bill Clinton on the eve of February's New Hampshire primary (which his wife lost). It continued with the unremarkable news that Clinton faced difficulties winning the nomination and honing her campaign message, and that her campaign staff worried about the optics of their decisions. The article admitted that "[a]lmost all campaigns calibrate stagecraft, speeches and strategy." Presumably for this to be news the Clinton campaign had to be spinning more than others, or in a more troubling way than others. Yet, the story offers no evidence, or even discussion, of that possibility. And it can't for a simple reason: *The New York Times* reporters read thousands of personal emails of one campaign and nothing from any other.

The Times wasn't even reading Clinton's emails. "The leak includes few emails from the candidate herself," the story noted. They were reading the emails of her aides, whom *The Times* describes as resembling the staff in Veep ("HBO's scabrous comedy dissecting the vanity and phoniness of Washington.") To prove the point, *The Times* describes a dozen campaign aides corresponding about whether Clinton should tell a joke about the hairstyles of Trump and Benghazi inquisitor, Rep. Trey Gowdy, during an Iowa dinner. Clinton didn't tell the joke (Chozick & Confessore, 2016a).[12] An earlier, web-only story, which seemed to be the product of five reporters reading the WikiLeaks site as quickly as possible, was no more illuminating: Her aides angled for influence in the campaign; Clinton explored a campaign two years before she entered the race; her aides worried about campaign details, including a single Twitter post; her aides liked when she talked about her mother (Chozick, Confessore, Eder, Alcindor, & Stockman, 2016). An October 11 story described the Clinton campaign debating how to handle policy announcements after the candidate had changed her position, with the Keystone XL pipeline flip serving as an example (Stockman, 2016).

The Post didn't focus on a mopey Bill Clinton, the advantages of mother talk, or the Keystone pipeline. It found news in a major donor's concern that the Clinton campaign hadn't reacted strongly enough to Trump's assertion in his announcement speech that Mexicans were rapists. *The Post* implied there might be something shady about the fact that Haim Saban, who donated $10 million to a pro-Clinton Super PAC, expressed those concerns at the same time he was majority owner and chair of Univision, an American Spanish language television network. "The emails reveal how a major donor had access to the highest levels of the Clinton campaign and was able to press top aides about an issue of major interest to his company," *The Post* wrote. Saban defended himself: "'As an immigrant myself, I am appalled by Mr. Trump's disturbing, un-American and non-inclusive stance,'" Saban, who grew up in Israel, was quoted saying. "I've been a supporter of Hillary Clinton and the Democratic Party long before my affiliation with Univision, and one thing has nothing to do with the other '" (Gold & Helderman, 2016).

Over the next two weeks in October, *The Times* published six inside stories based solely on the contents of the hacked emails (they were discussed in several others stories) and *The Post* published four—with no overlap in content between them. From *The Times*: Clinton aides didn't respect New York Mayor Bill De Blasio much; Clinton was "genial" in a paid speech hosted by Goldman Sachs, offering its chief executive advice on steps to take if he wanted to run for president (manage a soup kitchen); "Clinton liked covert action if it stayed covert" (the actual headline); and Clinton considered many possible running mates (Chozick, 2016a; Chozick & Confessore, 2016; Sanger, 2016a; Yee, 2016). "[T]he content of the messages [was] a measure short of astonishing so far," an October 19 story acknowledged (Flegenheimer & Alcindor, 2016).

The Post's stories veered in different, but no more compelling directions. The Center for American Progress, the liberal think tank Podesta founded and ran until he became the Clinton campaign chair, "played prominent behind-the-scenes roles assisting Clinton's campaign"; Clinton aides had trouble navigating "the treacherous politics of poverty"; and Jeb Bush's success in fundraising led Clinton to worry about her own. One story estab-lished the ordinariness of Podesta's personal life: he offered friends advice on making risotto, agreed to pick up his wife's prescription, and used profani-ties to refer to people he didn't like. (The latter story was tongue-in-cheek, yet still included much private information (Ehrenfreund, 2016; Gold & Narayanswamy, 2016; Gold, Wagner, & Phillip, 2016; Helderman & Hamburger, 2016a; Phillip & Wagner, 2016; Zak, 2016).

As had been the case with the earlier dump of DNC emails, news stories about the Podesta disclosure dragged in people with little connection to the campaign. Did the public really need to know that Clinton campaign staffers made disparaging comments about the head of a trial lawyers' trade group, a former conservative-turned-Clinton supporter, a former Clinton cabinet offi-cial, Clinton's brothers, and a lion-killing dentist?—all of whom were named or identifiable in the stories (Chozick & Confessore, 2016). At least one of the targets, Harvard law professor Lawrence Lessig, thought not. After news accounts described a Podesta aide disparaging Lessig's "smugness," and stating, "I fucking hate that guy," Lessig blogged: "I can't for the life of me see the public good in a leak like this … The burdens of public service are insane enough without the perpetual threat that every thought shared with a friend becomes Twitter fodder" (Weigel, 2016b). Similarly, did it matter that staffers fought among themselves, sometimes using profanity (Gearan & Wagner, 2016; Zak, 2016)? Both news organizations relied on the same rationale. "Though the WikiLeaks disclosures have not contained the sort of campaign-shaking bombshell that some Trump backers had hoped for," *The Post* explained, "the Podesta emails have provided an almost unprecedented historical archive of the inner workings of a major-party presidential cam-paign" (Helderman, 2016b). The WikiLeaks emails "provided a revealing glimpse into the inner works of Mrs. Clinton's campaign," echoed *The Times* (Chozick & Confessore, 2016). That it was the inner workings of just one of two major campaigns for president didn't seem to matter.

In addition to the stand alone stories about the contents of the emails, the WikiLeaks' disclosure infiltrated the news in other ways. *The Post* framed Clinton's final debate performance in terms of her ability to "respond to and explain what has been learned from the hacking" and "other recent revela-tions" (Balz, 2016a). A front-page follow-up suggested that she had failed, showing "discomfort in the face of scrutiny about her record" as revealed by the WikiLeaks emails (Wagner, 2016). Trump and his surrogates ham-mered away at the emails,[13] the first Podesta posting coming at a particu-larly opportune time for his campaign. "Following Mr. Trump's wishes, his advisers have aggressively pushed the Clinton camp emails in news media briefings and cable news appearances, bringing up the hacked messages to battle back from the questions about Mr. Trump's comments about women," *The Times* explained (Healy, Sanger, & Haberman, 2016). In a front-page story about Clinton campaign anxiety, *The Post* noted Trump's strategy to label the WikiLeaks revelations "'big stuff' and to 'repeatedly slam' Clinton over them. In a conference call with reporters, the Trump campaign highlighted a Clinton aide's comments that it characterized as anti-Catholic."[14] Although both newspapers tried to correct for overly negative characterizations of the emails' content, the Trump campaign still managed to use the emails to convey Clinton as plotting with international banks to destroy U.S. sovereignty and "to enrich these global financial powers, her special-interest friends and her donors" (Balz, 2016c; Grynbaum, 2016a; Martin & Burns, 2016; Rappeport & Burns, 2016; Weigel, 2016a, 2016d, 2016e).

The WikiLeaks' disclosures also found their way into the other email story, the one about Clinton's use of a private server while she was Secretary of State. Both news organizations wrote about WikiLeaks' October 25 release of emails that described campaign officials' reactions when they learned of the private server just as Clinton launched her campaign. The officials weren't happy and some blamed aides who worked at the State Department (Eder, 2016b; Helderman, 2016b). Three days later, the emails about the email server were trotted out again when FBI Director James Comey re-opened (and then later re-closed) his investigation (Helderman, Zapotosky, & Horwitz, 2016). In a front page story just two days before the election, *The Times* rehashed what the stolen emails said about certain key Clinton aides on the theory that they might follow her into the White House. (Flegenheimer & Landler, 2016).

Amidst all the elevating of the mundane into the monumental,[15] one serious topic emerged—the possibility that foreign government donations to the Clinton foundation might have had an impact upon State Department policy. *The Times* ran five stories on the Clinton foundation, including two on the front page (Chozick, 2016a; Creswell & Goodman, 2016; Eder, 2016a; Eder & Chozick, 2016; Mcintire, 2016). *The Post* ran three stories, one on the front page (Helderman & Hamburger, 2016b; Phillip, Sullivan, & Gold, 2016; Zapotosky, Helderman, & Hamburger, 2016). *The Times* and *Post* stories raised legitimate questions about unseemly behavior, such as representatives of the Qatar government donating $1 million to the foundation and then requesting five minutes with Bill Clinton (which doesn't seem to have been granted), or donors paying the former president huge amounts of money for speeches and to fund travel, or the former Secretary of State attending a foundation gathering in Morocco after its king had pledged $12 million to the charity. But the stories seem to relish the gossipy details (a former Clinton aide describing Chelsea Clinton as a "spoiled brat kid") and infighting among the staff as much as any actual wrongdoing. And none of the stories established any connection between the donations and State Department policies. As a *Times'* story acknowledged: "The emails ... have not contained evidence to support Republican contentions that Mrs. Clinton performed any favors for foundation donors" (Eder & Chozick, 2016). These articles come closest to establishing a public interest that might justify using stolen, private email correspondence. Indeed, outside campaign season, the questions-are-raised genre of news story might have been acceptable. It is harder to justify publishing insinuations without corroboration in the last weeks before a hotly contested presidential election.

Although the motivations of those who stole the emails and those who disclosed them made their way into the coverage of both news organizations, motives were not central to the stories.[16] *The Post* included allegations against Russia in 11 of its 20 stories on the DNC leaks and 10 of its 33 stories surrounding the Podesta leaks. *The Times* focused on the Russian connection heavily in the stories on the DNC leaks, 17 of 25 stories. But its interest flagged with the Podesta leaks, including the connection in only 9 of 32 stories, and only one of the last 17 stories before the election. (*The Post*'s last six stories before the election didn't mention the connection.) This loss of focus is particularly odd because the Russians' role became clearer as the campaign neared an end, and the possibility that the Trump campaign might have been involved grew greater.

Despite the intelligence community's confirmation of the earlier hacks, both news organizations tiptoed around the possibility that the Podesta hacks also could be the result of Russian maneuvering: *The Times* suggested it, while *The Post* merely noted the government was investigating (Gold & Narayan-swamy, 2016; Healy et al., 2016; Sanger, 2016a). *The Times* and *The Post* both discussed an FBI investigation into possible Trump campaign collusion with the Russians, but mostly to pour cold water on the idea. "Law enforcement officials say that none of the investigations so far have found any conclusive or direct link between Mr. Trump and the Russian government," *The Times* stated. "And even the hacking into Democratic emails, F.B.I. and intelligence officials now believe, was aimed at disrupting the presidential election rather than electing Mr. Trump." The story also implied that the investigation was conducted because "Hillary Clinton's supporters, angry over what they regard as a lack of scrutiny of Mr. Trump by law enforcement officials, pushed for these investigations" (Lichtblau & Myers, 2016). *The Post* published a story two days later that explained FBI Director Comey didn't want to accuse Russia of political hacking because the administration would appear too partisan too close to the election (Nakashima, 2016a).

The Clinton campaign worked mightily to push the storyline that the Russians were behind the disclosure, were seeking to elect Trump, and were perhaps cooperating with the Trump campaign. For the most part, *The Times* and *The Post* weren't buying it. They dutifully reported the accusations, but usually in the context of the Clinton campaign's response to the newest WikiLeaks revelations (Chozick, 2016c; Chozick & Confessore, 2016; Chozick, Confessore, et al., 2016; Gold & Helderman, 2016; Helderman, 2016b; Helderman & Hamburger, 2016a; Phillip & Wagner, 2016; Rappeport, 2016b; Wemple, 2016b). *The Post* took up the Clinton campaign's allegations in a separate story, but couldn't resist including "plenty of fodder for Clinton critics to seize upon" (Gearan & Wagner, 2016). *The Times* reported that private security firms had concluded that the Russian foreign intelligence service hacked Podesta's Gmail account but noted the lack of U.S. government confirmation, leaving it to the Clinton camp to sound the alarm. "'The new public data confirming the Russians are behind the hack of John Podesta's email is a big deal,'" a senior policy advisor said. "There is no longer any doubt that Putin is trying to help Donald Trump by weaponizing WikiLeaks" (Gold & Helderman, 2016: Perlroth & Shear, 2016). At least once, *The Post* explicitly denied the possibility that the Trump campaign was involved. After exploring Trump associate Roger Stone's possible advance knowledge of the Podesta dump, *The Post* concluded: "Clinton's team has repeatedly worked to reinforce the perception of links between the Russian government and her opponent, which this argument reinforces. So far though, the accusation seems a lot like the plane from which Podesta was speaking: ungrounded." (Bump, 2016)

Did *The Times* and *The Post* wrestle with publishing the contents of the stolen emails? Little in the pages of either newspaper suggests they did. The only news story that even raised the possibility that it might be wrong to rely upon stolen documents came in the form of Trump campaign manager Kellyanne Conway's defense of her campaign's use of the material. Conway dismissed "questions about spreading information that is stolen and in some cases unsubstantiated," *The Times* wrote. "Democrats 'say stuff all the time that's not verified,' Ms. Conway said" (Healy et al., 2016). It's understandable that in the midst of the disclosures neither organization ruminated in news articles about the ethical implication of its choices. What is less comprehensible is that neither organization engaged in much reflection in forums designated for press criticism. A few regular columnists did: *The Times'* Timothy Egan criticized the press for taking "the bait" in writing about "office gossip"

(Egan, 2016). Paul Krugman wrote that "the Russians judged, correctly, that the news media would hype the revelation that major party figures are human beings, and that politicians engage in politics, as somehow damning" (Krugman, 2016). Neither Margaret Sullivan nor Erik Wemple, *The Post*'s media columnists, considered the press' handling of the WikiLeaks material. Sullivan brushed up against the issue twice: in one column she advocated a pardon for Edward Snowden and in another she offered guarded criticism of Assange (Sullivan, 2016a, 2016b). But her focus was on how the government should treat leakers, not on how the press should treat leaks.

Times' media columnist Jim Rutenberg (2016) did lay out the media's conundrum in an October 24 column: "Run with the stolen and in many cases unverified correspondence and potentially assist an audacious Russian attempt to disrupt a presidential election, or decline to print it and betray their mission to combat the great political fog machine." Rutenberg ultimately punted, concluding transparency, however it is enabled and whatever is disclosed, is good for democracy. "In this, the year of the leak, the hackers are contributing to a phenomenon—raw transparency—that should make democracy stronger," he wrote. Tellingly, Rutenberg's Exhibits A and B for transparency weren't based on the WikiLeaks disclosure and neither example raised related ethical issues.[17] Rutenberg did return to WikiLeaks to acknowledge reporting on private emails is "incredibly fraught," but seemed to share the opinion of two journalists he quotes, Glenn Greenwald of *The Intercept* and Susan Glasser of *Politico*, that there was "too much of a public interest at stake" and that "the emails are out there" and couldn't be unknown. Rutenberg didn't directly explain the public interest at stake,[18] nor weigh it against possible harms, presumably because all disclosures are for the good. In retrospect, his conclusion can only be characterized as horrifyingly naïve. "[S]o far, the hacks have only proved that the United States system knows how to process reality and can handle the truth, which should encourage our leaders to offer more of it," Rutenberg concluded. "So for that much, I guess, thanks, Vladimir Putin. Now, ready to share your emails?"

The Times' then public editor, Liz Spayd (2016), didn't weigh in at all until November 6, two days before the election. That means for 15 weeks she determined there was no need to explain the leaks coverage to *The Times'* readers, a statement in itself. Spayd concludes *The Times* "acquitted itself well" in balancing privacy and public interest, and in avoiding being used by a foreign power; it didn't publish every email and tried to determine each's accuracy. Spayd devotes most of her column to criticizing *The Times* for not paying enough attention to the cyberwar aspects of the story, one of this election's "most chilling chapters." *The Times* "should have assembled a strike force" and made "this story its top priority," she wrote. Spayd let *The Times* off the hook, however, for its last-minute, now seemingly discredited story stating that no links had been found between the Trump campaign and the Russians.

Although *The Times'* and *The Post's* journalists didn't engage in much public reflection on their journalistic choices, outside commentators did.[19] Eric Chenoweth (2016), co-director of the Institute for Democracy in Eastern Europe, noted the breach of the first two norms: publishing information from stolen documents and publishing information stolen by a foreign adversary. "Would any self-respecting news editor take a call from the head of the GRU or the FSB (Russian military and state intelligence) and accept an offer to publish a cache of emails from the staff of a U.S. presidential candidate? This is essentially what every outlet covering this story has done," Chenoweth wrote for *The Post*. As for norm three, publishing information from a source with known bad motives, University of North Carolina Professor Zeynep Tufekci (2016) wrote in *The Times* that WikiLeaks should have been treated with much greater skepticism: "Taking one campaign manager's email account and releasing it with zero curation in the last month of an election needs to be treated as what it is: political sabotage, not whistle-blowing."

Only Fred Cantor (2016) of Westport, Connecticut, in a letter to the editor took on norms four and five, the lack of balance in the coverage, particularly at the end of a political campaign. "If there were hacked emails pertaining to both candidates, there might well be a valid argument for publicizing them," Cantor wrote to *The Times*. "But news coverage of private emails stolen from individuals with ties to only one candidate … seems highly questionable …"

There seems to be almost no consideration of norm six, the harm done to private individuals by disclosing their private communications. Both news organizations' decision to avoid the worst violations of privacy, publishing Social Security numbers and suicide attempts, seems to have immunized them from criticism for including merely embarrassing revelations.

No one took on directly an issue that challenges the very premise of both news organizations' coverage—that the private nature of the information may lessen, rather than enhance, its public value.[20] An important unacknowledged assumption permeated the press coverage—that people speaking in private are inherently more honest, and thus more newsworthy, than people speaking in public. In some instances, that's right (private recordings of presidential conversations are obvious examples[21]), and that certainly could be the case with some examples here. But it's also true that people who don't think their communications will be made public speak in a more freewheeling, even exaggerated fashion that doesn't necessarily reflect what they honestly think, or only reflects what they think in a moment that doesn't require reflection. That's one of the reasons why privacy is important. It allows people to vent, to strategize, to share, and then craft what they want to say in public. Yet, it is the very unguardedness of the comments that drives much of the coverage. What makes the emails newsworthy then is not their content but the fact that we get to see them. Another word for that is voyeurism.

Before discussing the consequences of violating journalistic norms in the absence of a potent public interest, it is worth considering other justifications for *The Times'* and *The Post'*s coverage. The journalists could argue that they presented enough information, both about the emails' contents and Russian and WikiLeaks involvement, that readers could decide for themselves whether the revelations were important. That argument, however, gives too little weight to the press' framing of the information and too much to readers' ability to understand context or even to go beyond headlines and leads. Journalists also might have figured that because Clinton was going to win (as all the polls indicated) they could afford, and maybe were even obliged, to be harder on her. In retrospect, that claim might provide the best rationale possible to strive for balance, even when it may seem unnecessary.

The final justification is that once the documents were "out there," the media had no choice but to report on them. Of course, many things are "out there" that the media doesn't report, including lots of information from WikiLeaks. The media also could have reported on the hacking without disclosing what the emails said, and certainly without publishing a new story with a new revelation every few days (as happened in October).

The French election in May 2017 serves as a powerful counterpoint. Russian hackers accessed the emails of Emmanuel Macron, the leading candidate for the French presidency, and planned to release them in the days before the election. An existing French law blocked the hacked information from being disseminated widely; the law prohibited disclosure of information that could sway the election in the last 44 hours (Brunet, 2016), a law that likely would be unconstitutional as an impermissible prior restraint in the United States. Still, the French government's warnings and the press' reaction had an impact. While right-wing social media spread the information, leading news organizations abided by the prohibition. *Le Monde*, France's leading newspaper, issued a forceful statement that it would not publish files that were disclosed "with the obvious purpose of damaging the sincerity of the ballot." The newspaper said after the election it would assess the documents' validity and only publish them "in accordance with our journalistic and ethical rules, without being made a tool of anonymous actors' publishing schedules."

The stolen emails seemingly had little effect on the election; Macron won in a landslide (Brunet, 2016; Masters, 2017; Palma, 2017; Schultheis, 2017; Stanglin, 2017).

The Times' and *The Post's* coverage of the WikiLeaks disclosures has had consequences beyond the impact upon any particular election.[22] The realization that mainstream news organizations would recklessly disseminate hacked private communications has only heightened concerns about the ability to speak candidly anywhere, anytime. Politicians and the people who work for them have probably already changed their behavior. "Without a zone of privacy in which we can talk freely to those who are close to us, no one is safe," Georgetown linguist Deborah Tannen (2016) warned. "That's the sense in which WikiLeaks is a threat not only to the presidential campaign of a particular candidate, but to us all."

In addition, the enormous play given to the stolen emails can only encourage hacking. During the campaign, Trump even taunted the press: "Russia, if you're listening, I hope you're able to find the 30,000 emails that are missing. I think you will probably be rewarded mightily by our press" (Parker & Sanger, 2016). Russia was indeed rewarded for its 2016 hacks, which at the least contributed to deepening divisions within the United States and at the most helped elect a president. And so far, Russia has incurred very little in the way of penalty. Amanda Hess (2016), who writes about Internet culture for *The Times*, predicted that, "we can expect only more hacks, leaks and sinister highlighting down the road." Paradoxically, more hacks might mean fewer leaks. "Wanton destruction of the personal privacy of any person who has ever come near a political organization is a vicious but effective means to smother dissent," University of North Carolina professor Tufekci (2016) argued in a *Times* column.

The disclosure of inconsequential information may also create a far less favorable legal and societal environment for leaks that are of far more importance. The 1971 Supreme Court decision in *United States v. New York Times* (better known as the Pentagon Papers case) marked the last time the government and the press faced off in a major legal confrontation over the publication of stolen, classified documents. Although a strong precedent didn't emerge from *U.S. v. New York Times*,[23] a powerful principle that the press can be trusted at least as much as the government to act in the public interest did. (more so in the concurring opinions of Justices Black and Douglas).[24] The principle has manifested itself in the fact that for more than 46 years and through eight administrations (five Republican, three Democratic), the federal government has not prosecuted a single journalist for publishing leaked information. The principle also has presented itself (less consistently but still significantly) in the government's reluctance to jail journalists for refusing to disclose the source of their leaks.[25] When the press lowers the bar for publication, as it did with the DNC and Podesta leaks, it threatens to erode the foundation of its own protections. And it does so at a particularly precarious time. President Trump has repeatedly threatened to go after journalists who publish leaked information; Attorney General Jeff Sessions refused to rule out the possibility of prosecuting journalists for publishing information (Borchers, 2017). The even more serious danger is that a judiciary less convinced of the press' noble intentions will diminish First Amendment protections and let them.

Notes

1. The Times admitted as much in a long post-election investigation into the Russian hacks. Deep in an 8,152-word article, *The Times* acknowledged that "every major publication, including *The Times*" became a "de facto instrument of Russian intelligence" (Lipton, Sanger, & Shane, 2016). See also Mullin (2016).
2. These revelations are coming at a furious pace. See, for example, Satter, Donn, and Day (2017) and Thielman (2017).
3. *Times* regular columnist Charles Blow shared this judgment. (Blow, 2016a, 2016b) *Times* regular columnist Nicholas Kristoff was more ambivalent. (Kristoff, 2016)
4. Two of *The Post*'s regular contributors challenged that line. (Capehart, 2016; Robinson, 2016).
5. More than two months later, *The Times* continued to describe the emails as showing Democratic officials "conspiring to sabotage" Sanders campaign. (Hirschfeld Davis & Harris, 2016).
6. An earlier *Post* story quoted an email from Brad Marshall, the DNC's chief financial officer: "'[f]or KY and WVA can we get someone to ask his belief … I think I read he is an atheist. … My Southern Baptist peeps would draw a big difference between a Jew and an atheist'"(Hamburger & Tumulty, 2016).
7. "'Wondering if there's a good Bernie narrative for a story, which is that Bernie never ever had his act together, that his campaign was a mess,'" [Mark] Paustenbach wrote to communications director Luis Miranda, who replied: "'True, but the Chair has been advised to not engage. So we'll have to leave it alone'" (Rappeport, 2016a). In another example, Clinton aides "quickly moved to gather information" to discredit one of Bill Clinton's accusers but then never responded publicly (Helderman, 2016b).
8. The names will not be reprinted here.
9. In a *Times* column, Alex Gibney (2016), who made a 2013 documentary about WikiLeaks, strongly defended the leaks as "clearly in the public interest" in showing the DNC tried to undermine Sanders and denied that Assange had any "animus" against Clinton. Gibney took Assange to task for posting Social Security and credit card numbers of private individuals.
10. *The Times* reported on the award within the body of a story about Russian cyberattacks (Lichtblau & Schmitt, 2016).

11. Take Clinton's comment that "the people that know the industry better than anybody are the people who work in the industry." That could be nothing more than a truism that doesn't speak to her preferred method of regulating. The justifiable criticism is that comments like that, for which Clinton is well known, can be taken both ways. The problem is the press took it one way to make it a story.

12. Both news organizations seemed a bit preoccupied with Clinton's joke telling. *The Post*'s media critic Erik Wemple devoted an entire online column to an email chain that recounted deliberations over a quip Clinton delivered at a political reporters' award dinner. (Wemple, 2016b).

13. A post-election analysis indicated that Trump mentioned WikiLeaks 164 times in the campaign's last month (Legum, 2017).

14. This email exchange, involving Clinton campaign communications director Jennifer Palmieri, who is Catholic herself, provides a perfect example of how easy it is to extract something negative from complicated communication, and how hard it is to provide appropriate context and background. Reporters who tried to summarize accurately what the Trump campaign had termed anti-Catholic comments couldn't, except in the vaguest of terms. *The Post*'s lead said emails showed "comments by an aide about Catholics" (Phillip & Wagner, 2016). *The Times*' story noted that the Trump campaign had flagged emails supposedly critical of Catholics (Healy et al., 2016). The reporters who went beyond meaningless summaries or the Trump campaign's claim of "vicious anti-Catholic bigotry" found themselves trying to explain religious divisions within Catholicism. All of this was completely unrelated to Hillary Clinton and her campaign. The exchanges took place in 2011 before there even was a Clinton campaign. Some of the more critical comments came from people who never had any role in the campaign. And yet the superficial, negative encapsulation stuck (Bailey, 2016; Horowitz, 2016a).

15. Several columnists also concluded WikiLeaks revelations didn't amount to much. *Post* columnist Richard Cohen (2016) dismissed the revelations as similar to "constantly finding gambling at Rick's." *Post* opinion writer Charles Lane (2016) wrote that "[m]uch if not most of the internal Clinton campaign deliberations" were "run-of-the-mill" transactional politics.

16. *Post* columnist E. J. Dionne Jr. (2016) advocated that "[a]ll journalism relying on WikiLeaks should note our government has accused Russia of trying to influence the American election." It didn't.

17. Exhibit A is a *People* magazine reporter's voluntary disclosure that "Trump forced his tongue down her throat and proposed having an affair." Exhibit B was an undercover video that purportedly showed a Democratic operative bragging about sending "troublemakers to Mr. Trump's rallies, to provoke Trump supporters into attacking them."

18. Rutenberg does describe the emails as showing "cynical approaches by Hillary Clinton and her team to fund-raising; a penchant for secrecy; a coziness with reporters that is too often the case with both parties in Washington; and a calculated approach to environmental issues, free trade and banking ... ."

19. Former George W. Bush speechwriter, Marc Thiessen (2016), wrote a confusing online column criticizing the press for not covering the emails' contents enough and focusing too much on "how the emails were hacked and leaked." And yet he griped about WikiLeaks and its tactics, which are hacking and leaking.

20. Georgetown linguist Deborah Tannen (2016) discussed this issue indirectly, noting that people speak differently in private, not necessarily more authentically. Tannen found the leaks' revelations themselves to be "benign" and suggests that, "commentators are straining to find something—anything—that justifies the voyeuristic thrill of reporting on them."

21. Even presidential tapes should be judged knowing that the fact the actors were speaking in private might color what was said and how it was said, though the presumption of newsworthiness is high even for strategic communications.

22. The well-respected site, *FiveThirtyEight*, tackled the question of WikiLeaks' impact upon the election and reached inconclusive results (Enten, 2016).

23. The lack of a majority opinion and six, separate concurring opinions made it a bit of a muddle. The only clear precedent to emerge—that the government bears a very heavy burden when it tries to stop publication of the news—has been overtaken by technology. The U.S. government didn't even seek to block any of WikiLeaks' disclosures given the ability to copy, post and distribute huge numbers of documents on the Internet and funnel them through overseas servers.

24. In an important and prescient law review article, Patricia Bellia (2012) analyzes the threat WikiLeaks, through its rejection of journalisitic norms, presents to the Pentagon Papers' framework that presumes an institutional press that will self-censor to avoid releasing harmful information.

25. There are obvious, important exceptions. See *In Re Grand Jury Subpoena v. Miller* 397 F.3d 964 (2005), in which the U.S. Court of Appeals for the D.C. Circuit ruled that *New York Times* reporter Judith Miller had to reveal the source of the leak of a name of a covert CIA agent. When she refused, Miller served 85 days in jail. But see also, *U.S. v. Sterling* 724 F.3d 482 (2013), in which the U.S. Court of Appeals for the Fourth Circuit ruled that *New York Times* reporter James Risen had to reveal his source in the criminal prosecution of a CIA agent for disclosing classified information. Having won the 2-1 decision, however, the Obama administration's Justice Department declined to call Risen to testify. In both cases, strong dissents advocated for a newsworthiness test of the value of the leaked information.

References

Bailey, S. (2016, October 13). WikiLeaks emails appear to show Clinton spokeswoman joking about Catholics and evangelicals. *The Washington Post*. Retrieved from https://www.washingtonpost.com/news/acts-of-faith/wp/2016/10/12/wikileaks-emails-show-clinton-spokeswoman-joking-about-catholics-and-evangelicals/?utm_term=.b5e9d24273e2

Balz, D. (2016a, October 16). Clinton's tasks: Allay leak fallout, make a positive case. *The Washington Post*, p. A2.

Balz, D. (2016b, July 26). First lady helps put gathering back on script. *The Washington Post*, p. A1.

Balz, D. (2016c, October 14). In a pair of searing speeches, the presidential race is crystallized. *The Washington Post*, p. A1.

Becker, J., Erlanger, S., & Schmitt, E. (2016, September 1). How Russia often benefits as Assange reveals secrets. *The New York Times*, p. A1.

Bellia, P. L. (2012). WikiLeaks and the institutional framework for national security disclosures. *Yale Law Journal, 121*, 1448–1536. Retrieved from https://papers.ssrn.com/sol3/papers.cfm?abstract_id=2033207

Blow, C. (2016a, October 24). Clinton's specter of illegitimacy. *The New York Times*, p. A21.

Blow, C. (2016b, July 25). More damned emails. *The New York Times*, p. A23.

Borchers, C. (2017, October 18). Sessions says he can't 'make a blanket commitment' not to jail journalists. *The Washington Post*. Retrieved from https://www.washingtonpost.com/news/the-fix/wp/2017/10/18/sessions-says-he-cant-make-a-blanket-commitment-not-to-jail-journalists/?utm_term=.90b5ea511bcb

Brunet, R. (2016, December 22). La Russie, acteur de la presidentialle francaise? *France 24*. Retrieved from http://www.france24.com/fr/20161222-france-election-presidentielle-interferences-russie-front-national-marine-le-pen-pret-cyber

Bump, P. (2016, October 12). Is there actually evidence that Trump allies had a heads-up on what WikiLeaks was doing? *The Washington Post*. Retrieved from https://www.washingtonpost.com/news/the-fix/wp/2016/10/12/is-there-actually-evidence-that-trump-allies-had-a-heads-up-on-what-wikileaks-was-doing/?utm_term=.a44998ee1c48

Cantor, F. (2016, October 29). To the editor. *The New York Times*, p. A18.

Capehart, J. (2016, July 26). Don't blame Wasserman Schultz for Sanders's political failures. *The Washington Post*, p. A19.

Chenoweth, E. (2016, November 2). Can U.S. democracy defend itself? *The Washington Post*, p. A17.

Chozick, A. (2016a, October 19). Email outlines Clinton's potential no. 2s. *The New York Times*, p. A15.

Chozick, A. (2016c, October 12). Podesta says Russia broke into emails to tilt race. *The New York Times*, p. A16.

Chozick, A., & Confessore, N. (2016a, October 11). Emails disclose Clinton's strain to hone message. *The New York Times*, p. A1.

Chozick, A., & Confessore, N. (2016b, October 16). Genial Clinton emerges in hacked transcripts of Goldman Sachs talks. *The New York Times*, p. A19.

Chozick, A., Confessore, N., & Barbaro, M. (2016, October 8). Leaked speech excerpts show Clinton at ease with Wall Street and free trade. *The New York Times*, p. A14.

Chozick, A., Confessore, N., Eder, S., Alcindor, Y., & Stockman, F. (2016, October 10). Highlights from the Clinton campaign emails: How to deal with Sanders and Biden. *The New York Times*. Retrieved from https://www.nytimes.com/2016/10/10/us/politics/hillary-clinton-emails-wikileaks.html?_r=0

Cockrum, Comer and Schoenberg v. Donald J. Trump for President Inc. and Roger Stone, in U.S. District Court for the District of Columbia, Civil Action No. 1:17-cv-1370-ESH.

Cohen, R. (2016, October 24). The result of WikiLeaks new transparency? Less transparency. *The Washington Post*, p. A15.

Confessore, N., & Eder, S. (2016, July 26). Hacked emails reveal how the party favors flow to wealthy donors. *The New York Times*, p. A11.

Creswell, J., & Goodman, J. (2016, October 23). Teneo's constellation of influencers. *The New York Times, Business News*, p. 1.

Dionne, Jr., E. J. (2016, October 17). Who is more Catholic than whom. *The Washington Post*, p. A15.

Eddy, M. (2016, October 5). Assange sets new schedule of disclosures. *The New York Times*, p. A6.

Eder, S. (2016a, October 16). Email about Qatari offer shows thorny ethical issues Clinton Foundation faced. *The New York Times*, p. A19.

Eder, S. (2016b, October 26). 'We need to clean this up,' Clinton aide frets in newly public email. *The New York Times*, p. A22.

Eder, S., & Chozick, A. (2016, October 27). Donations to foundation vexed Clinton's top aides. *The New York Times*, p. A1.

Editorial Board. (2016a, August 17). A break in the Assange saga. *The New York Times*, p. A18.

Editorial Board. (2016b, September 16). Answer Russia's cyberattack. *The Washington Post*, p. A16.

Editorial Board. (2016c, July 26). Russia's motives for meddling. *The Washington Post*, p. A18.

Editorial Board. (2016d, July 27). This is what democracy looks like. *The New York Times*, p. A26.

Editorial Board. (2016e, July 28). Trump bets on Russian spying. *The Washington Post*, p. A18.

Egan, T. (2016, July 30). The real plot against America. *The New York Times*, p. A21.

Ehrenfreund, M. (2016, October 18). Email hack reveals Clinton aides' concern about treacherous politics of poverty. *The Washington Post*, p. A11.

Englund, W. (2016, July 29). Putin and Clinton: The roots of a beef. *The Washington Post*, p. A13.

Enten, H. (2016, December 23). How much did WikiLeaks hurt Hillary Clinton? Retrieved from https://fivethirtyeight.com/features/wikileaks-hillary-clinton/

Flegenheimer, M., & Alcindor, Y. (2016, October 19). Sanders backers rue and opportunity lost. *New York Times*, p. A15.

Flegenheimer, M., & Landler, M. (2016, November 6). If Clinton moves to oval office, aides' baggage may be heavy. *The New York Times*, p. A1.

Gabriel, T. (2016, July 25). Supporters of Sanders rally before convention. *The New York Times*, p. A15.

Gearan, A., & Phillip, A. (2016, July 26). Boos fade into cheers as Democrats turn focus to fighting Trump. *The Washington Post*, p. A1.

Gearan, A., & Wagner, J. (2016, October 13). Clinton campaign: WikiLeaks hack gets 'closer to the Trump campaign'. *The Washington Post.* Retrieved from https://www.washingtonpost.com/news/post-politics/wp/2016/10/13/clinton-campaign-wikileaks-hack-gets-closer-and-closer-to-the-trump-campaign/?utm_term=.7575fba14952

Gibney, A. (2016, August 8). Can we still trust WikiLeaks? *The New York Times,* p. A23.

Gold, M. (2016, July 25). Leaked emails reveal inner workings of party fundraising. *The Washington Post,* p. A7.

Gold, M., & Helderman, R. (2016, October 11). Univision chair to aides of Clinton: Go on offense. *The Washington Post,* p. A6.

Gold, M., & Narayanswamy, A. (2016, October 24). Clinton embraced big-money system. *The Washington Post,* p. A1.

Gold, M., Wagner, J., & Phillip, A. (2016, October 16). Hacked email show how liberal group back-channeled advice to Clinton. *The Washington Post,* p. A4.

Grynbaum, M. (2016a, November 1). CNN cuts ties to analyst as emails show she tipped off Clinton allies. *The New York Times,* p. A16.

Grynbaum, M. (2016b, July 25). Ego clashes exposed in Democratic National Committee emails. *The New York Times,* p. A15.

Hamburger, T., & Tumulty, K. (2016, July 23). As Democrats' convention nears, hacked emails are posted online. *The Washington Post,* p. A8.

Healy, P., Sanger, D., & Haberman, M. (2016, October 13). Leaked emails about Clinton hearten rival. *The New York Times,* p. A1.

Helderman, R. (2016b, October 25). WikiLeaks reveals fears and frustration inside Clinton world. *The Washington Post,* p. A1.

Helderman, R., & Hamburger, T. (2016a, October 8). Hacked emails appear to reveal excerpts of speech transcripts Clinton refused to release. *The Washington Post,* p. A1.

Helderman, R., & Hamburger, T. (2016b, October 27). Top aide's leaked memo details 'Bill Clinton Inc.' *The Washington Post,* p. A4.

Helderman, R., Zapotosky, M., & Horwitz, S., (2016, October 29). Computer seized in Weiner probe prompts FBI to take new steps in Clinton email inquiry. *The Washington Post,* p. A1.

Hermann, P., & Williams, C. (2016, August 10). WikiLeaks offers reward for help finding DNC staffer's killer. *The Washington Post,* p. B5.

Hess, A. (2016, November 6). Memes, myself and I. *The New York Times Arts and Entertainment,* p. 16.

Hirschfeld Davis, J., & Harris, G. (2016, October 12). Obama considers `proportional' response to Russian hacking in U.S. election. *The New York Times.* Retrieved from https://www.nytimes.com/2016/10/12/us/politics/obama-russia-hack-election.html?_r=0

Horowitz, J. (2016a, October 19). Clinton hopes to woo white Catholic voters. *The New York Times,* p. A13.

Horowitz, J. (2016b, July 26). Debbie Wasserman Schultz is met with jeers at pre-convention breakfast. *The New York Times.* Retrieved from https://www.nytimes.com/2016/07/26/us/politics/debbie-wasserman-schultz-dnc.html

In Re Grand Jury Subpoena v. Miller 397 F.3d 964 (2005).

Kristoff, N. (2016, July 28). Putin, Trump, and our Election. *The New York Times,* p. A27.

Krugman, P. (2016, November 7). How to rig an election. *The New York Times,* p. A23.

Lane, C. (2016, October 13). Privacy and democracy. *The Washington Post,* p. A17.

Legum, J. (2017, January 8). Trump mentioned Wikileaks 164 times in last month of election, now claims it didn't impact one voter. *Think Progress.* Retrieved from https://thinkprogress.org/trump-mentioned-wikileaks-164-times-in-last-month-of-election-now-claims-it-didnt-impact-one-40aa62ea5002/

Lichtblau, E. (2016, July 30). Russian spies said to hack Clinton's bid. *The New York Times,* p. A1.

Lichtblau, E., & Myers, S. L. (2016, November 1). Investigating Trump, F.B.I. sees no clear link to Russian government. *The Washington Post,* p. A21.

Lichtblau, E., & Schmitt, E. (2016, August 11). Wider damage seen in hack of Democrats. *The New York Times,* p. A1.

Lipton, E., Sanger, D., & Shane, S. (2016, December 13). The perfect weapon: How Russian cyberpower invaded the U.S. *The New York Times,* p. A1.

Lowery, W., Loveluck L., & Achenbach, J. (2016, July 26). Sanders, immigrant rights, gun control, police brutality all topics of protest. *The Washington Post,* p. A5.

Martin, J., & Burns, A. (2016, October 19). Keys to debate: Trump's brand, Clinton's tone, and sexual harassment. *The New York Times,* p. A11.

Martin, J., & Rappeport, A. (2016, July 25). Leaks bring down a Democratic leader. *The New York Times,* p. A1.

Masters, J. (2017, April 28). Fears of Russian meddling as France prepares to go to the polls. *CNN.* Retrieved from http://www.cnn.com/2017/04/28/europe/french-election-russia/index.html

Mcintire, M. (2016, October 17). Line between public and private blurs for inner circle of Clinton. *The New York Times,* p. A1.

Mullin, B. (2016, December 13). New York Times says it was 'a de factor instrument of Russian intelligence.' *poynter.org.* Retrieved from https://www.poynter.org/news/new-york-times-says-it-was-de-facto-instrument-russian-intelligence

Myers, S., & Macfarquhar, N. (2016, July 26). Seeing in email breach a Trump-Putin alliance, *The New York Times,* p. A1.

Nakashima, E. (2016a, November 3). Comey advised against denunciation of Russia for hacks. *The Washington Post,* p. A4.

Nakashima, E. (2016b, July 28). Is there a Russian plan to install Trump in White House? Officials doubt it. *The Washington Post,* p. A9.

Nakashima, E. (2016c, June 21). Russian hacking of DNC is confirmed. *The Washington Post,* p. A14.

Nakashima, E. (2016d, October 8). U.S. officially condemns Russia over hacking. *The Washington Post*, p. A1.

Nakashima, E. (2016e, July 27). U.S. reveals game plan for when cyberattackers strike. *The Washington Post*, p. A2.

Nakashima, E. (2016f, September 11). White House is urged to call out Moscow over hacks. *The Washington Post*, p. A10.

Palma, B. (2017, May 10). Was the French election hacked by Russia? *Snopes*. Retrieved from https://www.snopes.com/2017/05/10/french-election-russian-hack/

Parker, A., & Sanger, D. (2016, July 27). Donald Trump calls on Russia to find Hillary Clinton's missing emails. *The New York Times*. Retrieved from https://www.nytimes.com/2016/07/28/us/politics/donald-trump-russia-clinton-emails.html?_r=0

Perlroth, N., & Shear, M. (2016, October 21). Private security group says Russia was behind hack of Clinton campaign chairman. *The New York Times*, p. A14.

Phillip, A., Sullivan, S., & Gold, M. (2016, October 28). Clinton doubles Trump's October haul. *The Washington Post*, p. A1.

Phillip, A., & Wagner, J. (2016, October 13). Hacked emails show anxiety over Clinton candidacy. *The Washington Post*, p. A1.

Rappeport, A. (2016a, August 2). 3 Top D.N.C. officials leave as upheaval after DNC breach continues. *The New York Times*. Retrieved from https://www.nytimes.com/2016/08/03/us/politics/dnc-email-hack-hillary-clinton-bernie-sanders.html

Rappeport, A. (2016b, September 14). A hacker releases Democratic documents. *The New York Times*, p. A16.

Rappeport, A., & Burns, A. (2016, October 21). Trump stays firm on having option to dispute vote. *The New York Times*, p. A1.

Robinson, E. (2016, July 26.) Can Democrats unite and get out of their own way? *The Washington Post*, p. A19.

Rutenberg, J. (2016), October 24). A reality TV campaign gets a dose of reality. *The New York Times*, p. B1.

Sanger, D. (2016a, October 17). Clinton liked covert action if it stayed covert, hacked transcript showed. *The New York Times*, p. A14.

Sanger, D. (2016b, July 26). F.B.I. examining if hackers gained access to Clinton aides' emails. *The New York Times*, p. A14.

Sanger, D., & Perlroth, N. (2016, July 25). In hacking, Russia is accused of playing in American politics. *The New York Times*, p. A1.

Sanger, D., & Savage, C. (2016, October 8). U.S. accuses Russia of directing hacks to influence election. *The New York Times*, p. A1.

Sanger, D., & Schmitt, E. (2016, July 27). Spy agency consensus grows that Russia hacked D.N.C. *The New York Times*, p. A1.

Satter, R., Donn, J., & Day, C. (2017, November 4). Inside story: How Russians hacked the Democrats' emails. *AP*. Retrieved from https://www.apnews.com/dea73efc01594839957c3c9a6c962b8a

Savage, C. (2016, July 27). Democratic email release was timed for convention. *The New York Times*, p. A17.

Savage, C., & Perlroth, N. (2016, July 28). Cybersecurity experts aren't sure if email hacker is a person or a front. *The New York Times*, p. A16.

Schmitt, E. (2016, September 1). Democrats' email and a murky trail. *The New York Times*, p. A10.

Schultheis, E. (2017, May 6). The Macron leaks probably came too late to change the French election. *The Atlantic*. Retrieved from https://www.theatlantic.com/international/archive/2017/05/france-macron-leak-hack/525738/

Shear, M., & Rosenberg, M. (2016, July 23). Emails suggest that Democratic officials scoffed at Sanders campaign. *The New York Times*, p. A10.

Sorkin, A. R. (2016, October 18). Clinton could be tough on Wall St., emails hint. *The New York Times*, p. B1.

Spayd, J. (2016, November 6). Covert election plot. Muted coverage. *The New York Times*, p. 8.

Stanglin, D. (2017, May 6). French media, citizens warned not to spread candidate's hacked data. *USA Today*. Retrieved from https://www.usatoday.com/story/news/2017/05/06/french-media-citizens-warned-not-spread-candidates-hacked-data/101364656/

Stockman, F. (2016, October 11). The stage-managing of Clinton's Keystone shift. *The New York Times*, p. A12.

Sullivan, M. (2016a, October 5). Assange's message gets lost in the bluster. *The Washington Post*, p. C01.

Sullivan, M. (2016b, September 21). Snowden's actions merit a pardon. *The Washington Post*, p. C01.

Sullivan, S. (2016, July 28). Trump tries to regain spotlight with hacking remarks. *The Washington Post*, p. A09.

Tannen, D. (2016, October 28) Why what you say in private looks bad in public, even if it isn't. *The Washington Post*, p. B05.

Thielman, S. (2017, November 16). What was happening while Donald Jr. was egging on Julian Assange. *Talking Points Memo*. Retrieved from *http://talkingpointsmemo.com/news/junior-and-julian-sitting-in-a-tree*

Thiessen, M. (2106, October 24). WikiLeaks is exposing Clinton's duplicity, but it's no hero. *The Washington Post*. Retrieved from https://www.washingtonpost.com/opinions/wikileaks-is-exposing-clintons-duplicity-but-its-no-hero/2016/10/24/563c3752-99e9-11e6-a0ed-ab0774c1eaa5_story.html?utm_term=.daa8d81d6dc8

Tufekci, Z. (2016, November 5). Whistle-drowning, not whistle blowing. *The New York Times*, A19.

United States v. New York Times 403 U.S. 713 (1971).

United States v. Sterling 724 F.3d 482 (2013).

Wagner, J. (2016, October 20). Clinton struggles under scrutiny. *The Washington Post*, p. A1.

Weigel, D. (2016a, October 9). A tumultuous day in the life of a GOP Senate candidate. *The Washington Post*, p. A10.

Weigel, D. (2016b, October 18). Clinton challenger attacked in hacked emails sees no `public good in WikiLeaks dump. *The Washington Post*. Retrieved from https://www.washingtonpost.com/news/post-politics/wp/2016/10/18/an-anti-corruption-activist-attacked-in-podesta-email-sees-no-public-good-in-wikileaks-dump/?utm_term=.92f2e92a806e

Weigel, D. (2016c, July 24). Democrats struggle with intraparty divisions days before convention opens. *The Washington Post*, p. A5.

Weigel, D. (2016d, October 27). House Republicans already preparing for years of Clinton investigations. *The Washington Post*, p. A6.

Weigel, D. (2016e, October 11). Pence asks Republicans to share WikiLeaks revelations about Clinton—But overstates what's in them. *The Washington Post*. Retrieved from https://www.washingtonpost.com/news/post-politics/wp/2016/10/11/pence-asks-republicans-to-share-wikileaks-revelations-about-clinton-but-overstates-whats-in-them/?utm_term=.d518cf817ec7

Wemple, E. (2016a, November 7). And now from WikiLeaks: A CNN non-scandal). *The Washington Post*, p. A15.

Wemple, E. (2016b, October 24). WikiLeaks: Clinton aide sought to give media an "ego boost." *The Washington Post*. Retrieved from https://www.washingtonpost.com/blogs/erik-wemple/wp/2016/10/24/wikileaks-clinton-aide-sought-to-give-media-an-egoboost/?utm_term=.b92af489e567

Yee, V. (2016, October 13). De Blasio's pleas to Clinton revealed in leaked emails. *The New York Times*, p. A22.

Zak, D. (2016, October 21). Well the truth is out there now. *The Washington Post*, p. C1.

Zapotosky, M., Helderman S., & Hamburger, T. (2016, October 31). FBI agents said to push for probe of Clinton Foundation. *The Washington Post*, p. A3.

8. The Media Was the Message: Gendered Coverage of Hillary Clinton's Historic 2016 Campaign for U.S. President

DIANNE BYSTROM AND KIMBERLY NELSON
Iowa State University

In her 2017 book, *What Happened*, Hillary Rodham Clinton—the first woman to win a major U.S. political party's nomination for president—summarized some of the factors that she believed led to her Electoral College defeat to New York City businessman Donald J. Trump in the 2016 presidential election.

> I also understand why there's an insatiable demand in many quarters for me to take all the blame for losing the election on my own shoulders and quit talking about [then FBI Director James] Comey, the Russians, fake news, sexism, or anything else. Many in the political media don't want to hear about how these things tipped the election in the final days. They say their beef is that I'm not taking responsibility for my mistakes—but I have, and I do again throughout this book. Their real problem is they can't bear to face their own role in helping elect Trump, from providing him free airtime to giving my emails three times more coverage than all the issues affecting people's lives combined. (Clinton, 2017, p. 393)

Although Democrat Clinton was leading in the national polls heading into the November 8, 2016, general election, she lost the presidency to Republican Trump by a 304–227 margin in the Electoral College (with a record seven electors voting for someone besides their party's nominee). Trump's Electoral College win was fueled by the 77,744 more votes he received than Clinton across three states—Michigan, Pennsylvania, and Wisconsin—while she won the national popular vote by almost 2.9 million ("Official 2016 Presidential Election Results," 2017).

In her book, Clinton describes her experiences as the first woman running on a major political party ticket for U.S. president in an election marked by controversy, unpredictable twists and turns, and an unconventional opponent. While acknowledging the mistakes she made, especially for the use of a private email server while U.S. secretary of state and giving paid speeches to banks, Clinton also blames her loss to a combination of other factors, including Comey's October 28, 2016 letter that the FBI was re-opening its investigation of her emails; Russia's attempts to influence the outcome of the election by hacking Democratic Party emails and the electoral databases of more than 20 states and spreading political propaganda on social media; sexism, misogyny, and white resentment; and the way in which the mainstream media, particularly the *New York Times*, covered the presidential race (Zurcher, 2017).

Perhaps not surprisingly, members of the mainstream media were quick to assess whether its coverage of the presidential campaign contributed to Clinton's loss. "I do think there's some validity to it," said Sarah Jones of *The New Republic*. "Major outlets like the *New York Times* kind of made a mistake by treating the email scandal with the same weight that they treated Trump's scandals, when in fact there is never as much evidence to support that anything too nefarious went on with Clinton and her emails. But I think she overstates its influence a little bit" ("Did the Media Cost," 2017). However, responding to criticism on Twitter about the wide and extensive coverage of Clinton's use of a private email server throughout the campaign by the *New York Times*, reporter Glenn Thrush shot back with a series of defensive tweets on August 21, 2017, including: "But hour-long speeches that should have been 10 minutes, but complacency, but Bernie, but generational apathy, but silly war with the media" (Scarry, 2017).

In this chapter, we report the results of a computer-assisted content analysis designed to assess Clinton's coverage in four national newspapers—the *New York Times, Wall Street Journal, Washington Post,* and *USA Today*—in the two-and-one half months leading up to the 2016 presidential election. Our analysis of Clinton's 2016 campaign coverage is based on the findings of previous research on women political candidates, particularly those who run for president and vice president, which have found gender differences in how the media covers their issues and images in comparison to their male opponents.

This chapter begins with a summary of research findings on the media coverage of women political candidates and Clinton's coverage in 2007, 2008, 2015, and 2016 as a presidential candidate and in 2016 as the Democratic Party nominee. Based on previous studies, we propose six research questions for our analysis followed by a description of our methodology and the presentation of our results. Finally, we discuss the implications of our results in terms of the 2016 presidential campaign as well as future elections that feature a female candidate.

Media Coverage of Women Political Candidates

Studies on the media coverage of women political candidates date back to the early 1990s. These studies found that newspapers not only stereotyped women candidates running for elected office in the 1980s and early 1990s by emphasizing feminine traits and issues, but also by giving them less coverage that often questioned their viability (Kahn, 1991, 1994a, 1994b; Kahn & Goldenberg, 1991). Beginning in the mid-to-late 1990s and continuing through the 21st century, researchers have found more equitable newspaper coverage of female and male candidates running for state executive and federal legislative office both in terms of the quantity and quality of coverage (Bystrom, Banwart, Kaid, & Robertson, 2004; Devitt, 1999; Hayes & Lawless, 2015; Smith, 1997).

Most notably, a content analysis of the newspaper coverage of female and male candidates running for the U.S. House of Representatives in 2010 found more similarities than differences (Hayes & Lawless, 2015). Both female and male candidates were equally likely to be associated with "men's" as well as "women's" issues in their newspaper coverage. Also, female and male candidates were equally as likely to be linked with the traits of competence, leadership, integrity, and empathy.

However, most recent studies have found some gender differences in the media coverage of female versus male political candidates. Some studies have found that women candidates were much more likely to be discussed in terms of their sex, marital status, and children (Bystrom et al., 2004). Other studies have found that men running for governor or the U.S. Senate were linked more often with masculine issues, such as taxes and foreign affairs, whereas women were associated more often with feminine issues, such as education and health care (Bystrom et al., 2004; Major & Coleman, 2008). Studies also have shown that women political candidates are more likely to be covered in an image, rather than issue, frame and discussed more than men in terms of their character traits (Meeks, 2012).

Although recent studies show that female and male candidates running for the U.S. Congress and governor are receiving more equitable media coverage—especially in terms of quantity and discussions of their viability, appearance, and personality—women candidates for president continue to receive more stereotyped coverage. For example, studies of Elizabeth Dole's campaign for the Republican nomination for president in 1999 found that she received less equitable coverage in terms of quality and, especially, quantity as compared to her male opponents (Aday & Devitt, 2001; Bystrom, 2006; Heldman, Carroll, & Olson, 2005).

Studies also show that media coverage of Clinton's 2008 bid for the Democratic Party nomination for president and Sarah Palin's campaign as vice president on the Republican ticket emphasized their images over issues, often in negative or stereotypical ways. For example, content analyses of Clinton's newspaper (Bystrom, 2008; Dimitrova & Geske, 2009; Lawrence & Rose, 2010) and television (Lawrence & Rose, 2010) coverage found that she was more likely to be "game-framed" in terms of her campaign strategies rather than her issue positions. An analysis of examples from print media, television, and social networking revealed that Palin was portrayed as a sex object while Clinton was attacked for her lack of femininity in the 2008 general and primary elections (Carlin & Winfrey, 2009).

A content analysis of television, newspaper, and political blog coverage of the 2008 vice presidential candidates found that Palin was often discussed in terms of her family, personal appearance, electability, and social issues (Bode & Hennings, 2012). Similarly, Fridkin, Carle, and Woodall (2012) found that Palin's coverage, especially on television, focused more extensively on her appearance and family; was more critical on personal as well as substantive issues; and reinforced gender stereotypes by focusing on feminine traits and issues, even though she emphasized masculine issues in her speeches.

In the race for the 2012 Republican nomination for president, Michele Bachmann received more equitable coverage than Clinton and Palin in 2008. A study comparing Bachmann's coverage on national network and cable television stations to six male opponents seeking the 2012 Republican nomination for president found mostly similarities and just a few differences (Bystrom & Dimitrova, 2014). Bachmann's image attributes (appearance, family, and marital status) received about the same amount of mentions as her male opponents. Also, she was twice as likely to be linked with masculine issues—primarily foreign relations and taxes—than feminine ones.

Five studies by Harvard University researchers on the media coverage of Clinton's campaign for president in 2015 and 2016 found that she was treated differently than the other Democratic and Republican primary contenders as well as Republican presidential nominee Trump in the general election. Harvard's Thomas E. Patterson published four faculty research working papers on the pre-primary, primary, national conventions, and general election stages of the 2016 presidential campaign. His content analyses focused

on the coverage by a mix of national network television and newspaper outlets—including ABC, CBS, Fox, NBC, the *Los Angeles Times*, the *New York
Times*, *USA Today*, the *Wall Street Journal*, and the *Washington Post*—during
these four stages of the 2016 presidential campaign.

In the year leading up to the 2016 primaries, Patterson (2016a) found
that Clinton received by far the most negative coverage as compared to all
other Democratic and Republican contenders. In 2015, two-thirds (61%) of
her media coverage was negative with one-third (31%) positive. Journalists
made more references to her past than they did for other candidates and
focused on the negative, rather than her tenure in the U.S. Senate—where
she earned praise from both sides of the aisle—or her successful actions as secretary of state. Moreover, the media's frequent mention of her scandals—the
Benghazi attack, marital issues dating back to her time as first lady, and especially her use of a private email server while secretary of state—contributed to
the negative tone of her coverage (Patterson, 2016a).

During the January 1 through June 7, 2016 primary stage of the presidential
campaign, Clinton's media coverage improved to 53% negative and 47% positive (Patterson, 2016b). Comparatively, her Democratic primary opponent—
U.S. Senator Bernie Sanders—received the most positive coverage of all
candidates from both political parties, with 54% positive compared to 46%
negative. Trump's coverage was also more positive than Clinton's with 51%
negative and 49% positive. Clinton's electoral success in the primary stage of
the election did not result in strong favorable coverage, Patterson (2016b)
noted. Instead, she continued to get mostly bad press about her character
and policy positions. Although Clinton was portrayed as the candidate best-
prepared to be president, she was also described as representing the politics
of the past, too closely tied to big money, distant and robotic, and less trustworthy (Patterson, 2016b).

In his analysis of the four weeks of media coverage surrounding the 2016
Republican and Democratic national conventions, Patterson (2016c) found
that both candidates were primarily covered in terms of their campaigns in
general as well as polls and predictions for their chances of winning. However, Clinton was twice as likely to be associated with the emails she sent
and received as secretary of state (8%) than her policy positions (4%) in her
coverage. Comparatively, 13% of Trump's convention stage media coverage
was about his policy positions, and he was quoted more often about Clinton's
policy proposals than she was. In addition to her emails, other alleged scandals from Clinton's past accounted for another 3% of her convention stage
media coverage, raising attention to allegations of wrongdoing to 11% of her
overall coverage (Patterson, 2016c).

During the general election phase of the campaign, Patterson's content analysis found that both Clinton and Trump received media coverage that was "overwhelmingly negative in tone and extremely light on policy" (2016d). He concluded that the media had subjected the candidates to a false equivalency that can mislead voters about the choices they face. For example, because journalists covering the 2016 presidential election reported "all the ugly stuff they could find" and made no serious efforts to distinguish between the significance of allegations about Clinton as compared to those about Trump, Patterson (2016d) said that "large numbers of voters concluded that the candidates' indiscretions were equally disqualifying and made their choice, not on the candidates' fitness for office, but on less tangible criteria—in some cases out of a belief that wildly unrealistic promises could actually be kept."

In addition to Patterson, a group of researchers affiliated with Harvard's Berkman Klein Center for Internet & Society Research published a study based on the results of online and human coding of 2 million stories about the 2016 presidential campaign from media, campaign, and government websites and blogs for the 18 months between May 2015 and November 2016. They found that the mainstream media coverage for both candidates was negative in tone, but followed Trump's agenda more closely than Clinton's. Whereas Clinton's coverage focused on scandals, primarily her emails and the Clinton Foundation, Trump's coverage focused more on such issues as immigration, jobs, and trade than on his personal scandals (Faris et al., 2017).

Based on the results of recent research on the media coverage of women running for U.S. president, including Clinton in 2008 and 2016, we were interested in several areas in which gender differences have been found: masculine vs. feminine issue mentions; electability; personal appearance; and family. In addition, given the findings of Patterson (2016a, 2016c, 2016d) and Faris et al. (2017) that much of Clinton's media coverage in 2015 and 2016 focused on scandals, we were interested in the number of mentions of her emails, the FBI investigation, and her husband's past sexual misconduct. Finally, as much of the commentary about the 2016 presidential campaign focused on various constituencies of voters, we were interested in the number of mentions of white, Hispanic/Latino, black, and women voters.

This study of articles about Clinton published in four national newspapers from Labor Day through Election Day 2016 was designed to answer the following research questions:

RQ1: How much of Clinton's newspaper coverage was associated with masculine vs. feminine issues?

RQ2: How much of Clinton's newspaper coverage was associated with her electability?

RQ3: How much of Clinton's newspaper coverage was associated with her personal appearance and health?

RQ4: How much of Clinton's newspaper coverage mentioned her family?

RQ5: How much of Clinton's newspaper coverage was associated with scandals?

RQ6: Which political constituencies were mentioned the most in Clinton's newspaper coverage?

Method

For this study, articles were collected from four national newspapers—the *New York Times*, *USA Today*, the *Wall Street Journal*, and the *Washington Post*—with a total circulation of 6.1 million people as of May 11, 2016 ("Top 10 U.S. Daily Newspapers," 2016). *USA Today* (2.3 million), the *New York Times* (2.1 million), and the *Wall Street Journal* (1.3 million) are the top three daily newspapers in the United States, and the *Washington Post* ranks seventh with a circulation of 356,768. We used two databases—Gale Infotrac Newsstand and Newspaper Source Plus—available through our university library to search for the newspaper articles published between September 6, 2016 (Labor Day) and November 8, 2016 (Election Day) containing the search term "Hillary Clinton" or "Hillary Rodham Clinton." Initially, 2,022 articles were collected. Upon further analysis, some of these articles were not explicitly about Clinton and were removed from the study. Opinion articles, editorials, and letters to the editor were also removed to focus on Clinton's news coverage. After the articles were cleaned up, a total of 1,126 articles (*Wall Street Journal*, 379; the *New York Times*, 291; *Washington Post*: 290; and *USA Today*, 166) were included in this study.

Once articles were retrieved from the online search and cleaned, they were placed in a text file and formatted for Yoshikoder. Yoshikoder is an open-source, computer-assisted content analysis software used to track word frequency within selected articles. It allows users to generate their own dictionaries, providing for a great deal of flexibility in what can be analyzed (Lowe, 2006). The use of a computer-assisted content analysis program allowed us to examine a larger sample of news coverage than traditional hand coding. Based on previous research, we constructed a dictionary of 248 words in 12 areas of interest, including seven policy areas (education, foreign policy, health care, taxes/economy, social issues, masculine issues, and women's issues); electability; personal appearance and health; family; scandals; and political constituencies. We also searched for mentions of Trump in Clinton's news coverage for a 13th category.

Two queries were run with Yoshikoder. The first was a word frequency query. This applied the dictionary words to each of the four newspapers' articles separately. The second query run was a concordance, which also was applied to each newspaper separately. The concordance supplied context to the words picked up from running the word frequency query and enabled us to delete references not relevant to our study as well as to move relevant references between categories (e.g., references picked up from the word "college" in the education category sometimes pertained to "non-college-educated white voters," which were moved to the political constituency category).

Results

First, we examined the mentions of our dictionary terms in Clinton's total coverage in the four newspapers selected for our study both with and without the word "Trump." Including the name of Clinton's opponent allowed us to see how often he was mentioned in her coverage. Excluding Trump's name from our analysis allowed us to zero in on the gendered categories of news coverage—masculine issues, feminine issues, electability, personal appearance and health, and family—as well as the scandals and political constituencies that seemed to dominate presidential campaign coverage in 2016. In addition to Clinton's overall coverage, we examined her coverage in each newspaper to look for differences and similarities in our categories of interest both with and without the word "Trump."

Including the word "Trump," we found 20,942 mentions of our dictionary terms in the 1,126 articles included in our study. Excluding the word "Trump," we found 12,620 mentions of our dictionary terms in the articles analyzed. Of our dictionary 249 terms, including Trump, we found that 144 of these words were included in Clinton's coverage in the four newspapers.

In response to RQ1, we were first interested in Clinton's issue coverage. We found that she was most often associated with words included in our dictionary for masculine issues as compared to feminine issues. Masculine issues included mentions of foreign policy or foreign affairs in general as well as such terms as Iraq, military, terrorism, and war; taxes and the economy as well as such related terms as jobs and trade; and other issues, such as crime and guns, which have been more often associated with male political candidates. Feminine issues included education in general and such terms as college, schools, and teachers; health care in general and also such words as insurance, Medicaid, and Medicare; social issues such as immigration, gay rights, and poverty; and women's issues such as abortion, equal pay, and family leave.

Including the word "Trump," which constituted 40% of the 20,942 mentions of dictionary terms found, masculine issue word mentions totaled 21%

compared to feminine issue word mentions at 8%. With "Trump" excluded from the analysis, masculine terms constituted 35% of the 12,620 words mentioned compared to feminine word mentions at 13% (see Table 8.1). Thus, like previous studies of women running for president (Bystrom & Dimitrova, 2014; Meeks, 2012), we found that Clinton's coverage in these four newspapers was almost three times more likely to be framed in masculine rather than feminine issues.

Looking more closely at the masculine issues mentioned, words associated with taxes and the economy were more almost twice as likely to be mentioned than terms linked with foreign policy. In terms of feminine issues, words were distributed more evenly between social issues, health care, and education. Such "women's issues" as abortion, equality, equal pay, and paid leave were rarely mentioned in Clinton's coverage in these four newspapers (see Table 8.1).

In comparing her coverage across each newspaper, we found that the *Wall Street Journal* and *USA Today* were most likely to include terms associated with masculine issues, especially taxes and the economy, in their articles about Clinton. Masculine words constituted 26% and 23% of the

Table 8.1: Overall Newspaper Coverage of Hillary Clinton by Interest Areas.

Interest Areas	Coverage with Trump (N = 20,942 words)	Coverage without Trump (N = 12,620 words)
Trump	8,322 (40%)	
Total Masculine Issues	4,479 (21%)	4,479 (35%)
Foreign Policy	1,676 (8%)	1,676 (13%)
Taxes/Economy	2,663 (13%)	2,663 (21%)
Other Masculine Issues	140 (<1%)	140 (1%)
Total Feminine Issues	1,616 (8%)	1,616 (13%)
Education	334 (2%)	334 (3%)
Health Care	424 (2%)	424 (3%)
Social Issues	682 (3%)	682 (5%)
Women's Issues	176 (<1%)	176 (1%)
Electability	305 (1%)	305 (2%)
Appearance	708 (3%)	708 (6%)
Family	381 (2%)	381 (3%)
Scandal	3,048 (15%)	3,048 (24%)
Political Constituencies	2,083 (10%)	2,083 (17%)

word mentions in the *Wall Street Journal* and *USA Today*, respectively, with Trump included in the analysis and 42% in each newspaper without Trump. Across all four newspapers, feminine terms constituted only 7% to 8% of the word mentions with Trump included and 11% to 14% with Trump excluded (see Tables 8.2 and 8.3).

In response to RQ2, we found that very little coverage of Clinton was associated with her electability, which included such dictionary terms as experience, historic, and viable. Of her overall coverage (excluding the word Trump), terms associated with her electability constituted 2% of the total 12,620 words and 2% to 3% in each of the four newspapers included (see Tables 8.1 and 8.3). Like Patterson (2016a), we found that Clinton's experience as a former first lady, senator, and secretary of state, as well as her historic nomination as the first woman nominated by a major political party, were rarely mentioned.

Previous research has found that women political candidates are still discussed more often than men in terms of their personal appearance. Although our study did not compare her coverage with Trump's, we can determine in

Table 8.2: Coverage of Hillary Clinton by Newspapers in All Interest Areas.

Interest Areas	New York Times (n = 6,714 words)	Wall Street Journal (n = 5,320 words)	Washington Post (n = 6,246 words)	USA Today (n = 2,662 words)
Trump	2,581 (38%)	2,036 (38%)	2,475 (40%)	1,230 (46%)
Total Masculine Issues	1,333 (20%)	1,384 (26%)	1,157 (19%)	599 (23%)
Foreign Policy	612 (9%)	261 (5%)	561 (9%)	242 (9%)
Taxes/Economy	686 (10%)	1,104 (21%)	546 (9%)	327 (12%)
Other Masculine Issues	35 (<1%)	19 (<1%)	50 (<1%)	36 (1%)
Total Feminine Issues	556 (8%)	367 (7%)	506 (8%)	187 (7%)
Education	99 (1%)	69 (1%)	146 (2%)	20 (<1%)
Health Care	126 (2%)	105 (2%)	128 (2%)	65 (2%)
Social Issues	257 (4%)	159 (3%)	190 (3%)	76 (3%)
Women's Issues	74 (1%)	34 (<1%)	42 (1%)	26 (<1%)
Electability	96 (1%)	74 (1%)	87 (1%)	48 (2%)
Appearance	326 (5%)	94 (2%)	195 (3%)	93 (4%)
Family	181 (3%)	50 (<1%)	124 (2%)	26 (<1%)
Scandal	904 (14%)	813 (15%)	1,000 (16%)	331 (12%)
Political Constituencies	737 (11%)	502 (9%)	702 (11%)	142 (5%)

Table 8.3: Coverage of Hillary Clinton by Newspapers in Interest Areas Except Trump.

Interest Areas	*New York Times* (n= 4,133 words)	*Wall Street Journal* (n= 3,284 words)	*Washington Post* (n = 3,771 words)	*USA Today* (n = 1,432 words)
Total Masculine Issues	1,333 (32%)	1,384 (42%)	1,157 (31%)	605 (42%)
Foreign Policy	612 (15%)	261 (8%)	561 (15%)	242 (17%)
Taxes/Economy	686 (17%)	1,104 (34%)	546 (15%)	327 (23%)
Other Masculine Issues	35 (1%)	19 (<1%)	50 (1%)	36 (3%)
Total Feminine Issues	556 (14%)	367 (11%)	506 (13%)	187 (13%)
Education	99 (2%)	69 (2%)	146 (4%)	20 (1%)
Health Care	126 (3%)	105 (3%)	128 (3%)	65 (5%)
Social Issues	257 (6%)	159 (5%)	190 (5%)	76 (5%)
Women's Issues	74 (2%)	34 (1%)	42 (1%)	26 (2%)
Electability	96 (2%)	74 (2%)	87 (2%)	48 (3%)
Appearance	326 (8%)	94 (3%)	195 (5%)	93 (7%)
Family	181 (4%)	50 (2%)	124 (3%)	26 (2%)
Scandal	904 (22%)	813 (25%)	1,000 (27%)	331 (23%)
Political Constituencies	737 (18%)	502 (15%)	702 (19%)	142 (10%)

response to RQ3 that 6% of her overall coverage (excluding the word Trump) were mentions of terms associated with her appearance and health. The *New York Times* was the most likely to include mentions of Clinton's appearance (8% of the total words) and the *Wall Street Journal* was the least likely to include terms associated with her appearance (3% of the total words) (see Tables 8.1 and 8.3). In all four newspapers studied, questions about Clinton's health—primarily when she fainted after the 2016 September 11 memorial event in New York City—dominated this category of news coverage. Overall, 73% of the word mentions in this category were associated with questions about her health.

According to previous research, women political candidates are more often associated with members of their family than male candidates in their media coverage. In response to RQ4, we found that members of Clinton's family were mentioned in 3% of her coverage overall (excluding Trump). References to her husband, former President Bill Clinton, comprised 59% of the words mentioned in the family category. Again, the *New York Times* was slightly more likely to include mentions of Clinton's family compared to the other three newspapers (see Tables 8.1 and 8.3).

Research by Patterson (2016a, 2016c) and Faris et al. (2017) found that Clinton was more likely to be associated with scandals than Trump. Again, although we did not compare Clinton's coverage to Trump's, in response to RQ5 we found that around a quarter of Clinton's coverage both overall and in each newspaper (without Trump) were words associated with the various scandals linked to her campaign—primarily her use of a private e-mail server while secretary of state (see Tables 8.1 and 8.3). Overall, her emails constituted 62% of the words mentioned in the scandal category in all four newspapers. The *New York Times* paid the most attention to Clinton's emails (76% of the terms associated with scandals) and *USA Today* had the fewest mentions of her emails (46% of the terms associated with scandals). However, *USA Today* was more likely to mention former President Clinton's past sexual misconduct in its coverage of his wife's campaign (15% of scandal mentions) and the *Wall Street Journal* was the least likely to mention her husband's transgressions (2%). Overall, 7% of the word mentions in the scandal category were associated with allegations of her husband's past sexual misconduct.

Finally, we wanted to examine the mentions of political constituencies in Clinton's newspaper coverage. We noticed that much of the 2016 campaign coverage focused on various groups of voters, including white working class, non-college-educated whites, college-educated whites, women, Hispanic/ Latinos, and blacks. While it appears that Trump was most often associated with white working class and non-college-educated white voters, Clinton seemed to be linked to women, college-educated whites, Hispanics/Latinos, and black voters. In response to RQ6, we analyzed which groups of voters were mentioned in Clinton's media coverage. Overall, mentions of political constituents constituted 17% of her overall coverage and ranged from 10% (*USA Today*) to 19% (*Washington Post*) of each newspaper studied with the term "Trump" excluded (see Tables 8.1 and 8.3).

We found that mentions of women and/or white voters dominated Clinton's coverage both overall and by newspaper. Overall, "women" comprised 29% and "white/s" were 28% of the words in the political constituency category in the articles analyzed, followed by Hispanics/Latinos (25%), and blacks (16%). Women voters constituted 44% of the political constituency mentions in *USA Today*, 42% in the *Wall Street Journal*, 26% in the *New York Times*, and 22% in the *Washington Post*. White voters constituted 35% of the political constituency mentions in the *Washington Post*, 30% in *USA Today*, 24% in the *New York Times*, and 21% in the *Wall Street Journal*. Hispanics/ Latinos received more word mentions than blacks in the *Washington Post* (32%–10%) and *Wall Street Journal* (22%–8%) in the overall political constituent mentions. Blacks received more word mentions than Hispanics/Latinos in the *New York Times* (27%–21%) and *USA Today* (20%–16%).

While our analysis has focused on the mentions of issues, electability, appearance, family, scandal, and political constituencies excluding the word "Trump," we note that his name dominated the majority of her coverage both overall (40%) and in each newspaper studied—ranging from 46% in *USA Today* to 40% in the *Washington Post* and 38% in both the *New York Times* and *Wall Street Journal* (see Tables 8.1 and 8.2). We did not find this surprising as newspapers often mention a political candidate's opponent in campaign coverage.

Next, we turn to a discussion of our results in terms of previous research as well as the 2016 presidential election and its aftermath.

Discussion

Our study contributes to the almost 30 years of research on the media coverage of women political candidates, particularly those who run for president, in several ways. First, it confirms the results of several recent studies that found that newspaper (Hayes & Lawless, 2015; Meeks, 2012) and television (Bystrom & Dimitrova, 2014) coverage of women running for state and federal office were more likely to include mentions of masculine issues over feminine issues.

We found that masculine issues were around three times more likely to be mentioned in newspaper articles about presidential candidate Clinton than feminine issues. Similarly, Hayes and Lawless (2015) found that 43% of the female and male candidates running for the U.S. House of Representatives in 2010 were linked to at least one men's issue and 16% were associated with at least one women's issue in their newspaper coverage. In her study of women political candidates—including Dole, Clinton, and Palin—and their male opponents, Meeks (2012) found that masculine issues were covered twice as much as feminine issues overall and three times more often in races for federal executive office. And, in their study of the 2012 Republican pre-primary presidential campaign, Bystrom and Dimitrova (2014) found that Bachmann was twice as likely to be linked with masculine issues, specifically foreign relations and taxes, than feminine issues in her national network and cable television coverage.

Associating women political candidates with masculine rather than feminine issues can be seen as a positive or negative, depending on the context of the campaign. If masculine issues—such as foreign policy, taxes, and the economy—are at the forefront of voters concerns, it would be positive for women political candidates to be discussed in terms of their views on such matters. According to a study by the Pew Research Center ("2016 Campaign," 2016), the economy and terrorism were the top two issues for voters in the 2016 presidential election. Pew found that 84% of registered voters said that the economy would be "very important" in making their decision about who to vote for in the 2016 presidential election; 80% said the issue of terrorism was very important. Other issues that ranked high in voters' concerns were foreign policy (75% very important), health care (74%), gun policy (72%), and immigration (70%). Of these issue concerns, our study found that words associated with taxes/the economy were mentioned the most frequently (21%) in articles about her campaign, followed by foreign policy (13%). However, words associated with health care—arguably a signature issue for Clinton along with her experience in foreign policy—constituted only 3% of her coverage. Thus, health care seems to have been a greater concern to voters in 2016 than it was accorded coverage in these newspapers during the presidential campaign, which could be perceived as detrimental to Clinton.

Our study also found that women are still covered in ways previous studies have shown that they receive more attention than male political candidates. We found that words associated with Clinton's personal appearance, overwhelmingly questions about her health, comprised 6% of her overall coverage; mentions of her family members, mostly her husband, were 3% of her coverage; and terms associated with her electability were 2% of her coverage.

Building on research by Patterson (2016a, 2016c, 2016d) and Faris et al. (2017), we also found that scandals associated with the Clinton campaign—primarily her use of a private server while U.S. secretary of state—comprised a large percentage of her media coverage. We found that words associated with scandals comprised 24% of her newspaper coverage overall—which was more than any single issue included in our analysis. Comparatively, Patterson (2016c) found that coverage of scandals constituted 11% of Clinton's television and newspaper coverage during the four weeks surrounding the national nominating conventions while attention to her policy positions comprised only 4%.

Finally, our study provides new information on the political constituencies associated with Clinton's campaign coverage. Notably, 17% of Clinton's overall coverage in the four newspapers studied was words associated with various constituencies of voters. Thus, the political constituency category ranked third overall, just behind scandals and taxes/economy, and ahead of any single issue in our analysis (excluding references to Trump). Perhaps not surprisingly, the word "women" comprised 29% of the political constituency mentions as Clinton appealed to female voters as part of her historic campaign as the first woman major political party presidential candidate. However, references to "white/s"—a group most associated with Trump's support—constituted 28% of words in this category. Two other constituencies key to Clinton's support—Hispanics/Latinos, who are becoming increasingly Democratic in their vote choice, and blacks/African Americans, who have long supported Democratic candidates—comprised only 25% and 16%, respectively, of the words in this category. Thus, despite the criticisms of Clinton for playing identity politics in her campaign, the media was more likely to mention white voters rather than Hispanics/Latinos and blacks in her newspaper coverage.

Exit polls showed that Clinton won the support of 54% of women voters overall, 94% of black women voters, 69% of Latina voters, and 62% of unmarried women voters. She also won the support of 82% of black men and 63% of Hispanic men. Although Trump received the support of 52% of white women, fueled largely by winning 61% of white women without a college degree, Clinton won the support of 51% of white women college graduates ("Historic Gender Gap," 2016).

In addition, her Electoral College loss to Trump appears to have inspired thousands of women to attend campaign training schools across the country as well as run for local and state office in 2017 and 2018 (Hillstrom, 2017). One year after the 2016 presidential election, Atlanta elected its first woman mayor, who is also African American, and Seattle elected its first woman mayor since 1926. The newly elected mayor of New Orleans is black and Seattle's new mayor is openly lesbian (Farmer, 2017). And in 2017, the most women candidates in at least a decade ran for state legislative seats in New Jersey and Virginia, increasing their representation in both. Notably, women candidates in Virginia flipped 11 of 16 Republican-held seats in the House of Delegates. In 2018, a record high 28 women are serving in the Virginia House (Farmer, 2017).

In addition, record numbers of women have announced their intent to run for the U.S. Congress in 2018. As of June 6, 2018, 361 women were running for or were likely to run for the House of Representatives nationwide—270 Democrats and 91 Republicans—breaking the record of 298 women in the primaries for the House in 2012. Likewise, 45 women—27 Democrats and 18 Republicans—were running for or likely to run for the U.S. Senate as of June 2018, breaking the record of 40 women set in 2016. Thus, 2018 appears to be on track to break records in terms of the number of women running for the U.S. Congress ("2018 Summary of Women Candidates," 2018).

As more women run for local, state, and federal elected office—many in response to Clinton's loss and Trump's victory in 2016—it is important to continue to study their media coverage especially in terms of the gendered presentation of their issues and images.

References

2016 campaign: Strong interest, widespread dissatisfaction. (2016, July 7). *Pew Research Center*. Retrieved from http://www.people-press.org/2016/07/07/201 `ampaign-strong-interest-widespread-dissatisfaction/

2018 summary of women candidates. (2018, June 6). Center for American Women and Politics. Retrieved from http://cawp.rutgers.edu/potential-candidate-summary-2018

Aday, S., & Devitt, J. (2001). *Style over substance. Newspaper coverage of female candidates: Spotlight on Elizabeth Dole*. Washington, DC: The Women's Leadership Fund.

Bode, L., & Hennings, V. (2012). Mixed signals? Gender and the media's coverage of the 2008 vice presidential candidates. *Politics & Policy, 40*(2), 221–257. doi:10.1111/j.1747-1346.2012.00350.x

Bystrom, D. (2006). Media content and candidate viability: The case of Elizabeth Dole. In Mitchell S. McKinney, Dianne G. Bystrom, Lynda Lee Kaid, & Diana B. Carlin (Eds.), *Communicating politics: Engaging the public in Democratic life* (pp. 123–133). New York, NY: Peter Lang Publishing.

Bystrom, D. (2008, August). *Gender and U.S. presidential politics: Early newspaper coverage of Hillary Clinton's bid for the White House*. Paper presented at the annual meeting of the American Political Science Association, Boston, MA.

Bystrom, D., Banwart, M. C., Kaid, L. L., & Robertson, T. (2004). *Gender and campaign communication: VideoStyle, webStyle and newsStyle*. New York, NY: Routledge.

Bystrom, D., & Dimitrova, D. V. (2014). Migraines, marriage, and mascara: Media coverage of Michele Bachmann in the 2012 Republican presidential campaign. *American Behavioral Scientist, 58*(9), 1169–1183. doi:10.1177/0002764213506221.

Carlin, D. B., & Winfrey, K. L. (2009). Have you come a long way, baby? Hillary Clinton, Sarah Palin, and sexism in 2008 campaign coverage. *Communication Studies, 60*(4), 326–343. doi:10.1080/10510970903109904

Clinton, H. R. (2017). *What happened*. New York, NY: Simon & Schuster.

Devitt, J. (1999). *Framing gender on the campaign trail: Women's executive leadership and the press*. Washington, DC: The Women's Leadership Fund.

Did the media cost Hillary Clinton the election? (2017, September 24). *Al Jazeera*. Retrieved from http://www.aljazeera.com/programmes/listeningpost/2017/09/media-cost-hillary-clinton-election-170923131221409.html

Dimitrova, D. V., & Geske, E. (2009, May). *To cry or not to cry: Media framing of Hillary Clinton in the wake of the New Hampshire primary*. Paper presented at the annual meeting of the International Communication Association, Chicago, IL. Retrieved from http://citation.allacademic.com/meta/p_mla_apa_research_citation/2/9/5/3/2/pages295321/p295321-1.php

Faris, R. M., Roberts, H., Etling, B., Bourassa, N., Zuckerman, E., & Benkler, Y. (2017). Partisanship, propaganda, and disinformation: Online media and the 2016 U.S. presidential election. *Berkman Klein Center for Internet & Society*. Retrieved from https://dash.harvard.edu/bitstream/handle/1/33759251/2017-08_election Report_0.pdf?sequence=9

Farmer, L. (2017, November 8). Election 2017 was a historic night for women. *Governing*. Retrieved from http://www.governing.com/topics/politics/gov-election-2017-historic-night-women-candidates.html

Fridkin, K., Carle, J., & Woodall, G. S. (2012). The vice presidency as the new glass ceiling: Media coverage of Sarah Palin. In Melody Rose (Ed.), *Women and executive office: Pathways and performance* (pp. 33–52). Boulder, CO: Lynne Rienner Publishers.

Hayes, D., & Lawless, J. L. (2015). A non-gendered lens: Media, voters, and female candidates in contemporary congressional elections. *Perspectives on Politics, 13*(1), 95–118. doi:10.1017/S1537592714003156

Heldman, C., Carroll, S. J., & Olson, S. (2005). "She brought only a skirt": Print media coverage of Elizabeth Dole's bid for the Republican presidential nomination. *Political Communication, 22*(3), 315–335. doi:10.1080/10584600591006564

Hillstrom, C. (2017, November 6). The Trump effect, one year later: Thousands of women are running for office. *Yes! Magazine*. Retrieved from http://www.yesmagazine.org/issues/solidarity/the-trump-effect-one-year-later-thousands-of-women-running-for-office-20171106

Historic gender gap isn't enough to propel Clinton to victory in 2016 presidential race. (2016, November 9). *Center for American Women and Politics*. Retrieved from http://cawp.rutgers.edu/sites/default/files/resources/post-election-gg-release-2016-presidential.pdf

Kahn, K. F. (1991). Senate elections in the news: Examining campaign coverage. *Legislative Studies Quarterly, 16*(3), 349–374. Retrieved from http://www.jstor.org/stable/440102

Kahn, K. F. (1994a). The distorted mirror: Press coverage of women candidates for statewide office. *Journal of Politics, 56*(1), 154–173. Retrieved from http://www.jstor.org/stable/2132350

Kahn, K. F. (1994b). Does gender make a difference? An experimental examination of sex stereotypes and press patterns in statewide campaigns. *American Journal of Political Science, 38*(1), 162–195. doi:10.2307/2111340

Kahn, K. F., & Goldenberg, E. N. (1991). Women candidates in the news: An examination of gender differences in the U.S. Senate campaign coverage. *Public Opinion Quarterly, 55*(2), 180–199. Retrieved from http://www.jstor.org/stable/2749288

Lawrence, R. G., & Rose, M. (2010). *Hillary Clinton's race for the White House: Genderpolitics and the media on the campaign trail*. Boulder, CO: Lynne Rienner Publishers.

Lowe, W. (2006, September). *Yoshikoder: An open source multilingual content analysis tool for social scientists*. Paper presented at the annual meeting of the American Political Science Association meeting, Philadelphia, PA. Retrieved from https://www.researchgate.net/publication/251551334_Yoshikoder_An_Open_Source_Multilingual_Content_Analysis_Tool_for_Social_Scientists

Major, L. H., & Coleman, R. (2008). The intersection of race and gender in election coverage: What happens when the candidates don't fit the stereotypes? *The Howard Journal of Communication, 19*(4), 315–333. doi:10.1080/10646170802391722

Meeks, L. (2012). Is she "man enough"? Women candidates, executive political offices, and news coverage. *Journal of Communication, 62*(1), 175–193. doi:10.1111/j.1460-2466.2011.01621.x

Official 2016 presidential election results. (2017). *Federal Election Commission.* Retrieved from https://transition.fec.gov/pubrec/fe2016/2016presgeresults.pdf

Patterson, T. E. (2016a, June 20). Pre-primary news coverage of the 2016 presidential race: Trump's rise, Sanders' emergence, Clinton's struggle. *Shorenstein Center on Media, Politics, and Public Policy.* Retrieved from https://shorensteincenter.org/pre-primary-news-coverage-2016-trump-clinton-sanders/

Patterson, T. E. (2016b, July 11). News coverage of the 2016 presidential primaries: Horse race reporting has consequences. *Shorenstein Center on Media, Politics, and Public Policy.* Retrieved from https://shorensteincenter.org/news-coverage-2016-presidential-primaries/

Patterson, T. E. (2016c, September 21). News coverage of the 2016 national conventions: Negative news, lacking context. *Shorenstein Center on Media, Politics, and Public Policy.* Retrieved from https://shorensteincenter.org/news-coverage-2016-national-conventions/

Patterson, T. E. (2016d, December 7). News coverage of the 2016 general election: How the press failed the voters. *Shorenstein Center on Media, Politics, and Public Policy.* Retrieved from https://shorensteincenter.org/news-coverage-2016-general-election/

Scarry, E. (2017, August 22). Hillary Clinton supporters still moaning about media coverage almost 10 months later. *Washington Examiner.* Retrieved from http://www.washingtonexaminer.com/hillary-clinton-supporters-still-moaning-about-media-coverage-nearly-10-months-later/article/2632175

Smith, K. (1997). When's all fair: Signs of parity in media coverage of female candidates. *Political Communication, 14*(1), 71–82. doi:10.1080/105846097199542

Top 10 U.S. daily newspapers. (2016, May 11). *Cision.* Retrieved from https://www.cision.com/us/2014/06/top-10-us-daily-newspapers/

Zurcher, A. (2017, September 13). What happened: The long list of who Hillary Clinton blames. *BBC.* Retrieved from http://www.bbc.com/news/world-us-canada-41244474

9. Goodbye Neighbor: Mexican News Coverage of the Trump Wall and U.S. Immigration Proposals

MELISSA A. JOHNSON
Department of Communication, North Carolina State University

HÉCTOR RENDÓN
Laboratory for Analytic Sciences, North Carolina State University

Relationships between countries around the globe and the United States have been tumultuous since Donald J. Trump became the U.S. president on January 20, 2017. Among the many nations subject to the White House's erratic comments and inconsistent policies has been Mexico, one of the United States' closest neighbors.

The trading relationship between the two nations is strong and vital to both economies, especially since the North American Free Trade Agreement (NAFTA) was enacted in 1994. Mexico is the second-largest importer of U.S. goods, which supports about 1.2 million jobs in the United States and accounts for 15.9% of all U.S. exports, according to the Office of the U.S. Trade Representative (2017). This is up 455% since 1993, pre-NAFTA. Mexico is also the second-largest trading partner in exports to the United States.

Human relations between the countries is equally robust. There were 11.7 million Mexican immigrants in the United States in 2014, with about half estimated as undocumented (Gonzalez-Barrera & Krogstad, 2017). However, from 2007 through 2014, immigration from Mexico decreased by approximately one million. Thus, while Mexican presence in the U.S. is strong, it has been dropping. In addition, an estimated million or more U.S. citizens live in Mexico, a popular spot for retirees (U.S. Department of State, 2017). Approximately 91% of Americans are in the country illegally, without proper residency visas (*Excelsior*, 2017; National Institute of Statistics and Geography, 2015).

Further, often unmentioned in the bilateral relations is the transmission of Mexican culture into the United States and U.S. culture into Mexico. For instance, as of 2011, there were 38,000 Mexican food restaurants in the United States. Mexican music, art, pottery, and the like are also well-diffused. Of note, Mexican musicians produced the top six Latin albums sold in the United States in 2016. Conversely, U.S. popular culture has spread into Mexico. An example is U.S. Halloween, which has been merged into Mexico's Day of the Dead celebrations (McDonnell, 2016). In addition, as Mexico is the fourth largest cinema-going nation in the world (by number of tickets sold), Mexicans see a plethora of U.S.-produced films, along with U.S. television shows that are widely available. In short, there is a vibrant, dynamic movement of products, services, people, and cultural products flowing both ways across the border.

The purpose of this research is to examine Mexican newspaper coverage of Donald Trump's first 100 days in office, focusing on issues related to immigration, the U.S.-Mexico border, and Trump's proposal to build a border wall. First-level and second-level agenda setting concepts serve as the theoretical foundation for the study. The goal is to gain knowledge of Mexican news organizations' reporting of U.S. President Trump, especially his assertions about immigration and the U.S.-Mexico relationship.

The following literature review discusses agenda setting theory, prior media studies related to immigration, and how this study extends the research. Also included is a brief overview of the Mexican media system in order to provide the political and economic contexts of the news coverage.

Agenda Setting Theory and Research

Decades of research based on agenda setting theory have demonstrated that what media organizations cover and deem salient influences the public agenda—what citizens think is important (Bryant & Miron, 2004; Cacciatore, Scheufele, & Iyengar, 2016; Kim, Scheufele, & Shanahan, 2002; McCombs, 2004). An early investigation known as the Chapel Hill study demonstrated that the composite news agenda of four local newspapers and five national media outlets strongly correlated ($r = .967$) with the top issues that local voters ranked as important (McCombs & Shaw, 1972). In short, the media scholars said, news consumers "learn in direct proportion to the emphasis placed" on various subjects (1972, p. 177). Agenda setting assumes that individual attitude formation is a media effect caused by attending to what journalists feature as the most important topics in society.

In addition, scholars such as Perloff (2015) have emphasized that agenda setting is central to democracy. The reasoning is that individuals and organizations jostle to influence the public agenda and thereby, guide public policy. As researchers have noted, an important function of media when they serve as referents is that they help citizens reach a consensus that benefits society (Bennett & Iyengar, 2008; McCombs, Shaw, & Weaver, 2014).

Intermedia Agenda Setting and Niche Agenda Setting

Of course, unlike in the 1970s news environment of the Chapel Hill study, social media, blogs and other digital media forms now impact the public agenda. But research shows that when consumers say they are getting their news from the Internet, it is often on platforms such as social media which lead them directly to newspaper or television websites. Facebook itself, for instance, does not employ journalists or produce news. In addition, platforms such as the *Huffington Post* aggregate news originating from legacy news organizations.

As studies have discovered, there are high degrees of intermedia agenda setting among traditional and new media (e.g., Sweetzer, Golan, & Wanta, 2008). However, questions that have arisen in international agenda setting studies are whether intermedia agenda setting is as robust in non-Western nations and whether there are global agenda setting effects (Du, 2013).

Although agenda setting was initially conceptualized as influencing "masses" of citizens, it is possible to break out news consumption patterns to examine how individual media potentially influence different sets of news readers (e.g., voters or influentials from different political parties, business leaders). Recognizing that the concept of mass audiences consuming the same media is outdated, Perloff termed this "niche agenda setting" (2015).

First-Level and Second-Level Agenda Setting

Standard agenda setting studies examine cross-lagged correlations between topics awarded salient by mediated communication and top issues on the public's agenda, as measured by public opinion surveys. First-level agenda setting is overall transference of an issue or individual salience from media to the public. For instance, in the classic Chapel Hill study, the researchers selected a three-week interview timeframe and studied media content that appeared a week before the interviews started, along with content appearing through completion of interviews (McCombs & Shaw, 1972).

The present study uses concepts from agenda setting theory to investigate topics in Mexico City newspapers but full-fledged agenda setting theory does not underpin the present research because public opinion data are based on secondary research, rather than primary research. In addition, as several scholars have noted (Bennett & Iyengar, 2008; Perloff, 2015; Tan & Weaver, 2013), "mass" opinion polls are imprecise measures when citizens are consuming niche media (news exposure diversity), rather than all attending to the same daily newspapers and/or television newscasts as was typical in the 20th century.

Second-level agenda setting is another term for attribute agenda setting (Kim & McCombs, 2007). This refers to transfer of specific characteristics regarding an issue or an individual from the media source to the public. For instance, Golan and Wanta's 2001 study demonstrated that presidential candidate traits featured in media were replicated in the candidate characteristics ascribed to them by the public. Another attribute study of U.S. presidential candidates—this one of 2012 television news coverage—also considered how niche audiences select different media (Hyun & Moon, 2016), finding that Fox's Special Report contained more negativity about then presidential candidate Barack Obama and was more positive toward Mitt Romney. Surveys showed that Fox News viewers had more polarized attitudes and results found that Fox had the most robust agenda setting function. This is in line with viewership studies that have indicated the Fox network has more conservative viewers and CNN has more liberal viewers (de Zúñiga, Correa, & Valenzuela, 2012; Hollander, 2008; Stroud, 2011). The authors asserted that their results show that transfer of salience of media to the public continues in the new media environment, albeit in narrower, more partisan contexts.

There are cognitive aspects in second-level agenda setting as well as affective traits, also known as substantive and affective dimensions of attributes (Kim & McCombs, 2007; Takeshita, 2005). As Kim and McCombs asserted, "Just as objects vary in salience, so do the attributes of each object" (2007, p. 300). For instance, an immigration article describing health, language, and education components of a policy would center on how a news consumer evaluated *cognitive* components. Conversely, an immigration story characterizing a policy as positive or negative would emphasize *affective* elements. They become the elements that citizens use to evaluate their support or non-support of public policy issues or individuals in the news.

Other factors affecting agenda setting research are the amount of news consumption, such as heavy versus light readership or viewership (Kim & McCombs, 2007); trust in the news organization or gatekeeper (Pingree & Stoycheff, 2013); and the psychological relevance of media messages (Lang, 2013), to name a few.

Agenda Setting Research in Latin America

As Du noted, most agenda-setting research examines the phenomena within one locale or nation-state, and non-Western studies such as those in Korea or Japan are largely influenced by U.S. agenda setting approaches (2013). Among the short list of agenda setting studies in Latin America, most rely on U.S. theorists McCombs and Shaw (e.g., Mont'Alverne & Marques, 2016; Stein & Kellam, 2014). For example, a longitudinal study of Chilean newspaper coverage found a high level of intermedia agenda setting between a popular newspaper and elite paper (Mellado & Humanes, 2017), providing a glimmer of evidence that intermedia agenda setting exists in at least some countries in Latin America. Conversely, in an analysis of editorials, not news, Mont'Alverne and Marques (2016) found divergent emphases.

A key study (McCombs, Llamas, Lopez-Escobar, & Rey, 1997) of second-level agenda setting in Spanish-language media was conducted to analyze political elections in Spain. The authors combined survey data with content analysis to explore the influence of media in relation to how the public perceived the candidates. In Latin America and specifically in Mexico, some scholars have studied issues related to local and international construction of agendas and the main topics disseminated by media outlets in a variety of contexts. One of these studies focuses on the coverage of the so-called war on drugs; the authors (Villanueva & Ortiz, 2015) analyzed several newspapers from England, Mexico, Spain, and the U.S. and found that the 2012 political transition in Mexico could have influenced a change in the topics used for coverage of drug-related stories. Another study (Alanis, 2013) investigated the possible relationship of media exposure to topics and surveys related to public concerns; the results suggest that only in the case of two topics was there a link between media topics and the salience of the same issues in the public's perception. Another recent study (Rosales, Rodríguez, Cárcamo-Ulloa, & Montecinos, 2017) dealt with social media analysis disseminated by Chilean news outlets in reference to Mexico and Mexicans to establish agenda setting patterns. The researchers found that in Chilean news the most relevant topics about Mexico are generally associated with a few topics like entertainment, drugs, and violence.

In English-language journals, for the most part, few agenda setting scholars have analyzed Latin American media outlets, and no comprehensive contemporary studies of Mexican media agenda setting were found. However, in Du's study of multinational agenda setting (2013), she found that Mexico was the only country of the 11 she examined where the media agenda had no significant correlation with the public opinion agenda. She speculated that because *El Universal* was the only Mexican newspaper in the database that she used at the time, its influence on public opinion may not have been as strong as the national newspapers in other countries. In addition, in Du's research, Mexico's media agenda was not associated with those of the 10 other countries. In other words, Mexico was the exception to the global intermedia agenda that she found among the other nations. Mexico was also an exception in a study of other nations in U.S. news, where among the group of nations viewed favorably by U.S. respondents, it was the only country receiving negative news (Wanta, Golan, & Lee, 2004).

Immigration Research

Much of the 21st century's media research in English-language publications about immigration has been underpinned with framing theory (Fryberg et al., 2012; Kim, Carvalho, Davis, & Mullins, 2011; Knoll, Redlawsk, & Sanborn, 2011; Lee, McLeod, & Shah, 2008; Merolla, Ramakrishnan, & Haynes, 2013; Quinsaat, 2014) or agenda setting theory (Funk & McCombs, 2017). Dekker and Scholten's (2017) analysis of Dutch immigration policy combined both, and Funk and McCombs (2017) also added community structure concerns to their study. Concepts related to threat are central to a third body of immigration studies in the social science tradition (Atwell Seate & Mastro, 2015; Fujioka, 2011; Watson & Riffe, 2013). The majority of research about immigration news has investigated how developed nations' media describe immigration vis á vis immigrants arriving from developing or war-torn nations. A few studies have also examined English- and Spanish-language media coverage related to immigration, but within the context of the United States (Avila, 2014; Branton & Dunaway, 2008; De Moya, Rendon, & Johnson, 2015).

The current study veers in a different direction. It investigates how bilateral government policies proposed by a political figure in a developed nation are covered by media of a less developed nation that is directly affected by the policies.

Mexican Media System

We know from international communication research that media systems differ by country and are especially affected by political systems (e.g., Cole, 1996; de Beer & Merrill, 2004; Hachten & Scotton, 2016). One 30-year study of six Mexican newspapers said that historically, Mexican media had been viewed as the "handmaidens of government" (Montgomery, 1984), especially because of the media-government relation norms under the long-term rule of the Institutional Revolutionary Party (PRI). However, changes in the 1990s, and early 2000s, including the disruption of the PRI dominance with two National Action Party (PAN) presidents, brought some new press freedoms that Hughes (2003) categorized as more "civic" than autocratic. Even so, forms of censorship such as control of newsprint, allocation of government advertising, or taxation policies can influence perceived freedoms or journalist self-censorship and still continue today (Hughes, 2003; Stevenson, 2004; Waisbord, 2002). Hughes also noted that NAFTA opened up relationships among Canadian, U.S., and Mexican journalists as the northern countries sent more reporters to cover Mexico. This, she said, along with journalism educational exchanges, also helped to influence changes in Mexican journalism.

Government corruption and organized crime, especially among narcotics and human traffickers, has made Mexican journalism a high-risk occupation, so risky that some banks won't give journalists credit and insurance companies won't sell them life insurance (Relly & González de Bustamante, 2014). At least 100 journalists have been murdered since 2000, according to Freedom House (2017). In 2016, the Mexican Supreme Court disallowed a legal limit on lawsuits, meaning that libel suits filed by politicians or other societal influentials could financially destroy journalists or news organizations. Scholars and journalism non-governmental organizations agree that Mexico is one of the globe's most dangerous places to be a journalist (Freedom House, 2017; Hachten & Scotton, 2016; Malkin, 2017).

A study comprised of 39 interviews with Mexican journalists in northern border states found both individual-level and organizational-level influences on journalism decisions (Relly & González de Bustamante, 2014). Although some news organizations—not all—provided security protections ranging from bulletproof glass to eliminating bylines, journalists self-censored to avoid being murdered, according to interviews conducted by the scholars (2014).

The authors said that fear of violence reduced the amount of Mexican investigative, or civic, journalism. Because various businesses reduced advertising so that they were not extortion targets, this also affected the news organizations' financial conditions. Some media outlets were once again dependent on government advertising to continue operating, which was "similar to the period before the transition to democracy" (Relly & González de Bustamante, 2014, p. 118). A consideration in the present study is whether this situation affected Mexico's coverage of the United States and its president.

As described earlier, researchers know that selective exposure to news outlets that align with one's personal beliefs is common (Hyun & Moon, 2016;

Stroud, 2011). In this study, newspapers were chosen knowing that their core audiences may have little overlap. Thus, the force of intermedia agenda setting may decrease in political systems such as Mexico's where media are strongly affiliated with different political parties or agenda.

Mexican Media Consumers

A recent survey by the Reuters Institute found that the main sources of news for Mexican citizens were television (65%), radio (33%), print sources (51%), and social media (72%). Seventy percent of the population access news via smartphones, with computer news penetration limited to 45% (Newman, 2017). In most Latin American countries, elites are the primary newspaper readers (Schroeder, 2017). According to the 2017 Study of Internet Users' Habits in Mexico, conducted by the Mexican Internet Association, 79% of the population frequently use their internet connection to visit news sites; this activity is the second most common among Mexican internet users, only surpassed by the use of social media platforms (97%). Given that digital readership statistics are generally higher than traditional circulation data, it is assumed that the majority of Mexican readers who read news articles access them via digital devices.

In summary, agenda setting concepts are useful for examining Mexican media coverage of Donald Trump's first 100 days. The review of the literature led to the following research questions for the present study:

First-Level Agenda Setting and Intermedia Agenda Setting

RQ1: What are the topics and subtopics associated with proposed U.S. immigration policies, the U.S.-Mexico border, and the proposed Trump wall?

RQ2: How do the three newspapers' agenda compare? Is there evidence of intermedia agenda setting among *La Jornada, Reforma*, and *El Universal*?

Second-Level Agenda Setting and Niche Agenda Setting

RQ3: How does each Mexican newspaper present cognitive and affective attributes of proposed U.S. immigration policies?

RQ4: How does each Mexican newspaper present cognitive and affective attributes of the U.S.-Mexico border controversy?

RQ5: How does each Mexican newspaper present cognitive and affective attributes of Donald Trump's proposed border wall?

Methodology

Sampling Design

Three Mexico City-based daily newspapers with national circulations were selected in a purposive approach aimed at gaining multiple viewpoints. *Reforma*, founded in 1993, is popular with the business community. *La Jornada*, founded in 1984, is considered one of the most relevant leftist publications in the country (Fromson, 1996). *El Universal* is a newspaper founded in 1916 that boasts a close relationship with the PRI, the political party of most of the Mexican presidents since the Revolution ended in 1920 (except for presidents Vicente Fox and Felipe Calderón). *Reforma*'s daily circulation is estimated at 126,000, *La Jornada*'s is 35,000, and *El Universal*'s is 170,000 (Editor & Publisher International Data Book, 2012).

These were also selected because one of the challenges of international news content analysis is gaining a complete sample, as Du's study showed (2013). Each of these publications is available via Lexis-Nexis, which enabled a comprehensive collection of coverage from January 20, 2017 through April 30, 2017.

The authors used a multi-stage sampling design. First, a census of all articles published within the first 100 days was collected, using the search terms, "Trump and migración or inmigración" and "Trump and muro or frontera" (Trump and migration or immigration; Trump and wall or border). Files were merged and duplicates were excluded. This resulted in 336 articles in *Reforma*, 365 in *La Jornada*, and 501 in *El Universal*. This sample was used for the second-level agenda setting study as described below. However, to make it manageable for coding the first-level agenda, editorials were excluded (although opinion columns were retained) and a systematic sample was generated selecting every third story from *Reforma* and *La Jornada*, and every fourth article from *El Universal*. The procedure resulted in a sample of 391 articles. Holding a degree in international relations, the coder was a Latin American native Spanish speaker who was trained by the authors for the coding project.

Measures—First-Level Agenda Setting and Thematic Analysis (Hand-Coding)

To examine general characteristics of the articles and allow for paper-to-paper comparisons, the publication date, dateline, authorship, and story length were coded. Only one newspaper (*La Jornada*) included section and page number of the article in the index, so this variable suggesting prominence was not tabulated. The headline and the first two paragraphs of the article, or the first six sentences if the paragraphs were shorter, were used as the unit of analysis to determine the main subject of the story, following similar protocols for main topic selection. Coding noted: 1) the topics and subtopics related to Trump, immigration and the border wall; 2) how Mexican newspapers described the effects in Mexico of President Trump's policies, along with effects in the United States and in the world.

Measures—Second-Level Agenda Setting, and Computer-Assisted Coding

In the second-level agenda setting phase, computer-assisted coding tabulated what attributes of Trump and descriptors of immigration-related proposals or policies (including the wall) were presented. Themes such as friend or neighbor (amigo o vecino) and characteristics such as crazy or cruel (loco o crueldad) were noted, using adjective families for characteristics (e.g., Funk & McCombs, 2017).

To conduct the second-level agenda setting the tool Voyant was employed. This platform specializes in text analytics. First, the datasets were divided by topic—i.e., articles related to migration issues, articles about the wall, and articles related to the border. Then a specific search within each one of those datasets was performed; in the migration dataset, the term roots used were migra* and immigra* (all the words that had those roots were included, for example migration, migrant, migrants). In the dataset about the wall the key root terms were muro*, valla*, barrera*, barda*. And for the articles with information concerning the border the key root term was fronter*. The search for each dataset was conducted separately.

After all the relevant words were identified, we explored the context in which those terms were used by taking the previous and following five words that were next to the relevant terms. Once the immediate context for each dataset was extracted, a word frequency analysis was run to find the most salient attributes used in connection with migration, the wall, and the border. Then, all the concepts that had fewer than three mentions and that had no attribute embedded in them (e.g. grammatical conjunctions) were removed. After this point it was possible to identify the different kinds of attributes. By doing a qualitative analysis, seven different categories of attributes and affective concepts were identified for each dataset: 1) economic attributes, 2) social attributes, 3) political attributes, 4) international attributes, 5) affective negative, 6) affective positive, and 7) affective neutral.

The following terms were identified as recurrent in the Mexican media coverage of the first 100 days of the Trump presidency in relation to the border, migration, and the wall.

Border, Wall, and Immigration Dictionaries

Economic attributes: Budget, brick, businesses, businessmen, cement/concrete, charge, commerce, commercial, cost, customs, design, dollars, economy, finance, funds, hire, import, infrastructure, investment, jobs, labor, metal, millions of dollars, money, NAFTA, negotiation, pay/payment, poverty, project, prototype, renegotiate, resources, salaries, Carlos Slim, tariffs, wealth, workers.

Social attributes: Agents, asylum, bishops, border, bridge, capital, children, citizens, city, college, community, compatriot, Conan O'Brien, crime, culture, development, doctors, drug trafficking, drugs, environmental, experts, family, flow, group, human, immigrants, immigration, inhabitants, limits, living, media, migrants, migration, migratory, military, ocean, offspring, parents, patrol, people, police, population, protest, public, refugees, repatriation, return, rights, routes, safety, security, services, shelter, social, survey, terrorism, transit, undocumented, unity, university students, women, young people.

Political attributes: Actions, administration, agencies, agenda, agreement, announcement, authorities, border, campaign, CBP, church, commitment, congress, consulates, cooperation, decision, declaration, decree, department, discussion, executive order, federal, foreign relations minister, government, government officials, governors, ICE, initiative, INM, institutions, judges, justice, John Kelly, law, lawyers, leader, legal, Andrés Manuel López Obrador, magnate, measures, message, mexiquenses, nation, national, nationality, organizations, party, Enrique Peña Nieto, poblanos, politics, position, president, priority, processes, promise, proposal, prosecute, public officials, reform, reinforcement, relations, report, republican, sanctuary cities, secretary, Segob, senator, Jeff Sessions, sign, statistics, strategy, system, territory, Donald Trump, union, veto, Luis Videgaray.

International attributes: Agreement, Africa, America, American, Arizona, Berlin, bilateral, binational, border, California, Canada, Canadian, Carolina, Central American, Central Americans, Chihuahua, Ciudad Juarez, Coahuila, common, country, Cuban, Guatemala, Haitians, international, Israel, Laredo, local, meeting, Mexican, Mexico, Muslims, national, nations, Benjamin Netanyahu, Nogales, north, region, relationship, river, separate, Sinai, Sonora, south, states, Tamaulipas, territory, Texas, neighbor, Tijuana, United States, Washington, world.

Affective negative: Expansion, absurd, accusations, against, aggression, anti-immigrants, attack, build/construction, captured, close, collapse, concern, condemn, containment, control, crimes, criminals, crisis, deport, deportation, deportees, detain, detention, difficult, divide, expulsion, fear, hostile, ignominy, illegal immigrants, impose, irregular, militarize, obstacle, offense, offensive, oppose, persecution, physical, problem, racism, raids, recover, reject, restrictions, shame, stop, stupidity, symbol, threat, toughen, unnecessary, useless, wall, weapons, worry, xenophobia.

Affective positive: Agreement, advise, assist, attention, defend, defense, demolish, dignity, good, protection, respect, solidarity, solution, strengthen, success, support.

Affective neutral: Accept, accompanied, achieve, act, adjustment, answer, avoid, cancel, causes, combat, coming, comply, conditions, context, correct, create, crossing, departed, documents, effectivity, entrance, essential, example, far, favor, figures, force, form, formalize, function, future, height, image, impact, impulse, increase, insist, integral, intention, joint, joking, lack, live, massive, natural, needs, open, origin, participate, petitions, phenomenon, possible, pretends, reason, reduce, search, situation, speak, start, wants, willing.

Results

First-Level Agenda Setting

In the first-level agenda setting analysis, coding procedures described earlier resulted in 35% of the sample from *El Universal*, 34% from *La Jornada*, and 31% from *Reforma*. Thirty-four percent of the articles were published from January 20 (inauguration day) through January 31, 37.9% in February, 17.6% in March, and 10.5% in April. This indicates that the highest attention to the Trump administration's effects on Mexican immigration was earliest in the presidency.

Regarding authorship, 47% of the articles were written by reporters identified with bylines and 11% by columnists. *Reforma* boasted the most bylined articles (66.4%), followed by *La Jornada* (39.1%) and *El Universal* (36.8%). Columnists expressing views about Trump and immigration were most frequent in *La Jornada* (17.3%) and *Reforma* (16.4%). Twenty-seven percent of the total articles were identified by the newspaper name only, or by "staff." The remainder were supplied by wire services, with the most dominant Agence France-Presse (3.3%) and the Associated Press (2.6%). Other wire services used by the organizations included Notimex, Deutsche Presse-Agentur, Reuters, Xinhua, and Sputnik.

The most frequently listed datelines were Mexico City (25.8%) and Washington, D.C. (11.3%). U.S. border states of California, Arizona, New Mexico, and Texas were the sites of 4.1% of the articles. Mexican border states (Baja California, Sonora, Chihuahua, Tamaulipas, Nuevo Leon, and Coahuila) were the locations for 2.8% of the coverage. Additional Mexican locations accounted for 4.6% of news and other United States settings comprised

1.5% of stories. Latin American locales excluding Mexico were datelines for 2.0% of the coverage, Europe for 1.5% of the news, and other world locations comprised less than 1%. Further, 46% of the coverage had no datelines listed.

Agenda Setting Topics and Subtopics

The first research question asked what topics and subtopics associated with the proposed U.S. immigration policies, the U.S.-Mexico border, and the Trump wall comprised the Mexican newspapers' agenda. The broad topics were announcements, speculations, or myths about US immigration policies— including border issues or the wall (25.9%); actions taken by Mexico related to U.S. proposals (21.5%); effects of Trump proposals and U.S. immigration policies on Mexico (12.4%); U.S. actions against Mexicans (6.1%); effects of Trump proposals and U.S. policies on the United States (6.9%); U.S.-Mexico bilateral actions or statements (16.6%); and multi-lateral relations (10.5%).

Table 9.1 details the most popular subtopics associated with coverage of Donald Trump and Mexican immigration. The most frequent were statements or thoughts by Mexicans about U.S.-Mexican bilateral relations under

Table 9.1: Main Subtopic in Mexican Newspaper Coverage of Donald Trump's Immigration Proposals, the U.S.-Mexico Border, and the Border Wall.

U.S. Immigration Proposals	Percent of Total Coverage
Trump Wall	10%
Statements by Notables or Celebrities	7.7%
Other Trump Proposals	3.6%
Trump's Qualifications or Personality	2.8%
Other (non-White House) U.S. Proposals	1.0%
Rumors/Myths	0.8%
U.S.-Mexico Bilateral Relations	
U.S.-Mexico Philosophies or Statements	10.7%
U.S.-Mexico Meetings or Conversations	5.9%
Actions by Mexico or Mexicans	
Protests or Activism	8.4%
Mexican Political/Economic Actions	3.1%
Mexico's Resources Provided to Migrants	2.8%

(Continued)

Table 9.1: (Continued)

Lawsuits Filed by Mexicans	0.3%
Other Mexican Actions	6.9%
Effects of Trump Proposals on Mexico	
Effects on Mexican Sovereignty, Dignity, Pride	4.3%
Increase in Central American Immigration in Mexico	1.5%
Effects on Mexican Sports, Entertainment, Tourism	1.5%
Effects on Mexican Business, Agriculture, Trade	1.3%
Remittances to Mexico Cut if Immigration Decreased	0.5%
Other Effects on Mexico	3.3%
Actions by United States against Mexicans	
Arrests or Deportations of Mexican Immigrants	2.0%
Other U.S. Actions against Mexicans	4.1%
Effects of Trump Proposals on United States	
U.S. Cities/States Defy Trump Including Sanctuary	1.3%
U.S. Businesses Defy Trump Proposals	1.0%
Lawsuits Filed by U.S. Citizens	0.3%
Other Effects on United States	4.3%
Trump Proposals and Other Relationships	
Global Multilateral Relations	8.7%
Mexico's Relations with U.S. Border States	1.8%
	99.9%*
N = 391	*due to rounding error

the Trump Administration (10.7%), Trump statements about the border wall (10%), and coverage of immigration-related protests or activism (8.4%), including concerts staged as protests. Although Trump had railed about the wall on the campaign trail, most of the news coverage about this issue appeared in March and April. Global effects of Trump's immigration policies, including multi-lateral relations, were discussed in 8.7% of articles. Opinions voiced by distinguished citizens (such as Mexican priests or governors) along with sentiments of Mexican celebrities such as Salma Hayek accounted for 7.7% of coverage. One interesting theme (4.3%) was the threat to Mexican sovereignty and the effects of Trump's statements and proposed policies on Mexican dignity. Trump's outlandish remarks about Mexican "rapists" and "bad hombres" were frequently quoted. Subtopics on the codesheet that were not the main topics of any articles included U.S. violence against immigrants or lack of jobs in Mexico for Mexicans deported from the United States. Although effecmts of policies on the Deferred Action for Childhood Arrivals (DACA)-qualified Mexican immigrants in the United States was mentioned, it was not a main agenda item in the sampling period, as originally anticipated.

Intermedia Agenda Setting

The second research question asked how the three newspapers' agenda compared and whether there was evidence of intermedia agenda setting among *La Jornada, Reforma*, and *El Universal*. Despite the differences in the editorial approach of the newspapers, for the most part the emphasis placed on topics or subtopics was similar. For instance, among popular topics in the entire sample, discussions of the proposed wall were similarly frequent in the three papers, as were articles about protests and activism.

However, a few subtopics were covered differently by the news organizations. Significant differences by newspaper were found for coverage of Trump's personality or qualifications (X^2 = 8.979, 2df, $p < .05$); statements related to bilateral relations (X^2 = 12.177, 2 df, $p < .05$); and other effects on Mexico (X^2 = 9.163, 2 df, $p < .05$). Regarding Trump himself, *La Jornada* and *Reforma* reported on his personality as a main topic (6% and 2.5% respectively), but no *El Universal* articles focused on his character. One possible reason is that columnists were the primary authors of such pieces (18.6% of Trump personality pieces; X^2 = 45.7, $p < .05$) and there were no *El Universal* columnists named in this sample. In respect to statements about how immigration announcements could impact bilateral relations, this was a main topic in significant numbers of *Reforma* (18%) and *El Universal* articles (10.3%), but in fewer *La Jornada* articles (4.5%). These were statistically significant (X^2 = 12.177, 2 df, $p < .05$). Other effects on Mexico as a main topic included stories such as currency value concerns or effects on art or theatre. *La Jornada* had none of these, but 6.6% of *El Universal* and 3.3% of *Reforma* articles highlighted other effects (X^2 = 9.163, 2 df, $p < .05$).

Some of these differences may have been due to news organization structures (e.g., Shoemaker & Reese, 1996). For instance, all *El Universal*'s Washington-based articles were written by Victor Sancho. Having a reporter regularly assigned to this beat would affect coverage of the White House. On the other hand, although it was not a statistically significant difference, *El Universal* had no stories based in U.S. border states in this sample, although its reporters wrote bylined articles from Mexican border states.

Regardless of these factors, because there were only statistically significant differences by newspaper among three of the 27 subtopics (11%), we can conclude that intermedia agenda setting was dominant (89%) in this sample of coverage.

Second-Level Agenda Setting

Next, we looked at specific characterizations of the topics within the broader sample of articles (n = 1,202). The third research question asked how each Mexican newspaper presented attributes of proposed U.S. immigration policies, focusing on articles about migration or immigration. Within *El Universal*, variations of the terms *migra* (such as migrantes, migratorio) and *inmigra* (inmigración, inmigrante) appeared 941 times. Among 938 cognitive attributes, political terms appeared most frequently (41.8%), followed by social (33.3%), international (17.7%), and economic characteristics (7.2%) (see dictionaries in Methodology section for examples). Negative descriptors were more dominant (59.4%) than positive (22.2%) or neutral (18.4%) words among 517 affective attributes. Following the same order as *El Universal*'s were cognitive attributes in *La Jornada*; comparing 334 migration and immigration terms, attributes related to the political (51.5%), international (21.1%), social (20.6%), and economic (6.8%) descriptors. Among affective attributes, negative characteristics were 52.3%, followed by positive (30.9%) and neutral (16.8%) traits in *La Jornada*, again mirroring patterns in *El Universal*. Finally, in connection with 190 migration/immigration words in *Reforma*, political terms were 56.6%, followed by international (22.4%), social (11.2%), and economic (9.8%) words. Among 38 affective attributes, 63.2% were negative and 36.8% were neutral. No positive attributes about migration or immigration surfaced in *Reforma* coverage. In short, despite the differences in the newspapers' orientations, the qualities associated with proposed White House or other U.S. immigration topics were similar.

The fourth research question addressed how each Mexican news organization presented attributes of the U.S. Mexico border—la frontera. Among 709 unique words with the root *fronter* (fronteriza, frontera, etc.), *El Universal* featured 676 cognitive attributes and 556 affective attributes. Among the cognitive, 52.8% were international, followed by social (22.6%), political (22.2%), and economic (2.4%). Regarding affective, 80.6% were negative, 16.2% neutral, and 3.2% positive. In *La Jornada*, variations on frontera appeared 765 times. Among 878 cognitive attributes, 50.2% were international, 26.3% social, 13.5% political, and 2.6% economic. Seventy-two percent of attributes were negative, 24.3% were neutral, and 3.7% positive. In *Reforma*, 473 unique words were based on *fronter*, with 428 cognitive attributes and 276 affective attributes. International attributes were 44.9%, followed by social (29.9%), political (18.7%), and economic (6.5%). Most affective attributes were negative (83.3%), with 8.4% neutral and 2.3% positive. Once again, reports about the border in the three news organizations revealed similar patterns. In relation to the border, negativity levels were even higher than those associated with immigration.

The last research question investigated the attributes of Donald Trump's proposed border wall. Terms include *muro, barda, barrera*, and *valla* (singular and plural). These surfaced 1,136 times in *El Universal*. Among 1,123 cognitive attributes, international descriptors emerged 39.6%, followed by political (28.8%), social (17.1%), and economic terms 14.5%). Descriptions were largely negative (70.3%), followed by neutral (28.4%) and positive (1.3%). In *La Jornada*, words related to the wall occurred 908 times. Again, international cognitive attributes comprised more than a third of the descriptors (36.6%), followed by social (30.3%), political (19.6%), which differed from *El Universal*'s patterns. However, economic terms (13.5%) surfaced similarly. As in *El Universal*, negative descriptors in *La Jornada* were dominant at 69.7%, with neutral terms occurring 27.3% and positive words revealed 2.9%. Finally, in *Reforma*, wall-related terms were found 757 times. The configurations of wall descriptions in *Reforma* varied slightly from the other newspapers, with international, political, and social cognitive attributes occurring almost equally at 27.6%, 27.1%, and 26.0% respectively. Economic terms were visible 19.2% of the time. However, affective attributes about the wall in *Reforma* resembled coverage in the other newspapers, with 70.2% negative, 27.9% neutral, and 2.0% positive. Similar to associations with the border, the three newspapers characterized the wall in very negative terms. Niche agenda setting was not manifest in second-level agenda setting; an intermedia agenda setting pattern was found among the attribute agenda, just as it was apparent in first-level agenda setting.

Effects of Media Agenda on Public Opinion

What was the potential influence on Mexican public opinion of the January–April coverage? While this was not a cross-lagged correlation study, and Mexico City citizens likely consumed other traditional or social media in addition to the news outlets investigated here, the second-level affective content of the three newspapers aligned with public opinion. A Pew Research Center study found that Mexican attitudes toward the United States dropped precipitously in 2017 (Pew Research, 2017). Sixty-five percent of Mexicans viewed the United States negatively, compared to 29% two years prior. In addition, 93% of Mexicans had no confidence in the U.S. president "to do the right thing" in world affairs, and 94% opposed Trump's idea of a border wall.

Similarly, according to Mexico City polling agency Parametría, 49% of Mexicans had a "bad" or "very bad" opinion of the U.S.—Mexico relationship (Brown, 2017). This contrasts with Parametria's survey in 2015, which found that 49% of Mexicans had a "good" or "very good" view of the relationship. Parametría's survey also found that migration was the most important issue to Mexicans in relation to the U.S., followed by trade (Brown, 2017). Eighty-five percent of Parametría respondents had an unfavorable view of Trump, although they differentiated their views of him from other Americans, whom they perceived favorably. In summary, as it can be assumed most Mexicans do not know Mr. Trump personally, these attitudes were most likely formed via mediated communication portrayals, including the coverage analyzed here.

Discussion

Despite the different histories and editorial approaches of the news organizations, intermedia agenda setting at both the first and second levels was robust. This included cognitive and affective attributes about proposed immigration policies, the border, and the wall.

Although dissimilar political leanings might influence coverage of domestic topics, the newspapers' sources and topics showed equal contempt for Trump's wall and the proposed immigration policies. Notably, Funk and McCombs (2017) observed that local identities can reduce intermedia second-level agenda setting because media coverage may vary depending on local demographic profiles. For instance, they found that in communities with high percentages of Hispanic-owned companies, the local newspapers used different vocabularies when covering immigration topics. Words related to hardship surfaced more often than ambivalence or accomplishment terms that were more prevalent in national media, or in newspapers located in communities with low percentages of Hispanic businesses. In the present study, among Mexican journalists or columnists, Mexican identity vis á vis Yankee identity surfaced when juxtaposed against Trump's statements or actions.

In addition, the dangers of reporting negatively about domestic government or business policies disliked by Mexican citizens did not apply to U.S. policies unfavorable to Mexicans. Thus, self-censorship by Mexican journalists observed in other studies (e.g., Relly & González de Bustamante, 2014) was not necessary with these topics. This also may account for the strong pattern of intermedia agenda setting.

Most articles expressing concern about Mexico's dignity or sovereignty appeared in January, with a few more in February and March and none in April, demonstrating that these trepidations were voiced while the shock of Trump's election win was being digested. According to the coverage, Trump's belittling comments triggered long-held resentments about Yankee imperialism, such as the loss of their Texas, California, Arizona, and New Mexico territories to the United States in 1845–1848, the U.S. invasion of 1914, and other injustices. Relations had been on the mend since NAFTA and the presidencies of Clinton, Bush, and Obama in the U.S. along with Zedillo, Fox, and Calderón in Mexico. Sources quoted in news articles, along with columnists' opinions, expressed anxiety that this progress would be destroyed.

The fear of relationship deterioration was expanded to other spheres of influence, like the entertainment industry and diplomacy with other countries. Two specific examples that surfaced in the second-level agenda setting were about TV host Conan O'Brien and the Prime Minister from Israel, Benjamin Netanyahu. In the first case, news outlets reported heavily on O'Brien's visit to Mexico City to shoot his TV show there, in an attempt to demonstrate that the U.S.-Mexico relationship was strong despite what politicians said. In the second case, Mexican coverage focused on the Israeli Prime Minister's comments praising Trump's idea to build a wall between Mexico and the U.S. Those reports showed that internal policies encouraged by the Trump administration had larger consequences that directly affected Mexico's diplomatic relations.

Of course, with his background in promoting wrestling, beauty contests, and reality television, Trump was savvy about how to get reporters—even in other nations like Mexico—to cover him regularly. His simplistic rhetoric, creating images of a wall in readers' minds rather than explicating a complex immigration proposal, made it easy to include him in the news agenda. His use of inflammatory language, such as "bad hombres," required a response because he effectively embedded the news value of conflict in his remarks and tweets.

Another divergence found in this coverage was the role of columnists as public intellectuals, especially given the elite readership of Mexico City newspapers. Columnists for the newspapers were not limited to writers whose primary profession was journalism. Examples included public intellectual and historian Enrique Krauze, and notable professors and authors such as Sergio Aguayo and Jorge G. Durand. Another columnist was Jorge Carrillo Olea, a retired army general and former governor. It is possible that their views may have held more sway among readers because of societal credibility beyond journalism's spheres.

Interestingly, even though *Reforma* is a newspaper mostly directed at the Mexican business community, their inclusion of economic attributes in their coverage was not larger than that of *El Universal* and *La Jornada*. Instead, *Reforma's* focus was similarly placed on international, political, social, and affective negative elements. This suggests that the threats perceived by Mexican journalists were more closely connected with Trump's rhetorical use of Mexico and Mexicans as a topic to mobilize his political base in the U.S.

Also, the agenda setting effects of the extended coverage of Trump's remarks disparaging Mexico seemed to have had an impact on public opinion. According to the Pew Research (2017) poll cited earlier, 93% of Mexicans have no confidence in Trump and 65% of the population has an unfavorable perception of the U.S.—a change from 29% two years ago. To add contrast, in another poll from *Reforma* (2017) published on January 21st, 2017, a day after Trump's inauguration, 66% of Mexicans felt pessimistic about the Trump presidency. Thus, in just a few months, Mexico's negative perception of Trump has increased, but more importantly for the long-term relationship, the image of the United States has taken a sharp decline. This might be related to the agenda setting effects produced by media coverage.

The limitations of this study were the short time period and small number of media organizations included in the sample. Researchers with access to a wider variety of Mexican media, including television, could provide additional observations.

The main contributions of this study were extending global intermedia agenda setting research (Du, 2013) and adding Mexican newspapers to the small number of agenda setting studies about Latin American media. Most important, the findings provide readers with a perspective on how Trump's nationalist views have the potential to damage the improved bilateral relations between Mexico and the United States that six presidents and countless other government officials, NGOs, and business executives have achieved in the past two decades.

References

Alanis, E. C. G. (2013). Analizando la elección presidencial del 2012 desde la perspectiva de la agenda setting en la prensa de Monterrey [Analyzing the presidential election of 2012 from the perspective of agenda setting in Monterrey press]. *Estudios sobre el Mensaje Periodístico, 19,* 793–801.

Atwell Seat, A., & Mastro, D. (2015). Media's influence on immigration attitudes: An intergroup threat theory approach. *Communication Monographs, 83*(2), 194–213.

Avila, A. J. (2014). Bienvenidos a Miami y mas: Immigration frames in English and Spanish newspapers during the 2012 Florida Republican primary. *#ISOJ Journal, 4*(1), 133–150.

Bennett, W. L., & Iyengar, S. (2008). A new era of minimal effects? The changing foundations of political communication. *Journal of Communication, 58*, 707–731.

Branton, R., & Dunaway, J. (2008). English- and Spanish-language media coverage of immigration: A comparative analysis. *Social Science Quarterly, 89*(4), 1005–1022.

Brown, M. (2017, March 2). Polls measure Americans', Mexicans' views of each other in Trump era. *CNS News*. Retrieved from https://www.cnsnews.com/news/article/mark-browne/polls-measure-americans-mexicans-views-each-other-country-trump-era

Bryant, J., & Miron, D. (2004). Theory and research in mass communication. *Journal of Communication, 54*, 662–704.

Cacciatore, M. A., Scheufele, D. A., & Iyengar, S. (2016). The end of framing as we know it ... and the future of media effects. *Mass Communication and Society, 19*, 7–23.

Cole, R. R. (1996). *Communication in Latin America: Journalism, mass media, and society*. Wilmington, DE: SR Books.

de Beer, A. S., & Merrill, J. C. (Eds.). (2004). *Global journalism: Topical issues and media systems* (4th ed.). Boston, MA: Allyn & Bacon.

De Moya, M., Rendon, H., & Johnson, M. A. (2015, May). *Frame building in immigration news: Ethnic and general market news about the Deferred Action for Childhood Arrivals Program*. Ethnicity and Race Division, International Communication Association, Puerto Rico.

de Zúñiga, H. G., Correa, T., & Valenzuela, S. (2012). Selective exposure to cable news and immigration in the U.S.: The relationship between FOX News, CNN, and attitudes toward Mexican immigrants. *Journal of Broadcasting & Electronic Media, 56*(4), 597–615.

Dekker, R., & Scholten, P. (2017). Framing the immigration policy agenda: A qualitative comparative analysis of media effects on Dutch immigration policies. *The International Journal of Press/Politics, 22*(2), 202–222.

Du, Y. R. (2013). Intermedia agenda-setting in the age of globalization: A multinational agenda-setting test. *Global Media & Communication, 9*(1), 19–36.

Editor & Publisher International Data Book. (2012). Irvine, CA: Duncan McIntosh.

Excelsior. (2017, February 28). Estadunienses ilegales en México aumentan 37.8%. *Excelsior*. Retrieved from http://www.excelsior.com.mx/nacional/2017/02/28/1149157

Freedom House. (2017). *Freedom of the press 2017: Press Freedom's Dark Horizon*. Retrieved from https://freedomhouse.org/report/freedom-press/freedom-press-2017

Fromson, M. (1996). Mexico's struggle for a free press. In R. R. Cole (Ed.), *Communication in Latin America: Journalism, mass media, and society* (pp. 115–138). Wilmington, DE: SR Books.

Fryberg, S. A., Stephens, N. M., Covarrubias, R., Markus, H. R., Carter, E. D., Laiduc, G. A., & Salido, A. J. (2012). How the media frames the immigration debate: The critical role of location and politics. *Analyses of Social Issues and Public Policy, 12*(1), 96–112.

Fujioka, Y. (2011). Perceived threats and Latino immigrant attitudes: How White and African American college students respond to news coverage of Latino immigrants. *The Howard Journal of Communications, 22*(1), 43–63.

Funk, M. J., & McCombs, M. (2017). Strangers on a theoretical train: Inter-media agenda setting, community structure, and local news coverage. *Journalism Studies, 18*(7), 845–865.

Golan, G., & Wanta, W. (2001). Second-level agenda setting in the New Hampshire primary: A comparison of coverage in three newspapers and public perceptions of candidates. *Journalism & Mass Communication Quarterly, 78*(2), 247–259.

Gonzalez-Barrera, A., & Krogstad, J. M. (2017, March 2). *What we know about illegal immigration from Mexico.* Pew Research Center. Retrieved from http://www.pewresearch.org/fact-tank/2017/03/02/what-we-know-about-illegal-immigration-from-mexico/

Hachten, W. A., & Scotton, J. F. (2016). *The world news prism: Digital, social and interactive* (9th ed.). Malden, MA: Wiley Blackwell.

Hollander, B. A. (2008). Tuning in or tuning elsewhere? Partisanship, polarization, and media migration from 1998 to 2006. *Journalism & Mass Communication Quarterly, 85*(1), 23–40.

Hughes, S. (2003). From the inside out: How institutional entrepreneurs transformed Mexican journalism. *The International Journal of Press/Politics, 8*(3), 87–117.

Hyun, K. D., & Moon, S. J. (2016). Agenda setting in the partisan TV news context: Attribute agenda setting and polarized evaluation of presidential candidates among viewers of NBC, CNN, and Fox News. *Journalism & Mass Communication Quarterly, 93*(3), 509–529.

Kim, K., & McCombs, M. (2007). News story descriptions and the public's opinions of political candidates. *Journalism & Mass Communication Quarterly, 84*(2), 299–314.

Kim, S.-H., Carvalho, J. P, Davis, A. G., & Mullins, A. M. (2011). The view of the border: News framing of the definition, causes, and solutions to illegal immigration. *Mass Communication and Society, 14*(3), 292–314.

Kim, S.-H., Scheufele, D., & Shanahan, J. (2002). Think about it this way: Attribute agenda-setting function of the press and the public's evaluation of a local issue. *Journalism and Mass Communication Quarterly, 79*(1), 1–25.

Knoll, B. R., Redlawsk, D. P., & Sanborn, H. (2011). Framing labels and immigration policy attitudes in the Iowa caucuses: "Trying to Out-Tancredo Tancredo." *Political Behavior, 33*(3), 433–454.

Lang, A. (2013). Discipline in crisis? The shifting paradigm of mass communication research. *Communication Theory, 23*, 10–24.

Lee, N. J., McLeod, D. M., & Shah, D. V. (2008). Framing policy debates issue dualism, journalistic frames, and opinions on controversial policy issues. *Communication Research, 35*(5), 695–718.

Malkin, E. (2017, April 25). *Edited by Drug Lords: Mexican journalists navigate threats and censorship by cartels.* Committee to Protect Journalists. Retrieved from https://cpj.org/2017/04/edited-by-drug-lords.php

McCombs, M. (2004). *Setting the agenda: The mass media and public opinion.* Cambridge: Polity.

McCombs, M., Llamas, J. P., Lopez-Escobar, E., & Rey, F. (1997). Candidate images in Spanish elections: Second-level agenda-setting effects. *Journalism & Mass Communication Quarterly, 74*(4), 703–717.

McCombs, M., & Shaw, D. L. (1972). Agenda-setting function of mass media. *Public Opinion Quarterly, 36*(2), 176–187.

McCombs, M. E., Shaw, D. L., & Weaver, D. H. (2014). New directions in agenda-setting theory and research. *Mass Communication & Society, 17*, 781–802.

McDonnell, P. J. (2016, October 30). How Mexico combines Halloween and Day of the Dead into one surreal celebration. *Los Angeles Times.* Retrieved from http://www.latimes.com/world/mexico-americas/la-fg-mexico-halloween-snap-story.html

Mellado, C., & Humanes, M. L. (2017). Homogeneity and plurality of the media agenda in Chile. A crosslongitudinal study of the national print press between 1990 and 2015. *Communication & Society, 30*(3), 41–60.

Merolla, J., Ramakrishnan, S. K., & Haynes, C. (2013). 'Illegal,' 'undocumented,' or 'unauthorized': Equivalency frames, issue frames, and public opinion on immigration. *Perspectives on Politics, 11*(3), 789–807.

Mexican Internet Association. (2017, August). *Estudio sobre los Hábitos de los Usuarios de Internet en México 2017.* Retrieved from https://www.asociaciondeinternet.mx/es/estudios

Mont' Alverne, C., & Marques, F. P. J. (2016). The agenda of the day: A study about the Brazilian Congress in editorials of *Folha de S. Paulo* and *O Estado de S. Paulo. Brazilian Journalism Research, 12*(2), 112–137.

Montgomery, L. F. (1984). Stress on government and press criticism of government leaders: Mexico 1951–1980. *Gazette, 34*(3), 163–174.

National Institute of Statistics and Geography, Mexico. (2015). Retrieved from http://en.www.inegi.org.mx/

Newman, N. (2017). *Digital news report 2017.* Reuters Institute for the Study of Journalism. Retrieved from http://www.digitalnewsreport.org/survey/2017/analysis-by-country-2017/

Office of the United States Trade Representative. (2017). *U.S.-Mexico trade facts.* Retrieved from https://ustr.gov/countries-regions/americas/mexico

Perloff, R. M. (2015). Mass communication research at the crossroads: Definitional issues and theoretical directions for mass and political communication scholarship in the age of online media. *Mass Communication and Society, 18*, 531–556.

Pew Research Center. (2017, September 14). Mexican views of the U.S. turn sharply negative. Retrieved from http://assets.pewresearch.org/wp-content/uploads/sites/2/2017/09/13094516/Pew-Research-Center_09.14.17_Mexico-Report.pdf

Pingree, R. J., & Stoycheff, E. (2013). Differentiating cueing from reasoning in agenda-setting effects. *Journal of Communication, 63*, 852–872.

Quinsaat, S. (2014). Competing news frames and hegemonic discourses in the construction of contemporary immigration and immigrants in the United States. *Mass Communication & Society, 17*(4), 573–596.

Reforma (2017, January 21). *Reinan pesimismo y desconfianza.* Retrieved from http://gruporeforma-blogs.com/encuestas/?p=7024

Relly, J. E., & González de Bustamante, C. (2014). Silencing Mexico: A study of influences on journalists in the Northern States. *The International Journal of Press/Politics, 19*(1), 108–131.

Rosales, D. C., Rodríguez, N. R., Cárcamo-Ulloa, L., & Montecinos, F. N. (2017). México, en la prensa chilena: análisis basado en minería de datos textuales en Twitter. *Revista Latina de Comunicación Social.* Retrieved from http://www.revistalatinacs.org/072paper/1199/49en.html

Schroeder, J. (2017, September 8). Mexicans: New climate, old habits. *World Press Online.* Retrieved from http://www.worldpress.org/specials/press/mexico.htm

Shoemaker, P. J., & Reese, S. D. (1996). *Mediating the message: Theories of influences on mass media content.* New York, NY: Longman.

Stein, E. A., & Kellam, M. (2014). Programming presidential agendas: Partisan and media environments that lead presidents to fight crime and corruption. *Political Communication, 31,* 25–52.

Stevenson, R. L. (2004). Freedom of the press around the world. In A. S. de Beer & J. C. Merrill (Eds.), *Global journalism: Topical issues and media systems* (4th ed., pp. 66–83). Boston, MA: Allyn & Bacon.

Stroud, N. J. (2011). *Niche news: The politics of news choice.* New York, NY: Oxford University.

Sweetzer, K. D., Golan, G. J., & Wanta, W. (2008). Intermedia agenda setting in television, advertising, and blogs during the 2004 election. *Mass Communication and Society, 11*(2), 197–216.

Takeshita, T. (2005). Current critical problems in agenda-setting research. *International Journal of Public Opinion Research, 18,* 275–296.

Tan, Y., & Weaver, D. H. (2013). Agenda diversity and agenda setting from 1956 to 2004. What are the trends over time? *Journalism Studies, 14*(6), 773–789.

U.S. Department of State. (2017, January 25). *U.S. Relations with Mexico.* Retrieved from https://www.state.gov/r/pa/ei/bgn/35749.htm

Villanueva, O. M. M., & Ortiz, Á. I. (2015). Agenda-setting'de medios en la guerra contra las drogas [Media agenda-setting on War on Drugs]. *Estudios sobre el Mensaje Periodístico, 21*(1), 403–420.

Waisbord, S. (2002). Antipress violence and the crisis of the state. *Harvard International Journal of Press/Politics, 7,* 90–109.

Wanta, W., Golan, G., & Lee, C. (2004). Agenda setting and international news: Media influence on public perceptions of foreign nations. *Journalism & Mass Communication Quarterly, 81*(2), 364–377.

Watson, B. R., & Riffe, D. (2013). Perceived threat, immigration policy support, and media coverage: Hostile media and presumed influence. *International Journal of Public Opinion Research, 25*(4), 459–478.

10. A "Political Novice" vs. the "Queen of War": How State-Sponsored Media Framed the 2016 U.S. Presidential Campaign

Nataliya Roman and John H. Parmelee
University of North Florida

U.S. presidential elections are arguably some of the most followed events in the world. Each four years, party conventions, presidential debates and other aspects of election campaigning result in extensive media coverage in the U.S. and abroad. Such overseas interest can be explained by the "outsized impact of U.S. economic, political and cultural strengths" (Kluver, n.d., para. 1). The U.S. is a major military power with the largest economy in the world (Gray, 2017; Haynie, 2017). The outcome of presidential elections can "affect the security and economic prosperity of other nations" (Haynie, 2017, para. 2).

At the same time, the way media frame U.S. presidential elections can affect how people see the U.S. and its values around the world (Kluver, n.d.). According to Entman (1993), "to frame is to select some aspects of a per- ceived reality and make them more salient in a communicating text, in such a way as to promote a particular problem definition, causal interpretation, moral evaluation, and/or treatment recommendation for the item described" (p. 52).

Framing analysis is especially interesting in the context of international broadcasters. These media organizations are public diplomacy efforts of their governments and are funded by their respective states. The goal of these international broadcasters is to provide information for overseas audiences and to share their interpretations of the events.

This study will look at the 2016 presidential candidates' portrayals in international news media organizations: Voice of America (U.S.) and Sputnik (Russia). Both of these media outlets have English-language websites and a vast network of reporters around the globe. While Voice of America (VOA) promises "accuracy, balance, comprehensiveness and objectivity" in its news coverage ("Mission and Values," n.d., para. 6), Sputnik just provides a generic statement about covering "global political and economic news" for international audience ("About Us," n.d., para. 3). Interestingly, earlier Sputnik described itself as "a provider of alternative news content," which "tells the untold" (Osipova, 2016, p. 349), however, this mission statement recently disappeared from its website.

Given the political, cultural and media differences between the U.S. and Russia, it is important to explore the differences in how VOA and Sputnik framed the 2016 U.S. presidential candidates. This chapter looks at the tone of coverage of the main presidential candidates. It assesses the volume of coverage of each candidate and examines the policies that were mentioned in relation to each of the candidates.

Framing Coverage of Candidates

Framing theory is a useful lens through which to examine how broadcasters from different countries and political perspectives portray candidates for elective office. This is especially true because there are few cross-national framing studies of election coverage (Strömbäck & van Aelst, 2010). Framing theory suggests that journalists and others create dominant story lines, or frames, which connect various types of visual and verbal information into an efficient package for audiences to interpret (Gamson & Modigliani, 1987; Gitlin, 1980). The framing of political candidates by journalists is important to study because, as Tankard (2001) notes, "the power of framing comes from its ability to define the terms of a debate without the audience realizing it is taking place" (p. 97). Frames can be seen as independent variables that can "influence the audience's perception of certain issues" (Scheufele, 1999, p. 108). So the manner in which broadcasters frame candidates can influence viewers' opinions about candidates. Because there are many frames that news outlets can use when covering candidates, the specific framing decisions made by news outlets can illustrate their perceptions of, and bias toward, the candidates involved.

Frames exist in four locations of the communication process: within the writer of a message, within the message, within the receiver, and within the culture (Entman, 1993). The present study is focused on the interaction between the first and second locations. In this case, the writers of the messages belong to organizations that are connected to the governments of the United States and Russia, which often have opposing policy agendas. The messages are the news stories that are published by the organizations. Framing theory suggests that the worldview, or cognitive frame, of a news organization's sponsoring government will influence how candidates are framed and what issues are emphasized in stories on the news sites.

Past research confirms that the cognitive frames that journalists and their news outlets have about politics tend to shape the messages in their stories. For example, an analysis of how newsmagazines with different political perspectives covered Ronald Reagan's presidency found that the magazines chose those frames that fit their already established perceptions, or cognitive frame, of Reagan and his party and ignored frames that clashed with their perceptions (Parmelee, 2006). News outlets' established ideological perceptions are not the only influence on how politics is framed. It also matters whether the media outlet is a commercial venture or is government funded as a public service. Strömbäck and van Aelst (2010) found that commercial TV news was more likely than public service broadcasters to frame elections as a game, as opposed to framing in terms of serious issues.

Regarding the second framing location in the communication process, the message, it is important to note that the emphasis on certain issues in news stories can trigger within viewers positive or negative feelings about candidates because of a process called priming. During the priming process, an individual's perceptions and memories about an issue are activated when the issue is discussed in news coverage (Richardson, 2002). So coverage that emphasizes issues that trigger negative memories can have harmful effects on those candidates associated with those issues, and persistent coverage of issues with positive perceptions can have the opposite effect.

The framing of messages in news stories can be examined in several ways. Messages can be analyzed by topic, presentation, cognitive attributes, and affective attributes (Ghanem, 1997). The present study examines the messages in news coverage in terms of topics, such as issues, and affective attributes, such as tone. Many framing studies have used content analysis to investigate the tone of messages. Research into framing during elections in various countries has measured the degree to which a positive, negative, or neutral in tone was used (Bichard, 2006; McCombs, Llamas, Lopez-Escobar, & Rey, 1997). Differences have been observed in the tone of news in countries that cover the same issues. For example, online news coverage of the U.S. invasion of Iraq was more positive in countries that officially supported the war than in countries opposing the war (Dimitrova, Kaid, Williams, &

Trammell, 2005). This finding suggests in the present study that the political views of the news organization's sponsoring government will be associated with how candidates are framed.

Analyzing what issues are contained in messages can also be useful in framing research. Looking at which issues are emphasized or ignored is consistent with Entman's (1993) assertion that "framing essentially involves selection and salience" (p. 52). Furthermore, revealing the issues that are most discussed in political coverage can indicate possible priming effects on viewers. Chong and Druckman (2007) provide an example of the priming effects on politicians when news coverage makes some issues the most salient:

> For example, individuals exposed to news stories about defense policy tend to base their overall approval of the president (or some other political candidate) on their assessment of the president's performance on defense. Thus, if these individuals believe the president does an excellent (or poor) job on defense, they will display high (or low) levels of overall approval. If, in contrast, these individuals watch stories about energy policy, their overall evaluations of the president's performance will tend to be based on his handling of energy policy. (pp. 114–115)

In terms of the present study, heavy news coverage of Trump related to, say, immigration should prime viewers' memories and perceptions of that issue, which will lead to a more positive or negative evaluation of Trump based on viewers' perceptions.

Media Coverage of Elections

Researchers have looked at different aspects of U.S. election media coverage. One way to do it is to examine the volume of media coverage about each candidate. Prior to 1998, male candidates dominated election coverage, however, it changed quickly in the following years (Atkeson & Krebs, 2008; Bystrom, Banwart, Kaid, & Robertson, 2004; Bystrom, Robertson, & Banwart, 2001; Kahn, 1994; Kahn & Goldenberg, 1991). Devitt (2002) and Atkeson and Krebs (2008) examined media coverage of gubernatorial and mayoral candidates. They found no evidence of gender bias in the volume of media coverage of female and male candidates (Atkeson & Krebs, 2008; Devitt, 2002).

Another way to examine election media coverage is to assess the tone of candidates' mentions. Rosenson (2015) looked at how newspapers covered state legislators. The researcher found that more than 80% of stories had a neutral tone and there was "no difference in tone when the newspaper's owners share the same partisan orientation as the state legislature compared to when they have different partisan orientation" (Rosenson, 2015, p. 1291). Benoit, Furgerson, Seifert, and Sargardia (2013) found more negative than positive stories in the coverage of Senate races, while the opposite was true for gubernatorial and mayoral races. Bystrom et al. (2004) revealed that while the tonality of female and male candidates coverage did not differ in 1998 and 2002 races, this was not the case for 2000 races. Female candidates received significantly more positive and less negative coverage than male candidates (Bystrom et al., 2004).

Benoit et al. (2013) looked at the focus of media coverage. They found that media were more likely to pay attention to the horse race aspect of the Senate and gubernatorial campaigns, while the discussions of candidates' character and issue positions were less prevalent (Benoit et al., 2013). Contrary, Dunaway, Lawrence, Rose, and Weber (2013) revealed that issues-oriented stories made up a larger share of media coverage than horse-race and character-oriented stories. They also discovered that races with female contenders had significantly more trait-oriented stories than races with male-only contenders (Dunaway et al., 2013).

Similarly, earlier research indicated that media were more likely to focus on personal characteristics of female candidates, while the coverage of male candidates was more focused on policy issues (Devitt, 2002). Female candidates' coverage had more mentions of their appearance, gender and marital status (Bystrom et al., 2004). However, Holt (2012) did not find any significant differences in the number of mentions about the appearance of Barack Obama and Hillary Clinton during the 2008 Presidential elections.

Finally, female candidates appeared more often in media coverage about "health care," "senior citizens issues," "women's issues" as well as "international affairs" (Bystrom et al., 2004, p. 181). Male candidates were more often mentioned during the discussions of "taxes, crime, dissatisfaction with government, and defense" (Bystrom et al., 2004, p. 181).

International Broadcasters and Public Diplomacy

The two organizations examined in this study are VOA and Sputnik. Both of them are public diplomacy endeavors of their respective governments. Public diplomacy "is a new subfield of global communication" with roots in the "Cold-War ideological struggle of the 20th century between the United States and the USSR" (McPhail, 2010, p. 87). According to Entman (2008), the goals of mediated public diplomacy are to advance government's foreign policies abroad via mass communication channels. International broadcasting serves as one of such conduits.

VOA is the U.S. international broadcaster with multimedia platforms available in more than 40 languages and an international audience of nearly 237 million ("VOA History," n.d.). The service was launched in 1942 to battle Nazi propaganda ("VOA History," n.d.). Even though VOA receives funding from the U.S. Congress, the U.S. government has limited ability to influence its media content (Golan & Himelboim, 2015). According to Freedom House (2017a, 2017b), generally, the U.S. enjoys a free press, while Russian media are not free.

Sputnik is a relatively new Russian multiplatform news agency that aims to reach global audiences. The media organization was launched in 2014. It presents information in more than 30 languages (About us, n.d.). According to the U.S. intelligence community report (National Intelligence Council, 2017), Sputnik is a part of "Russia's state-run propaganda machine" that aimed to influence the outcome of the 2016 U.S. presidential election (p. 3). The report concluded that, "Russia's goals were to undermine public faith in the US democratic process, denigrate Secretary Clinton, and harm her electability and potential presidency (National Intelligence Council, 2017, p. ii)."The investigation revealed that "state-owned Russian media made increasingly favorable comments about President-elect Trump as the 2016 US general and primary election campaigns progressed while consistently offering negative coverage of Secretary Clinton" (National Intelligence Council, 2017, p. 3).

Little is known about how VOA covered the U.S. 2016 Presidential election, and this study will try to fill this gap. Given VOA's mission and U.S. journalistic norms and traditions, we expect to see relatively neutral coverage of both candidates. Meanwhile, given Sputnik's role in the 2016 U.S. elections and U.S. intelligent findings, we expect to see more biased coverage of the candidates, especially Hillary Clinton. Thus, this study will examine the following research questions:

RQ1. What differences exist in the volume of coverage of Donald Trump and Hillary Clinton on the websites of VOA and Sputnik?

RQ2. What are the differences in the tone of coverage of the main presidential candidates?

RQ3. What are the differences in the types of policies discussed by the two presidential candidates?

Method

This study employed quantitative content analysis and a qualitative frame analysis. It looked at how the VOA and Sputnik websites portrayed the two

U.S. presidential candidates: Donald Trump and Hillary Clinton. Sputnik was chosen for this study because the website has archives with access to past election coverage. Meanwhile RT, a better-known Russian international broadcaster, allows access to only a limited number of articles.

Content Analysis

Sampling

The timeframe of the study included the general election campaign: September 5 (Labor Day)–November 8 (Election Day), 2016. The researchers used a two-step process to retrieve the articles about the candidates. First, they searched the websites using the keywords "US elections." After they retrieved all articles that contained these keywords, they checked whether these articles contained mentions of Donald Trump and Hillary Clinton. Articles that mentioned the candidates in the headline were automatically included. The content of other articles was searched using two keywords: "Clinton," and "Trump." Only articles that mentioned at least one of the candidates were selected for this study.

The search identified 933 Sputnik articles and 415 VOA articles that mentioned at least one of the candidates. A decision was made to code each 5th Sputnik article. As a result, 186 Sputnik articles were selected for the analysis. If the article was no longer available, the researchers replaced it with the next one in order from the original sample. Also, the researchers coded each 2nd VOA article. As a result, 207 VOA articles were included in the sample.

Coding Procedures

This study examined the tone of the coverage (whether the candidates were portrayed in positive, negative or neutral light). The researchers only looked at textual elements of the articles. Building upon Rosenson's (2015) research, this paper defined negative stories as those that showcased candidates as "incompetent, unethical, pursuing undesirable policies, or causing bad outcomes" (p. 1294). Also, stories, where other parties criticized candidates, including their opponents, depicted them in "unflattering light," or talked about candidates losing in election polls, were coded as negative (Rosenson, 2015, p. 1294). Positive stories included mentions about candidates "doing good job," winning in polls, "solving problems, making things better, working to address constituent concerns, or being worthy of praise for any reason" (Rosenson, 2015, p. 1294). Also, endorsements of candidates and statements about intention to vote or voting for candidates were coded as positive. Stories were coded as neutral if they were neither positive nor negative or included both positive and negative mentions about the candidates.

Also, this study quantified the number of Trump and Clinton mentions in each article using the Microsoft Word search function. In addition, this paper examined the issues that were mentioned in relation to each candidate. Previous research outlined a number of such issues: "foreign relations," "economy," "defense," "energy," "education," "healthcare," "welfare/poverty," and "civil rights" (Bystrom et al., 2004; Luo, 2009, p. 9). This study included two additional issues: "immigration" and "climate" giving the prominence of these topics in 2016 election campaign. The researchers searched the following keywords in each article using the Microsoft Word search function: foreign, international, "diplom" (for foreign policy), tax, business, job, "econom," trade (for economy), defense, terror', military (for defense), energy, oil, gas, coal, solar, renewable (for energy), education, school, university, college (for education), Obamacare, healthcare, med' (for healthcare), welfare, poverty (for welfare/poverty), civil rights, social justice (for civil rights/social justice), immigr' (for immigration), and climate (for climate).

Two researchers coded the content. Ten percent of the articles were chosen randomly to assess intercoder reliability. Krippendorff's Apha statistics was calculated for each variable. The researchers reached a 0.87 coefficient for Trump's tone, 0.89 for Clinton's tone, 0.98 for Trump's mentions, and 0.999 for Clinton's mentions. Krippendorff's Apha statistics for the issue variables ranged from 0.66 to 1 and in one instance equaled to "0". It is worth noting, that the researchers reached 95% or more percentage agreement for each category. However, because mentions of issues were relatively rare, even one disagreement in 40 coded articles could have brought the Krippendorrff's Alpha statistics to 0 as it happened in the case of the "healthcare" issue for Trump.

Frame Analysis

While a manifest content analysis can measure the degree to which certain types of tones or issues are present, a qualitative frame analysis is helpful at adding context and clarification to the tones and issues found. Several steps were taken in the frame analysis. As the articles were viewed, notes were taken guided by Entman's (1993) conception that frames can be found by looking for "keywords, stock phrases, stereotyped images, sources of information, and sentences that provide thematically reinforcing clusters of facts or judgments" (p. 52). Close attention was paid to how the words and phrases created a portrait of the candidates. The themes that were discovered emerged from the data.

Results

Content Analysis

RQ1 examined the number of Trump and Clinton mentions on the VOA and Sputnik websites. The analysis revealed that Clinton was mentioned more often in Sputnik coverage than Trump. While Clinton's name appeared 933 times in the articles, Trump was only mentioned 784 times. However, the independent-samples test did not reveal any statistically significant differences between the coverage of the two candidates ($t(370) = -1.43, p > 0.05$). The mean score of the Clinton' mentions ($m = 5.02, sd = 5.86$) was not significantly different from the mean score of the Trump's mentions ($m= 4.22, sd = 4.89$).

Another interesting finding (see Table 10.2) is that Clinton appeared in 11% more Sputnik stories than Trump. Nearly 22% of stories did not mention Trump, while only 11% did not mention Clinton.

At the same time, VOA devoted more attention to Trump than to Clinton (see Table 10.1). Trump appeared in 1,984, while Clinton in 1,485 stories (see Table 10.1). An independent t test confirmed that these differences were statistically significant ($t(412) = 2.22, p < 0.05$). Trump was mentioned more often ($m = 9.59, sd= 12.85$) than Clinton ($m=7.17, sd = 8.83$) in VOA coverage.

Unlike Sputnik, VOA featured Trump in 6% more stories than Clinton (see Table 10.2). More than 5% of stories did not mention Trump and nearly 11% of stories did not mention Clinton.

Table 10.1: Number of the Candidates' Mentions in Sputnik and VOA.

Medium/Number of Mentions	Trump	Clinton
Sputnik	784	933
VOA	1984*	1485

*Significant at p < 0.05

Table 10.2: The Tone of Trump and Clinton Coverage in Sputnik and VOA Articles.

	Trump Tone (Sputnik)	Clinton Tone (Sputnik)	Trump Tone (VOA)	Clinton Tone (VOA)
Neutral (0)	56% (105)	46% (85)	57% (117)	56% (115)
Negative (1)	17% (31)	33% (61)	29% (61)	14% (29)
Positive (2)	5% (9)	10% (19)	9% (18)	20% (41)
Not mentioned in the article	22% (41)	11% (21)	5% (11)	11% (22)
Total	N = 186	N = 186	N=207	N=207

RQ2 examined the tone of Trump and Clinton coverage on the websites (see Table 10.2). The analysis showed that about half of Sputnik stories about Trump and Clinton were neutral. In this study, we coded stories neutral when the tone of the articles was neutral in relation to the candidates, or when the stories contained positive and negative mentions about the candidates. Interestingly, there were nearly two times more negative stories about Clinton (33%) than about Trump (17%) in Sputnik coverage. Similarly, there were more positive stories about Clinton (10%) than about Trump (5%). Please note that mentions about the candidates winning in the polls made up a large share of these positive stories.

A chi-square test of independence was conducted to compare the tone of coverage of the two candidates in Sputnik coverage. A statistically significant relationship was found (χ^2 (3) = 21.91, p < 0.001, N = 372). The results remained statistically significant even when articles that only mentioned one candidate were removed from the study (χ^2 (2) = 14.23, p < 0.05, N = 310).

Neutral stories about Trump and Clinton also constituted more than a half of VOA coverage. Contrary to Sputnik, VOA featured almost twice as many negative stories about Trump (29%) than about Clinton (14%). Also, there were twice as many positive stories about Clinton (20%) than about Trump (9%). A chi-square test of independence revealed statistically significant differences in the tone of coverage of the two candidates (χ^2 (3) = 24.03, p < 0.001, N = 414). The results remained statistically significant even when the researchers removed the articles that only mentioned one candidate (χ^2 (2) = 20.06, p < 0.001, N = 381).

RQ3 looked at the types of policies discussed by the two candidates. Foreign relations, defense and economy were the most discussed policies by the two candidates in Sputnik coverage. Each of these topics appeared in nearly 9–13% of the articles about each candidate. Table 10.3 shows that Clinton was slightly more likely to discuss foreign relations and defense than Trump. At the same time, Trump was featured more often in articles that mentioned the economy, immigration, welfare/poverty, and climate. However, this study did not find any statistically significant differences in the types of policies discussed by the candidates.

The analysis of VOA coverage showed a slightly different picture. Chi-square test of independence (χ^2 (1) = 6.21, p < 0.05, N = 414) revealed that Trump (23%) talked significantly more often about economy than Clinton (14%). Similarly, a significant difference (χ^2 (1) = 12.56, p < 0.001, N = 414) was found between the number of Trump's (17%) and Clinton's (5%) mentions of the immigration issues. Also, Trump (8%) mentioned foreign policy issues more often than Clinton (4%). However, these differences were not statistically significant.

Table 10.3: Policies Discussed by Clinton and Trump in Sputnik and VOA Coverage.

Issue	Trump (Sputnik)	Clinton (Sputnik)	Trump (VOA)	Clinton (VOA)
Foreign relations	10.34% (15)	13.33% (22)	8% (15)	4% (7)
Economy	11.72% (17)	9.09% (15)	23% (45)*	14% (25)
Defense/military/terror	9.66% (14)	10.91% (18)	9% (17)	7% (13)
Energy	2.76% (4)	3.03% (5)	2% (3)	3% (5)
Education	0	0	2% (3)	1% (2)
Healthcare	0.69% (1)	0.61% (1)	3% (5)	3% (5)
Welfare/poverty	2.07% (3)	0.61% (1)	1% (1)	2% (4)
Civil rights	0.69% (1)	0	0	0
Immigration	4.83% (7)	1.21% (2)	17% (33)**	5% (10)
Climate	3.45% (5)	1.82% (3)	1% (2)	1% (1)
Total articles about a candidate	N = 145	N = 165	N = 196	N = 185

*Significant at p <0.05.
**Significant at p <0.001.

Frame Analysis

Qualitative analysis provided a more nuanced understanding of the candidates' portrayals. While both news organizations mentioned high unfavorable ratings of the two main presidential candidates, they differed significantly in how they portrayed Trump and Clinton.

Sputnik's Coverage: The "Populist" vs. the "Queen of War"

Trump always seemed to look as the "lesser of two evils"[1] in the Sputnik coverage. However, he did not always appear in a favorable light. Sputnik reported on Trump's lack of "expertise in foreign policy" and "consistent strategy," citing German Die Welt.[2] Another article quoted former chief of the U.S. National Foreign Trade Council William Reinsch, who called Trump an "unpredictable and relatively uninformed candidate."[3] Meanwhile, another Sputnik article called Trump's views "populist."[4]

Sputnik repeatedly mentioned Trump's comments about normalizing relations with Russia and reiterated expectations that Trump would likely "partially lift the [American] sanctions [against Russia]."[5] Interestingly, one of the articles also hinted that Trump might be a better candidate for the global community as he "does not seek a military confrontation with China,"[6] and is "less inclined to go to war."[7] The former quote belongs to the chief of staff of the Chinese Americans for Trump Mark Ma, while the latter to the former U.S. Congressman Dennis Kucinich.

Numerous articles and opinion pieces also denied the fact of the Russian interferences in the U.S. elections, including claims that Russia was "behind the Wikileaks' releases."[8] Moreover, the articles repeatedly refuted the links between the Trump's campaign and Russian officials.

Sputnik also brought up Trump's controversial statements on women and minorities, including the "'hot mic' tape," where Trump "lewdly boast[ed] about sexually assaulting women."[9] Other articles mentioned Trump's support among working-class people and even proclaimed that the billionaire was leading "a peasants' revolution to the White House."[10]

At the same time, Clinton was depicted as "more prepared," "robotic,"[11] and with "character and judgment [...] superior to Trump's."[12] The first two characteristics came from the mayor of Warren, Mich., Jim Fouts, and the third was brought up in an article about Pennsylvania poll results. In other articles, Clinton was also called "two-faced,"[13] a "liar,"[14] and "war hawk."[15] The second quote belongs to a Russian economist Vasily Koltashov, while the last to geopolitical analyst Steven MacMillan.

A large number of stories hinted that Clinton's victory would lead to war. Citing Green Party Presidential nominee Jill Stein and unnamed experts, Sputnik reported that there would be either "a thermonuclear war with Russia,"[16] or war with Russia and China.[17] The last statement belongs to constitutional lawyer Bruce Fein.

Sputnik opinion pieces and news articles portrayed the Democratic nominee as the "Queen of War,"[18] "the candidate of an endless war,"[19] and alluded that "she's looking forward to being a war president on day one."[20] The second quote came from former U.S. diplomat James George Jatras and last from a senior fellow at the Center for Preventive Action at the Council on Foreign Relations Micah Zenko.

Clinton was also criticized for her use of a private email server and her tenure as the Secretary of State. Sputnik reported that the Clinton's private server "had been penetrated by at least five foreign intelligence services."[21] Citing Wikileaks emails, the website claimed the Clinton campaign "disclos[ed] decisions in the Clinton State Department that favored large donors to the Clinton Foundation in what appear to be 'pay-for-play' schemes of selling access and influence."[22] Another story claimed that, "money of the Clinton Foundation was allegedly used to finance wedding of Clinton's daughter Chelsea."[23]

One story stood out in particular. It quoted "Dave Schippers, who served as the Chief Investigative Counsel for the House Judiciary Committee's probe into Bill Clinton's possible impeachment." The article brought up unfounded allegations that "a number of people linked to the Clintons 'disappeared,' citing the example of Deputy White House Counsel Vince Foster eventually found dead, killed by a gunshot."[24] The story further quoted Schippers, who suggested that, "Vince Foster was probably as close to Hillary as anybody on the face of the Earth. ... He knew all about the money she made, the $100,000 she made overnight in the commodities market. He knew everything. ... In my opinion, he was a weak link in the chain of evidence."

Finally, a number of stories questioned Clinton's ability to lead the country given the health issues she experienced during the campaign. The articles and opinion pieces hinted that Clinton might be "suffering a neurological condition,"[25] had an "attack of Parkinson's."[26] Also, one article quoted *News Junkie Post* editor Gilbert Mercier, who suggested that "as long as she [Clinton] can stand up and read a teleprompter without drooling all over her face, even if her health deteriorates further, she will remain president on paper while the first husband, Bill Clinton, actually runs the White House."[27] While no articles questioned Trump's health, one brought up speculations about Donald Trump "being a coke head."[28]

VOA's Coverage: A "Political Novice" vs. "Strong, Steady, and Tested"

VOA portrayed Clinton as experienced, "strong, steady and tested"[29] politician, who "never buckles under pressure,"[30] and is "smarter and funnier than former President Bill Clinton."[31] The latter quotes came from former President Barack Obama, First Lady Michelle Obama and Ron Fournier, a political journalist who reported on the Clintons in Arkansas and later in Washington, D.C. VOA often featured former president Obama campaigning for Clinton and urging voters "to uphold his presidential policies on numerous fronts, most of which Clinton has vowed to continue."[32]

A large share of negative mentions about Clinton focused on her private email server controversy and to a lesser extent on Wikileaks' Clinton Foundation revelations. VOA brought up Trump's remarks about Clinton "lack[ing] honesty and trustworthiness,"[33] her being "corrupt life-long politician,"[34] and cited Trump's allegations that Clinton's presidency could create an "unprecedented and protracted constitutional crisis,"[35] which would end in impeachment "over her emails and questions about the Clinton Foundation charity."[36] Unlike Sputnik, VOA often balanced these accusations with a statement about the results of the FBI investigation, which concluded, "in July [2016] that Clinton was 'extremely careless' in her use of a private email server, but her actions showed no criminal intent."[37] On another occasion, a post-debate fact-checking article explained that "it doesn't violate campaign rules for a nonprofit philanthropy to accept donations from foreign governments."[38]

The issue of Clinton's health was not a prominent topic in VOA. The website reported on Clinton's illness and even featured Trump's questioning of "whether Clinton has the stamina to serve as commander in chief."[39] However, VOA did not sensationalize this issue.

A large share of Trump's coverage mainly focused on his inflammatory rhetoric about immigrants, minorities and women as well as his character flaws. In one article, VOA described the candidate as a "celebrity businessman and political novice who capitalized on voters' economic anxieties, took advantage of racial tensions and overcame a string of sexual assault allegations on his way to the White House."[40] The media organization repeatedly brought up the tape, where "the Republican candidate boasts about groping women and makes other lewd comments,"[41] and in numerous articles mentioned the fact that "several women have accused Trump of sexual misconduct,"[42] however he denied these allegations.

Many articles also featured Trump's opponent questioning his "temperament" and "judgment."[43] Another article quoted President Obama calling Trump "uniquely unqualified"[44] for the job. In addition, Trump was criticized for his rhetoric about Russia, his praise of Russian President Vladimir Putin, and his doubts "about Russia's involvement in the hacking of the Democratic National Committee emails."[45]

Most positive mentions about Trump had to do with his business expertise. The candidate's supporters called him a tax "genius"[46] and a "straight-talker,"[47] who wants "to put people back to work"[48] and can make "better economic choices for all."[49] However, such positive mentions were rare.

Discussion

This study looked at how VOA and Sputnik framed the two major 2016 presidential candidates: Democrat Hillary Clinton and Republican Donald Trump. The differences in coverage framing matched the cognitive frames of the outlets and their sponsoring governments. Sputnik's tone was more negative toward Clinton and more neutral with Trump, while VOA's tone was more positive for Clinton and more negative toward Trump. In addition, Sputnik and VOA focused the heaviest amount of coverage on the same issues for each candidate, which invited readers to judge the candidates based on the same set of issues. The top three topics mentioned by Sputnik in campaign coverage were foreign relations, military issues, and the economy. On the other hand, VOA devoted the most coverage to immigration, the economy, and military issues. Frame analysis explored the context of how the issues were discussed, revealing that Sputnik's coverage of foreign policy and military issues painted Clinton as a "war hawk" and Trump as less inclined toward military adventures. VOA's extensive coverage of immigration highlighted Trump's plans to restrict access to the U.S. and Clinton's desire for a more open policy.

While this study did not find statistically significant differences in the number of mentions of the two candidates on Sputnik's website, these differences emerged in VOA coverage. Trump's name appeared more often than Clinton's in VOA articles. Are these findings a result of a gender bias typical for the campaign coverage of the past (Kahn, 1994; Kahn & Goldenberg, 1991) or are there other explanations for such differences? For example, could the number of mentions be driven by the negativity of candidates' campaigns? Also, it is worth pointing out that Trump only appeared in 6% more VOA stories than Clinton. Thus, if we use a different measure to quantify the media coverage, we can see that these disparities are less prominent. In contrast, Clinton appeared in 11% more Sputnik stories than Trump.

This study also found that about a half of Sputnik and VOA stories portrayed both candidates in a neutral light. This number of neutral stories was significantly smaller than in previous studies (Bystrom et al., 2001; Rosenson, 2015). Such differences could stem from the variations in the definition of the term neutral. Also, these differences could have emerged due to the varying levels of campaigns: state legislature, governor and senate versus presidential elections.

In line with our expectations, Clinton received more negative coverage than Trump on Sputnik's website (National Intelligence Council, 2017). Similar to intelligence community findings, this study revealed that a large share of negative stories about Clinton on Sputnik's website focused on Wikileaks' revelations, corruption allegations, her alleged war appetites and ties to terrorism as well as alleged health issues (National Intelligence Council, 2017). VOA also featured negative stories about Clinton, however, they mainly focused on her email controversy and often provided context.

At the same time, VOA featured more negative stories about Trump and significantly less about Clinton. Trump's negative mentions generally focused on his rhetoric about women and minorities. Interestingly, while negative stories about Trump were less prevalent in Sputnik coverage, they still constituted nearly one fifth of the overall coverage. Sputnik repeatedly mentioned Trump's character flaws and lack of political experience, thus carefully crafting a believable image of a candidate with faults.

Another interesting finding is that Clinton received more positive coverage than Trump on both the Sputnik and VOA websites. These results were possibly driven by frequent mentions of Clinton winning in the polls on both websites. It is worth noting that during the election campaign pollsters estimated Clinton's chance of winning the election between 71% and 99%, and even Donald Trump's own pollsters were surprised by the outcome of the election (AAPOR, n.d.). Some of Clinton's VOA positive coverage also came from President Obama's and other political figures' endorsements. To sum up, VOA coverage of Clinton appeared rather balanced and factual with only slight positive bias in a form of frequent mentions of then-President Obama campaigning for Clinton and praising her qualities and expertise.

Finally, this study found that Trump mentioned the economy and immigration more often than Clinton in VOA coverage. The findings about the economy are in line with previous research on candidate gender and media coverage (Bystrom et al., 2004). However, it is possible that these differences had nothing to do with the gender of the candidates, but could be rather explained by candidates' own agendas or agendas of their parties.

Limitations and Future Research

This study employed quantitative and qualitative types of content analysis. While the former allows researchers to calculate occurrences of certain categories, the latter lets researchers examine the context of the frames. However, content analysis does not shed a light on the reasons behind the choice of frames or their effects. Future research can focus on in-depth interviews with VOA and Sputnik journalists. Researchers can also conduct experiments involving the audiences of the respective media organizations.

Notes

1. https://sputniknews.com/us/201611051047095326-trump-chinese-americans/
2. https://sputniknews.com/politics/201611081047191786-germany-clinton-trump-election/
3. https://sputniknews.com/us/201611051047095326-trump-chinese-americans/
4. https://sputniknews.com/politics/201611071047135560-us-election-clinton-trump/
5. https://sputniknews.com/analysis/201611041047077147-next-us-president-russia/
6. https://sputniknews.com/us/201611051047095326-trump-chinese-americans/
7. https://sputniknews.com/us/201611081047166959-us-russia-elections-new-president-advisors/
8. https://sputniknews.com/analysis/201611041047077147-next-us-president-russia/

9. https://sputniknews.com/radio_the_bradcast/201610111046257039-al-gore-trump-clinton/

10. https://sputniknews.com/politics/201609241045670122-poll-trump-republican-free-trade/

11. https://sputniknews.com/us/201609271045753841-clinton-trump-tweets-debate/

12. https://sputniknews.com/us/201611011046962991-clinton-trump-poll/

13. https://sputniknews.com/radio_connecting_the_pieces/201610211046594232-should-the-messenger-be-blamed/

14. https://sputniknews.com/politics/201611071047135560-us-election-clinton-trump/

15. https://sputniknews.com/politics/201609191045470004-hillary-clinton-hawk/

16. https://sputniknews.com/us/201611031047015061-usa-president-cantidades-account-war-rethoric/

17. https://sputniknews.com/politics/201609081045102627-clinton-us-exceptionalism-global-war/

18. https://sputniknews.com/columnists/201609211045561397-us-election-circus/

19. https://sputniknews.com/politics/201609161045362244-clinton-president-russia-war/

20. https://sputniknews.com/politics/201609191045470004-hillary-clinton-hawk/

21. https://sputniknews.com/us/201611051047089422-usa-penetration-russian-infrastructure/

22. https://sputniknews.com/us/201611051047089422-usa-penetration-russian-infrastructure/

23. https://sputniknews.com/us/201611061047120487-clinton-foundation-chelsea-wedding/

24. https://sputniknews.com/analysis/201611061047125921-clinton-impeachment-elections/

25. https://sputniknews.com/politics/201610011045909477-hillary-health-clinton-walking-stairs/

26. https://sputniknews.com/columnists/201609211045561397-us-election-circus/

27. https://sputniknews.com/politics/201610141046342123-us-nofly-zone-syria-clinton/

28. https://sputniknews.com/radio_unanimous_dissent/201609281045772219-democrats-accuse-trump-being-coke-head/

29. https://www.voanews.com/a/clinton-trump-make-last-minute-appeals-to-voters-as-election-day-arrives/3586089.html

30. https://www.voanews.com/a/hillary-clinton-hoping-to-crack-ultimate-glass-ceiling-presidency/3579966.html

31. https://www.voanews.com/a/hillary-clinton-hoping-to-crack-ultimate-glass-ceiling-presidency/3579966.html

32. https://www.voanews.com/a/two-days-from-election-trump-clinton-head-to-states-where-they-trail/3583381.html

33. https://www.voanews.com/a/donald-trump-urges-early-voters-change-ballots/3575589.html

34. https://www.voanews.com/a/stress-us-presidential-election-donald-trump-hillary-clinton/3536824.html

35. https://www.voanews.com/a/obama-tries-to-rally-support-for-clinton-among-black-voters/3577302.html
36. https://www.voanews.com/a/hillary-clinton-says-donald-trump-always-puts-himself-first/3579924.html
37. https://www.voanews.com/a/obama-tries-to-rally-support-for-clinton-among-black-voters/3577302.html
38. https://www.voanews.com/a/hillary-clinton-donald-trump-fact-check-presidential-debate/3558833.html
39. https://www.voanews.com/a/trump-weight-health/3509394.html
40. https://www.voanews.com/a/us-election-congress-senate-house/3586879.html
41. https://www.voanews.com/a/us-candidates-look-to-put-october-surprises-behind-them/3574243.html
42. https://www.voanews.com/a/many-conservative-christians-accept-trump-s-moral-flaws/3568237.html
43. https://www.voanews.com/a/hillary-clinton-donald-trump-foreign-policy-issues/3585984.html
44. https://www.voanews.com/a/obama-tries-to-rally-support-for-clinton-among-black-voters/3577302.html
45. https://www.voanews.com/a/us-accuses-russia-of-hacking-attempts-on-political-groups/3541461.html
46. https://www.voanews.com/a/trumps-tax-returns-roil-us-presidential-race/3534832.html
47. https://www.voanews.com/a/virginia-especially-loudoun-county-could-decide-next-president/3530765.html
48. https://www.voanews.com/a/both-candidates-at-home-in-farmville-va-for-vice-presidential-debate/3535906.html
49. https://www.voanews.com/a/iranian-americans-unswayed-recent-headlines-trump-clinton/3579758.html

References

AAPOR. (n.d.). *An evaluation of 2016 election polls in the U.S.* Retrieved from http://www.aapor.org/Education-Resources/Reports/An-Evaluation-of-2016-Election-Polls-in-the-U-S.aspx

About Us. (n.d.) *Sputnik.* Retrieved from https://sputniknews.com/docs/about/index.html

Atkeson, L. R., & Krebs, T. B. (2008). Press coverage of mayoral candidates: The role of gender in news reporting and campaign issue speech. *Political Research Quarterly,* (2), 239. doi:10.1177/1065912907308098

Benoit, W. L., Furgerson, J., Seifert, J., & Sargardia, S. (2013). Newspaper coverage of senate, gubernatorial, and mayoral elections. *Human Communication, 16*(4), 215–229.

Bichard, S. (2006). Building blogs: A multi-dimensional analysis of the distribution of frames on the 2004 presidential candidate web sites. *Journalism & Mass Communication Quarterly, 83*(2), 329–345.

Bystrom, D. G., Robertson, T. A., & Banwart, M. C. (2001). Framing the fight: An analysis of media coverage of female and male candidates in primary races for governor and U.S. Senate in 2000. *American Behavioral Scientist, 44*(12), 1999.

Bystrom, D. G., Banwart, M. C., Kaid, L. L., & Robertson, T. (2004). *Gender and campaign communication: VideoStyle, webStyle and newsStyle.* New York, NY: Routledge.

Chong, D., & Druckman, J. N. (2007). Framing public opinion in competitive democracies. *American Political Science Review, 101,* 637–655.

Devitt, J. (2002). Framing gender on the campaign trail: Female gubernatorial candidates and the press. *Journalism & Mass Communication Quarterly, 79*(2), 445–463.

Dimitrova, D. V., Kaid, L. L., Williams, A. P., & Trammell, K. D. (2005). War on the web: the immediate news framing of Gulf War II. *The International Journal of Press/Politics, 10,* 22–44.

Dunaway, J., Lawrence, R., Rose, M., & Weber, C. (2013). Traits versus issues: How female candidates shape coverage of senate and gubernatorial races. *Political Research Quarterly, 66*(3), 715.

Entman, R. M. (1993). Framing: Towards clarification of a fractured paradigm. *McQuail's Reader in Mass Communication Theory, 43*(4), 51–58.

Entman, R. M. (2008). Theorizing mediated public diplomacy: The US case. *The International Journal of Press/Politics, 13*(2), 87–102. Retrieved from http://journals.sagepub.com/doi/pdf/10.1177/1940161208314657

Freedom House. (2017a). *United States.* Retrieved from https://freedomhouse.org/country/united-states

Freedom House. (2017b). *Russia.* Retrieved from https://freedomhouse.org/report/freedom-world/2017/russia

Gamson, W. A., & Modigliani, A. (1987). The changing culture of affirmative action. In R. G. Braungart & M. M. Braungart (Eds.), *Research in political sociology* (Vol. 3, pp. 137–177). Greenwich, CT: JAI Press.

Ghanem, S. (1997). Filling in the tapestry: The second level of agenda setting. In M. McCombs, D. Shaw, & D. Weaver (Eds.), *Communication and democracy: Exploring the intellectual frontiers in agenda-setting theory* (pp. 3–14). Mahwah, NJ: Lawrence Erlbaum.

Gitlin, T. (1980). *The whole world is watching: Mass media in the making and unmaking of the new left.* Berkeley, CA: University of California Press.

Golan, G. J., & Himelboim, I. (2015). Can world system theory predict news flow on Twitter? The case of government-sponsored broadcasting. *Information Communication & Society, 19*(8), 1150–1170.

Gray, A. (2017). The world's 10 biggest economies in 2017. *World Economic Forum.* Retrieved from https://www.weforum.org/agenda/2017/03/worlds-biggest-economies-in-2017/

Haynie, D. (2017, March 7). These are the world's most influential countries. *U.S. News & World Report.* Retrieved from https://www.usnews.com/news/best-countries/best-international-influence

Holt, L. F. (2012). Hillary and Barack: Will atypical candidates lead to atypical coverage? *Howard Journal of Communications, 23*(3), 272–287. doi:10.1080/10646175.201 2.695629

Kahn, K. F. (1994). The distorted mirror: Press coverage of women candidates for statewide office. *The Journal of Politics,* 56 (1), 154.

Kahn, K. F., & Goldenberg, E. N. (1991). Women candidates in the news: An examination of gender differences in U.S. senate campaign coverage. *Public Opinion Quarterly, 55*(2), 180–199.

Kluver, R. (n.d.). *Media coverage of the US election in Arabic, Chinese, and Russian media.* Retrieved from http://www.electionanalysis2016.us/us-election-analysis-2016/section-5-overseas/media-coverage-of-the-us-election-in-arabic-chinese-and-russian-media/

Luo, Y. (2009). Agenda building: Web site campaigning, newspaper coverage, and candidate stereotypes in the 2008 Democratic presidential campaign. *Conference Papers— International Communication Association,* 1–31.

McCombs, M., Llamas, J., Lopez-Escobar, E., & Rey, F. (1997). Candidate images in Spanish elections: Second-level agenda setting effects. *Journalism & Mass Communication Quarterly, 74*(4), 703–717.

McPhail, T. L. (2010). *Global communication: Theories, stakeholders, and trends.* Malden, MA: Blackwell Pub.

Mission and Values. (n.d.). *VOA public relations.* Retrieved from https://www.insidevoa.com/p/5831.html

National Intelligence Council. (2017). *Background to "Assessing Russian activities and intentions in recent US elections": The analytic process and cyber incident attribution.* Retrieved from https://www.dni.gov/files/documents/ICA_2017_01.pdf

Osipova, Y. (2016). Indigenizing soft power in Russia. In N. Chitty, L. Ji, G. D. Rawnsley, & C. Hayden (Eds.), *The Routledge handbook of soft power* (pp. 346–358). Abingdon: Routledge. Retrieved from https://books.google.com/books?id=3i0lDwAAQBA-J&pg=PA349&lpg=PA349&dq=sputnik,+alternative+news&source=bl&ots=_OSM91mApM&sig=x9KsAc7GkrLEmuBe0gl6MqZNQws&hl=en&sa=X&ved=0ahUKEwixjOjmtu7XAhUCWCYKHQaXBngQ6AEIWTAI#v=onepage&q=sputnik%2C%20alternative%20news&f=false

Parmelee, J. H. (2006). Understanding symbolism in magazine coverage of President Reagan. *Florida Communication Journal, 34*(2), 54–69.

Richardson, G. (2002). *Pulp politics: How political advertising tells the stories of American politics.* Landham, MD: Rowman & Littlefield.

Rosenson, B. A. (2015). Media coverage of state legislatures: Negative, neutral, or positive?. *Social Science Quarterly (Wiley-Blackwell), 96*(5), 1291–1300. doi:10.1111/ssqu.12211

Scheufele, D. A. (1999). Framing as a theory of media effects. *Journal of Communication, Winter*, 103–122.

Strömbäck, J., & Van Aelst, P. (2010). Exploring some antecedents of the media's framing of election news: A comparison of Swedish and Belgian election news. *International Journal of Press/Politics, 15*(1), 41–59.

Tankard, J. W. (2001). The empirical approach to the study of media framing. In S. D. Reese, O. H. Gandy, & A. E. Grant (Eds.), *Framing public life* (pp. 95–106). Mahwah, NJ: Lawrence Erlbaum.

VOA History. (n.d.). Retrieved from https://www.insidevoa.com/p/5829.html

11. "Judicious Skepticism:" Fact-Checking Trump

BETH KNOBEL
Fordham University

There's an old joke that goes, "How do you know if a politician is lying? His lips are moving." Although honest politicians do exist, polls show that Americans think politicians lie often (Just 4%, 2014). And Donald J. Trump has arguably lied more than any other politician in American history, creating more need than ever before for the media and politically oriented citizens to fact-check the words of the president. Trump's tendency to prevaricate has been well documented both during the presidential campaign of 2015–2016 and since Trump assumed the presidency in 2017. "Mr. Trump is trafficking in hyperbole, distortion and fabrication on practically a daily basis," asserted the *New York Times* (Stolberg, 2017). "A lot of what he himself says is as fake, misleading, and as inaccurate as it comes," explained *Mashable* (Lekach, 2017). Even one of the president's Republican colleagues admitted Trump shows "flagrant disregard for truth and decency" (Flake, 2017). This never-before-seen level of prevarication has provoked a response from the media, which has traditionally seen the watchdog role as being critical to its mission (Cater, 1959; Jones, 2009; Knobel, 2018). Given that the president lies more than five times per day on average according to a *Washington Post* estimate (Kessler, Kelly, & Lewis, 2017), fact-checking Trump has become a central element of presidential coverage.

To track the truthfulness of presidential statements, journalists at both mainstream and digital news outlets have created new features and tools aimed at assessing the veracity of the president's statements. The sheer volume of lies coming from the president means that news consumers have more appetite for fact-checking and news organizations have more reason than ever to pursue it:

> Media outlets are more aggressively fact-checking political statements—a func-
> tion often pushed into the background when campaigns end—finding innovative
> new formats and seeing keen interest among consumers. An administration that
> views the press as the opposition is reinvigorating it. (Bauder, 2017)

Digital news organizations, particularly ones that specialize in verification, have taken a large role in fact-checking the president's many assertions.
Newspapers have also responded strongly to the need for constant presidential fact-checking under Trump. Interestingly, the newspapers have largely
used digital tools to present their fact-checking work, underlining the evolution of American newspapers over the past two decades into robust digital news organizations. But fact-checking Trump has not ended there. Even
individual citizens have also developed new tools to fact-check the president's
words. The digital nature of all these tools gives people around the world the
ability to assess Trump's assertions for themselves, providing new avenues for
accountability that will last far after the 45th president of the United States
has left office.

Although fact-checking is now fueled by the digital revolution, philosophers and psychologists have been mulling the nature of veracity for thousands of years. The father of Western philosophy, Socrates, was one; he was
driven by the search for truth and clear that lying had serious consequences.
"False words are not only evil in themselves, but they infect the soul with
evil," he wrote (Plato & Jowett, 1914, p. 445). Although a vast number of
political philosophers have addressed the issues of truth and lies, the most
relevant philosophers for the Trump era would be the two who dominated
the 17th Century, René Descartes of France and Baruch Spinoza of the
Netherlands. Each of these men specifically considered what happens when
someone utters a non-truth and how the process of discernment happens by
those who hear it. Although their theories were formed hundreds of years
ago in a vastly different world from the wired one we know today, the philosophers made arguments that apply directly to the process of sorting out the
barrage of lies coming from the American president.

Descartes and Spinoza disagreed about how people decide what to believe
and what to disbelieve. Descartes argued that people can take in and understand ideas without making a decision as to their veracity. To put that another
way, he argued that people do not automatically assume that a statement is
true before moving to evaluate it. "Under this view, there is an initial period
of non-decision and then evaluation; that is, a one-step evaluative process"
(Street & Richardson, 2015, p. 228).

On the other hand, Spinoza argued that the people believe the things they
hear, even for a split second, before launching a second process to evaluate

the veracity, changing their minds if the evidence becomes compelling. "The 'Spinozan' account … proposes that understanding an assertion means having first to accept it as true automatically. It is only after the initial acceptance that people can consider rejecting the idea. In that sense, cognition is considered a two-step process where the 'unbelieving' stage follows automatic acceptance" (Street & Richardson, 2015, p. 228). In the Spinozan world, "the evaluative phase is more cognitively effortful than the automatic belief stage" (Street & Richardson, 2015, p. 228).

So while both philosophers would likely find usefulness in a process that helps to fact-check statements, Descartes's Cartesian model suggests that a person reading or writing a fact-checking article would not have made a decision as to its veracity, while a Spinozan model suggests the person writing or checking would have accepted its truthfulness, even briefly, before looking for information to check to see if that decision was correct.

Harvard psychologist Daniel Gilbert has taken the Descartes-Spinoza debate into the 21st Century, and his work supports the Spinozan viewpoint. Gilbert, now well known for appearing in commercials that urge Americans to plan for retirement, has done a number of psychological studies that suggest that in our modern information ecosystem, people tend towards the Spinozan model. Gilbert argues that people today tend to accept that statements may be true, even for a brief moment, before launching critical thinking skills to evaluate and, potentially, reject the statement if it is untrue:

> For instance, if someone were to tell us—hypothetically, of course—that there had been serious voter fraud in Virginia during the presidential election, we must for a fraction of a second accept that fraud did, in fact, take place. Only then do we take the second step, either completing the mental certification process (yes, fraud!) or rejecting it (what? no way). (Konnikova, 2017)

Like Spinoza, Gilbert argues that the first step, acceptance, happens naturally as part of the way people think. However, for him as for Spinoza, the second step takes *work*—information and effort. And if no one puts in the work to debunk a false statement, Gilbert says that people may well fail to identify a lie. As Gilbert puts it, "when faced with shortages of time, energy, or conclusive evidence, [human minds] may fail to unaccept the ideas that they involuntarily accept during comprehension" (Gilbert, 1991, p. 115). The process of evaluating and identifying lies is particularly important because psychology has identified a "truth bias," meaning people lean toward accepting something someone says as true (McCornack & Parks, 1986). This makes the work of fact-checking all the more important.

Whether or not one leans toward the Cartesian model and believes that people are agnostic when evaluating statements for truthfulness, or whether one leans towards the Spinozan view and believes that people start by accepting a notion as true before evaluating it, the fact-checking work of journalists clearly provides the raw material necessary for analysis. These fact-checking sites and features facilitate the process of evaluation by centralizing information in easy-to-locate places. They also aid the process by providing verified and detailed analyses. The beauty in fact-checking comes from the details that such news organizations are able to present, which I will outline in this chapter. Through text, graphics, and hyperlinks, these fact-checking outlets present a wealth of information and analysis, including documents, testimonials, audio files, video files, and tweets. Fact-checking output is exactly the kind of journalistic work that Gilbert and, in fact, Spinoza had in mind to permit citizens to exercise the "judicious skepticism" necessary to counteract truth bias (Schaefer, 2013). They facilitate the investment of time and effort that Gilbert argues is necessary to separate political truth from fiction.

Yet because of President Trump's outrageous behavior since becoming president, we now need to consider that neither the Cartesian nor Spinozan models accurately reflect the way some people think today. The President's perpetual lies have likely created a third model to consider: that people now automatically *reject* the words of the President when first uttered and need to be convinced that something he says is true. The work of academics like Dr. Bella DePaulo, a psychologist at the University of California at Santa Barbara, supports this assertion. DePaulo, whose research focuses on lying, writes that Trump has told so many untruths that he has caused some people to remove the usual "default setting" of a truth bias:

> By telling so many lies, and so many that are mean-spirited, Trump is violating some of the most fundamental norms of human social interaction and human decency. Many of the rest of us, in turn, have abandoned a norm of our own—we no longer give Trump the benefit of the doubt that we usually give so readily. (DePaulo, 2017)

For simplicity, I shall call this third group the "AILs" (short for "Assume It's Lies")—those who initially assume that what they hear coming from the president is untrue before analyzing his statements for truthfulness. (Conveniently, this term echoes the name of Roger Ailes, the founder of Fox News Channel.) The people who assume a politician is always lying are the modern-day mirror images of the Spinozans, who assume truth before exploring a statement's veracity.

Public opinion polls suggest that a sizeable portion of the American populace may have become AILs in the Trump era. A Politico/Morning Consult poll from January 2018 showed that only 35% of voters believed that Trump was honest, while 49% said he was not (Morning Consult + Politico, 2018,

p. 9). Similarly, a Quinnipiac University poll that same month showed 37% of voters thought Trump was honest, compared with 60% who thought he was not (Quinnipiac University Poll, 2018).

DePaulo finds this a shockingly high number, and suggests that the high quantity and low quality of Trump's lies have eroded public trust in the president:

> The sheer frequency of Trump's lies appears to be having an effect, and it may not be the one he is going for … For fewer than 40 percent of American voters to see the president as honest is truly remarkable. Most humans, most of the time, believe other people. That's our default setting. Usually, we need a reason to disbelieve. (DePaulo, 2017)

While liberals were likely the first to have adopted the AIL mindset, Trump's lies have become so egregious that moderates and even conservatives have had to admit that they cannot believe all he says. Commenting about the barrage of lies concerning the president's relationship with the adult film actress known as Stormy Daniels, even the ultra-conservative *Wall Street Journal* editorial page warned that the president:

> is compiling a record that increases the likelihood that few will believe him during a genuine crisis—say, a dispute over speaking with special counsel Robert Mueller or a nuclear showdown with Kim Jong Un. Mr. Trump should worry that Americans will stop believing anything he says. (Editorial Board, 2018)

As with Cartestians and Spinozans, fact-checking sites and services also serve this third population, the AILs, by presenting convincing evidence that citizens are correct when they assume that the president is lying. But they also serve public policy by correcting that view when the President is being truthful.

Therefore, fact-checking creates a historical record that serves all people who care to invest the time and effort to find out whether Trump is uttering the truth, half-truth, or fiction. Fact-checking is also useful to this varied audience because it creates a nuanced approach, not just labeling statements "true" or "false" but explaining to what degree things might be considered partial truths or partial lies. For the Cartesians, who go in with an open mind, these fact-checking sites help enable a determination about truth and accuracy. For the Spinozans and the AILs, who are more likely to have a pre-disposition about truthfulness, fact-checking outlets can either reinforce a worldview already held or challenge citizens to reexamine their assumptions. Although I will document in the next sections of this paper the varied ways that fact-checking work is being done today, I do so knowing that there are limits to the usefulness of fact-checking. The problem is that Trump's most ardent supporters are not often swayed to change their political behavior by fact-checking his many lies—at least not yet.

Pre-Digital Fact-Checking

For media organizations, "fact-checking" can mean one of two things. One is the public-facing work done by journalists to check the accuracy of politicians' statements. Most of this chapter concerns this kind of political fact-checking. But fact-checking also refers to the internally focused work that news organizations do to make sure that what they write and say has been checked and double-checked for accuracy. These two different kinds of fact-checking operations are related. A news organization gains credibility if its work meets high standards for truthfulness and precision, making its assertions about politicians more trustworthy. "Accuracy is the foundation upon which everything else is built—context, interpretation, debate and all of public communication" (Kovach & Rosenstiel, 2014, p. 57). Many publications like the *New Yorker* still employ fact-checkers on staff to help ensure that everything published is completely factual. Others rely on reporters and editors to get it right. No matter how it is done, a journalistic organization's in-house commitment to accuracy adds credibility to the kind of public fact-checking that holds officials accountable.

Internal fact-checking at American newspapers came of age at the same time that journalism was moving out of the era of sensationalism and partisanship into one of objectivity. "It was around the turn of the 20th century, between the sensational yellow journalism of the 1890s and muckraking in the early 1900s, that the American journalism industry began to really focus on facts" (Fabry, 2017). The news business became more professional about the same time, as codes of ethics and professional organizations became popular. "And, as objective journalism caught on, ideals of accuracy and impartiality began to matter more than ever" (Fabry, 2017). To make sure that articles contained truthful depictions, publications started to amp up their fact-checking operations. For instance, Joseph Pulitzer's son Ralph opened a "Bureau of Accuracy and Fair Play" at the family-owned New York *World* in 1913 to help distinguish "that which is true and that which is false" (Silverman, 2007). The magazine *Time* suggests that the earliest published use of the phrase "fact-checker" may be found in one of its advertisements from 1938, which stated that *Time* had expanded its research staff from 10 to 22 (Fabry, 2017). Lucas Graves, who wrote an outstanding book about political fact-checking, points out that this kind of internal fact-checking targets the reporter, while political fact-checking has an external source as its focus—"the people being reported on" (Graves, 2016, p. 7).

Political fact-checking took several forms in the pre-digital era. One was to produce straightforward articles and broadcast stories, which laid out the facts and then assessed their veracity. Among the most famous of these was Edward R. Murrow's famous 1954 episode of *See It Now*, which examined the career of Senator Joseph McCarthy (Murrow, 1954). To gather the material for that broadcast, CBS News crews spent a year following the senator around and filming his speeches. Murrow's method was to fact-check McCarthy by showing him telling lies, using the films taken all over the country, and then debunk the senator's statements with specific, convincing evidence to prove to the audience that McCarthy was bending the truth. "When he [Murrow] finally decided on the means of covering McCarthy it was a simple one, to let McCarthy destroy McCarthy" (Halberstam, 1979, p. 143). The power came not only from Murrow throwing his considerable credibility behind his investigation, but also from the power of the images of McCarthy telling lies. "It was the first time McCarthy's allegations had been systematically dissected in the full glare of the mass media" (Sperber, 1986, p. 437).

A second form of political fact-checking in the pre-digital era came from commentary, both print and broadcast. Because they could voice an opinion, commentators were able to point out lies more easily than some of their more objective colleagues. American commentators have criticized pretty much every major politician in history. The inclusion of more than a dozen newspaper columnists on President Richard Nixon's famed Enemies List sprung from their criticism, which grew harsher and harsher as Nixon hurtled towards resignation (Feldstein, 2010). Until the digital era began in the late 1990s, political fact-checking was generally done by news organizations using one of these two methods, as there were few other tools available to journalists. Graves points out that today's political fact-checking combines "traditional reporting tools and a commitment to objectivity with the annotated, critical style first associated with bloggers" (Graves, 2016, p. 10). By combining straight reporting with commentary, today's fact-checkers have extended the values and traditions of old-school journalism into the digital era.

Digital Fact-Checkers

There can be no question that the digital age provides new possibilities for journalistic organizations to gather the information to check the veracity of the president's statements and also to disseminate the results. Graves explains that, "The emergence of the Internet as a vehicle of professional journalism really makes it possible for these dedicated organizations to practice fact checking in a different way" (Scriber, 2016). Graves calls political fact-checking "a new style of journalism," (Graves, 2016, p. 10) and I'm not entirely sure I agree, given the very long history of news organizations testing politicians' claims for truthfulness. But the digital era certainly provides ways for citizen journalists and non-governmental organizations to build and share account-ability tools. Trump is a digital president, brought into office on a wave of 140 character tirades and viral video clips. So, it seems apt that the digital medium is at the heart of the fact-checking work being done by journalists, organizations, and citizens.

Much of the work to verify Trump's statements is being done by digital news organizations, particularly ones that came into existence specifically to perform the fact-checking role. Most of these organizations started work before Trump entered politics. One 2015 estimate counted 22 active fact-checking outfits in the United States (Adair & Thakore, 2015), and a few more have started work since then. There is even an International Fact-Checking Network (IFCN), a forum for fact-checkers worldwide (Poynter, 2018). Founded in 2015, the IFCN is housed at the Poynter Institute in Florida, a well-respected non-profit journalism think tank. These digital fact-checking organizations have been "built upon an idea that people want to hold their politicians accountable for the claims they make. And in a world with lots of misinformation, readers, viewers, and voters are looking for places that can quickly sort facts from falsehoods" (Sharockman, 2017). While there are numerous digital news organizations fact-checking President Trump, two of the highest-profile organizations, FactCheck.org and PolitiFact, have both been kept particularly busy by the 45th president.

FactCheck.org, launched in 2003, is "a pioneer of fact-checking" (Adair, 2017). Run out of the Annenberg Public Policy Center at the University of Pennsylvania, the organization was founded by political communications professor Kathleen Hall Jamieson and Brooks Jackson, a long-time political reporter for the Associated Press, the *Wall Street Journal,* and CNN. The organization not only tries to distinguish truth from falsity based on its own reporting, but says it tries to check with the person or group making a claim if veracity is called into question. "We systematically go through transcripts and videos looking for statements based on facts. Once we find a statement that we suspect may be inaccurate or misleading, we will engage–or attempt to engage–with the person or organization that is being fact-checked. The burden is on the person or organization making the claim to provide the evidence to support it" (Our Process, 2018). The Trump administration, it must be said, has shown little interest engaging with news organizations that are trying to check whether presidential statements are factual. The treatments by FactCheck.org tend to be lengthy and detailed, with multiple hyperlinks.

Articles end with a "Share The Facts" summary that provides a verdict like "Distorts the facts" or "Lacks context" that can easily be posted by readers on social media.

Surprisingly, FactCheck.org does not feature Trump prominently on its home page. Readers must navigate to content about the president by going to an Archives tab, where Trump is the first choice. That leads to a Donald Trump home page, where all the site's recent stories on Trump are located (Donald Trump, 2018). FactCheck.org also has two features that are not found on all similar sites. One is a section where some presidential speeches are annotated and checked for truth (Trump Transcripts, 2018). In this feature, FactCheck.org highlights certain lines of the speech transcript in yellow, and when the reader clicks on them, a box appears with a verdict on the truthfulness and some context. Unfortunately, only a few presidential speeches per month get this fact-checking treatment. The other unique feature is a weekly "online fact-checking video" on the FactCheck.org site produced in partnership with *CNN*'s Jake Tapper, host of the political talk show *State of the Nation* (State of the Nation, 2018). This partnership between *CNN* and FactCheck.org has been active since 2015. A majority of the videos are about Trump or his Republican colleagues.

PolitiFact (2018) is another large and highly active fact-checking organization. Founded in 2007, PolitiFact is run by the *Tampa Bay Times*, one of the nation's most respected newspapers—no doubt due in part to its ownership by the non-profit Poynter Institute. PolitiFact tried to take FactCheck.org's model and go it one better by adding additional features to improve content. "We could make fact-checking more accessible to a larger audience by rating claims on a Truth-O-Meter and tallying candidates' records," wrote the site's founder (Adair, 2017). In addition to providing a detailed examination of facts, PolitiFact staffers rate politicians' statements on their trademarked "Truth-O-Meter" from true to false, with at least three editors reviewing each rating. "The most ridiculous falsehoods get the lowest rating, Pants on Fire" (Adair & Holan, 2013). Similarly, the site also monitors whether politicians have changed positions with a "Flip-O-Meter" and assesses whether they are delivering on their stated promises. PolitiFact, which won the 2009 Pulitzer Prize for National Reporting for its coverage of the 2008 election, says it draws about 8.6 million page views per month with over 4.7 million unique visitors as of November 2017 (Audience, 2018).

PolitiFact examines the president's actions in several ways. On its home page, it features a link to its "Trump-O-Meter," where readers can quickly see how the president is doing on fulfilling his agenda. As of May 2018, the tally showed just 9 of 102 promises kept, 7 broken, 46 in the works, and 33 stalled

(Trump-O-Meter, 2018). For deeper accountability, users can go to a tab titled "People" on the site's home page, where Trump is the first name listed. A click there directs to the Donald Trump main page (Donald Trump's file, 2018), which has several features. One is the "PolitiFact scorecard," which summarizes the organization's fact-checking of Trump's statements. For instance, the site examined Trump's November 7, 2017 statement that Chicago is "the city with the strongest gun laws in our nation." PolitiFact dubbed this a "pants on fire" lie. Its analysis concluded: "The statement is years out of date. After a Supreme Court ruling, Chicago residents can own handguns and carry them unseen on the streets. A national gun control group puts seven states above Illinois in regulating gun ownership" (Greenberg, 2017). As of May 2018, PolitiFact found almost 80% of the Trump state-ments examined classified as "Mostly False" (22%), "False" (32%), or "Pants on Fire" (15%). Of course, PolitiFact did not vet all presidential statements, only ones it felt worthy of examination. But this is still an astoundingly high number of non-truths.

Extending the "Trump Bump"

Like newspapers that reported a "Trump bump" or a gain in circulation after the election of 2016, many fact-checking organizations have seen an increase in donations in the Trump era. PolitiFact not only saw its web traffic continue to rise since Trump's election, but it raised $105,000 in less than three weeks in response to several Trump tirades through a paid membership program. "Perks include the opportunity to listen in on the staff as they decide the Truth-O-Meter rating of a fact-checked claim, 'virtual coffees,' and access to a closed Facebook group" (Mantzarlis, 2017). Another fact-checking digital news operation, Snopes.com, which describes itself as "the oldest and largest fact-checking site on the Internet" (About Snopes.com, 2018) having been founded in 1994, also benefited from a financial surge after Trump arrived. "In one day, Snopes received more than $500,000 worth of donations from nearly 20,000 people on GoFundMe in order to keep its doors open" (Funke, 2017). Management issues related to Snopes's parent company so drained the website that it had to appeal directly to readers to stay alive. Although the website's appeal letter did not mention Trump specifically, the stories in Snopes actively fact-check both the president and members of his administration.

These are hardly the only digital news organizations to spend part of their energy on fact-checking Trump. Nate Silver's renowned data-centered blog FiveThirtyEight (2018) also created a new feature called "TrumpBeat" to centralize all its stories on the president in one place (TrumpBeat, 2018). FiveThirtyEight has mostly focused its Trump coverage on policies rather than politics, at least during Trump's first year in office, with health care, environment, and immigration as the most-covered topics (Casselman, 2017). Interestingly, the FiveThirtyEight staff held a web-chat amongst its top editors in October 2017, allowing readers to share the staff's frustration about covering this particular president. "The media has lots of problems in how it covers Trump. We've just scratched the surface here. But these problems are also hard to solve and figuring them out in real time is tough," Silver explained (Silver, 2017). Like other journalists doing fact-checking, FiveThirtyEight editors worried that they are inadequately covering some parts of the administration, like federal agencies, because too much of their coverage is based on Trump's tweets and off-the-cuff statements.

ProPublica (2018), another Pulitzer Prize-winning digital news organization focused on accountability journalism, has reacted to the challenges of covering Trump by increasing its collaborations with partner news orgs. For instance, when the Trump administration announced in March 2017 that its staffers had filed financial disclosure forms, it made them very hard to obtain. "It was like dealing with the world's worst customer service department— only we were trying to wrangle purportedly public information," explained ProPublica (Umansky, 2017). So it decided the issue called for a collaborative approach: "One of our editors, Tracy Weber, had an idea: Why not call our friends at other outlets and coordinate. Within minutes, The New York Times and Associated Press had agreed to work with us and post all the documents we gathered" (Umansky, 2017). ProPublica also has done more crowdsourcing under the 45th president:

> Last month, the Trump administration disclosed donors who funded the president's $100 million inauguration committee. The administration posted them as super-unhelpful, non-searchable PDFs. So reporters got together to fix that, turning the documents into data. Then, the Huffington Post's Christina Wilkie invited readers to dig in and background the donors. It turns out, some of the names were straight-up fake. (Umansky, 2017)

Like some other digital news organizations, ProPublica also saw a significant spike in donations after Trump's election (Mullin, 2016).

In a similar vein but using somewhat different technology, the non-profit Internet Archive (Archive, 2018) has added to the work of some of these digital news sites by curating videos that address specific claims investigated by what has been called the "big three" of fact-checking (Martzarlis, 2016): PolitiFact, FactCheck.org, and the *Washington Post*'s Fact Checker. The Internet Archive site cross-references articles by one of those three fact-checking organizations to videos that show the claim under investigation being made. For instance, on October 26, 2017, Trump claimed during an interview with Lou Dobbs on Fox Business Network that the U.S. loses almost every lawsuit it brings against the World Trade Organization. The Internet Archive made it easy to find both the interview (Lou Dobbs Tonight, 2017) and a FactCheck.org article debunking the claim, which explains that in actuality, the U.S. wins almost every claim it brings against the WTO (Farley, 2017). The Internet Archive also has gathered Trump's speeches, debates, rallies and other television appearances into one searchable database (Trump Archive, 2018), creating a very useful resource for those who want to police the president's statements.

Legacy Media Leans Digital

Although digital media and citizen journalists have jumped into action to fact-check Trump, legacy media have also dedicated significant resources to keeping the president honest. Even mainstream publications that usually stay out of politics like *Scientific American* have addressed Trump's lying. "The traditional mechanisms for identifying the truth about politics come from mainstream media and its fact checking," it wrote (Tsipursky, 2017). While radio and television news outlets have dedicated significant resources to fact-checking the president, I will focus here on newspapers, particularly the large nationally focused ones—which have had the resources to dedicate significant time and effort to this effort. Like their digital counterparts, American newspapers have also created new and creative ways to fact-check the 45th president.

Years before Trump's arrival in politics, back in 2007, the *Washington Post* launched its own specialized fact-checking website and column (Fact Checker, 2018). The *Washington Post* Fact Checker mimics the work of FactCheck.org and PolitiFact in some key ways. For one, the *Washington Post* approaches its work much like FactCheck.org, producing detailed and well-researched stories that evaluate statements. Also, like PolitiFact, the *Post* uses ratings, but its scale features "Pinocchios," named for the fictional puppet whose nose grew when he told a fib. One Pinocchio is for "Some shading of the facts," whereas four Pinocchios means a "whopper" of a lie (Kessler, 2013). The *Post* adds two more symbols to its list of ratings: a "Geppetto Checkmark," named for Pinocchio's puppet master, for statements that represent "the truth, the whole truth, and nothing but the truth," and an upside-down Pinocchio, representing a flip-flop on an issue (Kessler, 2013). The site is run by the *Washington Post*'s award-winning former State Department correspondent, Glenn Kessler. Most of Kessler's work appears online, but he does publish a column in the Sunday print edition. Although the *Post* Fact Checker does not focus only on Trump, much of its 2017 content covered the president. That is likely the reason why "the number of unique visitors has exploded, especially this year, with new readership records set month after month" (Kessler, 2017).

The *Post* fits an enormous amount of data into its digital fact-checking features. For instance, its interactive list of all the claims made by the president during his first 100 days (Lee, Kessler, & Shapiro, 2017) includes the claim, when made and repeated, the source, and a paragraph of analysis. If the *Post* had a story on the claim or covered the event where it was made, the database also presents a hyperlink to the article. The site also includes a master calendar where each day is color-coded, from white for no misleading or false claims by the president, to dark red for more than 20 claims made on a particular day. Similarly, the *Post* continues the follow the president with an "ongoing database" of false or misleading claims (Kessler, Kelly, Rizzo, & Lee, 2018). The *Washington Post* Fact Checker is also monitoring the president's promises (Trump Promise Tracker, 2018), although it seems to watch fewer of them than some other sites. By mid-2018, the *Post* reported that about half of the 60 promises tracked had been resolved, albeit with about the same number of promises kept as broken.

The *New York Times* has also moved aggressively into fact-checking the president, often using new graphic tools to do so. For instance, the *Times* created an interactive list of Trump's lies about six months into his term (Leonhardt & Thompson, 2017). Each non-truth on its list is followed by a hyperlink giving more information about what the president said that was not factual. The *Times* also keeps a log of the hundreds of people insulted by the president (Lee & Quealy, 2017). Of course, the *Times* covers the news, and its team of reporters on Trump has produced thousands of inches of fact-based accountability coverage. The emphasis on holding the president accountable has led to a gain of thousands of new paying consumers. "For the last two quarters, the *Times* has added almost 600,000 digital subscribers, a growth rate that is almost 500% faster than the rate for the previous seven quarters. *Times* executives initially downplayed the impact of Trump's unpopularity among the paper's readers, but now acknowledge it is the major factor in the explosion" (Gerth, 2017). This surge suggests that some citizens still rely heavily on the mainstream media to play the watchdog role.

Added Accountability?

There can be little question that journalistic fact-checking has exploded under Trump, with more outlets and more digital tools available than ever before to monitor the president's statements. The detailed descriptions of what each of these sites can do leave little doubt that the fact-checking genre enables interested citizens to find the information they need to do the kind of digging that Gilbert, following Spinoza, describes as a necessary process to separate lies from truth. This chapter has not even described every fact-checking site, nor all the work done by legacy and digital media that can be considered fact checking. Trump may accuse any outlet that tries to hold him accountable as spreading "fake news," but the fact of the matter is that the President's lies are being debunked by the media and private citizens on a daily basis.

But does fact-checking this president actually work? Graves (2016, pp. 175–176) suggests there are three ways in which political fact-checking can have an effect, each affecting a different audience. For citizens, Graves says that new information can change their thinking on political issues, which could lead to changed political behavior. For journalists, Graves posits that fact-checking can actually encourage colleagues and competitors to dig harder into the work of verification. And for officials, Graves argues fact-checking can discourage lying. However, the evidence about the efficacy of these three different types of effects is mixed.

Let's start with the effect on citizens. For fact-checking to work, people have to see it. Millions of Americans are seeing the main fact-checking sites every month and consuming articles either on the Web or in print that check presidential statements for veracity. But there are many reasons to believe that Trump supporters are less likely to see or seek out fact-checking articles than moderates or liberals who do not support the president or are politically neutral. One reason is because Americans are increasingly choosing to consume media that align with their political views (Mitchell, Gottfried, Kiley, & Matsa, 2014). Conservatives and Republicans are more likely to get their news from outlets that do not provide much credible fact-checking, like Fox News Channel (Mitchell et al., 2014). These people may easily miss fact-checking work that holds Trump accountable. Other studies suggest that conservative Republicans are largely eschewing the mainstream media, meaning they are less likely than moderates and liberals to come across the kind of fact-checking done by newspapers (Faris et al., 2017; Thompson, 2016).

That said, academic studies have concluded that fact-checking can have effects on citizens when they do see it (Weeks, 2015). People are apparently open to having their minds changed when convincing fact-checking evidence is presented. This appears to apply to Trump supporters as well as non-supporters, meaning those with Cartesian, Spinozan, or AIL belief systems:

> Think fact-checking can't change minds? Researchers recently presented participants four Trump falsehoods and asked people to say whether they believed

them. After demonstrating with credible sources that Trump's claims were false, belief in them fell among all groups, including Trump supporters. (Sharockman, 2017)

This finding is notable because "a respectable body of scholarship confirms that humans are likely to scrutinize claims that challenge deeply held beliefs while uncritically embracing those that comport with existing dispositions" (Gottfried, Hardy, Winneg, & Jamieson, p. 1561). It is encouraging that belief systems can still be affected by facts and that some people are willing to question their own assumptions.

But another recent study suggests that changes in political behavior may not follow from changes in knowledge. It found that Trump voters were not willing to give up their support of the president just because they had been convinced that he was untruthful (Nyhan, Porter, Reifler, & Wood, 2017). This study was based on two experiments that corrected misleading claims that Trump made during his Republican National Convention acceptance speech and in the first general election debate with Hillary Clinton. The study concluded that although Trump supporters had more accurate views of the truth after they heard the false claims being debunked, their positive attitude towards the president was unchanged after learning that he had lied:

> Trump supporters were willing to accept the factual correction and update their beliefs. ... In neither study did exposure to a correction affect Trump supporters' attitudes about Trump himself. ... Respondents—particularly Trump supporters—took the corrections literally, but apparently not seriously. (Nyhan et al., 2017, pp. 16–17)

Apparently, those who like Trump seem likely to continue to support him, no matter how much he lies. Harvard Psychology professor Steven Pinker explained this phenomenon as "raw tribalism: when someone is perceived as a champion of one's coalition, all is forgiven" (Edsal, 2018).

But fact-checking is important in myriad ways beyond just challenging the president's supporters to be better informed. It reminds people of the real meaning of journalism in this "post-truth" era, which is to serve as a watchdog over the government and separate objective truth from the lies and half-truths that some people try to pass off as the whole truth. As *Washington Post* editor Marty Baron put it, "holding the most powerful to account is what we are *supposed* to do. If we do not do that, then what exactly *is* the purpose of journalism?" (Baron, 2016).

In fact, the verification movement appears to be continuing to grow (New studies on political fact-checking, 2016). The American Press Institute, for one, leads a project to connect existing fact-checking organizations and to encourage more to begin (American Press Institute, 2018). The organization not only offers free fact-checking resources, but also an online training course to teach verification skills. Trump's lies are actually inducing more accountability journalism to debunk those lies. This would seem to back up Graves' assertion that good fact-checking begets more of the same.

And those who run these digital accountability sites say that their work does indeed make a difference by inducing political actors to behave better. "Some politicians have responded to fact-checking journalism by vetting their prepared comments more carefully and giving their campaign ads extra scrutiny" (Holan, 2015). Furthermore, academic research also suggests that politicians seem to be more responsible when being fact-checked. One study investigated the effect on a diverse group of state legislators from nine U.S. states in the months before the November 2012 election. All their states had an affiliate of PolitiFact at work, meaning the threat to subject the politicians to rigorous fact-checking was real:

> In the experiment, a randomly assigned subset of state legislators were sent a series of letters about the risks to their reputation and electoral security if they are caught making questionable statements. The legislators who were sent these letters were substantially less likely to receive a negative fact-checking rating or to have their accuracy questioned publicly, suggesting that fact-checking can reduce inaccuracy when it poses a salient threat. (Nyhan & Reifler, 2014)

It is important to note that this effect was seen on the state level. There seems to be little evidence that the current chief of the Executive Branch is feeling any pressure from the fact-checking work being done on his statements.

Nor is there reason to think that the current occupant of the White House is being induced to act more ethically by those fact-checking him. President Trump does not seem to be picking his words more carefully because they are being scrutinized, given the continued high pace of his prevaricating. The lies just keep coming and coming, no matter how quickly they are debunked.

Trump may be immune so far, but Americans generally hold the work of fact-checking politicians in high esteem. One recent poll found more than 8 of ten respondents with a positive view of this type of work (New studies on political fact-checking, 2016). And that is a good thing, since there seems little reason to think that the need to fact-check the president will fade as long as Trump remains president. President Trump lies so much that, sadly, an entire army of fact-checkers is necessary to keep up. "If things continue at this pace, fact-checkers will come out of this presidency bleary-eyed and in need of a very long vacation," predicted one critic (Lekach, 2017).

Digital news organizations, legacy media, and individuals should all keep contributing to the effort to keep Trump's lies in the spotlight so that the president's own "fake news" can be identified and real news strengthened. And Americans must remember Gilbert's argument that it takes effort to discern what is true and what is not. With so many different news organizations creating myriad tools to fact-check presidential assertions, Americans need not break a sweat to do the work of becoming an informed citizenry. But they do have to be skeptical, and question what they hear and read.

These fact-checking organizations invest considerable time and energy into their work so that the American people don't have to. Everything one needs to be a "judicious skeptic" is just a few mouse clicks away. Americans would be well served to take notice, and use fact-checking sites to become more educated consumers—or rejectors—of presidential rhetoric.

References

About Snopes.com. (2018). *Snopes.com*. Retrieved from https://www.snopes.com/about-snopes/

Adair, B. (2017, August 21). Behind the unlikely success of PolitiFact and the Truth-O-Meter. *Columbia Journalism Review*. Retrieved from https://www.cjr.org/first_person/politifact-fact-checking-anniversary.php

Adair, B., & Holan, A. D. (2013, November 1). Learn how PolitiFact does its work. *PolitiFact.com*. Retrieved from http://www.politifact.com/truth-o-meter/article/2013/nov/01/principles-politifact-punditfact-and-truth-o-meter/

Adair, B., & Thakore, I. (2015, January 19). Fact-Checking census finds continued growth around the world. *Duke Reporters' Lab*. Retrieved from https://reporterslab.org/fact-checking-census-finds-growth-around-world/

American Press Institute. (2018). Fact-Checking Project. *American Press Institute*. Retrieved from americanpressinstitute.org/category/fact-checking-project/

Audience. (2018). *PolitiFact*. Retrieved from http://politifactmediakit.hotims.com/r5/showkiosk.asp?listing_id=5218545&category_code=audi&category_id=78544

Baron, M. (2016, November 30) Washington Post editor Marty Baron has a message to journalists in the Trump era. *Vanity Fair*. Retrieved from www.vanityfair.com/news/2016/11/washington-post-editor-marty-baron-message-to-journalists

Bauder, D. (2017, February 8). Media fact-checking more aggressive under Trump. *Associated Press*. Retrieved from https://apnews.com/b88b5b272b584642a5e09a9345a39e77

Casselman, B. (2017, August 25). What I learned from 7 months of watching the Trump White House. *FiveThirtyEight*. Retrieved from https://fivethirtyeight.com/features/what-i-learned-from-7-months-of-watching-the-trump-white-house/

Cater, D. (1959). *The fourth branch of government*. Boston, MA: Houghton Mifflin.

DePaulo, B. (2017, December 8). I've studied liars. I've never seen one like President Trump. *Washington Post*. Retrieved from https://www.washingtonpost.com/outlook/i-study-liars-ive-never-seen-one-like-president-trump/2017/12/07/4e529efe-da3f-11e7-a841-2066faf731ef_story.html?utm_term=.cce4de7f4fbd

Donald Trump. (2018). *FactCheck.org*. Retrieved from http://www.factcheck.org/person/donald-trump/

Donald Trump's file. (2018). *PolitiFact*. Retrieved from http://www.politifact.com/personalities/donald-trump/

Edsal, T. B. (2018, January 25). Is President Trump a stealth postmodernist or just a liar? *New York Times*. Retrieved from https://www.nytimes.com/2018/01/25/opinion/trump-postmodernism-lies.html

Fabry, M. (2017, August 24). Here's how the first fact-checkers were able to do their jobs before the Internet. *Time*. Retrieved from http://time.com/4858683/fact-checking-history/

FactCheck.org. (2018). *FactCheck.org*. Retrieved from factcheck.org

Fact Checker. (2018). *Washington Post*. Retrieved from washingtonpost.com/news/fact-checker/

Faris, R. M., Roberts, H., Etling, B., Bourassa, N., Zuckerman, E., & Benkler, Y. (2017, August). Partisanship, propaganda, and disinformation: Online media and the 2016 U.S. Presidential election. Berkman Klein Center for Internet & Society Research Paper. Retrieved from https://dash.harvard.edu/bitstream/handle/1/33759251/2017-08_electionReport_0.pdf

Farley, R. (2017, October 27). Trump wrong about WTO record. *Factcheck.org*. Retrieved from http://www.factcheck.org/2017/10/trump-wrong-wto-record/

Feldstein, M. (2010). *Poisoning the press: Richard Nixon, Jack Anderson and the rise of Washington's scandal culture*. New York, NY: Farrar, Straus and Giroux.

FiveThirtyEight. (2018). *FiveThirtyEight*. Retrieved from fivethirtyeight.com.

Flake, F. (2017, October 24). *Speech on floor of US Senate*. Retrieved from https://www.nytimes.com/2017/10/24/us/politics/jeff-flake-transcript-senate-speech.html

Funke, D. (2017, July 25). Snopes met its $500k fundraising goal. Now what? *Poynter*. Retrieved from https://www.poynter.org/news/snopes-met-its-500k-fundraising-goal-now-what

Gerth, J. (2017, June 29). For The New York Times, Trump is a sparring partner with benefits. *Columbia Journalism Review*. Retrieved from https://www.cjr.org/special_report/trump_new_york_times.php

Gilbert, D. (1991, February). How mental systems believe. *American Psychologist, 46*(20). Retrieved from https://pdfs.semanticscholar.org/cca6/6fa588bacd2793ed7ffb64a6920aa9c6129d.pdf

Gottfried, J. A., Hardy, B. W., Winneg, K. M., & Jamieson, K. H. (2013, November). Did fact checking matter in the 2012 campaign? *American Behavioral Scientist, 57*(11), 1558–1567.

Graves, L. (2016). *Deciding what's true: The rise of political fact-checking in American journalism*. New York, NY: Columbia University Press.

Greenberg, J. (2017, November 7). Donald Trump wrongly repeats that Chicago has strongest gun laws. *PolitiFact.com*. Retrieved from http://www.politifact.com/truth-o-meter/statements/2017/nov/07/donald-trump/trump-wrongly-repeats-chicago-has-strongest-gun-la/

Halberstam, D. (1979). *The powers that be.* New York, NY: Knopf.

Holan, A. D. (2015, December 11). All politicians lie. Some lie more than others. *New York Times.* Retrieved from https://www.nytimes.com/2015/12/13/opinion/campaign-stops/all-politicians-lie-some-lie-more-than-others.html

Jones, A. (2009). *Losing the news.* New York, NY: Oxford University Press.

Just 4% Say Candidates Keep Their Campaign Promises. (2014). *Rasumussen reports.* Retrieved from http://www.rasmussenreports.com/public_content/politics/general_politics/november_2014/just_4_say_candidates_keep_their_campaign_promises

Kessler, G. (2013, September 11). About the fact-checker. *Washington Post.* Retrieved from https://www.washingtonpost.com/news/fact-checker/about-the-fact-checker/?utm_term=.faf72098e426

Kessler, G. (2017, September 19). Happy 10th birthday Fact Checker. *Washington Post.* Retrieved from https://www.washingtonpost.com/news/fact-checker/wp/2017/09/19/happy-10th-birthday-fact-checker/?utm_term=.699519456cb5/

Kessler, G., Kelly, M., & Lewis, N. (2017, November 14). In 298 days, President Trump has made 1,628 false and misleading claims. *Washington Post.* https://www.washingtonpost.com/news/fact-checker/wp/2017/11/14/president-trump-has-made-1628-false-or-misleading-claims-over-298-days/?tid=sm_fb&utm_term=.583af4ccccae

Kessler, G., Kelly, M., Rizzo, S. & Lee, M. Y. H., (2018, April 30). In 466 days, President Trump has made 3,001 false and misleading claims. *Washington Post.* Retrieved from

Knobel, B. (2018). *The watchdog still barks: How accountability reporting evolved for the digital era.* New York, NY: Fordham University Press.

Konnikova, M. (2017 January/February). Trump's lies versus your brain. *Politico.* Retrieved from http://www.politico.com/magazine/story/2017/01/donald-trump-lies-liar-effect-brain-214658

Kovach, B., & Rosenstiel, T. (2014). *The elements of journalism: What newspeople should know and the public should expect* (3rd ed.). New York, NY: Three Rivers Press.

Lee, J., & Quealy, K. (2017, November 17). The 394 people, places and things Donald Trump has insulted on Twitter: A complete list. *New York Times.* Retrieved from https://www.nytimes.com/interactive/2016/01/28/upshot/donald-trump-twitter-insults.html?mcubz=1&ex_cid=SigDig&_r=0

Lee, M. Y. H., Kessler, G., & Shapiro, L. (2017, February 27). 100 days of Trump claims. *Washington Post.* Retrieved from https://www.washingtonpost.com/graphics/politics/trump-claims/?tid=a_inl&utm_term=.61cdeda3732c

Lekach, S. (2017, November 14). Trump is on pace to lie 8,000 times by the end of his first term. *Mashable.* Retrieved from http://mashable.com/2017/11/14/trump-lies-falsehoods-washington-post-tracker/#jwwBoBDeZPq9

Leonhardt, D., & Thompson, S. A. (2017, July 21). Trump's lies. *New York Times.* Retrieved from https://www.nytimes.com/interactive/2017/06/23/opinion/trumps-lies.html?_r=0

Lou Dobbs Tonight. (2017, October 25). *Internet Archive*. Retrieved from https://archive.org/details/FBC_20171026_020000_Lou_Dobbs_Tonight/start/625/end/657.5

Martzarlis, A. (2016, November 10). Fact-checking under President Trump. *Poynter*. Retrieved from https://www.poynter.org/news/fact-checking-under-president-trump

Mantzarlis, A. (2017, February 7). PolitiFact raised $105,000 in 20 days through its newly launched membership program. *Poynter*. Retrieved from https://www.poynter.org/news/politifact-raised-105000-20-days-through-its-newly-launched-membership-program

McCornack, S. A., & Parks, M. R. (1986). Deception detection and relationship development: The other side of trust. In Margaret L. McLaughlin (Ed.), *Communication yearbook 9*. Newbury Park, CA: Sage.

Mitchell, A., Gottfried, J., Kiley, J., & Matsa, K. E. (2014, October 21). Political polarization & media habits. *Pew Research Center*. Retrieved from http://www.journalism.org/2014/10/21/political-polarization-media-habits/

Morning Consult + Politico. (2018, January 18–20). National tracking poll, project 180111. Retrieved from https://www.politico.com/f/?id=00000161-34ea-daac-a3e9-3feb1c800001

Mullin, B. (2016, Nov. 14). ProPublica is seeing a surge in donations after John Oliver's Trump segment. *Poynter*. Retrieved from https://www.poynter.org/news/propublica-seeing-surge-donations-after-john-olivers-trump-segment

Murrow, E. R. (1954, March 9). A report on Senator Joseph R. McCarthy. *See It Now*. Columbia Broadcasting System. Transcript retrieved from http://www.lib.berkeley.edu/MRC/murrowmccarthy.html

New studies on political fact-checking. (2016, September 16). *American Press Institute*. Retrieved from https://www.americanpressinstitute.org/fact-checking-project/new-research-on-political-fact-checking-growing-and-influential-but-partisanship-is-a-factor/

Nyhan, B., Porter, E., Reifler, J., & Wood, T. (2017, June 29). *Taking corrections literally but not seriously? The effects of information on factual beliefs and candidate favorability*. Research paper. Retrieved from https://papers.ssrn.com/sol3/papers.cfm?abstract_id=2995128

Nyhan, B., & Reifler, J. (2014). *The Effect of Fact-checking on Elites: A field experiment on U.S. state legislators*. Research paper. Retrieved from https://www.dartmouth.edu/~nyhan/fact-checking-elites.pdf

Our process. (2018). *FactCheck.org*. Retrieved from http://www.factcheck.org/our-process/

Plato, & Jowett, B. (1914). *The dialogues of Plato*. New York, NY: Charles Scribers Sons.

PolitiFact. (2018). *PolitiFact*. Retrieved from politifact.com

Poynter (2018). International Fact Checking Network. *Poynter*. Retrieved from poynter.org/tags/international-fact-checking-network

ProPublica. (2018). *ProPublica*. Retrieved from propublica.org

Quinnipiac University Poll. (2018, January 25). Trump is no role model for children, U.S. voters say 2–1; Quinnipiac university national poll finds; he does not provide moral leadership, voters say. Retrieved from https://poll.qu.edu/national/release-detail?ReleaseID=2516

Schaefer, J. (2013, June 26). Truth Bias: A psychological cloak for deception. *Psychology Today*. Retrieved from https://www.psychologytoday.com/blog/let-their-words-do-the-talking/201306/truth-bias

Scriber, B. (2016, September 8). Who decides what's true in politics? A history of the rise of political fact-checking. *Poynter*. Retrieved from https://www.poynter.org/news/who-decides-whats-true-politics-history-rise-political-fact-checking

Sharockman, A. (2017, June 13). The power of fact-checking in today's world. *PolitiFact*. Retrieved from http://www.politifact.com/truth-o-meter/article/2017/jun/13/power-fact-checking-todays-world/

Silver, N. (2017, October 5). Does the media cover trump too much? Too harshly? Too narrowly? *FiveThirtyEight*. Retrieved from https://fivethirtyeight.com/features/does-the-media-cover-trump-too-much-too-harshly-too-narrowly/

Silverman, C. (2007). *Regret the error: How media mistakes pollute the press and imperil free speech*. New York, NY: Union Square Press.

Snopes.com. (2018). *Snopes*. Retrived from snopes.com

Sperber, A. M. (1986). *Murrow: His life and times*. New York, NY: Freundlich.

State of the Nation. (2018). *FactCheck.org*. Retrieved from http://www.factCheck.org/state-of-the-union-with-jake-tapper/

Stolberg, S. G. (2017, August 7). Many politicians lie. But Trump has elevated the art of fabrication. *New York Times*. Retrieved from https://www.nytimes.com/2017/08/07/us/politics/lies-trump-obama-mislead.html?_r=0

Street, C. N. H., & Richardson, D. C. (2015). Descartes versus Spinoza: Truth, uncertainty, and bias. *Social Cognition, 33*(3), 227–239.

Thompson, A. (2016, December 8). Parallel narratives. *Vice News*. Retrieved from https://news.vice.com/en_us/article/d3xamx/journalists-and-trump-voters-live-in-separate-online-bubbles-mit-analysis-shows

Trump Archive. (2018). *Internet archive*. Retrieved from http://archive.org/details/trumparchive&tab=collection

TrumpBeat. (2018). *FiveThirtyEight*. Retrieved from https://fivethirtyeight.com/tag/trumpbeat

Trump-O-Meter. (2018). *PolitiFact*. Retrieved from http://www.politifact.com/truth-o-meter/promises/trumpometer/

Trump Promise Tracker. (2018). *Washington Post*. Retrieved from https://www.washingtonpost.com/graphics/politics/trump-promise-tracker/?utm_term=.01df768fa6b5

Trump Transcripts. (2018). *FactCheck.org*. Retrieved from https://transcripts.factcheck.org

Tsipursky, G. (2017, June 15). How to address the epidemic of lies in politics. *Scientific American*. Retrieved from https://blogs.scientificamerican.com/observations/how-to-address-the-epidemic-of-lies-in-politics/

Umansky, E. (2017, May 8). How we're learning to do journalism differently in the age of Trump. *ProPublica*. Retrieved from https://www.propublica.org/article/how-were-learning-to-do-journalism-differently-in-the-age-of-trump?utm_source=pardot&utm_medium=email&utm_campaign=dailynewsletter

Weeks, B. E. (2015). Emotions, partisanship, and misperceptions: How anger and anxiety moderate the effect of partisan bias on susceptibility to political misinformation. *Journal of Communication, 65*(4), 699–719

12. Trump, the Press Critic: Unethical and Ineffective

ARTHUR S. HAYES
Fordham University

When President Donald Trump (2017d) tweeted, "Network news has become so partisan, distorted and fake that licenses must be challenged and, if appropriate, revoked. Not fair to public," in early October 2017, the response from the news media was mostly measured (Blake, 2017). Most observers recognized that Trump's call to sic the Federal Communications Commission (FCC) on NBC was unworkable.

The FCC licenses television and radio stations, not networks such as NBC (Media Bureau, 2008, p. 8). True, the FCC has a broadcast news distortion policy, empowering it to investigate a station "if it receives documented evidence ... from individuals with direct personal knowledge that a licensee or its management engaged in the intentional falsification of the news" (Media Bureau, 2008, p. 14). But plaintiffs lost in the only two news distortion cases to reach appeals courts, *Galloway v. FCC* (1985) and *Serafyn v. FCC* (1998), though the FCC often receives complaints of inaccurate or one-sided news reports. Generally, the FCC "will not intervene in such cases because it would be inconsistent with the First Amendment to replace the journalistic judgment of licensees with our own" (Media Bureau, 2008, p. 14).

Empty threat of a crackdown or not, most observers noted that the tweet marked a turning point in Trump's more than two-year diatribe against the mainstream news media, particularly those labeled liberal by conservatives and Republicans (Calderone & Robinson, 2015). Though just about every president has complained about unfair press coverage, and Richard Nixon used surrogates to bring ultimately unsuccessful challenges against broadcast stations (see Hazlett & Sosa, 1998, p. 50), no president before Trump had publicly advocated the use of regulatory power to censor news media for their unfavorable and allegedly inaccurate coverage. Instead, Presidents Nixon and

Franklin Roosevelt retaliated against unfavorable press coverage by signaling privately to federal regulators to launch investigations or to disapprove proposed corporate deals (Stamm, 2011, p. 111). Many, however, suspect that Trump has used the more subtle approach, too. Such accusations surfaced during fall 2017 when the U.S. Justice Department reviewed AT&T's proposed merger with Time Warner, which owns CNN, a frequent target of Trump's most bitter attacks (Peters, 2017).

This chapter offers a unique perspective on Trump's fake news campaign against mostly legacy news organizations—analysis of Trump as a press critic through the lens of press criticism theory. Tested against the tenets of journalism criticism outlined by journalism scholar Jay W. Jensen (1960) and communication theorist James W. Carey (1974), Trump's fake news campaign does not qualify as valid criticism. Nor does Trump's criticism qualify as legitimate under a key tenet of journalism professor Marion Tuttle Marzolf's (1991) norms. Communication ethics scholar Wendy Wyatt (2007) wrote the first book-length study of press criticism. Trump's campaign against fake news outlets does not meet her norms of discursive democracy.

In *Press Critics are the Fifth Estate: Media Watchdogs in America* (Hayes, 2008), this author developed a theoretical framework and norms for analyzing the ethical legitimacy and effectiveness of press critics based on a First Amendment concept of democratic discourse. Under this theory and norms, Trump's suggestion that the FCC should start license-revocation proceedings against NBC is unethical because it is coercive speech, which is unacceptable in public democratic discourse. Under the standards I devised, a critique of the press must be fair, accurate, coherent and fact-based. Here, too, as this chapter documents, Trump's criticism comes up short.

The First Amendment concept of democratic discourse press criticism theory, however, accepts uncivil speech as legitimate on the belief that excluding incivility wrongly limits the diversity of speakers in the marketplace of ideas. Therefore, Trump's petty ad hominem attacks on journalists, though widely condemned for their tone, are acceptable under this theory of democratic public discourse though other forms of logical fallacies such as circular arguments, dogmatism, hasty generalizations and non-sequiturs are not.

The personal attacks and, indeed, the overwhelming majority of his criticism, however, does not meet the standards for my "prescription for effective press criticism in a democracy," which is derived from my study of effective press critics (Hayes, 2008, pp. 135–140). As this chapter will show, Trump's failure to persuade the so-called liberal press to conform to his standards of journalism—indeed their rebuke of his critique shown in their rejection of narrowly defined objectivity, false equivalency, pundits' retorts and the rise of fact-checking sites, combined with the support for the news media shown in public opinion polls—underscores the soundness of my criteria for determining when a press critic is effective. This chapter will show that Trump is something of a poster boy for ineffectual press criticism.

Trump's Campaign Against the News Media: Nixonian and Machiavellian

By September 2015, four-and-a-half months into his candidacy for the Republican Party presidential nomination, Trump had attacked the news media 43 times (Calderone & Robinson, 2015). That year, he had yet to tar his targets with the "fake news" smear. But a pattern soon developed that continued into his presidency. He attacked as biased anyone—even leading conservative pundits and Fox news personalities—who did not give him favorable coverage in highly subjective, vague and extremely irrelevant personal terms. At the same time, however, he "received more media attention than any 2016 candidate" as Sunday shows and cable networks made "every effort to accommodate him," and editors lined "up to get him on the cover" (Calderone & Robinson, 2015). As Trump approached his 100th day in office, Trump or his administration had attacked the news media at least 130 times, used the smear fake news 30 times on Twitter, yet he had appointed four former Fox News personalities to his administration (Alderman, 2017).

How does Trump define fake news? In one tweet he defined it as news outlets that rely on "phony unnamed sources & highly slanted & even fraudulent reporting, #Fake News is DISTORTING DEMOCRACY in our country" (Trump, 2017c). Yet, he is not averse to using unnamed sources to bolster his agenda (see Holpuch, 2017).

Apparently, Trump sees in any unfavorable report about him, his actions and policies by mostly CNN, *NBC*, *ABC*, the *Washington Post* or the *New York Times* a conspiracy, an intentional effort to undermine his presidency and betray Americans—no matter how trivial the inaccuracy or whether the report is objectively accurate. "The FAKE NEWS media (failing *@nytimes*, *@NBCNews*, *@ABC*, *@CBS*, *@CNN*) is not my enemy, it is the enemy of the American People!" (Trump, 2017a). In short, Trump considers liberal mainstream media outlets as fake news and perceives them as fraudulent, vicious and incompetent (Weber, 2017). As the Pulitzer prize-winning fact-checking outlet Politifact (Holan, 2017) concluded:

> When PolitiFact fact-checks fake news, we are calling out fabricated content that intentionally masquerades as news coverage of actual events. When President Donald Trump talks about fake news, he means something else entirely. Instead

of fabricated content, Trump uses the term to describe news coverage that is unsympathetic to his administration and his performance, even when the news reports are accurate.

Sebastian Gorka, former deputy assistant to the president, offered a disturbing Machiavellian rationale for Trump's campaign against the news media, one that, if true, is clearly censorial and reeks of Nixonian paranoia. In a democracy, no government official should be off-limits to public scrutiny based on status or public popularity. Moreover, fact-supported unfavorable coverage is not concocted coverage. But Gorka argued that,

> There is a monumental desire on behalf of the majority of the media, not just the pollsters, the majority of the media to attack a duly elected President in the second week of his term. That's how unhealthy the situation is and until the media understands how wrong that attitude is, and how it hurts their credibility, we are going to continue to say, "fake news". (Massie, 2017)

Theories of Press Criticism

There is a paucity of scholarship defining well-substantiated and coherent principles and norms for understanding the purpose and role of press critics in democratic societies. As Wyatt (2007, p. 3) noted, "Only a handful of journalism and communication scholars, a few journalists, an art critic, and a philosopher have contributed ideas about what the agenda—the terms and bounds—of criticism should be."

Jensen (1960, p. 262) argued that criticism was not synonymous with "petty faulty—criticism of the carping, captious, censorious, caviling type … criticism that is not based upon understanding is not criticism at all … it must be conducted in an objective manner." As documented below, Trump's approach is not true criticism gauged by Jensen's standards.

Trump's criticism of the news media does not qualify as legitimate under Carey's criteria listed below:

- "The press requires a strong critical tradition that makes an active and continuous response in terms of factual detail, unemotional language and articulate values to the materials presented to the public" (1974, p. 231).
- "But attack is not criticism, and it is the absence of substantial criticism that makes the sporadic attacks on the press by government and others so telling" (p. 235).
- "This criticism must be based upon precise observation, clear procedure, unemotional language, subject to the cooperative correction of

others, and occurring in the public forum where all affected by the institution can at least observe and can comment on the critical process" (p. 235).

• "I am arguing that press criticism is essentially the criticism of language ... it requires therefore close public attention to the methods, procedures and techniques of journalistic investigation and the language of journalistic reporting" (p. 244).

Marzolf argued that press criticism should take its cue partially from literary and art criticism. "The press critic would also work on the same three levels set forth by literary critics: the individual, personal response; the interpretive or explanatory response for the audience; and the evaluative response that judges quality" (Marzolf, 1991, p. 198). Marzolf said the press critic's purpose is to serve society and the profession by encouraging public debate about news media performance on an analytical and intellectual level. Of course, she could not have anticipated Trump's current volleys against the news media, but she warned (p. 198), "Too much press criticism in the past has attacked the writer or publisher for evil intentions or character defects rather than examining the institutional performance or social utility of the reportage," which is an apt description of one of the shortcomings of his press criticism.

Wyatt's theory is grounded in Jurgen Habermas's public sphere theory of deliberative democracy and argues that the "ultimate purpose of deliberative democracy is mutual understanding" (2007, p. 111). Thus, her theory doesn't allow for a critic like President Trump who does not engage in rationale exchanges with the news media about press performance but instead delivers his commands and barbs through tweets and at press conferences. Press critics, Wyatt (2007, p. 145) argues, are citizens who have taken "a lead in facilitating the process of criticism" and engages in public discourse that is primarily face-to-face "and aims toward mutual understanding, which is the goal of all communicative action and a requirement for intersubjectively formed opinions."

The First Amendment Concept of Democratic Discourse Press Criticism Theory

The First Amendment concept of democratic discourse press criticism theory adds something new to press criticism theory: an emphasis placed on effectiveness. Implicit in all public criticism is the notion of the public good; that the critic's goal is to educate the public, to monitor influential and powerful institutions and individuals and to persuade those institutions and individuals to meet their own professed social obligations (Hayes, 2008, p. 4).

The First Amendment concept of democratic discourse press criticism theory, however, rejects some key prerequisites of the Habermasian model of public sphere discourse and deliberation. It does not require that press critics communicate in a public sphere that meets all of Habermas's structural requirements: "What Habermas has in mind with his account of the public sphere and what tends to be assumed, even if only tacitly, in invocations of the public, are actors meeting face to face according to legal or rational deliberative procedures in order to come to agreement on a matter of national interest" (Dean, 2003, p. 96).

Though civility and rational discourse is preferred, the First Amendment concept of democratic discourse theory does not exclude speakers who rely on hyperbole, parody, profanity, sarcasm and other forms of irreverent, offensive and abusive language. In a true democracy, eloquence cannot be a prerequisite for participation (Hayes, 2008, pp. 13–14) because "individuals must be free within public discourse from the enforcement of all civility rules, so as to be able to advocate and to exemplify the creation of new forms of communal life in their speech." Moreover, under the First Amendment concept of democratic discourse theory, hyperbole, parody, profanity, sarcasm and other forms of irreverent, offensive and abusive speech are protected (Hayes, 2017, p. 154).

The theory recognizes that the Internet serves as a basis for a participatory democratic communication. It operates as a public sphere allowing grassroots press watchdog groups and individuals to galvanize public opinion via email and blog conversations and arrive at consensus that can be used as leverage to hold news media outlets accountable to news consumers. "Most generally put, the public sphere is the site and subject of liberal democratic practice. It is the space within which people deliberate over matters of common concern, matters that are contested and about which it seems necessary to reach consensus" (Dean, 2003, p. 95).

Habermas argues that, generally, the Internet does not function as a public sphere. But he seems to carve out an exception for press critics. "Within established national public spheres, the online debates of web users only promote political communication when news groups crystallize around the focal points of the quality press, for example, national newspapers and political magazines" (Habermas, 2006, p. 426).

Trump's Coercive Speech

Coercive speech, however, is unethical under Habermasian discourse ethics and argumentation theories, which Habermas draws upon, and the First

Amendment concept of democratic discourse theory. "In rational discourse," we assume that conditions of communication obtain that "exclude every kind of coercion—whether originating outside the process reaching understanding or within it—other than that of the better argument, so that all motives except that of cooperative search for truth are neutralized" (Habermas, 1996, p. 273).

In argumentation theory, coercive speech falls under the category of the illogical fallacy, ad baculum. "Literally, 'an argument to the stick', the *ad baculum* is an argument which turns on a threat or reference to dire consequences ... the fallacy of deferring to the opinions of those of superior rank for fear of offending them and landing oneself in difficulties" (Woods, 1998, p. 493–494).

Generally, First Amendment free speech principles also recognized that coercive speech is constitutionally unprotected speech (Hayes, 2008, p. 14). Specifically, a series of rulings stand for the proposition that "a public official who tries to shut down an avenue of expression of ideas and opinions through 'or threatened imposition of government power or sanction' is violating the First Amendment" (*BackPage LLC vs. Thomas Dart*, 2015, p. 230). Of course, as noted above, broadcasting networks are not under direct licensing control by the FCC. Consequently, NBC has no grounds to file an injunction against Trump. Moreover, Trump later "claimed that he was not calling for restrictions on the press. He merely wants the press to 'speak more honestly'" (Estepa, 2017).

Thus, the importance of the ethical critique: Drawing from those free speech principles, I maintain that press criticism by an elected or government official is presumptively inappropriate in a democracy because typically it is more than a mere equal exchange of opinions between the government official and the news outlet.

> Where press critics are concerned, I add the direct and indirect threat of the coercive power of government action to the list of coercive speech. A press critic in a position to invoke the coercive power of the state against a media outlet poses a threat to a free exchange of ideas, and that is what we seek, an honest discourse among critics, the public, and the news media. But when a government official scolds the press there is almost always a tacit threat of censorship via criminal prosecution or regulatory sanctions or approvals. Thus, such a scolding can coercively intrude into the editorial integrity of a news organization, restricting the options the organization has a right to expect. (Hayes, 2008, p. 14)

Twice Trump has explicitly attempted to coerce the news media into bending to his will by threatening the use of regulatory or legislative actions. As discussed above, Trump raised the prospect of an FCC crackdown on broadcasting networks. As a candidate for the Republican Party presidential nomination, Trump vowed (Gold, 2016):

One of the things I'm going to do if I win, and I hope we do and we're certainly leading. I'm going to open up our libel laws so when they write purposely negative and horrible and false articles, we can sue them and win lots of money. We're going to open up those libel laws. So when *The New York Times* writes a hit piece which is a total disgrace or when *The Washington Post*, which is there for other reasons, writes a hit piece, we can sue them and win money instead of having no chance of winning because they're totally protected.

Once in office, Trump went after the *New York Times* again. "The failing @nytimes has disgraced the media world. Gotten me wrong for two solid years. Change libel laws" (Trump, 2017b)? Like his wish to use federal regulatory authority to target broadcasters, Trump's desire to revise libel laws to use as a cudgel against the press is vague and rhetorical. He would have to persuade "Congress to create a federal libel, as it has always been state law" (See Chemerinsky, 2017, p. 563). As noted above, coercive speech is unethical and undemocratic because it can rob an individual of rational free choice. On that measure alone, Trump's fake news campaign is morally bankrupt. Yet, at least in the U.S., where freedom of the press is guaranteed under the First Amendment, government's browbeating of the news media has proved largely ineffective.

How an Effective Press Critic Operates

Press Critics are the Fifth Estate profiled effective press critics. The press critics were chosen based on the following criteria, with emphasis placed on the top four standards (Hayes, 2008, p. 4).

1. Has the critique led to the dismissal, resignation, or reassignment of a reporter, broadcast public affairs personality, editor, or news executive?
2. Has the critique led to content or programming changes consistent with widely acknowledged journalism ethical standards?
3. Has the critique led to a reform of a news organization's standards and practices?
4. Has the critique spurred public debate in public forums and in the news media about news media performance or the business of mass media, helping to shape public opinion on the issue?
5. Do news media outlets quote the individual or organization as an authority on news media ethics and performance?
6. Does the individual or organization have a longtime and substantial following, measured in viewers, books sales, or Web site hits?
7. Has the individual or organization inspired a movement?

8. Has the individual or organization established standards of inquiry, analysis, or proposals used by other critics?
9. Have the individual's critiques gained currency among other critics and scholars who point to the individual as a groundbreaking activist or thinker in news media criticism?

The research showed that the effective press critic adopted a non-combative adversarial relationship with the news media, confronted news media outlets with fact-based arguments, offered critical analysis based on a news' organization's failure to comply with the implicit or explicit terms of its social contract or ethical codes, and galvanized public support for its arguments (Hayes, 2008, pp. 135–140).

Under my theory, a legitimate press critic may have an ideological or political agenda. What matters is the content of the critique. Thus, *The Daily Show*'s Jon Stewart, for example, ranks as a highly effective press critic because the liberal's satirical jabs, delivered in print and on the *Daily Show*, and his on-air interviews with journalists held news media outlets and specific journalists accountable based on their own professional standards and professed obligations to served the public good, spurred discussion about journalism performance among the public, scholars and the industry and, in one remarkable instance, galvanized public opinion that led to the cancelling of CNN's *Crossfire* political debate show (Hayes, 2008, pp. 135–140). Reagan conservative Reed Irvine ranks as highly effective largely because of his success in persuading PBS, which under the Public Broadcasting Act of 1967 is obligated to fairness and balance, to run a rightwing rebuttal to *Vietnam: A Television History* in 1985 (Hayes, 2008, pp. 21–24).

Trump's Ineptitude

In stark contrast, Trump's approach is combative because adversaries seek a common goal, which is, in this context, to improve press performance consistent with the mainstream media's obligation to provide the public with accurate and fair reporting about important civic issues and powerful individuals, institutions and groups. That does not appear to be Trump's objective, evidenced, in part, by his denouncing certain news outlets as enemies of the people:

> A press critic that sees its target as an enemy does not seek to engage the news outlet and its personnel in a discussion or debate because the enemy is to be eliminated … There is little incentive for a news organization to engage in a constructive dialogue with a press critic who attacks it as an enemy to vanquish. (Hayes, 2008, p. 135)

Trump's criticism is devoid of critical analysis and nuance. He talks about bias, but he has not defined it beyond his belief that a report is unfavorable to him. He denounces the use of anonymous sourcing, but does not articulate when its use is appropriate and when it is not. The Society for Professional Journalist Code of Ethics, for example, endorses the use of anonymity and advises that journalists, "Consider sources' motives before promising anonymity. Reserve anonymity for sources who may face danger, retribution or other harm, and have information that cannot be obtained elsewhere. Explain why anonymity was granted" (SPJ Code of Ethics, 2014).

At least two of the president's biggest claims of media inaccuracy have been baseless fantasies. On January 21, 2017, a day after the inauguration, Trump claimed the media had misrepresented the number of people attending his inauguration and Press Secretary Sean Spicer labeled the news accounts as shameful, wrong and dishonest (Cillizza, 2017). He claimed it "was the largest audience to ever witness an inauguration—period—both in person and around the globe" (Cillizza, 2017). Politifact, however, rated his assertion as "pants on fire" (Qiu, 2017), meaning the claim was ridiculous and inaccurate (About Politifact, 2017).

Trump claimed that the news media were not reporting terrorist attacks in the U.S. and Europe. Politifact, however, "found no support for the idea that the media is hushing up terrorist attacks on U.S. or European soil. ... There is plenty of coverage of [sic] in the American media of terrorist attacks. We rate the statement Pants on Fire!" (Jacobson, 2017). If Trump occupied the status of a professional press critic such as *Politico*'s Jack Shafer, *CNN Reliable Sources* Brian Stelter or *NPR*'s Eric Deggans, it is unlikely that he would still have his job after publishing such whoppers. But no one can fire the president for spreading false information about news coverage.

There have been occasions when Trump's charges of inaccurate reporting were correct. For example, a week before Trump moved into the White House, *Time*'s Zeke Miller's observation that a bust of Martin Luther King was removed from the White House was reported by another reporter. "More decorating details: Apart from the return of the Churchill bust, the MLK bust was no longer on display" (Gibbs, 2017). But that was untrue.

The Trump Administration, however, tried to assign ill will as a motive for the journalistic slip-up. At a press conference, Spicer called the mistake "deliberately false reporting." Later, Trump said, "So Zeke, Zeke from *Time* magazine, writes a story about 'I took down.' I would never do that because I have great respect for Dr. Martin Luther King. But this is how dishonest the media is" (Schreckinger & Gold, 2017). Miller, however, never claimed that Trump took the statue down or ordered that it be removed. Miller quickly apologized publicly and the story was retracted, but *Time* was not cowered by the White House's mischaracterization of the motives behind the mistake:

> No news organization ever wants to make an error, but we all have procedures for handling them when we do. Zeke moved quickly to correct the record, and we stand behind him for taking responsibility for the mistake. He and our other reporters will continue to cover the new Administration thoroughly, fairly and fearlessly. (Gibbs, 2017)

Journalism scholar Michael Schudson (2017) lists, "willingness to retract, correct, and implicitly or explicitly apologize for misstatements in a timely manner," and "an interest in contrary evidence" as earmarks of trustworthy and quality journalism. Thus, by Schudson's measure, *Time* and other outlets that apologize and run retractions when presented with evidence that their reports are inaccurate cannot reasonably be said to be involved in a fake news conspiracy to undermine the presidency.

As 2017 drew to a close, Trump's demands that management fire journalists yielded no direct results. Most notably, ESPN did not meet the White House's demands to fire host Jemele Hill for tweeting that Trump was a White supremacist (Stelter, 2017a). News outlets, however, took it upon themselves to discipline reporters who in their Trump-related news reports or tweets showed gross carelessness or intentional bias. The *Los Angeles Times* dismissed a freelancer who tweeted, "@TIME I would rather see Donald Trump's life end" (Edgar, 2016). CNN took the initiative in firing three reporters who reported an erroneous story about a probe into a pre-inaugural meeting between a Trump associate and a Russian investment fund head without prompting from Trump (Stelter, 2017b). ABC News suspended Brian Ross, its chief investigative correspondent, for four weeks without pay for his erroneous report about Michael Flynn and Trump, which the network called a serious error (Wang, 2017).

Trump's attacks have not eroded trust in the news media for a majority of Americans, according to polling results. He has failed to galvanize public opinion to support his claims against the news media. In July 2017, the results of Axios's poll found that "89% of Republicans" viewed "President Trump as more trustworthy than CNN, and 91% of Democrats think the opposite. Among all adults, trust for CNN is 7 points ahead of Trump. Among independents, CNN wins by 15 points" (Allen, 2017). In November 2017, the Quinnipiac University poll ("Trump Approval Rating At Near-Record Low," 2017) reported that,

> American voters disapprove 58–38 percent of the way the media covers Trump, but trust the media more than Trump 54–34 percent to tell the truth about

important issues. Voters say 53–42 percent that the media focuses too much on negative stories about Trump, but do not believe 57–39 percent that the media makes up negative stories about him.

Citing the results of a Morning Consult/Politico poll, *Broadcasting & Cable*'s John Eggerton (2017) observed, "It may be some comfort to news media incessantly hammered by the President as 'fake' and 'enemies' that more respondents trusted them (45%) than trusted the President (35%)."

Public support for the accused fake news outlets can be measured in higher subscriptions and ratings.

> The *New York Times* added 154,000 digital-only subscriptions in the last quarter, bringing its total digital subscriptions to about 2.5 million … The *Washington Post*, bird-dogging the Trump administration and the Russia investigation with equal intensity, has seen its digital subscriptions pass the 1 million mark. Cable TV ratings and revenues have surged as well. (Shafer, 2017)

Trump's combative, hyperbolic and largely unsubstantiated attacks upon the news media have proved counterproductive as evidenced in several outlets' bold response to Trump's lies. Journalism historian Mitchell Stephens (2017) took note of the shift away from reliance on key tenet's of 20th-century objective journalism brought on by Trump's harangues:

> The big news in American journalism today has been that reporters, editors and producers at legacy journalism organizations have become so eager to dispute the more questionable pronouncements and proposals of the Trump administration. Increasingly, they are prepared to label the president's wilder statements and tweets "falsehoods" or even "lies." The big news is that many of our best journalists seem, in news coverage, not just opinion pieces, to be moving away from balance and nonpartisanship.

The *Washington Post* added a slogan beneath its online masthead in February 2019—"Democracy Dies in Darkness." Management said it wasn't a direct response to Trump (Farhi, 2017). An opinion writer for the *Washington Examiner*, however, observed that, "Many readers will find it difficult to believe that the introduction of 'democracy dies in darkness' was spurred by new tech platforms and not, say, by the presence of Donald Trump in the White House" (York, 2017).

Juliane A. Lischka, (2017 p. 1) a postdoctoral student, conducted a critical discourse analysis of *New York Times* news articles about fake news accusations and found a prideful rebuke by Times journalists and columnists of Trump's fake news accusations.

> First, the accusations are taken as a "badge of honor" for professional journalism but are morally evaluated to damage journalism's role as the fourth estate in

democracy. Second, using sarcasm, the articles criticize President Trump's capacity to govern and thus question his legitimacy. Third, reporting implies that fake news accusations aim at suppressing critical thinking as in authoritarian regimes. Fourth, accusations are described as irrational responses to professional reporting or proven factually wrong, when possible.

Individually, on-air news and talk show hosts have struck back. During the Thanksgiving weekend, Trump criticized CNN International by saying the network lies and represents the U.S. poorly to the world. CNN's Wolf Blitzer retorted, "CNN and CNN International are not sponsored by any state or autocrat or any political organization. Despite the constant criticism of the president, we are unwavering in our mission—free and independent, as the press should be" (Bauder, 2017).

Conclusion

This chapter has made an argument grounded in press criticism theory for rejecting President Trump's fake news campaign as unethical and undemocratic discourse. Under Jensen's theory, Trump's campaign does not rank as true criticism because it is subjective, carping, censorious and fails to demonstrate that he understands journalistic values and practice. Similarly, under Carey's theory, which distinguishes attack from criticism, Trump is not engaging in legitimate press criticism. Marzolf warned against press criticism that subscribed evil motives and character defects. Trump has dubbed his fake news targets enemies of the people. The president's rants against the news media on Twitter and at rallies are not public dialogue designed to reach mutual understanding with the press and, therefore, do not conform to Wyatt's conception of press criticism. This author's press criticism theory holds that any press criticism from a president is presumptively coercive because of the potential a government official has to exercise regulatory means to win compliance. Coercive speech is undemocratic. There is, however, no need to presume bad intentions by Trump; he has been explicit in threatening to use regulatory and legal authority to get the news media to bend the press to his will.

This author's press criticism theory also establishes norms for determining effectiveness. Because Trump has failed to engage in a rational, fact-based conversation with the press, one that identifies an understanding of the profession's accepted practices and ethical norms, and its widely accepted role in a democratic society, no news organization has agreed to his calls to fire journalists or to change the standards and practice of anonymous sourcing. Moreover, the results of three polls show that he has not persuaded even a majority of voters that he is more credible than the news outlets he paints as fake.

The targets of his attacks have rightly chosen to defy Trump by publicly documenting the accuracy of news accounts that he says are fake and characterizing his rhetoric as an authoritarian threat to free press values. The results of this analysis provide the news media and others with another critique of his fake news campaign: by the standards of democratic discourse, it is an unscrupulous, but thankfully, ineffective tactic.

References

About Politifact. (2017). *Politifact.* Retrieved from http://www.politifact.com/about/

Alderman, J. (2017, April 28). By the numbers: 100 days in, a look at the Trump Administration's conflicted relationship with the media. *Media Matters for America.* Retrieved from https://www.mediamatters.org/blog/2017/04/28/numbers-100-days-look-trump-administrations-conflicted-relationship-media/216205

Allen, M. (2017, July 4). Exclusive: Astonishing poll about Trump and the media. *Axios.* Retrieved from https://www.axios.com/exclusive-astonishing-poll-about-trump-and-media-2453120782.html

BackPage LLC vs. Thomas Dart, 807 F. 3d 229 (7th Cir., 2015). Retrieved from https://scholar.google.com/scholar_case?case=11419977392901106820&q=Back-Page+LLC+vs.+Thomas+Dart&hl=en&as_sdt=8003

Bauder, D. (2017, November 27). CNN Wolf Blitzer fights back against attacks. *Boston.com.* Retrieved from https://www.boston.com/news/media/2017/11/27/cnns-wolf-blitzer-fights-back-against-trumps-attack

Blake, A. (2017, October 11). Trump's threat to NBC's license is the very definition of Nixonian. *Washington Post.* Retrieved from https://www.washingtonpost.com/news/the-fix/wp/2017/10/11/trumps-threat-to-nbc-license-is-exactly-what-nixon-did/?hpid=hp_hp-top-table-main_trump-nbc-1150am%3Ahomepage%2Fstory&tid=a_inl&utm_term=.5dd68b11e68a

Calderone, M., & Robinson, J. (2015, September 28). 43 times Donald Trump has attacked the media as a presidential candidate. *Huffington Post.* Retrieved from https://www.huffingtonpost.com/entry/donald-trump-has-attacked-the-media-many-many-times_us_56059e0de4b0af3706dc3cce

Carey, J. W. (1974, April). Journalism and criticism: The case of an undeveloped profession. *The Review of Politics, 36*(2), 227–249.

Chemerinsky, E. (2017). The First Amendment in the era of Trump. *Denver Law Review, 94*(4), 553–566. Retrieved from http://static1.1.sqspcdn.com/static/f/276323/27675140/1504552788037/Vol94_Issue4_Chemerinsky_PRINT.pdf?token=fO6wqJkIapvS3DcbDFGoeEHKpd8%3D

Cillizza, C. (2017, January 2). Sean Spicer held a press conference. He didn't take questions. Or tell the whole truth. *Washington Post.* Retrieved from https://www.washingtonpost.com/news/the-fix/wp/2017/01/21/sean-spicer-held-a-press-conference-he-didnt-take-questions-or-tell-the-whole-truth/?utm_term=.f631ed381ccd

Dean, J. (2003) *Constellations,10*(1), 95–112. Retrieved from http://pages.uoregon.edu/koopman/courses_readings/phil123-net/intro/dean_net_publicsphere.pdf

Edgar, D. (2016, November 3). L.A. Times ends relationship with freelancer who sent Trump tweet. *Los Angeles Times.* Retrieved from http://www.latimes.com/local/readers-rep/la-rr-donald-trump-tweet-freelancer-20161103-htmlstory.html

Eggerton, J. (2017). Survey says: News media more trusted than Trump. *Broadcasting & Cable.* Retrieved from http://www.broadcastingcable.com/news/washington/survey-says-news-media-more-trusted-trump/170473

Estepa, J. (2017, October 11) Trump threatens NBC and other networks after nuclear arsenal story. *USAToday.* Retrieved from https://www.usatoday.com/story/news/politics/onpolitics/2017/10/11/trump-suggests-nbc-and-other-networks-should-penalized-after-nuclear-arsenal-story/753373001/

Farhi, P. (2017, February 24). The Washington Post's new slogan turns out to be an old saying. *Washington Post.* Retrieved from https://www.washingtonpost.com/lifestyle/style/the-washington-posts-new-slogan-turns-out-to-be-an-old-saying/2017/02/23/cb199cda-fa02-11e6-be05-1a3817ac21a5_story.html?utm_term=.d08f8a5e6ce1

Galloway v. FCC, 778 F. 2d 16 (D.C. Cir. 1985).

Gibbs, N. (2017, January 24). A note to our readers. *Time.* Retrieved from http://time.com/4645541/donald-trump-white-house-oval-office/

Gold, H. (2016, February 26). We're going to open up libel laws. *Politico.* Retrieved from https://www.politico.com/blogs/on-media/2016/02/donald-trump-libel-laws-219866

Habermas, J. (1996). *Between facts and norms: Contributions to a discourse theory of law and Democracy.* Cambridge, MA: The MIT Press. Retrieved from http://blogs.unpad.ac.id/teddykw/files/2012/07/J%25C3%25BCrgen-Habermas-Between-Facts-and-Norms.pdf

Habermas, J. (2006). Political communication in media society: Does democracy still enjoy an epistemic dimension? The impact of normative theory on empirical research. *Communication Theory, 16*, 411–426.

Hayes, A. S. (2008). *Press critics are the fifth estate: Media watchdogs in America.* Westport, CT: Praeger.

Hayes, A. S. (2017). *Sympathy for the cyberbully: How the crusade to censor hostile and offensive online speech abuses freedom of expression.* New York, NY: Peter Lang.

Hazlett, T. W., & Sosa, D. W. (1998). "Chilling" the Internet? Lessons from FCC regulation of radio broadcasting, *Michigan Telecommunication and Technology Law Review, 4*(35). Retrieved from https://repository.law.umich.edu/cgi/viewcontent.cgi?article=1162&context=mttlr, https://repository.law.umich.edu/mttlr/vol4/iss1/2

Holan, A. D. (2017, October 18). The media's definition of fake news vs. Donald Trump's. *Politifact.* Retrieved at http://www.politifact.com/truth-o-meter/article/2017/oct/18/deciding-whats-fake-medias-definition-fake-news-vs/

Holpuch, A. (2017, August 17). Trump tweets Fox News story with anonymous sources after criticizing practice, *The Guardian*. Retrieved from https://www.theguardian.com/us-news/2017/aug/08/donald-trump-news-tweet-north-korea-fox-and-friends

Jacobson, L. (2017, February 6). Donald Trump wrong that media is not reporting on terrorism anymore. *Politifact*. Retrieved from http://www.politifact.com/truth-o-meter/statements/2017/feb/06/donald-trump/donald-trump-wrong-media-not-reporting-terrorism-a/

Jensen, J. (1960, June). A method and a perspective for criticism of the mass media. *Journalism Quarterly, 37*, 261–266.

Lischka, J. A. (2017, September 17). A badge of honor? How the New York Times discredits President Trump's fake news accusations. *Journalism Studies*. doi:10.1080/1461670X.2017.1375385

Marzolf, M. T. (1991). *Civilizing voices: American press criticism 1880–1950*. New York, NY: Longman.

Massie, C. (2017, February 7). WH official: We'll say "fake news" until media realizes attitude of attacking the president is wrong. CNN. Retrieved from http://www.cnn.com/2017/02/07/politics/kfile-gorka-on-fake-news/index.html

Media Bureau. (2008, July). The public and broadcasting: How to get the most service from your local station. *Federal Communications Commission*. Retrieved from https://apps.fcc.gov/edocs_public/attachmatch/DA-08-940A2.pdf

Peters, J. (2017, November 13). If Trump White House is meddling in AT&T deal, it wouldn't be unprecedented. *Columbia Journalism Review*. Retrieved from https://www.cjr.org/united_states_project/att-deal-cnn-trump.php

Qiu, L. (2017, January 21). Donald Trump had biggest inaugural crowd ever? Metrics don't show it. *Politifact*. Retrieved from http://www.politifact.com/truth-o-meter/statements/2017/jan/21/sean-spicer/trump-had-biggest-inaugural-crowd-ever-metrics-don/

RBR-TVBR (2013, December 31). How to lose your station's FCC license. *Radio & Television Business Report*. Retrieved from http://www.rbr.com/how-to-lose-your-stations-fcc-license/

Schreckinger, B., & Gold, H. (2017, May/June). Trump's fake war on fake news. *Politico*. Retrieved from https://www.politico.com/magazine/story/2017/04/23/trump-loves-media-reporters-white-house-215043

Schudson, M. (2017, February 23). Here's what fake news looks like. *Columbia Journalism Review*. Retrieved from https://www.cjr.org/analysis/fake-news-real-news-list.php

Serafyn v. FCC, 149 F. 3d 1213 (1998).

Shafer, J. (2017, December 27). Who's winning Trump's war with the press? *Politico*. Retrieved from https://www.politico.com/magazine/story/2017/12/27/trump-press-war-winning-216160

SPJ Code of Ethics. (2014, September 6). Society of Professional Journalists. Retrieved from https://www.spj.org/ethicscode.asp

Schreckinger, B. and Gold, H. (2017, May/June). Trump's fake war on fake news. *Politico.* Retrieved from https://www.politico.com/magazine/story/2017/04/23/trump-loves-media-reporters-white-house-215043

Stamm, M. (2011). *Sound business: Newspapers, radio, and the politics of new media.* Philadelphia, PA: University of Pennsylvania Press.

Stelter, B. (2017a, June 27). Three journalists leaving CNN after retracted article. *CNN Media.* Retrieved from http://money.cnn.com/2017/06/26/media/cnn-announcement-retracted-article/index.html

Stelter, B. (2017b, September 14). ESPN says it accepts Jemele Hill's apology after anti-Trump tweets. *CNN Media.* Retrieved from http://money.cnn.com/2017/09/13/media/jemele-hill-espn-white-house/index.html

Stephens, M. (2017, June 26). Goodbye nonpartisan journalism. And good riddance. Disinterested reporting is overrated. *Politico.* Retrieved https://www.politico.com/magazine/story/2017/06/26/goodbye-nonpartisan-journalism-and-good-riddance-215305

Trump approval rating at near-record low, Quinnipiac University national poll finds; Roy Moore should drop out, voters say almost 3–1. (2017, November 14). Retrieved from https://poll.qu.edu/national/release-detail?ReleaseID=2500

Trump, D. [Donald J. Trump] (2017a, February 17). The FAKE NEWS media (failing @nytimes, @NBCNews, @ABC, @CBS, @CNN) is not my enemy, it is the enemy of the American People! [tweeted]. Retrieved from https://twitter.com/realdonaldtrump/status/832708293516632065?lang=en

Trump, D. [Donald J. Trump] (2017b, March 30). The failing @nytimes has disgraced the media world. Gotten me wrong for two solid years. Change libel laws? [tweeted]. Retrieved from https://twitter.com/realDonaldTrump/status/847455180912181249

Trump, D. [Donald J. Trump] (2017c, July 16). With all of its phony unnamed sources & highly slanted & even fraudulent reporting, #Fake News is DISTORTING DEMOCRACY in our country! [tweeted]. Retrieved from https://twitter.com/realdonaldtrump/status/886544734788997125?lang=en

Trump, D. [Donald J. Trump] (2017d, October 11). Network news has become so partisan, distorted and fake that licenses must be challenged and, if appropriate, revoked. Not fair to public! [tweeted]. Retrieved from https://twitter.com/realDonaldTrump/status/918267396493922304

Wang, V. (2017, December 7). ABC suspends reporter Brian Ross over erroneous report about Trump. *The New York Times.* Retrieved from https://www.nytimes.com/2017/12/02/us/brian-ross-suspended-abc.html

Weber, J. (2017, December 9). Trump says CNN was "caught red handed" with fake news on Wikileaks email. *Fox News.* Retrieved from http://www.foxnews.com/politics/2017/12/09/trump-says-cnn-was-caught-red-handed-with-fake-news-on-wikileaks-email.html

Woods, J. (1998, November). Argumentum ad baculum. *Argumentation, 12*(4), 493–504. doi:10.1023/A:1007779930624

Wyatt, W. N. (2007). *Critical conversations: A theory of press criticism*. Cresskill, NJ: Hampton Press.

York, B. (2017, February 22). Byron York: Washington Post adopts new motto, "democracy dies in darkness," says it has nothing to do with Trump. *Washington Examiner*. Retrieved from http://www.washingtonexaminer.com/byron-york-washington-post-adopts-new-motto-democracy-dies-in-darkness-says-it-has-nothing-to-do-with-trump/article/2615453

Part IV

Why Twitter and Facebook May Never Be the Same

13. Tweeting the Election: Comparative Uses of Twitter by Trump and Clinton in the 2016 Election

FLORA KHOO AND WILLIAM BROWN
Regent University

(*We would like to thank Rebecca John for her time and assistance as a coder for inter-rater reliability. This chapter would not have been possible without her help.*)

"Such a beautiful and important evening! The forgotten man and woman will never be forgotten again. We will all come together as never before" (Trump, 2016). This was the first tweet by property mogul, Donald Trump, after being successfully elected as president of the United States (U.S.) in the 2016 elections (see Figure 13.1). Trump's tweet was liked 629,307 times and retweeted 225,429 times.

Donald J. Trump ✔
@realDonaldTrump
🐦 Follow

Such a beautiful and important evening! The forgotten man and woman will never be forgotten again. We will all come together as never before

6:36 AM - 9 Nov 2016

↩ 🔁 225,429 ♥ 629,307

Figure 13.1: Donald Trump's First Tweet After Being Elected President.

Social media such as Twitter, Facebook and Instagram have become an essential part of political campaigns. The first presidential election in which Twitter was heavily used was in 2012, as it was sometimes referred to as the "Twitter election" (McKinney, Houston, & Hawthorne, 2014). Both the public and journalists used Twitter to send and receive news and political analysis on the election. Consider the final presidential debate between Barack Obama and Mitt Romney, which generated 6.5 million tweets the evening of the event in the 2012 election (Sharp, 2012). Such a large volume of tweets provides the potential to influence public opinion. Twitter was created in 2006 and currently has 317 million monthly active users worldwide (Statista, 2016). The significant rise in the use of Twitter in political campaigns has made this social media platform an increasingly important area for communication research. The purpose of the present study is to analyze the Twitter messages from two celebrity presidential candidates, Hillary Clinton and Donald Trump, during a critical period in the fall of 2016 coinciding with the presidential debates.

Literature Review

Studies show that there is a relationship between traditional media and the Twitter feeds of political candidates and parties (Conway, Kenski, & Wang, 2015). In the 2012 presidential primary, researchers found that news media influenced candidate and party reactions on Twitter as well as vice versa. Their research indicated that Twitter can both lead and follow traditional media. Twitter has become a means to bypass media gatekeepers; it serves as a "new source for journalistic content" (Conway, Kenski, & Wang, 2015, p. 364) and a source of influence on public opinion.

Tweeting during the presidential and vice presidential debates can influence attitudes towards candidates and the perceptions of political debates (Houston, Hawthorne, Spialek, Greenwood, & McKinney, 2013). Viewers who tweeted during a televised political event during the 2012 election such as a debate generated more favorable attitudes toward the candidates, in particular Barack Obama. Such live tweeting is driven by engagement and careful processing of debate content rather than by tweeting for enjoyment (Houston et al., 2013).

Landreville, White, and Allen (2015) examined the on-screen visuals shown during the final 2012 presidential debate on ABC-Yahoo news live-streaming online coverage to understand what visuals the viewers saw during the debate. Their study revealed that on-screen visuals such as instant poll results and Twitter feeds were dependent on elite sources such as public figures and media professionals. This elite source bias affirms the viewers' tendency to perceive the gatekeeper with more credibility and stronger analytical skills.

In the 2012 presidential election, researchers found a positive association between the number of times a candidate was mentioned by traditional media and the number of mentions of the candidate on Twitter. However, the candidates' Twitter activities did not impact the number of mentions about them on Twitter (Hong & Nadler, 2012).

Drawing on six theories that address uses and gratifications, word-of-mouth communication, selective exposure, framing, diffusion of innovations and the continuity-discontinuity framework, Parmelee and Bichard (2012) analyzed how tweets framed policies and personalities of politicians. Using a mixed methods approach that included interviews and content analysis of tweets, they found that the leaders' tweets influenced the followers' political views much more than the views of their family and friends. Their findings suggest that digital text messages were perceived as important and carried as much influence as a face-to-face meeting, especially in instances that had a perceived agreement on political opinion between the leader and follower.

Campaign tweets are an important part of impression management in political campaigns (Meeks, 2016). Meeks' study centered on Leary and Kowalski's (2016) model on impression motivation and impression construction. Political candidates are strongly motivated to impression-manage in order to get elected. Since the candidate's performance influences voters' perception of their self-presentation, they are thus spurred to impression-manage. This is especially the case since they are reliant on voters for approval and their votes. The candidate would thus determine their appearance, body language and verbal rhetoric on political issues and character traits in order to construct their image and self-presentation (Meeks, 2016).

In the 2016 presidential campaign, Wang, Li, and Luo (2016) analyzed the follower demographics of the presidential candidates, discovering that Trump supporters were more polarized in terms of social influence. Trump supporters either had a substantial amount of influence or little influence; and they also were found to be very young or very old. The research also revealed that Clinton supporters were more racially diverse and there was no gender affinity effect for Clinton. The percentage of female supporters for Clinton was 45.36% and Trump was 45.40%. This showed that there was no significant difference in female Twitter supporters between the two candidates, which contradicts the perception that Clinton had a stronger female base of online supporters.

Political tweets have persuasive power (Bichard & Parmelee, 2011). Trump used Twitter to set his agenda in the election campaign (Balsley,

2016) and whenever he had limited media coverage, he would strategically unleash "tweets storms" (Wells et al., 2016, p. 672). Other studies indicated that pro-Trump tweets were retweeted more often than pro-Clinton tweets and Trump had more support throughout most of the campaign, especially in October as well as a few days just before the election (Magdy & Darwish, 2016).

Social media offer famous idols the opportunity to turn their "celebrity capital into political influence" (Brown & Fraser, 2004). President Obama is a political celebrity with 79.2 million Twitter followers and ranks among the top four people with the most Twitter followers (Twitter, n.d.).The former president capitalizes on his popularity by tweeting policy issues and updates to his wide base of followers. He indicates that he does not do his own tweeting (Milian, 2009). His @BarackObama account is run by the Organizing for Action staff (Rampton, 2015), and any tweet by Obama is signed off as "bo" (Ho, 2011; Rampton, 2015).

Building celebrity status through a popular medium like Twitter may produce political capital. Arnold Schwarzenegger's stunning victory in the California recall election was strongly linked to the power of his celebrity status (Brown & Fraser, 2004). While in office, the former Governor of California provided direction for the content of the tweets, but had his staff write and send the tweets (Jones, 2010). Other politicians such as Clinton and Singapore Prime Minister Lee Hsien Loong similarly utilized the power of social media to engage with the public. When Lee personally tweeted, he signed off with his initials, LHL (Lee, n.d.). The former Secretary of State signs her tweets with—H (Twitonomy, October 24).

Gender and Race in Election Campaigns

The 2016 campaign saw Mrs. Clinton making her bid to be the first female U.S. president, thus making gender a pertinent issue to address at the polls. Lakoff (1973) found that the identity of women is "linguistically submerged" and that women experience "linguistic discrimination" both through the way in which females are taught to use language and in the way language treats them (pp. 45–46). The linguistic discrimination that Mrs. Clinton faced in the 2016 campaign could be found in the way Twitter users referenced her. For example, 13 days before Election Day, Mrs. Clinton posted a tweet from a year ago. She tweeted, "Happy birthday to this future president" along with a black-and-white photo of herself as a young girl (see Figure 13.2). Her tweet generated more criticisms than birthday wishes from Twitter users, which encouraged discussion about her in a negative way. Critics tweeted, "Too bad her mother didn't have one." (@LindaTraitz, 2016). Donald Trump Jr.

Happy birthday to this future president.

6:03 AM - 26 Oct 2016

60,028 Retweets 117,725 Likes

♡ 16K ⟲ 60K ♡ 118K

Figure 13.2. Hillary Clinton's Birthday Tweet Before 2016 Election Day.

wrote, "A year later the arrogance and entitlement in this tweet is exactly why it was never going to happen" (2016). Lakoff (1973) notes how the language of the favored group or the group that holds power is adopted by the other group and not vice versa.

Herrnson, Lay, and Stokes (2003) found that gender stereotypes impact voters' perceptions. A woman candidate could capitalize on gender stereotypes by focusing on issues that are favorable to them as women and by targeting woman voters. For instance, in past elections, voters perceived females as more suitable to handle what were stereotypically perceived as feminine issues such as education and child care, and were perceived to be less proficient in handling responsibilities stereotypically perceived as masculine issues like war and the economy (Shapiro & Mahajan, 1986). Although such stereotypes have likely changed in the past 30 years, being a woman political leader could have strategic advantages in campaigning on salient issues in which women are believed to have greater expertise and experience (Herrnson, Lay, & Stokes, 2003). Research also has found that women voters may feel positively towards female candidates and moderate their perceptions of female candidates through the lens of their political party affiliation (Dolan, 2008). Other studies found that the interaction of gender and party showed mixed results. Cook (1998) noted that women would likely vote for Republican female candidates and feminists would more likely favor Democratic women candidates. The perception of a candidate's viability could also impact the election results. If a voter favors a woman candidate but perceives that she may lose the election, the voter might choose to strategically vote for a male candidate in order to attach oneself to the winning candidate (Smith, Paul, & Paul, 2007).

Social compassion strategy in political campaigns, including those not directly connected to women's interest, steer the gender gap in influencing voting behavior on election day (Hutchings, Valentino, Philpot, & White, 2004). Compassion issues often involve the plight of socially vulnerable groups such as ethnic minorities and women. How compassionate a candidate appears towards vulnerable social groups may influence male and female voters differently. "Compassionate conservativism" was the Republican Party's new catch phrase during the 2000 campaign in its efforts to reach out to minority voters, and George Bush became the first Republican presidential nominee to address the National Association for the Advancement of Colored People (NAACP) at its Baltimore convention in 12 years (Philpot, 2010, p. 1). However, studies on compassion strategies in elections showed mixed results. Hutchings, Valentino, Philpot and White (2004) found that women had a higher evaluation of Bush than men when they were exposed to the same message of racial inclusion at the 2000 Republican National Convention (RNC).

Theoretical Framework

Framing theory is relevant to explaining the 2016 presidential election campaign because it demonstrates how frames embedded in tweets can shape the way individuals think about a candidate and how they understand what issues are at stake. Frames influence how one thinks by highlighting certain aspects of reality and renders other aspects obscure. Entman (1993) states "to frame is to select some aspects of a perceived reality and make them more salient in a communicating text, in such a way as to promote a particular problem definition, causal interpretation, moral evaluation, and/or treatment recommendation for the item described" (p. 52).

Lecheler, de Vreese, and Slothus (2009) emphasize how framing effects differ in magnitude and process, depending on the importance of an issue.

Each person is affected differently by the information received if it is an issue of which he or she cares deeply. The importance of the issue is a key component of opinion and attitude formation. Both persuasion scholars and agenda-setting scholars acknowledge importance as a "moderator of opinion change" (Lecheler et al., 2009, p. 401).

Some studies have examined issue-specific and generic frames (de Vreese, 2002; Semetko & Valkenburg, 2000). Issue-specific frames refer to a specific topic, while generic frames could encompass a broad selection of topics. Iyengar (1991) distinguishes between episodic and thematic framing. He found that framing effects vary, depending on the nature of the issue. This aspect of issue importance could be the deciding factor in terms of what makes one frame stronger than another (Chong & Druckman, 2007).

When an issue is framed in terms of values, it is likely to impact opinion formation of the individual. Value frames link value positions to how political debate is constructed and provides an interpretative lens to the policy conflict. They also portray debates on public policy issues as "clashes of deep-rooted values" (Schemer, Wirth, & Matthes, 2011, p. 335).

Another important framing question is whether political knowledge impacts the scope and processing of a framing message. Scholars have found mixed results when it comes to accessing if individuals with less knowledge are more susceptible to framing effects. Since political knowledge does not necessarily moderate framing effects, it may be the availability of relevant knowledge and the actuality of prior opinions on that issue that moderate effects (Lecheler et al., 2009). Druckman (2001) indicates that every political message comes with a messenger and therefore the framing effects may be limited by the trustworthiness of their source.

Schmuck, Heiss, Matthes, Engesser, and Esser (2017) discuss how the *strategic game* frame applies to political news coverage. The *game* frame focuses on who is winning or losing, the candidates' standing in the election polls, and the fight for public opinion and approval (Iyengar, Norpoth, & Hahn, 2004). On the other hand, the *strategy* frame looks at the candidates' motives, strategies and tactics in reaching for their political goals (Aalberg, Stromback & de Vreese, 2012). In a highly competitive environment, *strategic game* framing transits from issue-oriented to a focus on winning or losing. The *strategic fame* frame centers on the political process whereas the *issue* frame focuses on content and policies.

Priming effects occur when mental constructs influence how individuals perceive a candidate or policy. Campaign framing of issues that points to the opponent's character or integrity can prime voters to form opinions about the candidate's integrity and evaluate policy issues in ethical terms (Domke,

Shah, & Wackman, 1998). Issues influence voting behavior directly, which is a result of the voter's acceptance or rejection of candidates' positions on the issue. Issues also have an indirect influence due to priming effects such as voters' thoughts on the issues. This "carryover" shapes the perception of a candidate as well as other issues in the election campaign (Domke, Shah, & Wackman, 1998, p. 70). In the 2016 presidential election, candidates' framing of issues and character information on Twitter was fostered by highlighting certain information favorable toward a candidate and excluding certain information unfavorable toward the candidate, thus, creating priming effects.

Research Questions

In our study, we seek to analyze both framing and priming effects of Twitter messages by the Clinton and Trump campaigns. We pose the following research questions:

RQ 1: What frames were used by the two presidential candidates in their campaign tweets?

RQ 2: How did Clinton and Trump frame issues in their campaign tweets to advance their campaigns?

RQ 3: To what extent were Clinton and Trump attacking their opponents versus promoting themselves through their campaign tweets?

Methodology

We designed a content analytical study to investigate the use of frames by the two presidential candidates in their campaign tweets during the 2016 presidential election campaign. Quantitative content analysis seeks to identify the key relationships or patterns in the content analyzed (Riffe, Lacy, & Fico, 2014). Using Twitter Advanced Search, Clinton and Trump's campaign tweets during the period from September 5, 2016 to November 8, 2016 were downloaded for analysis. This period was selected as it was about two months before the Election Day on November 9, 2016, and was expected to be the most intensive period of the campaign to clinch votes. A total of 1,163 tweets were identified (see Table 13.1). They comprised 760 tweets by Clinton and 403 tweets by Trump. These candidates were selected as they were both leading in the election polls and were considered the two primary candidates.

Population and Sampling

The sample size for the study comprised 478 campaign tweets, 239 by Clinton and 239 by Trump (@HillaryClinton, @RealDonaldTrump). On

Table 13.1: Clinton and Trump's 2016 Election Campaign Tweets.

2016 Campaign Tweets			
Month	Clinton	Trump	Total
September 5–30	294	120	414
October 1- 31	347	242	589
November 1–8	119	41	160
Total	760	403	1,163

average, every fourth tweet was selected, and these 478 tweets were chosen randomly within the sample frame of all the tweets disseminated by the two key presidential nominees over a two-month period. A random sample of 100 tweets per candidate for the months of September and October, and 39 tweets for November were coded. This comprised a total of 239 tweets per candidate. Photos in the tweets were coded, but videos were omitted from the study.

Unit of Analysis

The entire tweet was taken as a unit of analysis irrespective of whether a photograph or other visual display accompanied the tweet.

Measurement of Tweet Frames

Tweets from @HillaryClinton and @RealDonaldTrump were perused to get a sense of the frames. In the content analysis of Clinton and Trump's tweets, 13 main frames and sub-frames were identified. The frames were defined as follows:

Patriotism Frame

The *Patriotism* frame is indicated by statements that describe the greatness of America and strong belief in the nation. For example, "America is big-hearted, not small-minded" or "build a better and stronger America" were coded within this frame. It could also include references to remembering 9/11 tragedy as it was a landmark date in the history of America, which brought out patriotic feelings of America.

The *Patriotism* frame also is indicated by images of American national flags, red, blue and white colors or by campaign slogans such as Stronger Together, #MakeAmericaGreatAgain, #AmericaFirst or Americans standing shoulder-to-shoulder.

Criticism Frame

The criticism frame is divided into three sub-frames dealing with policy, character and/or scandal, and other criticisms.

a. **Policy.** The *Policy Criticism* frame is indicated by critiquing the current president or the opponent's allegedly failed policies such as unemployment, immigration, Obamacare, or Obama-Clinton *ISIS* strategy. He/she would make a negative comparison of the opponent's policies in contrast to the positive benefits of his/her own proposed policies.

It could also be indicated by negative statements such as America has been hit by slow growth, "that is a reason not to vote for Hillary Clinton," "Tim Kaine has a pay-to-play problem just like crooked Hillary Clinton," or "someone please fact check her coal statements," "maybe for you, it's his dangerous statement about using nuclear weapons" or build bridges, not walls.

Images in the *Policy Criticism* frame could also include unappealing visuals of the opponent such as non-smiling expressions or graphics highlighting "Hillary's bad tax habit" and how "Clinton voted for higher taxes 98 times."

b. **Character/Scandal.** The *Character/Scandal Criticism* frame is indicated by critiquing the opponent's character and/or scandals. This could include Clinton's use of personal server, CGI's financial accountability issues, hacked emails from Wikileaks or negative labelling of American voters such as "deplorables," or Trump's mistreatment of women, his previous bankruptcies and tax evasion. Phrases or slogans that critique character could include Crooked Hillary, Love Trumps Hate or America is better than Donald Trump. The *Character/Scandal Criticism* frame could also include unflattering visuals of the opponent such as tired or angry facial expressions.

c. **Other.** The *Other* criticism frame indicates other types of criticisms not characterized as policy issues or character flaws.

Endorsement Frame

Four *Endorsement* frames were categorized, the first dealing with leadership and celebrity endorsement, the second dealing with American voter endorsements, the third representing appreciation, and the fourth representing other types of endorsements.

a. **Leadership/Celebrity.** The *Leadership/Celebrity* frame is defined as self-endorsing statements using poll results or endorsements from celebrities or presidential nominees who are endorsing their running mates and their policies.

In terms of visuals, the endorsement frame would be indicated by the image of the running mates or the presidential candidates standing alongside their vice-presidential nominee or the use of poll statistics in their favor.

b. American Voter. The *American Voter* endorsement frame is defined by statements, photos or letters from American voters who are endorsing their favorite candidate. This frame may be indicated by the American voters wearing campaign pin/badges, Trump caps or holding placards showing endorsement of the candidate.

c. Appreciation. The *Appreciation* frame is indicated by thanks and appreciation of the candidates for the support/endorsement of the voters in the election campaign.

d. Others. The *Others* frame captures other types of endorsements not represented in the first three endorsement frames.

Voting Frame

The *Voting* frame is indicated by the statements encouraging people to vote in the election, and references to the coming election day. Images could include the American national flag, campaign rallies, and statements such as "I will vote" or "register to vote."

Policy Frame

The *Policy* frame is indicated by statements that refer to policies the candidates are promoting such as equal pay for men and women, immigration reform for Hispanic residents, and national educational support and environmental protection.

FBI & Security Frame

The *FBI and Security* frame refers to the FBI's investigation of Clinton's emails and private server. This is indicated by then-FBI Director James Comey's statements on the case. The visuals could include the image of Comey.

Social Compassion Issues Frame

The *Social Compassion Issues* frame refers to issues faced by vulnerable, social groups. This frame includes ethnic minority group issues and gender and

LGBT kids' issues not directly related to specific policies. This could include references to one being judged by the color of one's skin, Charlotte shooting of Keith Scott who is a Black man, the Central Park jogger's case, Trump's renting of apartments to African Americans and marking their applications with the letter, "C" to represent colored, and tensions between police and ethnic minorities and/or the lack of respect for each other. Additionally, this frame maybe indicated by references to the woman's right to vote, the 19th Amendment, parents concerned about their daughters being in a Donald Trump America, and LGBT kids who should not be seen as different, but accepted as normal kids. This frame could also be referenced by statements as such as being an "inclusive America where everyone counts."

Others

The *Others* frame is reserved for all other tweets that could not be categorized in the seven major content frames.

Inter-Coder Reliability

Two researchers coded a total of 478 campaign tweets from the Clinton and Trump. Inter-coder reliability was calculated by dual coding of 51 tweets, which was approximately 10% of total number of tweets using Cohen's Kappa. This statistic was calculated to determine consistency among coders, and the total observed agreement of the overall inter-coder reliability ranged from .780 to 1.00.

Results

We content analyzed 13 frames in Clinton and Trump's campaign tweets (see Tables 13.2 and 13.3). Overall results showed significant differences in six text frames:

(1) the *Patriotism* frame, $\chi^2(1, N = 478) = 13.3 \, p < .001$, (2) the *Character/scandal* frame, $\chi^2(1, N = 478) = 4.58$, $p < .05$, (3) the *Others – Criticism* frame, $\chi^2(1, N = 478) = 22.1$, $p < .001$, (4) the *Appreciation Endorsement* frame, $\chi^2(1, N = 478) = 35.4$, $p < .001$, (5) the *Voting* frame, $\chi^2(1, N = 478) = 6.6$, $p < .05$, and (6) the and *Social Compassion Issues* frame, $\chi^2(1, N = 478) = 25.65$, $p < .001$. In addition, differences also were found for three photo frames: (1) the *Patriotism* frame, $\chi^2(1, N = 478) = 10.5$, $p < .01$, (2) the *Policy* frame, $\chi^2(1, N = 478) = 6.4$, $p < .05$, and (3) the *Social Compassion Issues* frame, $\chi^2(1, N = 478) = 13.4$, $p < .001$.

Table 13.2: Clinton and Trump's 2016 Campaign Tweets: Major Themes.

Frames	Clinton		Trump		Total within Frame		Pearson Chi-squares and p-values	
	Text	Photo	Text	Photo	Text	Photo	Text	Photo
	Frequencies/Percentages							
Patriotism Within Candidate	5 2.1%	11 4.6%	24 10%	30 12.6%	29 6.1%	41 8.6%	$\chi^2 = 13.25$ **p = .000	$\chi^2 = .10.55$ **p = .005
Policy Criticism Within Candidate	18 7.5%	4 1.7%	20 8.4%	7 2.9%	38 7.9%	11 2.3%	$\chi^2 = .11$ p = .74	$\chi^2 = .84$ p = .36
Character/ Scandal Criticism Within Candidate	90 37.7%	25 10.5%	68 28.5%	15 6.3%	158 33.1%	40 8.4%	$\chi^2 = 4.58$ *p =.032	$\chi^2 = 2.73$ p = .099
Others—Criticism Within Candidate	18 7.5%	7 2.9%	55 23%	6 2.5%	73 15.3%	13 2.7%	$\chi^2 = 22.13$ **p =.000	$\chi^2 = .08$ p = .779
Policy Within Candidate	13 5.4%	11 4.6%	7 2.9%	2 0.8%	20 4.2%	13 2.7%	$\chi^2 = 1.88$ p = .170	$\chi^2 = 6.41$ *p = .011
FBI & Security Within Candidate	1 0.4%	1 0.4%	2 0.8%	4 1.7%	3 0.6%	5 1.0%	$\chi^2 = .34$ p = .562	$\chi^2 = 1.82$ p = .177
Social Compassion Issue Within Candidate	27 11.3%	13 5.9%	1 0.4%	0 0%	28 5.9%	13 2.7%	$\chi^2 = 25.65$ **p =.000	$\chi^2 = 13.36$ **p = .000
Others Within Candidate	19 7.9%	3 1.3%	32 13.4%	3 1.3%	51 10.7%	6 1.3%	$\chi^2 = 3.71$ p = .054	$\chi^2 = .000$ p = 1.00

*p < .05; **p < .01; ***p < .001.

To find out what frames were used by the two presidential candidates in their tweets as indicated by the first and second research questions, and to what extent they attacked their opponents versus promoting themselves as mentioned in research question three, the most frequently occurring frame was identified. The highest-ranking frame across candidates was the *Character / Scandal Criticism* frame. At 37.7%, Clinton was more likely to criticize her opponent's character and highlight his scandals as compared to Trump (28.5%). There were more critical photos in Clinton's tweets (10.5%) than in Trumps tweets (6.3%) that drew attention to her opponent's character flaws and scandals. Across both candidates, 33.1% of tweets indicated this frame was used intensively and accounted for much of the mudslinging that occurred in the election campaign. These differences are statistically significant (χ^2 (1, N = 478) = 4.6, p < .05).

Another critical frame, *Others – Criticism*, was the second highest occurring frame. Trump (23%) was more likely to criticize other people or organizations compared to Clinton (7.5%). For example, he blamed *The New York Times*, *CNN* and the voting machine for affecting his image or his chances of winning the elections. This frame showed significance across candidates (χ^2 (1, N = 478) = 22.1, p < .001).

The Policy – Criticism frame was the sixth highest ranking frame, but it was not statistically significant (c^2 (1, N = 478) = 11, p > .05). Trump (8.4%) was a little more likely than Clinton (7.5%) to criticize the policies of the current president. Across both candidates, it occurred in merely 7.9% of the tweets.

The *Patriotism* frame ranked as the fifth lowest ranking frame, but it showed significant differences across candidates (χ^2 (1, N = 478) = 13.25, p < .001). Trump (10%) was more likely to demonstrate patriotism in his tweets compared to Clinton (2.1%). A common feature in Trump's tweet was the hashtag, #MAGA, also known as #MakeAmericaGreatAgain.

Results showed that the *Social Compassion Issues* frame differed significantly across candidates (χ^2 (1, N = 478) = 25.65, p < .001). Clinton (11.3%) was more likely to use the *Social Compassion Issues* frame to confront her opponent on his lack of empathy for vulnerable social groups. Trump (0.4%), on the other hand, gave this frame little attention. He (0%) did not utilize any socially compassionate photos in this frame, while Clinton (5.9%) did. The *Social Compassion Issues* photo frame showed significance (χ^2 (1, N = 478) = 13.4, p < .001). These results are illustrated in Table 13.2.

The *Policy* frame was the third lowest ranking frame. Clinton (5.4%) was more likely to state her policies in her tweets than Trump (2.9%). Clinton (4.6%) also had more photos demonstrating her policy stand compared to Trump (0.8%). This *Policy* photo frame indicated these differences were significant (χ^2 (1, N = 478) = 6.41, p < .05).

The *FBI & Security* frame was on par with the *Others Endorsement* frame as the lowest ranking frame and neither was the difference in this frame statistically significant (χ^2 (1, N = 478) = .34, $p > .05$). The *FBI & Security* frame received scant attention from both candidates and occurred 0.4% in Clinton's tweets and 0.8% in Trump's tweets. These results also are illustrated in Table 13.2.

Endorsement and Voting Frames

Results indicated that the *Leadership/Celebrity Endorsement* frame was the third highest ranking frame. Clinton (17.2%) used the *Leadership/Celebrity Endorsement* frame more often compared to Trump (13%). President Obama, First Lady Michelle Obama and pop celebrities such as Beyonce were frequently mentioned in Clinton's tweets. The same frame for photos occurred more often in Trump's tweets (12.6%) and Clinton trailed slightly behind at 9.2%. Trump had the tendency to use the visual communication of polls

Table 13.3: Clinton and Trump's 2016 Campaign Tweets: Endorsement and Voting Frames.

Frames	Clinton		Trump		Total within Frame	Total within Frame	Pearson Chi-squares and p-values	
	Text	*Photo*	*Text*	*Photo*	*Text*	*Photo*	Text	Photo
	Frequencies/Percentages							
Leadership / Celebrity Endorsement Within Candidate	41 17.2%	22 9.2%	31 13%	30 12.6%	72 15.1%	52 10.9%	χ^2 = 1.64 p =.201	χ^2 = 1.38 p = .240
American Voter Endorsement Within Candidate	3 1.3%	6 2.5%	5 2.1%	14 5.9%	8 1.7%	20 4.2%	χ^2 = .51 p = .476	χ^2 = 3.34 p = .068
Appreciation Endorsement Within Candidate	12 5%	5 2.1%	58 24.3%	7 2.9%	70 14.6%	12 2.5%	χ^2 = 35.42 **p = .000	χ^2 = .34 p = .559
Others Endorsement Within Candidate	1 0.4%	0 0%	2 0.8%	1 0.4%	3 0.6%	1 0.2%	χ^2 = .34 p = .562	χ^2 = 1.002 p = .317
Voting Within Candidate	23 9.6%	6 2.5%	9 3.8%	10 4.2%	32 6.7%	16 3.3%	χ^2 = 6.56 *p = .010	χ^2 = 1.04 p = .309

*$p < .05$; **$p < .01$; ***$p < .001$.

results in his favor to show he had the winning edge as compared to Clinton. This frame, however, did not show statistical significant differences across the two candidates (χ^2 (1, N = 478) = 1.64, p > .05).

The *Appreciation Endorsement* frame was the fourth highest ranking frame and differed significantly across both candidates (χ^2 (1, N = 478) = 35.4, p < .001). Trump (24.3%) showed the most appreciation to his supporters compared to Clinton (5.0%).

The *American Voter Endorsement* frame was the second lowest ranking frame and it was not statistically significant (χ^2 (1, N = 478) = .51, p > .05). This frame received little attention and it occurred 2.1% in Trump's tweets and 1.3% in Clinton's tweets.

The *Others Endorsement* frame was the lowest ranking frame. It appeared 0.4% in Clinton's tweets and 0.8% in Trump's tweets. This frame did not show any statistical significant differences (χ^2 (1, N = 478) = .34, p > .05). These results are illustrated in Table 13.3.

The *Voting* frame showed statistically significant differences across candidates (χ^2 (1, N = 478) = 6.6, p < .05). Clinton used this frame more frequently (9.6%) than did Trump (3.8%). The former Secretary of State had a link, hillaryclinton.com/makeaplan, inserted into her tweets. This link led to a website which allowed people to find out where and when to vote. *Make a plan* was the motto and part of Clinton's campaign's to encourage citizens to head to the polls. Trump, on the other hand, did not have such a plan. These results also are illustrated in Table 13.3.

Discussion

What was most notable about these results was the top-ranking frame, *Character / Scandal Criticism* frame. Clinton and Trump focused on attacking each other and deliberately heightened the spotlight of the opponent's scandals without reservation. This value frame primed voters to consider not only the candidate who was being attacked, but also the messenger of the tweet. Clinton used this frame most often, and it most likely cast her in a negative light from the voters' point of view. While Trump did use the *Character / Scandal Criticism* frame, he also utilized the *Appreciation Endorsement* frame which positioned him in a more positive light with voters. For example, it was commonplace for Trump to say thank you to his supporters, especially after he finished speaking at a campaign rally. Clinton did not emphasize the *Appreciation Endorsement* frame in her tweets, which may have emotionally distanced her from voters, especially her supporters and those are still undecided about who to vote for on Election Day.

Clinton emphasized the *Social Compassion Issues* frame more in her tweets. There were multiple references to issues faced by socially vulnerable groups such as women, ethnic minorities, and LGBT kids. She emphasized gender issues such as the women's right to vote and the importance of 19th Amendment. Clinton's tweets paid off in terms of getting the women and Latino vote. More women supported Clinton over Trump by 54% to 42% according to Pew Research (2016, para. 5). President Obama successfully won 55% of the women's vote in 2012 (Luhby, 2016, para. 20). In terms of the minority vote, 65% of Latinos voted for Clinton, while 29% of Latinos supported Trump (Luhby & Agiesta, 2016, para. 5), and 88% of Black African American voters supported the former Secretary of State versus 8% for Trump. Clinton's emphasis on gender issues, however, may have caused more men to consider Trump as a viable candidate who could represent their needs and hence, voted for him. Pew Research indicates that by 53% to 41%, more men supported Trump than Clinton (2016, para. 6). Trump's win among men was similar to Bush's performance in the 2004 and 2000 elections. Bush won the men by 11 points in both elections (Pew Research, 2016).

Clinton utilized the *Leadership / Celebrity* frame more than Trump, but it did not give her the upper hand in the election campaign. Her association with President Obama may have linked her to the rising costs of the unpopular policy, Obamacare. The importance of this issue was something that Clinton did not consider and may have hurt her support among voters who were frustrated with the rising costs of the Affordable Care Act. On the other hand, Trump's strategic use of favorable polls to endorse himself could have heightened the perceived win factor in his campaign.

Implications for Theory and Research

The strategic use of Twitter by both the Clinton and Trump political campaigns has important implications for communication theory and research. The attribute salience and exploration of how certain issues have been framed by both campaigns is certainly fodder for theoretical development. Consider negative portrayal of the candidates. How much did the public, if at all, perceive the caricature of Clinton as a rich privileged elite who abused the power of her position to enrich herself? What about the caricature of Trump as an unethical aggressive businessman who would do or say anything just to build his empire, and took liberties with the vulnerable women around him? Answering these questions will move scholars into the realm of third level agenda-setting research, which focuses on how the media bundles objects and attributes in the minds of media consumers (Vu, Guo, & McCombs, 2014).

Social media tools like Twitter have great potential for transferring the salience of relationships among a set of elements of a story that formulates a set of character attributes in the minds of the public of specific candidates. Consider two important positive narratives constructed by the Clinton and Trump campaigns. Clinton worked hard to share her life story as a seasoned public servant and leader with exceptional diplomatic skills that enabled her to achieve her political agendas for the good of the country, especially for women. This narrative reached its climax in her acceptance speech at the Democratic National Convention. She made salient her many roles not only as a Secretary of State, U.S. Senator, and political confidant of two U.S. Presidents, but she also attempted to connect the salience of her roles as a wife, mother and grandmother. Unexpectedly, her attempts to capitalize on the favorable images as a strong, independent, accomplished woman did not seem to energize enough independent women voters.

Conversely, Trump's narrative as a bright college graduate who pursued his entrepreneurial vision to turn his father's modest business into a commercial empire, revitalizing decaying areas of New York City by harnessing the power of blue collar workers in the construction industry, seemed to resonate with a fidelity that voters could believe, especially men. Such complex sets of attributes need to be explored through third level agenda-setting studies.

Future research also should continue to explore the growing use of Twitter for agenda building in political campaigns. Parmelee (2014) found that political leaders now have the ability to influence journalists and how they cover political events and discourse. Clearly, the continued novelty of a sitting president's strategic use of Twitter to bypass the traditional gatekeeping function of journalists will provide much new data.

Limitations and Conclusion

Twitter continues to play an important role in political campaigns. For Trump, Twitter was a strategic campaign megaphone to transmit his message on his values and issues of concern to him. One limitation of this study is that we did not identify which policies were most mentioned in the candidates' tweets. The importance of values issues to voters could be evaluated in terms of the number of shares, comments, reactions and retweets addressing each issue. A second limitation is the sample size of this study was moderate given the number of tweets that were available to analyze. Third, we did not explore the complex sets of elements in the Twitter messages that may have bundled attributes of the candidates in the minds of the public.

Did Twitter use overall favor Trump? While there were some meaningful results from the content analysis that seem to favor Trump's twitter campaign, there was no conclusive evidence that Trump's use of Twitter led to his successful bid for the highest office in the nation. Such a determination requires the addition of a more robust analysis, an online survey among voters who are Twitter users, for example, could measure the public perceptions of both candidates with respect to their Twitter use.

Despite the limitations, this study did indicate that both Clinton and Trump framed their campaigns differently on Twitter, matching the campaign strategies used in their overall campaigns. Thus, it does seem that Trump's use of Twitter positively contributed to his campaign's success. It is also important to recognize that Twitter is only one aspect of any candidates' social media strategy. We agree with the observations of Rachel Balsley after her study of Trump's Twitter's use, who concluded that "Trump's Twitter is a part of his larger, overall strategy that stretches across multiple platforms" to extend social networking beyond the Internet by increasing the engagement of his supporters (Balsley, 2016, p. 23).

Twitter, as well as other social media, can no longer be conceptualized as only echo chambers for already finely-tuned messages by political candidates. As President Trump has already discovered, playing with a powerful social medium like Twitter is like playing with fire that cannot so easily be controlled.

References

Aalberg, S., & Vreese, H. (2012). The framing of politics as strategy and game: A review of concepts, operationalizations and key findings. *Journalism, 13*(2), 162–178. doi:10.1177/1464884911427799.

Balsley, R. (2016). How is social media used by politicians? A content analysis of how Donald Trump uses Twitter to engage voters leading up to the 2016 "Super Tuesday" primary. Unpublished paper. Washington, DC: American University. Retrieved from https://scholar.googleusercontent.com/scholar?q=cache:qYisf4IhPnEJ:scholar.google.com/+rachel+balsley&hl=en&as_sdt=1,47&as_ylo=2013

Bichard, S., & Parmelee, J. (2011). *Politics and the Twitter revolution: How Tweets influence the relationship between political leaders and the public.* MD: Lexington Books.

Brown, W., & Fraser, B. (2004). *Turning celebrity capital into political influence: Lessons from Governor Schwarzenegger's gubernatorial election in California.* Paper presented at the Political Communication Division, 89th Annual Conference of the International Communication Association, New Orleans, Louisiana.

Chong, D., & Druckman, J. N. (2007). Framing public opinion in competitive democracies, *American Political Science Review, 101*, 637–655.

Clinton, H. (2016, October 26). Happy birthday to this future president. [Tweet]. Retrieved from https://twitter.com/HillaryClinton/status/791263939015376902

Conway, B., Kenski, K., & Wang, D. (2015). The rise of Twitter in the political campaign: Searching for Intermedia agenda-setting effects in the Presidential Primary. *Journal of Computer-Mediated Communication, 20*(4), 363–380. doi:10.1111/jcc4.12124/full

Cook, E. A. (1998). Voter reaction to women candidates. In Sue Thomas and Clyde Wilcox (Eds.), *Women and elective office: Past, present and future* (pp. 56–72). New York: Oxford University Press.

De Vreese, C. H. (2002). *Framing Europe: Television news and European integration.* Amsterdam: Aksant Acadeic.

Dolan, K. (2008). Is there a gender affinity effect in American politics? *Political Research Quarterly, 61*(1), 79–89. doi:10.1177/1065912907307518

Domke, D., Shah, D., & Wackman, D. (1998). Media priming effects: Accessibility, association and activation. *International Journal of Public Opinion Research, 10*(1), 51–74. doi:10.1093/ijpor/10.1.51

Druckman, J. (2001). On the limits of framing effects: Who can frame? *The Journal of Politics, 63*(4), 1041–1066. Retrieved from http://www.jstor.org/stable/2691806

Entman, R. (1993). Framing: Toward clarification of a fractured paradigm. *Journal of Communication, 43*, 51–58. doi:10.1111/j.1460-2466.1993.tb01304.x

Herrnson, P., Lay, C., & Stokes, A. (2003). Women running as women: Candidate gender, campaign issues and voter-targeting strategies. *Journal of Politics, 65*(1), 244–255. doi:10.1111/1468-2508.t01-1-00013

Ho, E. (2011, June 20). Obama is actually writing his own tweets now. Time. Retrieved from http://techland.time.com/2011/06/20/obama-is-actually-writing-his-own-tweets-now/

Hong, S., & Nadler, D. (2012). Which candidates do the public discuss online in an election campaign?: The use of social media by 2012 candidates and its impact on candidate salience. *Government Information Quarterly, 29*, 455–461. Retrieved from https://papers.ssrn.com/sol3/papers.cfm?abstract_id=2323214

Houston, B., Hawthorne, J., Spialek, M., Greenwood, M., & McKinney, M. (2013). Tweeting during the presidential debates effect on candidate evaluations and debate attitudes. *Argumentation and Advocacy, 49*, 301–311. doi:10.1080/00028533.2013.11821804

Hutchings, V., Valentino, N., Philpot, T., & White, I. (2004). The compassion strategy: Race and the gender gap in campaign 2000. *Public Opinion Quarterly, 68*(4), 512–541. doi:10.1093/poq/nfh038

Iyengar, S. (1991). *Is anyone responsible? How television frames political issues.* Chicago, IL: University of Chicago Press.

Iyengar, S., Norpoth, H., & Hahn, K. S. (2004). Consumer demand for election news: The horserace sells. *Journal of Politics, 66*(1), 157–175. doi:10.1046/j.1468-2508.2004.00146.x

Jones, B. (2010, January 13). More *governors* finding Twitter tweets sweet. *USA Today.* Retrieved from www.usatoday.com/tech/hotsites/2010-01-13-governors-tweet-Twitter_N.htm

Lakoff, R. (1973). *Language and woman's place. Language in Society,* 2(1), 45–80. Retrieved from http://www.jstor.org/stable/4166707

Landreville, K., White, C., & Allen, S. (2015). Tweets, polls and quotes: Gatekeeping and bias in on-screen visuals during the final 2012 presidential debate. *Communication Studies,* 66(2), 146–164. doi:10.1080/10510974.2014.930919

Lecheler, S., de Vreese, C., & Slothmus, R. (2009). *Issue importance as a moderator of framing effects. Communication Research,* 36(3), 400–425. doi:10.1177/0093650209333028

Lee, Hsien Loong. (n.d.). @leehsienloong. Retrieved from https://twitter.com/leehsienloong? lang=en

Luhby, T. (2016). How Hillary Clinton lost. *CNN.* Retrieved from http://www.cnn. com/2016/11/09/politics/clinton-votes-african-americans-latinos-women- white-voters/

Luhby, T., & Agiesta, J. (2016, November 9). Exit polls: Clinton fails to energize African-Americans, Latinos and the young. *CNN.* Retrieved from http://www.cnn. com/2016/11/08/politics/first-exit-polls-2016/

Magdy, W., & Darwish, K. (2016). *Trump vs Hillary: Analyzing viral tweets during U.S. presidential elections 2016.* Retrieved from https://arxiv.org/abs/1610.01655

McKinney, M. S., Houston, J. B., & Hawthorne, J. (2014). Social watching a 2012 Republican presidential primary debate. *American Behavioral Scientist,* 58(4), 556–573.

Meeks, L. (2016). Aligning and trespassing: Candidates' party-based issue and trait ownership on Twitter. *Journalism & Mass Communication Quarterly,* 93(4), 1050–1072. doi:10.1177/1077699015609284

Milian, M. (2009, November 16). President Obama: 'I have never used Twitter.' *LA Times.* Retrieved from http://latimesblogs.latimes.com/washington/2009/11/obama- never-used-twitter.html

Parmelee, J. H. (2014). The agenda-building function of political tweets. *New Media & Society,* 16(3), 434–450. doi:10.1177/1461444813487955

Parmelee, J. H., & Bichard, S. (2012). *Politics and the Twitter revolution: How Tweets influence the relationship between political leaders and the public.* Lanham, MD: Lexington Books.

Philpot, T. (2010). *Race, Republicans and the return of the party of Lincoln.* Ann Arbor: University of Michigan.

Rampton, R. (2015, May 18). Obama tweets, and a million follow: It's Barack. Really! *Reuters.* Retrieved from https://www.reuters.com/article/us-usa-obama-twitter/ obama-tweets-and-a-million-follow-its-barack-really-idUSKBN0O31RV20150518

Riffe, D., Lacy, S., & Fico, F. (2014). *Analyzing media messages: Using quantitative content analysis in Research.* New York, NY and London: Routledge.

Schemer, C., Wirth, W., & Matthes, J. (2011). Value resonance and value framing effects on voting intentions in direct-democratic campaigns. *American Behavioral Scientist,* 56(3), 334–352. doi:10.1177/0002764211426329

Schmuck, D., Heiss, R., Matthes, J., Engesser, S., & Esser, F. (2017). Antecedents of strategic game framing in political news coverage. *Journalism,* 18(8), 937–955. doi:10.1177/1464884916648098

Semetko, H. A., & Valkenburg, P. M. (2000). Framing European politics: A content analysis of press and television news. *Journal of Communication, 50*, 93–109. doi:10.1111/j.1460-2466.2000.tb02843.x

Shapiro, R., & Mahajan, H. (1986). Gender differences in policy preferences: A summary of trends from the 1960s to the 1980s. *Public Opinion Quarterly, 50*(1), 42–61. doi:10.1086/268958

Sharp, A. (2012). *The final 2012 presidential debate*. Retrieved from https://blog.twitter.com/2012/the-final-2012-presidential-debate

Smith, J., Paul, D., & Paul, R. (2007). No place for a woman: Evidence for gender bias in evaluations of presidential candidates. *Basic and Applied Social Psychology, 29*(3), 225–233. doi:10.1080/01973530701503069

Statista. (2016, December 12). *Number of monthly active Twitter users worldwide from 1st quarter 2010 to 3rd quarter 2016*. Retrieved from https://www.statista.com/statistics/282087/number-of-monthly-active-twitter-users/

Traitz, L. (2016, October 26). Too bad her mother didn't have one. [Tweet]. Retrieved from https://twitter.com/LindaTraitz/status/923700571151798273

Trump, D. (2016, November 9). Such a beautiful and important evening! The forgotten man and woman will never be forgotten again. We will all come together as never before. [Tweet]. Retrieved from https://twitter.com/realDonaldTrump/status/79631564030760738

Trump, D., Jr. ((2016, October 26)). A year later the arrogance and entitlement in this tweet is exactly why it was never going to happen. #maga. [Tweet]. Retrieved from https://twitter.com/DonaldJTrumpJr/status/923615257687461888

Twitonomy. (2016, October 24). @HillaryClinton's profile. Retrieved from http://twitonomy.com/profile.php?sn=HillaryClinton

Twitter. (n.d.). Twitter milestones. Retrieved from https://about.twitter.com/company/press/milestones

Tyson, A., & Maniam, S. (2016, November 9). Behind Trump's victory: Divisions by race, gender, education. *Pew Research*. Retrieved from http://www.pewresearch.org/fact-tank/2016/11/09/behind-trumps-victory-divisions-by-race-gender-education/

Vu, H. T., Guo, L., & McCombs, M. E. (2014). Exploring "the world outside and the pictures in our heads" A network agenda-setting study. *Journalism & Mass Communication Quarterly, 91*(4), 669–686. doi:10.1177/1077699014550090

Wang, Y., Li, Y., & Luo, J. (2016). *Deciphering the 2016 U.S. presidential campaign in the Twitter sphere: A comparison of the Trumpists and Clintonists*. Retrieved from https://arxiv.org/pdf/1603.03097.pdf

Wells, C., Shah, D., Pevehouse, J., Yang, J., Pelled, A., Boehm, F., … Schmidt, J. (2016). How Trump drove coverage to the nomination: Hybrid media campaigning. *Political Communication, 33*(4), 669–676. doi:10.1080/10584609.2016.1224416

14. The Commander in Tweets: President Trump's Use of Twitter to Defend

JEFFREY DELBERT
Lenoir-Rhyne University

The notion of political rhetoric and democratic dialogue may be impossible without a coherent community in which individuals can interact. Tulis (1987) claimed the President of the United States acts as our rhetor-in-chief, exercising the "office through the medium of language" (p. 3). As the rhetorical leader of our country, the president can make appeals to the entire union, which can alter citizens' attitudes, beliefs, and behaviors in ways that particular individuals cannot accomplish alone. Moreover, the president encourages deliberation not only within government, but also within the citizenry. As such, the executive branch has the power and platform to teach a polity how to "talk politics," providing direction in the public dialogue.

Donald Trump, the 45th President of the United States (POTUS), has been criticized for his public discourse, especially his use of Twitter. After assuming the presidency, Trump tweeted using the official @POTUS Twitter account, as well as his pre-presidential and personal handle @realDonaldTrump. This is a direct departure from both Presidents Bush and Obama and has allowed President Trump to maintain two personas.

Moreover, the president frequently tweeted early in the morning with seemingly off-the-cuff, erratic discourse that conflicted with previous messages or positions espoused by his cabinet members. For instance, @realDonaldTrump wrote in a June 16, 2017 tweet, "I am being investigated for firing the FBI Director by the man who told me to fire the FBI Director! Witch Hunt." Such discourse often lacked concrete evidence and used ad hominem attacks to defend his position, undermining efforts for the White House to focus on stated objectives.

President Trump's use of Twitter to defend himself and his positions offers an interesting space to explore the grounds on which he has encouraged public deliberation during his presidency. By examining his first 100 days in office, this analysis aims to uncover patterns in his rhetoric, especially his attempts at interpretive dominance in the *polis*. Unraveling how Trump interacts and manages information will illustrate his overall leadership style, as well as how he models discussion in the public sphere. Furthermore, the chapter seeks to offer insight on how political leaders can use social media to develop rhetorical defense strategies to respond to attacks from opponents, citizens, political institutions, and media outlets.

Rhetorical Defense and Political Media

Since President Trump's election in 2016, he has faced an onslaught of attacks against his person, proposals, and ideals from aggrieved publics and alienated media outlets. These discourses occur amidst a chorus of praise from an extremely supportive base. Such dichotomous discourses discussing "fascist policies" and "liberal tears" occur on a myriad of social media. However, the president happens to be an active participant on one, Twitter. Trump frequently retweeted (RT) supporters' comments, while blocking or censuring detractors personally. Such involvement prompts this study to ask how President Trump's involvement in personally responding to criticisms impacts both the Office of the President, as well as the state of democratic dialogue itself. Accordingly, this study is grounded in the extant literature of rhetorical defense and the importance of medium in political messaging.

Many studies have considered the ways in which public figures can defend themselves. Foundationally, Plato's "The Apology of Socrates" serves as a model of how arguments work to logically present a case to citizens (Smith, 1956). After being accused of corrupting the youth and rejecting the gods, Socrates' defense takes place in two parts. In the first, he defended his character by arguing the accusations stem from a false reputation circulated about him. In the second, he cross-examined his accuser and led Meletus to contradict himself. In this first-person, conversational discussion, Plato illustrated how one might use honest and virtuous dialogue to make one's point clear. Although the dialogue did not save Socrates, this illustrates how defenses can provoke citizens by embarrassing accusers and how to argue against claims that one is disrupting the political stasis.

Defense has continued to be a primary focus in rhetorical and argumentation studies (see, e.g., Benoit, 2015; Coombs, 1995; Hearit, 1994; Rowland & Jerome, 2004; Ware & Linkugel, 1973). In fact, Perelman and

Olbrechts-Tyteca (1969) featured defense as a primary consideration of how to formulate an argument, especially its order and construction. First, the authors claimed the extensiveness of one's argument is related to its likelihood of being refuted. For instance, statements that relate to arguments that are difficult to disprove should be kept brief, in order "to ensure its prominence" in the dialogue (p. 486). Furthermore, the presence of recalcitrant audiences requires an "accumulation of arguments" to address the numerous hearers (p. 477). Thus, Perelman and Olbrechts-Tyteca illustrated how some arguments in a defense that may appear as inconsistent and superfluous are rhetorically necessary in an arena where recalcitrant audiences may exist.

For instance, Twitter's 328 million users are certainly diverse globally, economically, and generationally (Aslam, 2017), which leads to a host of recalcitrant audiences. Thus, Perelman and Olbrechts-Tyteca's perspective on rhetorical defense may illustrate how users on a medium such as Twitter can employ contradictory ideas to make strong arguments across a variety of situations and audiences by repeating and amplifying arguments across single and multiple Twitter accounts. Although repetition of an argument might make a specific argument more present, its repetition also amplifies that claim for particular audiences.

Perelman and Olbrechts-Tyteca also asserted the order of an argument matters in defensive statements, as "some arguments can only be understood and accepted if other arguments have already been stated" (p. 494). Following Quintilian's advice, they stated a defense may begin by refuting an:

> accusation that raised a continuing doubt as to the moral integrity of the defendant, unless minor arguments against him were obviously false, in which case they should be refuted first, in order to discredit the prosecution by demonstrating their falsity. (p. 500)

In this sense, the order matters as it can provide information by which all other information can be coded and understood. Changing the order of a defense changes the argument itself.

Many current explorations of defenses deal with self-defense. Ware and Linkugel (1973) offered four categories that the accused can use to respond to accusations of misdeeds: denial, differentiation, bolstering, and transcendence. Ryan (1982) asserted that defenses could be made in terms of policy or character. Benoit (2015) developed the theory of image repair, which focused "exclusively on messages designed to improve images tarnished by criticism and suspicion (it is also possible to try to preempt anticipated criticism)" (p. 3).

Image repair theory developed a clear vocabulary to discuss a rhetor's defensive strategies. The theory consists of five broad categories (denial, evasion of responsibility, reducing offensiveness, corrective action, and mortification) and each category is broken down into specific variants. For instance, when a defender denies an accusation, they may use simple denial (e.g., I am not responsible) or may shift the blame (e.g., It wasn't me, it was him). When evading responsibility for an act, one may use provocation (e.g., I did it because of another wrongful act), defeasibility (e.g., I didn't know), attempt to establish it was an accident, or to claim the act was done with good intentions.

Overall, Benoit argued rhetorical defense is a goal-directed activity in which the accused are attempting to maintain a favorable reputation by addressing audiences' perceptions. Although there might be multiple and/or unclear goals, the aim is to maintain face to continue to operate in society and have access to limited resources. This can be difficult, as the accused may need to respond to multiple audiences, some of which may operate at cross-purposes, resonating with Perelman and Olbrechts-Tyteca's ideas.

Stein (2008) complicated self-defense strategies by introducing the concept of *antapologia*, or attacking a defense. He suggested that although a rhetor may successfully weaken or undermine an opponent's defense, some of the accused would never publicly accept the wrongdoing. Thus, antapologia is a strategy to defend against defenses, which may not undermine the actions themselves, but rather seek to undermine the credibility of the accused.

Analyzing Trump's language on Twitter helps contextualize how he hopes to characterize his presidency, opponents, and vision. Although rhetors may want to focus solely on their strengths, defensive rhetoric and negativity can force discussion of broader issues (Geer, 2006). In terms of a burden of proof, people rarely ask for evidence to support a positive claim about oneself. However, negative claims about another person require more evidence, considering one is guilty until proven innocent. As Geer (2006) argued, public opinion is linked to the type of trait and issue appeals made by a candidate, especially when considering competence, integrity, and caring. Thus, considering his defensive rhetoric on Twitter reveals which issues he finds most important, as well as how he attempts to justify his competency as a leader.

Trump's tweets also must be considered alongside the medium on which they are presented. Although it may seem trite to argue the medium is the message, Twitter has changed the possibilities of how presidents can connect with constituents, including timeliness, directness, and speed of transmission. Previous studies have considered the use of medium as a substantial force in communicating messages as times change. In 1992, Postman wrote:

> ... technological competition ignites total war, which means it is not possible to contain the effects of a new technology to a limited sphere of human activity ...

technological change is neither additive nor subtractive. It is ecological ... A new technology does not add or subtract something. It changes everything. (p. 18)

In short, technologies shape the landscape in which we can express our attitudes, beliefs, and behaviors. They change what our symbols mean, as well as the symbols themselves. Accordingly, he argues,

> In a technocracy, tools play a central role in the thought-world of the culture. Everything must give way, in some degree, to their development. The social and symbolic worlds become increasingly subject to the requirements of that development. Tools are not integrated into the culture; they attack the culture. They bid to become the culture. As a consequence, tradition, social mores, myth, politics, ritual, and religion have to fight for their lives. (p. 28)

As Twitter becomes a central mode of expression for citizens, media, and political actors, it cannot be considered as a passive communication tool for the president. Instead, as Postman suggested, the tool, Twitter, begins to fight older modes of communication, to attack and subvert old methods and cultures, and to shape the way we think, act, and understand events in our world.

As media types change, different types of information become accessible to citizens. In addition to providing first-person information, Twitter provides a chorus of voices to support or denounce users' statements. George (1972) and Mutz (2002) argued better decisions are made when participants disagree, enabling citizens to empathize with opponents' viewpoints through exposure to "cross cutting views" (p. 118). Geer (2006) asserted democracies actually require negativity, as citizens need to understand both positives and negatives to advance a debate. Twitter allows this type of democratic dialogue, enabling citizens to cross-compare issues and rank them hierarchically.

However, Mark (2006) argued the power of third party validators has diminished, as people "feel like you can find something in print anywhere to support your point" (p. 234). Such ideas resonate with Marcuse's (2002) notions about the limitedness of technology. He wrote, "the total mobilization of all media for the defense of the established reality has coordinated the means of expression to the point where communication of transcending contents becomes technically impossible" (p. 71). Although we might all have the ability to communicate our ideas directly, and to the source, Marcuse would argue our communication media have begun to restrict our modes of expression, making it difficult or impossible to challenge dominant thoughts. In such a technopoly, the problems and disputes faced by a society become buried under the sheer size and speed of technological changes themselves, as we attempt to accommodate the new modes of technology.

This chapter does not argue that technology shapes society in a unidirectional manner. However, the schizophrenic use of the term media itself results from the concept that media use in society produces unconscious consequences for peoples and their cultures. This collective word *media*, which stands in for a host of communicative outputs in society, illustrates the innocuous way the technology itself creates an interactive environment that is difficult to define. Certainly such technologies are not created in a vacuum and are derivative of our societies. However, the influence of society on technology, and vice versa, is important in considering technology is not an innocent influence on our society.

In technology's mediation, media amplify, refract, and distort the representations passing through their form and begin to influence many levels of our lives, including our governing structures. In fact, after the 2016 Presidential election, the media representations of our political system began to worry U.S. citizens and productivity dropped (Boddy, 2017). Accordingly, the analysis must consider how President Trump's use of Twitter changes the shape, size, and speed of conversations occurring in the United States. An analysis of Trump's Twitter accounts will reveal not only the nature of the political environment created by new social media technologies, but also the specific practices a president can use to defend one's policies, personas, and her or his political standing.

Method

The current study analyzes President Donald Trump's tweets to understand his use of rhetorical defense on Twitter. Accordingly, this study investigates both of President Trump's Twitter accounts, @realDonaldTrump and @POTUS, during his first 100 days in office, spanning from January 20, 2017 to April 29, 2017. This time period was chosen because U.S. Presidents typically set the tone of their presidencies early on in their administrations. During this time period, Mr. Trump tweeted 516 times with @realDonaldTrump and 500 times with @POTUS.

The tweets were coded as attacks, acclaims, and defenses. Then, the defenses were coded according to themes. These themes were then organized by ideas and analyzed to understand the relationship among the various themes. Each theme was considered with regard to the particular account, re-tweets (RTs), the time of the president's tweets, as well as President Trump's "likes" during this period of time. Furthermore, the events surrounding the Tweets were considered to understand what events Trump chose to ignore or highlight.

Analysis

Assessing the ways in which President Trump's rhetorical devices challenge political and media communities is important to understanding how Trump wields the power of public office. Although both of President Trump's Twitter accounts reveal similar information, he mostly used @POTUS to champion and acclaim his accomplishments. Thus, the bulk of this analysis will focus on his personal account, @realDonaldTrump, which served as his platform to address his grievances with public and media dialogues. However, examining both accounts shows how he encourages people to think and act, especially by directly questioning whether individuals are able to trust major institutions. Overall, the analysis assesses whether a coherent rhetorical strategy was present across President Trump's tweets.

The analysis first focuses on President Trump's personal account, @realDonaldTrump (@DJ), which contained 61 defenses. These statements included a wide range of themes, including a defense about a non-existent terrorist attack in Sweden (Bradner, 2017) and his plans about building a border wall between the U.S. and Mexico. Primarily, Trump's statements defended his image, especially how he was portrayed in the media and his interpretation of events.

A majority of his defenses, 29 on @DJ and 5 on @POTUS, address #FAKE news. Although the concept of bogus news stories is not new, this concept has reemerged in the digital news era (Soll, 2016). According to Google Analytics, the rise of the search term "fake news" immediately preceded Trump's 2016 presidential election victory over Hillary Clinton. Perhaps furthering interest in the term, President-elect Trump shouted, "You are fake news" at CNN's James Acosta during a January press conference (Savranksy, 2017). Since November 2016, many of the related Google search terms to fake news are associated with President Trump, Russia, and the news organization CNN, which coincide with many of the themes present in Trump's defensive Twitter statements.

Many of these tweets simply attack media as perpetuating fake poll numbers, favoring the Clintons, and propagating false election results. For example, nearly six months after his victory, on April 24 (2017c), Donald Trump tweeted at 12:48 p.m., "New polls out today are very good considering that much of the media is FAKE and almost always negative. Would still beat Hillary in. ..." He continued seven minutes later, "...popular vote. ABC News/Washington Post Poll (wrong big on election) said almost all stand by their vote on [sic] me & 53% said strong leader" (Trump, 2017d). This defense responds to media outlets releasing polls that his public approval numbers were dropping. These tweets attempt to bolster his image as a strong and validly elected leader, as well as clamors that he actual won the popular vote.

It is worthwhile to mention the time delay in Trump's tweets, which is not uncommon. His thoughts have taken minutes or hours to complete. Trump also tweeted on April 24 (2017a) at 5:28 a.m., "The Wall is a very important tool in stopping drugs from pouring into our country and poisoning our youth (and many others)! If." Then, three hours later at 8:31 a.m., "....the wall is not built, which it will be, the drug situation will NEVER be fixed the way it should be! #BuildTheWall" (Trump, 2017b). This message defends his desire to build a wall by reasoning it will also stop drugs from flowing in from Central and South America. The delay makes this message even more curious, as it seems he needed several hours to strengthen his rationalization, which rests uncomfortably on an either-or fallacy and no substantiated data.

Trump's defenses related to fake media also emerge when discussing his relationship with Russia. For example, on March 28, 2017 Trump tweeted, "Why doesn't Fake News talk about Podesta [sic] ties to Russia as covered by @FoxNews or money from Russia to Clinton—sale of Uranium?" Additionally, on April 29, 2017, he retweeted @foxnation saying, "@TuckerCarlson: #Dems Don't Really Believe #Trump Is a Pawn of #Russia—That's Just Their Political Tool." In both instances, he never denies his personal relationship with Russia or its leaders, but instead tries to undermine other groups and institutions as equally culpable by shifting the blame. These defenses are not trying to resolve any issues, but instead attempt to protect Trump's brand and absolve him of responsibility, while shifting any wrongdoing to the Democrats and the media's reporting practices.

During his more optimistic days, his thoughts on Russia simply attempt to transcend the debate altogether. On April 13, 2017, @realDonaldTrump tweeted, "Things will work out fine between the U.S.A. and Russia. At the right time everyone will come to their senses & there will be lasting peace!" Such optimism merely dismisses the debate and fails to address citizens' and pundits' concerns about these issues. Instead, the public is expected to believe Trump at his word that his negotiation skills will resolve all potential and existing conflicts with Russia.

Although Trump frequently criticized CNN and the *New York Times* specifically when discussing fake news, Trump's belief that the media is betraying him runs much deeper. Trump's tweets frequently make the case that he is a victim of some deep state or media conspiracy. For instance, a tweet on @ DJ from April 21, 2017 states, "No matter how much I accomplish during the ridiculous standard of the first 100 days & it has been a lot (including S.C.) media will kill [sic]!" Additionally, on February 18, 2017, Trump cried,

"Don't believe the main stream (fake news) media. The [sic] White House is running VERY WELL. I inherited a MESS and am in the process of fixing it." Both instances highlight Trump's insistence that news media are distorting his administration's actions intentionally and maliciously. On February 25, he writes, "The media has not reported that the National Debt in my first month went down by $12 billion vs a $200 billion increase in Obama first mo." In an attempt to justify his version of events, he attacks the entire media as malicious, instead of as merely mistaken.

These defenses might seem innocuous, but, intentional or not, they are undermining the checks and balances that support the American system of information exchange. Trump's need to attack while defending illustrates a need not just to correct, but to punish what he views as unfavorable coverage. He suggests the media might not just stop a story, but "will kill." He may have run out of his 180 characters, but the distinction seems important for the Commander-in-Chief to make.

Although the media bore the brunt of Trump's ire, Trump's defenses also frequently attacked the intelligence community. On February 26, @DJ tweeted, "Russia talk is FAKE NEWS put out by the Dems and played up by the media in order to mask the big election defeat and the illegal leaks!" He continued on April 2, 2017, writing, "The real story turns out to be SURVEILLANCE and LEAKING! Find the leakers." These tweets illustrate the larger conspiracy he perceives to be against him and his administration. By linking supposed fake media stories with intelligence leaks, he simultaneously undermines two institutions and blames negative coverage on corruption rather than on perceived incompetence. This shift in blame to a corrupt deep state, an enemy within, fits well with the narrative he conceived about the institution of government during his presidential campaign.

These shifts in blame seem to be grounded in an assumption that executive branch offices and the media should kowtow to Trump's personal agenda. After media outlets attacked his surrogate speakers, such as Kellyanne Conway, on various media outlets in March, Trump (2017, March 13) tweeted, "It is amazing how rude much of the media is to my very hard working representatives. Be nice you will do much better!" His defense of his surrogates implies that questioning the actions of his administration, and of Trump himself, will result in communication being blocked. Such arguments seem to divide institutions among communication lines; you either talk with us or without us. By suggesting flattery is the key to getting answers, he attempts to transcend public criticism for his actions and instead shifts the blame to the superficial manner in which these conversations occur. Yet again, Trump makes himself a victim.

A series of tweets posted on March 2, 2017 really underscore Trump's defense of his persona and actions. In the tweets, he attacks the Democrats, the intelligence community, and the media for their treatment of Jeff Sessions's congressional testimony. In an attempt to evade responsibility for contact with Russian officials and protect his administration's image as non-colluders with Russia, Trump wrote:

> 6:22 p.m.: "Jeff Sessions is an honest man. He did not say anything wrong. He could have stated his response more accurately, but it was clearly not. ..."
> 6:27 p.m.: "... intentional. This whole narrative is a way of saving face for Democrats losing an election that everyone thought they were supposed. ..."
> 6:35 p.m.: "... to win. The Democrats are overplaying their hand. They lost the election, and now they have lost their grip on reality. The real story ..."
> 6:38 p.m.: "... is all of the illegal leaks of classified and other information. It is a total "witch hunt!"

President Trump attempts to correct Sessions's alleged perjury to Congress regarding his contact with Russian officials during the election (Goggin, 2017). His defense here attempts to evade responsibility for these posts by suggesting there is not enough information to substantiate the claims made by the media and the Democrats. His statements suggest these institutions are merely propagating such stories for their own political gain, instead of attempting to check governmental actions. Here, Trump undermines the very institutions he has sworn to defend. Declaring a witch-hunt attempts to minimize claims of collusion on the grounds that Sessions was merely not careful with his words. Trump then infers his base should shift the blame to nasty media coverage and Democrat politicking, rather than the Trump campaign's or administration's ineptitude.

Another notable element within Trump's defenses is his insistence that he, and he alone, has the answers to dilemmas facing the United States. A February 6, 2017 tweet illustrates such an attempt to bolster his supposed reliability: "I call my own shots largely based on an accumulation of data and everyone knows it. Some FAKE NEWS media in order to marginalize lies!" Although many tweets infer President Trump has the perspective of perspectives when evaluating data, this tweet clearly clarifies Trump's belief that he alone knows the path forward and does not need to explain his reasoning to anyone.

For instance, on February 1, 2017, he writes, "Everybody is arguing whether or not it is a BAN. Call it what you want it is about keeping bad people (with bad intentions) out of country!" Then, on February 11, 2017, he writes across two tweets: "I am reading that the great border WALL will cost more than the government originally thought, but I have not gotten involved in the. ...", "... design or negotiations yet. When I do, just like with the F-35 FighterJet [sic] or the Air Force One Program, price will come WAY DOWN!" This defense rests on his egomania; I alone have the key to save the future of the United States. The purpose here is to defend his promises, while undermining criticism by stating the true cost cannot be determined without his involvement.

Trump's insistence that he can correct government ills sometimes extends beyond the powers afforded to his office, illustrating a lack of knowledge of presidential duties. For instance, after an anonymous report circulated in March 2017 about President Trump's ties with Russian President Vladimir Putin, Trump took to Twitter to demand satisfaction. Trump (2017, March 5) wrote, "Who was it that secretly said to Russian President 'Tell Vladimir that after the election I'll have more flexibility?' @foxandfriends." Additionally, when Snoop Dogg's video for the remixed version of "Lavender" was released, Trump fired back about the video illustrating a Trump Clown being shot by a toy gun. He wrote on March 15, 2017, "Can you imagine what the outcry would be if @SnoopDogg failing career and all had aimed and fired the gun at President Obama? Jail time!" Both of these instances, whether the initial actions were justified or not, demonstrate a president willing to interfere in the justice process by shouting for particular sentences to be rendered. Such statements illustrate Trump's use of intimidation to sway the opinion of his base, potential jurors, as well as to help discourage further attacks against his character, his actions, or his associates. These defenses are rallying cries to defend Trump's honor.

Trump's presidential account, @POTUS, had fewer defenses and focused mostly on acclaiming his accomplishments. Most of the defenses were exact copies of those posted to his personal account. Interestingly, however, they were not retweeted. Instead, they were posted separately, but hours apart. For instance, both @POTUS and @realDonaldTrump (2017, March 18) posted these two tweets: "Despite what you have heard from the FAKE NEWS I had a GREAT meeting with German Chancellor Angela Merkel. Nevertheless Germany owes ...,", "... vast sums of money to NATO & the United States must be paid more for the powerful, and very expensive, defense it provides to Germany!" However, @realDonaldTrump tweeted this message about three hours before @POTUS.

It is difficult to imagine what possesses a president to take this sort of communicative action. As this particular tweet dealt with international intimidation of foreign governments, it appears President Trump wanted this defense of his agenda to be recorded on his official presidential channel, noted by leaders abroad, and taken seriously. As this was early in his presidency, leaders had yet to learn how to deal with Trump. This tweet may have been an attempt to show the world how serious he was about putting "America First."

Another @POTUS tweet from March 29, 2017 stated, "If the people of our great country could only see how viciously and inaccurately my administration is covered by certain media!—DJT." This tweet features an interesting aspect that appears at the end of eleven of @POTUS's messages; the president signs his words. These initials signal to users that he endorses that particular idea. The infrequency of such initialing indicates that the president had a need to let citizens know when the messages were his own. These signatures provide some evidence that Trump maintains a personal Twitter page to fulfill communicative needs. It allows him to maintain and cultivate his own voice during his presidency. Accordingly, Trump likely uses Twitter as a channel to cultivate his base's support and satisfy his need to be heard, letting supporters, voters, and the world know his personal thoughts on current issues.

Although many of Trump's tweets could not be coded as defenses, it is worth noting that a good defense starts with a solid offense. Trump often attacked the Democrats and other detractors for not supporting his policies, which often began a cycle of defending his ideas further. Additionally, President Trump often repeated acclaims, whether true or false, in an attempt to validate his supposed successes. Again, these were largely to claim he was doing well, translating attacks against him and avoiding the need to defend the outcries against him.

Conclusion

President Trump's Twitter accounts reveal a coherent strategy for how the Office of the President can use social media platforms to manage one's administration and public persona. President Trump was able to use the medium not only to attack detractors and acclaim his successes, he was able to use the medium to recontextualize and defend his agenda. His use of Twitter encourages consideration about the future of presidential discourse and how social media are shifting our society.

Trump's strategy seems to hinge on four parts. First, his messages seem intent on dismantling traditional information sources. As the rhetor in chief, President Trump has set a precedent that one can shift the blame, dismiss long-standing institutions, and simply deny accusations without moving through traditional gatekeepers. Trump continually bypassed traditional media outlets to provide the real news to his base. When not receiving the press coverage he desired, he simply transcended the debate by going to Twitter, decrying fake news, and making outlandish accusations about their true intentions.

Twitter and other social media offer presidents the ability to respond to events in real time, as well as control how messages are framed. However, without an independent media to fact check sources, citizens have no recourse on whom to believe. During Trump's presidency, he has been able to undermine, or at least politicize, traditional and trusted modes of information exchange citizens use. According to Dugan and Auter (2017), Trump's tweets and public statements have polarized Democrats' and Republicans' trust in the media. Their poll revealed that while Democrats believe the media "get their facts straight" 62% of the time, Republicans believed this same idea only 14% of the time.

Although trust in the media has been at a historical low for several years, the power of the presidency to alter the citizenry's trust of institutions, and particular news outlets, is alarming. This is especially true when considering President Trump has demonstrated that a U.S. President can champion particular news outlets simply because they support his version of events and then only provide presidential access to those outlets. Outwardly bragging about such preferential treatment on Twitter certainly has altered the ways the press deal with the president, as well as how citizens treat the press.

Second, Trump claims there is deep state interference in all U.S. affairs. Such charges imply that information provided about him and his decisions are not to be trusted. Trump then asserts he has insider information and can fix the situation. Considering how frequently citizens are Googling fake news, it seems discussions about Trump's messaging, at least in part, are influencing citizens' perceptions about the legitimacy of the structures around them. With top-level governing officials uttering conspiracy theories about foreign interference and underground conspirators, citizens are encouraged to question the security of our information channels. Trump's words show the president has the power to alarm and discourage citizens about the scope of potential seditions in our government and intensify many of the previously fringe conversations about a corrupt U.S. government.

Third, Trump demonstrates that a U.S. President can run a permanent political campaign by simply recording his or her thoughts on a public medium. Contrary to Mark's (2006) assertion that third party validators are no longer politically relevant, Twitter allows opinion leaders to manage surrogate publics to fight ongoing digital battles in support of the leader's cause. In the case of Trump, his Twitter teaches the polity how to talk politics, which means never wavering from your ideals and then waiting for third party validators to echo your concerns. In this political and media environment, the users with the most "likes" or "retweets" win. Despite the fact that much of this digital support may have been manufactured, the numbers—the perception—matter.

Fourth, President Trump illustrates that a president can foster a pre-viously held persona while in office. Trump's lack of personal posts on @ POTUS differed from previous presidents, but his signature on specific posts provided clues as to why he persists in using @realDonaldTrump. His strat-egy to post as the "real" Trump, not a politician or U.S. president, helps him express his personal thoughts through his carefully cultivated identity, allowing Trump to manage the image that gained him fame and success. This form of communication is an interesting change for the presidency and may continue in an era where presidents compete for likeability with previously cultivated personas.

Of course, many still clamor that Trump's tweets have hurt his presi-dency. A Quinnipiac poll from August "found that 69 percent of Americans—including 54 percent of Republicans—thought that Trump should stop using his personal Twitter account" (Silver, 2017). Similarly, an NBC/WSJ poll found that "66 percent of Americans disapprove of Trump's use of Twitter … includ[ing] … 46 percent of Republicans" (Todd, Murry, & Dann, 2017, para. 8). Yet, not even Silver (2017) could find a reliable correlation between Trump's "tweetstorms" and the administration's low approval rating and inability to push legislation through Congress.

Trump's tweets still seem to serve as a distraction from major issues, as well as a way for him to recontextualize and defend his agenda. In fact, Silver (2017) notes Trump's tweets "dictate news cycles and amplify controver-sies" (para. 10). Accordingly, the public's annoyance toward Trump's tweets is based upon the amplification and repetition of messages with which they already disagree or with the fact that pertinent issues only get attention on Trump's terms. Additionally, the response against Trump's tweets also seems like a technological preference and one about presidential decorum rather than the messaging itself. Although some Tweets may temporarily hurt his approval rating (Silver, 2017), Trump's tweets do not seem to hurt his politi-cal popularity and overall goals, at least with the current Republican majority in Congress.

President Trump provides evidence as to how combining the power of the presidency and Twitter can alter our communicative environment. Trump's Twitter coverage has dominated the headlines since he first declared he would run for office. Such coverage, alongside the actual messages, has shifted people's moods and started discord with strangers and leaders abroad. As Marcuse (2002) suggested, the tool begins to overpower discussion, mak-ing it difficult to challenge dominant thoughts. His tweets are powerful, as would be anyone's who has access to classified information and discussions with world leaders. With an indiscriminate tongue, Trump's words make us question all the ways we are able to communicate, especially those that foster trust in the processes that guarantee our rights.

References

Aslam, S. (2017, August 12). Twitter by the numbers: Stats, demographics, & fun facts. *Omnicore*. Retrieved from https://www.omnicoreagency.com/twitter-statistics/

Benoit, W. L. (2015). *Accounts, Excuses, and apologies* (2nd ed.). Albany, NY: SUNY Press.

Boddy, J. (2017, February 15). Feeling way more stressed out? You're not alone. *NPR*. Retrieved from https://www.npr.org/sections/health-shots/2017/02/15/515366975/feeling-way-more-stressed-out-youre-not-alone

Bradner, E. (2017, Febuary 20). Trump's Sweden comment raises questions. *CNN*. Retrieved from http://www.cnn.com/2017/02/19/politics/trump-rally-sweden/index.html

Coombs, W. T. (1995). Choosing the right words: The development of guidelines for the selection of the "appropriate" response strategies. *Management Communication Quarterly, 8*, 447–475.

Fox Nation [foxnation]. (2017, April 28). @TuckerCarlson: #Dems Don't Really Believe #Trump Is a Pawn of #Russia—That's Just Their Political Tool bit.ly/2qeO8iP [Tweet]. Retrieved from https://twitter.com/foxnation/status/857997724133842944

Geer, J. G. (2006). *In defense of negativity*. Chicago, IL: The University of Chicago Press.

George, A. L. (1972). The case for multiple advocacy in making foreign policy. *American Political Science Review, 56*, 751–785.

Goggin, B. (2017, November 2). A timeline of Jeff Sessions' alleged perjury. *Digg*. Retrieved from http://digg.com/2017/jeff-sessions-russia-perjury

Hearit, K. M. (1994). From "we didn't do it" to "it's not our fault": The use of *apologia* in public relations crises. In W. Elwood (Ed.), *Public relations inquiry as rhetorical criticism: Case studies of corporate discourse and social influence* (pp. 117–131). Westport, CT: Praeger.

Kramer, M. R., & Olson, K. M. (2002). The strategic potential of sequencing apologia stases: President Clinton's self-defense in the Monica Lewinsky scandal. *Western Journal of Communication, 66*, 347–367.

Marcuse, H. (2002). *One-Dimensional man: Studies in the ideology of advanced industrial society*. New York, NY: Routledge Classics.

Mark, D. (2006). *Going dirty: The art of negative campaigning*. Lanham, MD: Rowman & Littlefield Publishers.

Mutz, D. C. (2002). Cross-cutting social networks: Testing democratic theory in practice. *American Political Science Review, 96*, 111–126.

Perelman, C., & Olbrechts-Tyteca, L. (1969). *The new rhetoric: A treatise on argumentation*. Notre Dame: University of Notre Dame Press.

Postman, N. (1992). *Technopoly*. New York, NY: Vintage Books.

POTUS. (2017). President of the United States Twitter feed. Retrieved from https:// twitter.com/POTUS.

Rowland, R. R., & Jerome, A. M. (2004). On organizational *apologia*: A reconceptualiza-tion. *Communication Theory, 14*, 191–211.

Ryan, H. H. (1982). *Kategoria* and *apologia*: On their rhetorical criticism as a speech set. *Quarterly Journal of Speech, 68*, 256–261.

Savransky, R. (2017, January 11). Trump berates CNN reporter: "You are fake news." *The Hill*. Retrieved from http://thehill.com/homenews/administration/313777-trump-berates-cnn-reporter-for-fake-news

Silver, N. (2017, September 28). Never tweet, Mr. president. *FiveThirtyEight*. Retrieved from https://fivethirtyeight.com/features/never-tweet-mr-president/

Smith, T. V. (Ed.). (1956). *Philosophers speak for themselves: From Thales to Plato*. Chicago, IL: The University of Chicago Press.

Soll, J. (2016, December 18). The long and brutal history of fake news. *Politico*. Retrieved from https://www.politico.com/magazine/story/2016/12/fake-news-history-long-violent-214535

Stein, K. A. (2008). *Apologia, antapologia*, and the 1960 Soviet U-2 incident. *Communi-cation Studies, 59*, 19–34.

Todd, C., Murray, M., & Dann, C. (2017, October 2). Trump's Twitter habit is hurt-ing his presidency. *NBC News*. Retrieved from https://www.nbcnews.com/politics/first-read/trump-s-twitter-habit-hurting-his-presidency-n806506

Trump, D. J. [POTUS]. (2017a, March 18). Despite what you have heard from the FAKE NEWS I had a GREAT meeting with German Chancellor Angela Merkel. Never-theless Germany owes... [Tweet]. Retrieved from https://twitter.com/POTUS/status/843138446646501376

Trump, D. J. [POTUS]. (2017b, March 18). ... Vast sums of money to NATO & the United States must be paid more for the powerful, and very expensive, defense it provides to Germany! [Tweet]. Retrieved from https://twitter.com/POTUS/status/843138551239905281

Trump, D. J. [POTUS]. (2017c, March 29). If the people of our great country could only see how viciously and inaccurately my administration is covered by cer-tain media! -DJT [Tweet]. Retrieved from https://twitter.com/POTUS/status/847077970900602881

Trump, D. J. [realDonaldTrump]. (2017a, February 1). Everybody is arguing whether or not it is a BAN. Call it what you want it is about keeping bad people (with bad intentions) out of country! [Tweet]. Retrieved from https://twitter.com/realDonaldTrump/status/826774668245946368

Trump, D. J. [realDonaldTrump]. (2017b, February 6). I call my own shots largely based on an accumulation of data and everyone knows it. Some FAKE NEWS media in order to marginalize lies! [Tweet]. Retrieved from https://twitter.com/realDonaldTrump/status/828575949268606977

Trump, D. J. [realDonaldTrump]. (2017c, February 11). I am reading that the great border WALL will cost more than the government originally thought, but I have not gotten involved in the. .... [Tweet]. Retrieved from https://twitter.com/realDonaldTrump/status/830405706255912960

Trump, D. J. [realDonaldTrump]. (2017d, February 11). ... design or negotiations yet. When I do, just like with the F-35 FighterJet or the Air Force One Program, price will come WAY DOWN! [Tweet]. Retrieved from https://twitter.com/realDonaldTrump/status/830407172747988992

Trump, D. J. [realDonaldTrump]. (2017e, February 18). Don't believe the main stream (fake news) media. The White House is running VERY WELL. I inherited a MESS and am in the process of fixing it. [Tweet]. Retrieved from https://twitter.com/realdonaldtrump/status/832945737625387008

Trump, D. J. [realDonaldTrump]. (2017f, February 25). The media has not reported that the National Debt in my first month went down by $12 billion vs a $200 billion increase in Obama first mo. [Tweet]. Retrieved from https://twitter.com/realDonaldTrump/status/835479283699224576

Trump, D. J. [realDonaldTrump]. (2017g, February 26). Russia talk is FAKE NEWS put out by the Dems and played up by the media in order to mask the big election defeat and the illegal leaks! [Tweet]. Retrieved from https://twitter.com/realdonaldtrump/status/835916511944523777

Trump, D. J. [realDonaldTrump]. (2017h, March 2). Jeff Sessions is an honest man. He did not say anything wrong. He could have stated his response more accurately, but it was clearly not. ... [Tweet]. Retrieved from https://twitter.com/realDonaldTrump/status/837488402438176769

Trump, D. J. [realDonaldTrump]. (2017i, March 2). ... Intentional. This whole narrative is a way of saving face for Democrats losing an election that everyone thought they were supposed. ... [Tweet]. Retrieved from https://twitter.com/realDonaldTrump/status/837489578193846278

Trump, D. J. [realDonaldTrump]. (2017j, March 2c). ... To win. The Democrats are overplaying their hand. They lost the election, and now they have lost their grip on reality. The real story ... [Tweet]. Retrieved from https://twitter.com/realDonaldTrump/status/837491607171629057

Trump, D. J. [realDonaldTrump]. (2017k, March 2d). ... is all of the illegal leaks of classified and other information. It is a total "witch hunt!" [Tweet]. Retrieved from https://twitter.com/realDonaldTrump/status/837492425283219458

Trump, D. J. [realDonaldTrump]. (2017l, March 5). Who was it that secretly said to Russian President "Tell Vladimir that after the election I'll have more flexibilty?" [Tweet]. Retrieved from https://twitter.com/realDonaldTrump/status/838353481526312961

Trump, D. J. [realDonaldTrump]. (2017m, March 13). It is amazing how rude much of the media is to my very hard working representatives. Be nice you will do much better! [Tweet]. Retrieved from https://twitter.com/realDonaldTrump/status/841270741060464648

Trump, D. J. [realDonaldTrump]. (2017n, March 15). Can you imagine what the outcry would be if @SnoopDogg failing career and all had aimed and fired the gun at President Obama? Jail time! [Tweet]. Retrieved from https://twitter.com/realDonaldTrump/status/841967881516679168

Trump, D. J. [realDonaldTrump]. (2017o, March 18). Despite what you have heard from the FAKE NEWS I had a GREAT meeting with German Chancellor Angela Merkel. Nevertheless Germany owes ... [Tweet]. Retrieved from https://twitter.com/realDonaldTrump/status/843088518339612673

Trump, D. J. [realDonaldTrump]. (2017p, March 18). ... vast sums of money to NATO & the United States must be paid more for the powerful, and very expensive, defense it provides to Germany! [Tweet]. Retrieved from https://twitter.com/realDonaldTrump/status/843090516283723776

Trump, D. J. [realDonaldTrump]. (2017q, March 28). Why doesn't Fake News talk about Podesta ties to Russia as covered by @FoxNews or money from Russia to Clinton—sale of Uranium? [Tweet]. Retrieved from https://twitter.com/realDonaldTrump/status/846854703183020032

Trump, D. J. [realDonaldTrump]. (2017r, April 2). The real story turns out to be SURVEILLANCE and LEAKING! Find the leakers. [Tweet]. Retrieved from https://twitter.com/realdonaldtrump/status/848529014667055105

Trump, D. J. [realDonaldTrump]. (2017s, April 13). Things will work out fine between the U.S.A. and Russia. At the right time everyone will come to their senses & there will be lasting peace! [Tweet]. Retrieved from https://twitter.com/realDonaldTrump/status/852510810287075329

Trump, D. J. [realDonaldTrump]. (2017t, April 21). No matter how much I accomplish during the ridiculous standard of the first 100 days & it has been a lot (including S.C.) media will kill [Tweet]. Retrieved from https://twitter.com/realDonaldTrump/status/855373184861962240

Trump, D. J. [realDonaldTrump]. (2017u, April 24). The Wall is a very important tool in stopping drugs from pouring into our country and poisoning our youth (and many others)! If [Tweet]. Retrieved from https://twitter.com/realdonaldtrump/status/856484873133060101

Trump, D. J. [realDonaldTrump]. (2017v, April 24).....the wall is not built, which it will be, the drug situation will NEVER be fixed the way it should be! #BuildTheWall [Tweet]. Retrieved from https://twitter.com/realDonaldTrump/status/856531163799859201

Trump, D. J. [realDonaldTrump]. (2017w, April 24). New polls out today are very good considering that much of the media is FAKE and almost always negative. Would still beat Hillary in. ... [Tweet]. Retrieved from https://twitter.com/realDonaldTrump/status/856233279841849344

Trump, D. J. [realDonaldTrump]. (2017x, April 24). ... Popular vote. ABC News/ Washington Post Poll (wrong big on election) said almost all stand by their vote on me & 53% said strong leader. [Tweet]. Retrieved from https://twitter.com/ realDonaldTrump/status/856234989591121922

Trump, D. J. [realDonaldTrump]. (2017y, April 29). ... Popular vote. ABC News/ Washington Post Poll (wrong big on election) said almost all stand by their vote on me & 53% said strong leader. [Tweet]. Retrieved from https://twitter.com/ realDonaldTrump/status/856234989591121922

Trump, D. J. [realDonaldTrump]. (2017z, June 16). I am being investigated for firing the FBI Director by the man who told me to fire the FBI Director! Witch Hunt. [Tweet]. Retrieved from https://twitter.com/realDonaldTrump/status/ 875701471999864833

Tulis, J. K. (1987). *The rhetorical presidency*. Princeton, NJ: Princeton University Press.

Ware, B. L., & Linkugel, W. A. (1973). They spoke in defense of themselves: On the generic criticism of *apologia*. *Quarterly Journal of Speech*, *59*, 273–283.

15. Are Algorithms Media Ethics Watchdogs? An Examination of Social Media Data for News

Tao Fu
University of International Business and Economics, China

William A. Babcock
Southern Illinois University Carbondale

With the increasing role of the Internet, ethical interrogation of it has been focused on computer ethics, machine ethics and artificial intelligence (AI) ethics, which are closely related fields. Computer ethics is a broader and more generic term. Machine ethics, in particular, address issues related to "the behavior of machines toward human users and other machines" (Anderson, Anderson, & Armen, 2005, p. 1). AI ethics focuses on thinking machines with machine learning algorithms (Bostrom & Yudkowsky, 2014). Moor (2006) offered reasons for studying machine ethics: Human beings want to be well-treated by machines, especially as they are becoming increasingly powerful and sophisticated.

Ethical discussions concerning computers, machine learning, and AI often recommend designing algorithms to solve problems. This study argues algorithms per se have their own problems that merit further ethical exploration. Technological development calls for a paradigm shift in media ethics. The current study focuses specifically on the use of computer algorithms, as part of the data science in journalism and communication studies. In the following sections, the researchers introduce big data and algorithms, ethical issues concerning algorithms inferred from recent news reports about Facebook. These are followed by W. D. Ross's (1930/2002) theory of prima facie duties, which has been used in both social science research and media ethics (Fairfield & Shtein, 2014). Then the researchers apply Ross's duties of non-*maleficence*, beneficence and self-improvement to analyze Facebook's fake news and news rankings and recommendations during the 2016 U.S. presidential campaign and discuss its possible consequences that might affect Americans' political decision-making and participation using gatekeeping theory.

Big Data, Algorithms, and Social Media

During recent years, data techniques have increasingly been used in many areas besides financial journalism (Fairfield & Shtein, 2014). "Big data" is used to "reference the cultural dimensions of data analytics, technological development, and organizational shifts" (Barocas, Rosenblat, boyd, Gangadharan, & Yu, n.d., p. 2). The main sources for big data include business transactions, logistics, retail, social media, video surveillance, and sensors widely used in industries such as healthcare, life sciences, and telecommunications (Villars, Olofson, & Eastwood, 2011).

Advanced analytic techniques such as machine learning, data mining, text mining, predictive analytics, and natural language process are used to draw values from data. Specifically, machine learning is the mathematical process by which recommendations are offered and results are monitored to improve future results. The purpose of data mining is to discover unforeseen patterns, while text analytics analyze text data such as emails, blogs, tweets, and online comments to draw insights that otherwise would be undetected. Predictive analytics identifies what likely would happen based on analysis of historical and recent data.[1] Natural language process deals with the interaction between computers and human languages to make computers better understand human languages used in natural settings such as services including machine translation and speech recognition.

Data analytics would be impossible without running an algorithmic process to draw patterns or insights from random data sets. Algorithms used for collecting results, generating recommendations, and making predictions may impact Internet users both as citizens and consumers. In this study, algorithms are operationalized as the "specified sequences of logical operations designed to accomplish a particular task" (Barocas et al., n.d.).

Algorithms have a strong mathematical and statistical basis. "Every algorithm, however it is written, contains humans, and therefore editorial, judgments," Bell (2012) noted. She (Bell, 2012) warned, while journalists and Internet users are faced with the deluge of data, how individuals and organizations respond to the data would to a large extent affect journalism's sustainability. Boyd and Crawford (2012) also argued even though the use of big data seems to offer quantitative and objective methods, it does not guarantee objective truth, especially in the case of social media messages. The Center for Internet and Human Rights (CIHR, 2015) proposed three attributes of algorithms, in particular, making them an object worthy of ethical examination: complexity and opacity, gatekeeping functions, and subjective decision-making.

The use of big data and algorithms in analytics calls for ethical consideration when employed in communications. Accordingly, using prima facie duties and gatekeeping as the theoretical framework, this study examines the algorithmic use of data in fake news and news ranking and recommendation in social media represented by Facebook.

Conceptual Foundation

Prima Facie Duties

Ross elaborated on the deontological concept of duty as enunciated by philosopher Immanuel Kant some 200 years earlier. Kant reasoned that only an action taken from self-imposed duty could be considered ethical. His "categorical imperative" thus assumed that what was ethical for a person to do was what that person would will everyone do. Ross's (1930/2002) prima facie is an intuition-based deontological theory. Ross (1930/2002) proposed a list of seven prima facie duties: fidelity, reparation, gratitude, justice, beneficence, self-improvement, and non-maleficence. This list does not have a ranked order as Ross (1930/2002) argues each individual case should be judged based on its unique context and circumstances. Among these, the duties of non-maleficence, beneficence, and self-improvement are particularly crucial and relevant to the current study. According to Ross (1930/2002), non-maleficence, also known as non-injury, refers to the duty not to harm others, including people's health, security, intelligence, character, or happiness. Beneficence means to do good to others or to improve conditions of others with respect of virtue, intelligence, or pleasure (Ross, 1930/2002). We should improve other people's health, wisdom, security, happiness, and moral goodness. Self-improvement refers to the duties to improve our own health, wisdom, security, happiness, and moral goodness.

Fairfield and Shtein (2014) argued that "Ross's duty-based approach both provides stability in the face of rapid technological change and flexibility to innovate to achieve the original purpose of basic ethical principles" (p. 38). Deontological ethics often denotes inflexibility. But Ross's list of prima facie duties is open-ended and context-sensitive which makes it an ethical tool particularly fit for technological change (Fairfield & Shtein, 2014). In their study of Ross's duties, Fairfield and Shtein (2014) identified beneficence, together with autonomy and justice, as one of the principles particularly applicable to solve emerging issues in the ethics of data science and data journalism.

Ross's prima facie duties were also implemented as a foundation for the study of machine ethics (Anderson et al., 2005). But this assumes "machine ethics" exists. As Moor (2006) says, it is more difficult to program a computer to act ethically than it is to have a computer play chess, and the concept of learning what is right and wrong is at best elusive for machines.

Given his philosophy has been influential in both the Belmont Report, which provides ethical guidelines for doing research with human subjects, and media ethics, "Ross therefore serves as a bridge and a way to translate ethical discourse between the two disciplines" (Fairfield & Shtein, 2014, p. 40). But there remains a large gulf between being able to translate ethical discourse and acting ethically, and any bridge between the two is at best shaky. Accordingly, this study applies Ross's deontological system to examine emerging ethical issues in algorithm-driven results of social media.

Gatekeeping Theory

Gatekeeping theory was first articulated by Lewin (1947) who argued gatekeepers were decision-makers charged with determining what information to pass along and what to keep out. It then was used to refer to the journalistic practice of wire editors who selected what to publish (White, 1950). In this decision-making process, gatekeepers "have the power to affect the flow of information," the proper function of which "will yield unbiased news" (Reese & Ballinger, 2001, p. 647).

In fact, "gatekeeping in mass communication can be seen as the overall process through which the social reality transmitted by the news media is constructed" (Shoemaker, Eichholz, Kim, & Wrigley, 2001, p. 233). Later developers of this theory suggested gatekeeping also include shaping and manipulating information (Shoemaker et al., 2001). Forces affecting gatekeepers' decision-making are more complicated than simply determining whether or not information was truthful and newsworthy (Gieber, 1999; White, 1950). These forces might include organizational stance and professional routines, norms, and structural constraints (Singer, 2010)—for example, policies about how to cover some topics, pressures from interest groups or government (Shoemaker et al., 2001). Gatekeepers could be either individuals or sets of routine procedures (Shoemaker et al., 2001).

The gatekeeping role of the media has been challenged with the proliferation of the Internet, which allows everyone to produce, publish, and distribute information online. The roles of gatekeepers then became less about selecting stories but more about "bolstering the value that they disseminate" (Singer, 1997).

When algorithms produce, trend, and recommend results, they raise several ethical questions to consider. Are algorithms the gatekeeper of stories circulating in social media like Facebook? Are algorithms taking the role of former news editors as they are performing the curation function? Has newsworthiness—traditionally decided by editors and reporters—been replaced by "trending-worthiness," or whether or not a topic has the potential to be popular, produced by algorithms?

Shoemaker and Vos (2009) identified three channels for gatekeeping: source, media, and audience. If algorithm-produced results and social media are the first two gatekeepers in the process of information flow, the gatekeeping role of social media users as the audience also merits examination. The audience allows attention-grabbing information to pass through, leaving newsworthiness unconsidered (Shoemaker & Vos, 2009). This is a fundamental divergence from traditional media's gatekeeping consideration, which is newsworthiness.

In the following case study and discussion, the duties of non-maleficence and beneficence were selected to examine social media's role as gatekeeper, and the duty of self-improvement for social media users.

Fake News, Biased News, and Social Media's Duties

Facebook had 1.86 billion monthly active users globally by the end of 2016 (Fiegerman, 2017) with about 167 million in the US (Nunez, 2016). According to a survey conducted in March and April 2016 by Pew Research Center, 79% of Americans use Facebook, much more than they do any other social media service (Geiger, 2016).

In the 2016 U.S. presidential campaign year, criticism of Facebook has targeted on fake news, trending, and recommending news showing political stance acceptable to particular Facebook users. The researchers argue when increasingly more Americans turn to Facebook as their sole news source, Facebook is the de facto gatekeeper, and algorithms the tool. Circulating fake news harms American political life and its citizens as this can impact voting. Facebook should take actions to cause the least harm guided by the non-maleficence duty.

But by trending and feeding stories recommended by algorithms, Facebook helped create the information cocoons in which American voters were selectively exposed to biased political opinions and voices. As the source of news many Americans rely on, Facebook should perform the duty of benef-icence to bring about the greatest good possible and improve their politi-cal wisdom. The researchers also argue Facebook users, as the audience, are gatekeepers responsible for deciding what news to engage. They have the self-improvement duty to develop their own talents and abilities to the fullest.

Post-Truth, Fake News, and Non-Maleficence

The year 2016 saw significant decisions made that might restructure the world order, including the Brexit referendum and Donald Trump's election. Oxford Dictionaries called "post-truth" the word of the year, and defined it as "relating to or denoting circumstances in which objective facts are less influential in shaping public opinion than appeals to emotion and personal belief." The word was said to have captured the "ethos, mood, or preoccupa-tions" of 2016 and "have lasting potential as a word of cultural significance," according to a *Washington Post* report (Wang, 2016). 2016 also was the year of "post fact" news, post-new news, and of the algorithmic timeline (Kibred, 2016). Consequently, stories recommended on Facebook, Twitter, or Insta-gram are not in a linear time-order but follow an algorithmic timeline based on correlating factors such as what the user's preferences are and what his or her friends are reading. Stories trending in social media, personalized and recommended by algorithms, foster like-minded bubbles among users who shared similar views and blocked them from diversified voices and opinions. Many such stories may be fake, misleading, or biased news, hoaxes, or even clickbait—web content encouraging users to click on a link to a particular web page.

Even though Mark Zuckerberg, chief of the social media giant, has repeat-edly emphasized that Facebook is just a technology company, not a media com-pany (Dwoskin, Dewey, & Timberg, 2016), it has become an important source for news for millions of people. A Pew Research Center survey found about six of 10 Americans get news from social media (Gottfried & Shearer, 2016). With 66% of Facebook users getting news on its own site, slightly behind Reddit's 70%, this means 44% of Americans get news from Facebook. Facebook saw the largest growth in use of social media for news from 2013 to 2016 (19%).[2] But the percentage of Facebook users who access news via other media was rela-tively low, ranging from 15% for print newspapers to 39% for local TV. Thus, Americans are flocking in large numbers to social media for news—in some cases as their only news source—rather than to the traditional media.

Buzzfeed found during the last three months of the presidential cam-paign 20 top-performing fake stories on Facebook generated more shares, comments and reactions than 20 top news stories produced by 19 major news organizations combined such as the *New York Times* and NBC (Silverman, 2016). Some examples of top fake election stories on Facebook include: Pope Francis shocks world, endorsed Donald Trump for President, releases statement; WikiLeaks confirms Hillary sold weapons to ISIS, then drops another bombshell; It's over: Hillary's ISIS email just leaked & it's worse than anyone could have imagined; Just read the law: Hillary is disqualified from holding any federal office; FBI agent suspected in Hillary email leaks found dead in apparent murder-suicide. The made-up Pope endorsed Trump story was shared, reacted to or commented on Facebook for nearly one million times with other stories being engaged for at least more than half a million times. Such huge traffic means increased advertising income for Facebook.

In the wake of the 2016 U.S. presidential election, Pew Research Center's survey found most American adults said fake news left them with a great deal of confusion (64%) and some confusion (24%) about basic facts of some issues and events regardless of demographic differences such as income, education and partisan affiliation (Barthel, Mitchell & Holcomb, 2016). In particular, some Americans (32%) say political news stories online are fabricated. The Pew Research Center's survey also found about one-fifth of Americans had shared fake news, and that 14% of them were aware the news was made-up. As to the prevention of the spread of fake news, 71% of U.S. adults said social networking sites and search engines need to take some or a great deal of responsibility.

In mid-December 2016 Facebook announced its measures to combat fake news amid criticism it might have affected the U.S. electorate. Facebook users could flag news stories they suspect are false. Facebook then will turn to third parties such as Snopes and Politifact for fact-checking and flag them as "disputed." Such stories might be banned from its advertising system. In mid-January 2017, Facebook announced it would replicate the same measures in Germany as part of its test before the German election to be held in September (McGoogan, 2017).

For journalism, a lofty ideal is the communication of truth (Patterson & Wilkins, 2008). The Society of Professional Journalists' (SPJ) (2014) Code of Ethics lists "seek truth and report it" as its first principle and standard of practice. But with the development of communication technologies such as machine learning and the massive user-generated content (UGC), telling and seeking truth have become more complicated.

At a time of increasing use of social media as a major news source, especially by members of the millennial generation, truth-telling is a growing concern. But should there be an expectation that social media be truthful? After all, there are no major and/or longstanding traditions of professionalism in social media as there were in legacy journalism, stemming from the Commission on Freedom of the Press (1947). This body, usually referred to as the Hutchins Commission, launched the concept of social responsibility, which in turn laid the foundation for or popularized a number of media accountability tools. Such tools included ethics codes, ombudsmen, and press councils, which served as ethics gatekeepers for the professional media for the remainder of the 20th century, ensuring the media act, and be seen as acting, in a truthful, hence professional manner. Social media have no such historical—or ethical—tradition and thus there has been no widespread consensus that social media users have an obligation to truth telling.

But, as indicated by Pew's survey findings, fake news disseminated on Facebook had confused American voters about basic facts concerning the presidential election, thus affecting their decision-making ability (Barthel, Mitchell, & Holcomb, 2016).

News media are supposed to seek and present truth to the audience so that the audience might make informed decisions as seen in the SPJ's Code of Ethics. In traditional news operations, gatekeepers such as fact checkers, and line and copy editors, even legal counsel sometimes, screen news accounts for inaccuracies. At Facebook, algorithms have taken the role of gatekeepers. But Facebook has been ambivalent as to whether or not it should play the editorial role. Making its content subject to censorship is part of the concern. As reported in the *New York Times*, Facebook is a "content provider that does not produce its own content—that is, as a platform, not a media company" (Rutenberg & Issac, 2017). Adam Mosseri, Facebook's VP of News Feed, maintains Facebook cannot become arbiters of truth. Accordingly, Facebook recently appointed Campbell Brown as "head of news partnerships" whose main duties are to co-ordinate relationships between Facebook and media companies rather than working as an editor, Facebook's new move to combat fake news (Rutenberg & Issac, 2017).

By non-maleficence Ross (1930/2002) means one should act so as to cause the least harm. As one of the main stakeholders, especially when an increasingly growing number of Americans are turning to social media such as Facebook for news, and even use it as the only news source, fake news on Facebook likely may have affected the outcome of the election. Although Zuckerberg claimed 99% of the content people see on Facebook is authentic, fake news during the campaign season may have seriously harmed American democracy.[3]

News Trending, Biased News, and Beneficence

Algorithm-driven automated recommendation and search-results ranking are two key methods for Internet companies to gain profits. At Google, how its algorithms crawl and index results is as much a top secret as is Coca-Cola's recipe, or probably even more so. But the use of algorithms by Netflix and Kroger provides some insight into how social media companies exploit the programs. Netflix, for instance, relies on recommendations that are results of machine learning of users' preferences and history. The recommender system, running on a collection of algorithms, was acknowledged as a key pillar of Netflix, bringing $1 billion a year (Gomez-Uribe & Hunt, 2015). Altogether, recommendations affect 80% of the audience's choice at Netflix and 20% of search, according to Gomez-Uribe & Hunt (2015). Kroger, a U.S. grocery store chain, mailed personalized coupons to its customers based on their analysis of loyalty-card data, according to a report from the Economist Intelligence Unit (EIU, 2013). The recommendation is based on what the customer had bought over the past two years (Groenfeldt, 2013).

Facebook relies on trending and recommendation in the same vein. News Feed and Trending Topics are two core services. News Feed is a 12-year-old service providing personalized stories that matter most to each individual user of Facebook. Trending was added to Facebook in 2014 offering breaking news and popular content to its users (Facebook, 2016). As Facebook's (2016) update in August said, it is based on pages an individual user liked, his or her location, previous trending topics clicked, or browsed plus topics trending at Facebook. Both of these services need algorithms to rank and recommend results.

Trending originally employed human reviewers, "news curators" as they were called internally, whose tasks were to add a story description to what was trending. Since May 2016, Facebook has been accused of suppressing conservative news. According to a Gizmodo report, curators' responsibilities included artificially "injecting" stories to ensure inclusion (though they might not be popular enough) and subjectively avoiding conservative stories unless they were covered by mainstream news outlets (Nunez, 2016). As Zuckerberg has emphasized that Facebook is not a media company and therefore does not function as a gatekeeper to exert editorial control of content and topics circulating on Facebook, Facebook came under fire after the curators were reported to manually remove stories with pro-Trump agenda.[4] But afterward, these contractors were all fired in August 2016.[5] Facebook currently only has engineers check if algorithm-driven topics are newsworthy (Wong, Gershgorn, & Murphy, 2016). While algorithms prioritize what is popular, it is difficult to distinguish what is truthful and what is a hoax. And while curators were allowed to cross-reference with Google News and reject trends produced by algorithms, engineers had limited freedom (Dewey, 2016).

The ethics question is whether social media should be news gatekeepers. As stories recommended by algorithms are the sources for users of social media, algorithms are in fact the gatekeeping tool. But algorithms are based on mathematical and statistical computations programed by engineers. Algorithms are amoral, without moral sense or principles, and thus incapable of distinguishing between right and wrong. It is human beings who affect the seemingly neutral and objective algorithms. Research has found historic biases and prejudices from human culture would be reified by machine learning (Caliskan-Islam, Bryson, & Narayanan, 2016). Another study of search engines found Google and Baidu ranked results of politically sensitive queries—many of which were blocked by China's great Internet firewall—differently (Fu & Babcock, 2014). Google's algorithms got most of the results from pro-human-rights sites and from mainstream Western media, following its freedom-based ethical values. Baidu, on the other hand, by generating most results from media headquartered in China and its Hong Kong Special Administrative Area, fulfilled its role to maintain social harmony.

When Facebook fired its human curators, who to some extent played the role of news editors, algorithms became de facto gatekeepers of stories circulating in Facebook. In such an ethics Wild West, algorithms are determining and filtering the news. Consequently, the concept of newsworthiness traditionally decided by editors and reporters has been replaced by "trending-worthiness" produced by algorithms.

Issues of fairness and accountability are all ethics based. While algorithms may be employed in a fair and accountable manner, algorithms are not inherently ethical. Rather, they simply are gatekeeping tools. *How* algorithms are used as gatekeepers is the key.

Therefore, Facebook, as the designer and owner overseeing the running of algorithms, should take actions to fulfill the duty of beneficence. Given the context that algorithms are top secrets to Internet companies, a demand for transparency of algorithms might be hard to achieve at this point. Even if Internet companies had the intent to disclose their algorithms, they likely would be too professional and complicated for most Internet users as laymen to understand.

In these circumstances, then, Facebook should adjust its algorithms to be inclusive to both liberal and conservative voices. It should provide American voters with fair stories to help improve their wisdom and make informed decisions. Biased opinions favoring any political stance would have been a threat to American democracy whose repercussions might be subtle and long running. To re-employ human editors might also be something for Facebook to consider. After all, the purpose of using amoral algorithms in machine learning and data mining is to make human beings well-treated, as argued by Moor (2006). This good treatment connotes the intellectual well being of American voters faced making big political decisions such as choosing a president. Without unbiased, inclusive and diversified information and opinion provided by the media, especially social media, American voters' ability to make informed voting decisions would be greatly impaired.

Facebook Users as Gatekeeper and Self-Improvement

Facebook users, the audience of social media news, have their own duties as gatekeepers. They decide what news to share, react to, or comment on. Increasingly, the public—especially individuals focused primarily on social media for their news and information—are not exposing themselves to a true "marketplace of ideas," but instead are doing their media "shopping" in smaller, selective venues. In such a silo-type media environment, users tend to "talk" with and get information from people largely like themselves. As seen in the recent U.S. presidential election, Facebook followers of Trump were certain that Clinton lied. Clinton's Facebook fans were just as certain Trump fabricated "facts" on a regular basis, especially in his tweets. Democrats using social media as their major news and information sources assumed Clinton would easily defeat Donald Trump. In this way, Clinton supporters acted as their own algorithms, essentially not accepting data indicating Trump could or would win.

While it may be impossible for all Facebook users to identify all fake news from truthful news accounts, they at the very least might detect what news is biased. To be better educated citizens, it is time Facebook and other social media users be exposed to political stories showing a variety of political stances. It is also time Facebook users regain their trust in traditional media, gatekeepers of what is newsworthy and true, and organizations guided by professional codes of ethics.

Conclusion

Algorithms, modern-day gatekeeping tools, have vastly expanded the concept of gatekeeping. Where gatekeepers inherently were intertwined with ethics, algorithms inherently are not so interrelated.

Algorithms are designed to in some manner censor. Censorship to promote the greater good can be of utilitarian ethical value. As a result, monitoring of algorithm gatekeepers is necessary to ensure that such tools are used in an ethical manner.

While it is clearly understandable that media ethics of previous decades had a cherished tradition and were rightfully revered for helping to make media of the second half of the 20th century more professional and fair, that era is in many respects over. Media ombudsmen are an endangered species given the economics of journalism. No more press councils exist in the U.S. Only a few journalism reviews still are published, either in print or online. Media editors/reporters are rare in traditional journalism. As a result, such media ethics tools are in danger of becoming little more than historical relics. Algorithms have pretty much become *the* media watchdogs. They are the new ethics tools not only for social media, but for much professional media as well. Algorithms, despite their seeming neutrality and objectivity, are subject to personal whim and bias. The hope is that these new electronic tools will be used in an ethical fashion.

Social media played a new trend-setting role in the 2016 U.S. presidential election and the Brexit referendum, as compared to how social media affected our understanding of the Arab Spring, the Occupy Movement and Barack Obama's first presidential campaign. Technological development calls for paradigm shift in media ethics. A new algorithm model is needed, especially for Facebook and social media—one that reconceptualizes the media ethics toolbox of the 21st century—which traditionally include ethics codes, ombudsmen, media critics, news councils, journalism reviews, and public/civic journalism initiatives.

This explorative study focused primarily on the deontological system Ross posits. As mentioned earlier, the prima facie duties outline what social media companies such as Facebook and what social media users should do in the context that more Americans depend on social media for news. Too, Facebook was criticized for fake news and biased news trending. Future studies may meld Ross with a teleological utilitarian such as John Stuart Mill to better suit to the 21st century's consideration of how to approach algorithms. Employing algorithms as mere censors or filters and disregarding the consequences of such actions would be in every respect unethical. Mill promotes a utilitarian concept of the greatest good for the greatest number. As a result, algorithms have the utility of serving the greatest good by satisfying the social needs of audience members, and thus promoting harmony. Thus, algorithms would perform both a gatekeeping and media ethics function formerly performed both by journalists and media ethics tools.

Notes

1. See Barocas et al. (n.d.), and SAS (2016) for more details.
2. This number is much higher than other social networking sites such as Reddit (8%), Twitter (7%), Instragram (10%), LinkedIn (6%), Vine (5%), Tumblr (2%), and YouTube (1%).

3. One study by Allcott and Gentzkow (2017) said fake news did not affect the outcome. Or refer to Concha (2017) at http://thehill.com/homenews/media/317646-fake-news-did-not-change-result-of-2016-election-study
4. This was denied by Facebook.
5. Some reports believed this move showed Facebook's confidence of its machine learning.

References

Allcott, H., & Gentzkow, M. (2017). Social media and fake news in the 2016 election. *Journal of Economic Perspective, 31*(2), 211–236. Retrieved from https://web.stanford.edu/~gentzkow/research/fakenews.pdf

Anderson, M., Anderson, S. I., & Armen, C. (2005). Towards machine ethics: Implementing two action-based ethical theories. AAAI Press. Retrieved from http://www.aaai.org/Papers/Symposia/Fall/2005/FS-05-06/FS05-06-001.pdf

Barocas, S., Rosenblat, A., boyd, d, Gangadharan, S. P., & Yu, C. (n.d.). Data & civil rights: Technology primer. Retrieved from https://perma.cc/X3YX-XHNA

Barthel, M., Mitchell, A., & Holcomb, J. (2016, December 15). Many Americans believe fake news is sowing confusion. Pew Research Center. Retrieved from http://www.journalism.org/2016/12/15/many-americans-believe-fake-news-is-sowing-confusion/

Bell, E. (2012). Journalism by numbers. *Columbia Journalism Review*. Retrieved from http://www.cjr.org/cover_story/journalism_by_numbers.php

Bostrom, N., & Yudkowsky, E. (2014). The ethics of artificial intelligence. In K. Frankish & W. M. Ramsey (Eds.), *The Cambridge handbook of artificial intelligence* (pp. 316–334). Cambridge: Cambridge University Press.

boyd, d., & Crawford, K. (2012). Critical questions for big data: Provocations for a cultural, technological, and scholarly phenomenon. *Information, Communication, & Society, 15*(5), 662–679.

Caliskan-Islam, A., Bryson, J. J., & Narayanan, A. (2016). Semantics derived automatically from language corpora necessarily contain human biases. Retrieved from http://randomwalker.info/publications/language-bias.pdf

CIHR. (2015). The ethics of algorithms: From radical content to self-driving cars. Retrieved from https://cihr.eu/ethics-of-algorithms/

Commission on Freedom of the Press. (1947). *A free and responsible press: A general report on mass communication: newspapers, radio, motion pictures, magazines, and books*. Chicago, IL: The University of Chicago Press.

Concha, J. (2017, February 2). Fake news did not change result of 2016 election: Study. Retrieved from http://thehill.com/homenews/media/317646-fake-news-did-not-change-result-of-2016-election-study

Dewey, C. (2016, October 12). Facebook has repeatedly trended fake news since firing its human editors. *Washington Post*. Retrieved from https://www.washingtonpost.com/news/the-intersect/wp/2016/10/12/facebook-has-repeatedly-trended-fake-news-since-firing-its-human-editors/?utm_term=.c9a3e0e12f72

Dwoskin, E., Dewey, C., & Timberg, C. (2016, November 15). Why Facebook and Google are struggling to purge fake news. *Washington Post*. Retrieved from https://www.washingtonpost.com/business/economy/why-facebook-and-google-are-struggling-to-purge-fake-news/2016/11/15/85022897-f765-422e-9f53-c720d1f20071_story.html

EIU. (2013). After the Big Bang: How retailers can harness the big data explosion. Retrieved from http://www.retailwire.com/public/braintrust-resources/B18CB83E-19B9-EB12-B0A73EBDCE9150A2.pdf

Facebook. (2016, August 26). Search FYI: An update to trending. Retrieved from http://newsroom.fb.com/news/2016/08/search-fyi-an-update-to-trending/

Fairfield, J., & Shtein, H. (2014). Big data, big problems: Emerging issues in the ethics of data science and journalism. *Journal of Mass Media Ethics, 29*(35), 38–51.

Fiegerman, S. (2017, February 1). Facebook is closing in on 2 billion users. CNN. Retrieved from http://money.cnn.com/2017/02/01/technology/facebook-earnings/index.html

Fu, T., & Babcock, W. A. (2014). "Search engines and online censorship in China: An ethics approach." Paper presented at the 97th Annual Conference of the Association for Education in Journalism and Mass Communication, Media Ethics Division. Montreal, Canada.

Geiger, A. (2016, December 21). 16 striking findings from 2016. Retrieved from http://www.pewresearch.org/fact-tank/2016/12/21/16-striking-findings-from-2016/

Gieber, W. (1999). News is what newspapermen make it. In H. Tumber (Ed.), *News: A reader* (pp. 218–223). Oxford: Oxford University Press.

Gomez-Uribe, C. A., & Hunt, N. (2015). The Netflix recommender system: Algorithms, business value, and innovation. *ACM Transactions on Management Information Systems, 6*(4), Article 13. doi:10.1145/2843948

Gottfried, J., & Shearer, E. (2016, May 26). News use across social media platforms 2016. Retrieved from http://www.journalism.org/2016/05/26/news-use-across-social-media-platforms-2016/

Groenfeldt, T. (2013, October 28). Kroger knows your shopping pattern better than you do. *Forbes*. Retrieved from http://www.forbes.com/sites/tomgroenfeldt/2013/10/28/kroger-knows-your-shopping-patterns-better-than-you-do/

Kibred, R. (2016, December 25). Why 2016 was the year of the algorithmic timeline? Retrieved from http://motherboard.vice.com/read/why-2016-was-the-year-of-the-algorithmic-timeline

Lewin, K. (1947). Frontiers in group dynamics: II. Channels of group life, social planning, and action research. *Human Relations, 1*(2), 143–153.

McGoogan, C. (2017, January 16). Facebook combating fake news in Germany ahead of election. *The Telegraph*. Retrieved from http://www.telegraph.co.uk/technology/2017/01/16/facebook-combating-fake-news-germany-ahead-election/

Moor, J. H. (2006, July/August). Machine ethics: The nature, importance and difficulty of machine ethics. *IEEE Intelligence System, 21*(4), 18–21.

Nunez, M. (2016, May 9). Former Facebook workers: We routinely suppressed conservative news. Retrieved from http://gizmodo.com/former-facebook-workers-we-routinely-suppressed-conser-1775461006

Patterson, P., & Wilkins, L. (Eds.). (2008). *Media ethics: Issues and cases* (6th ed.). Boston, MA: McGraw Hill Higher Education.

Reese, S. D., & Ballinger, J. (2001). The roots of a sociology of news: Remembering Mr. Gates and social control in the newsroom. *Journal of Mass Communication Quarterly, 78*(4), 641–658.

Ross, W. D. (1930/2002). *The right and the good.* P. Stratton-Lake (Ed.). Oxford: Clarendon Press.

Rutenberg, J., & Issac, M. (2017, January 6). Facebook hires Campbell Brown to lead news partnerships team. *New York Times.* Retrieved from http://www.nytimes.com/2017/01/06/business/media/facebook-campbell-brown-media-fake-news.html

SAS. (2016). Big data analytics: What it is and why it matters. Retrieved from http://www.sas.com/en_us/insights/analytics/big-data-analytics.html

Shoemaker, P., & Vos, T. (2009). *Gatekeeping theory.* London: Routledge.

Shoemaker, P. J., Eichholz, M., Kim, E., & Wrigley, B. (2001). Individual and routine forces in gatekeeping. *Journalism and Mass Communication Quarterly, 78,* 233–246.

Silverman, C. (2016, November 17). This analysis shows how fake election news stories outperformed real news on Facebook. BuzzFeedNews. Retrieved from https://www.buzzfeed.com/craigsilverman/viral-fake-election-news-outperformed-real-news-on-facebook?utm_term=.sc2qojJkz#.daZXbplEB

Singer, J. B. (1997). Still guarding the gate? The newspaper journalist's role in an online world. *Convergence, 3*(1), 72–89.

Singer, J. B. (2010). Quality control: Perceived effects of user-generated content on newsroom norms, values and routines. *Journalism Practice, 4*(2), 127–142.

SPJ. (2014, September 6). SPJ code of ethics. Retrieved from http://www.spj.org/ethicscode.asp

Villars, R. L., Olofson, C. W., & Eastwood, M. (2011). Big data: What it is and why you should care. IDC. Retrieved from http://sites.amd.com/us/Documents/IDC_AMD_Big_Data_Whitepaper.pdf

Wang, A. B. (2016, November 16). "Post-truth" named 2016 word of the year by Oxford Dictionaries. *Washington Post.* Retrieved from https://www.washingtonpost.com/news/the-fix/wp/2016/11/16/post-truth-named-2016-word-of-the-year-by-oxford-dictionaries/?utm_term=.aa7e9f9b80ac

White, D. M. (1950). The "Gate Keeper": A case study in the selection of news. *Journalism Quarterly, 27,* 383–390.

Wong, J. I., Gershgorn, D., & Murphy, M. (2016, Augst 26). Facebook is trying to get rid of bias in Trending news by getting rid of humans. *Quartz.* Retrieved from http://qz.com/768122/facebook-fires-human-editors-moves-to-algorithm-for-trending-topics/

16. Emerging Free Speech and Social Media Law and Policy in the Age of Trump

ARTHUR S. HAYES

Fordham University

President Donald Trump's tweeting—calculated it seems to stir controversy for almost every news cycle—is likely to lead to long-term constitutional and regulatory reassessments of social media use the president never intended. Almost the same thing can be said about the controversies leading up to the U.S. Senate Judiciary Committee hearings on Russian election interference held in late October and early November 2017 (Romm, 2017). Few during the race to the presidency—including the winner, no doubt—would have predicted that tech companies would be the targets of calls for increased government regulation, particularly with the champions of deregulation controlling the U.S. House, Senate and the Presidency.

In 2017, plaintiffs brought two separate lawsuits against Trump that challenged his right to block access to his Twitter account and to delete his and others tweets. The president blocks citizens from his Twitter account simply because they criticize him. Consequently, ten months into his presidency, Trump tried to persuade a judge to throw out a lawsuit brought by the Knight First Amendment Institute at Columbia University challenging his practice of blocking users based on their viewpoints as unconstitutional under the First Amendment (*Brief for the Knight First Amendment Institute at Columbia University v. Trump*, 2017).[1]

The online censorship controversy, however, is bigger than Trump. Increasingly, local government officials use social media to communicate with their constituents. Like Trump, a number of elected officials do not want to hear bad news and they block critics or delete their posts. First Amendment advocates argue that such censorship deprives citizens of participating in vital public forums for political debate and discussion and the censorship makes it difficult to hold government officials accountable. In that vein, and about the same time that the Knight First Amendment Institute filed its lawsuit, the ACLU, through its various state branches, brought similar lawsuits against the governors of Kentucky, Maine and Maryland (Bernstein, 2017).

Thus, the Knight First Amendment Institute lawsuit is likely to play a major role in shaping the development of constituent communications. The rise of digital technologies has altered how elected officials communicate with voters. In the past, elected officials communicated with voters via mail, telephone calls, press releases, television and radio press conferences, and through news interviews. Face-to-face town hall meetings provided the rare forums for direct and publicly shared interaction between constituents and elected officials. Social media has altered that imbalance by providing interactivity, which enhances citizens' ability to hold their representatives accountable and transparent. If left uncensored, Twitter, for example, provides the online equivalent of a town hall meeting. As Congressional Research analysts noted, "Constituent communication is one of the basic building blocks of a representative democracy" (Straus & Glassman, 2016, p. 1).

Meanwhile, two government watchdog groups, Citizens for Responsibility and Ethics in Washington and the National Security Archive, brought a lawsuit against Trump, identifying his deletion of tweets from his account as one of several practices that allegedly violated the Presidential Records Act (PRA) (Presidential Libraries, 2017) and the U.S. Constitution by evading transparency and government accountability (*Citizens for Responsibility and Ethics v. Trump*, 2017). Under the PRA, presidential records are not private property, and although the records are not subject to public access requests during the President's term of office, the Act makes presidential records publicly available five years after a President leaves office when the records are handed over to the National Archivist (American Historical Association v. National Archives and Records Administration, 2007). The (PRA) "remains the United States' most noticeable effort at asserting public ownership of and access to the records of public officials (in this case the president of the United States)" (Sezzi, 2005, Introduction).

In another attempt to achieve the same goal, a House Democrat introduced legislation—the Communications Over Various Feeds Electronically for Engagement (COVFEFE) Act—to amend the Act to include social media (Uchill, 2017).[2] Like the Knight First Amendment Institute lawsuit, these legal actions seek to hold President Trump accountable to public scrutiny.

By fall 2017, the failure of social media to police fake news and fake ads, the subject of U.S. Senate Judiciary Committee hearings on Russian election interference, sparked a great deal of chatter about the merits of government regulation of private social media sites to police fake news and advertisements (Caplan, 2017). Before the year's end, the U.S. Senate and House introduced their "Honest Ads Acts," legislation that would require social media companies to keep publicly available records of the political ads they publish, their advertisers and the targets of the ads (S. 1989-Honest Ads Act, 2017–2018). The bills are essentially the same. By making online platforms store political ads, the legislators hope to achieve transparency and accountability. Voters would be able to size up the legitimacy of political ads by seeing who paid for them, and, supposedly, make better-informed decisions at the voting booth as a result.

This chapter examines the lawsuits, proposed legislation and debates about social media law and regulatory policy that are linked directly and indirectly to Trump, both as a candidate and as president. Here, I argue that the plaintiffs suing the president for blocking access to his Twitter account in *Knight First Amendment Institute v. Trump* have a strong chance of prevailing based largely on the only precedent that is directly on point, *Davison v. Loudoun* (2017). A key part of Trump's defense is his contention that his tweets are personal because the president uses his personal account, @realdonaldtrump, and, consequently, the online account cannot be a public forum to which everyone has a right of access. The court in *Davison v. Loudoun*, however, rejected a similar argument from a local official.

Trump also argues, among other points, that his personal ownership of his Twitter account exempts him from complying with the Presidential Records Act (Cushing, 2017). Apparently, Trump will have to distinguish his case from a line of rulings that can reasonably read to allow judicial review of guidelines outlining "what is, and what is not, a 'presidential record'" in contrast to decisions about the "creation, management and disposal" of records (*Crew v. Cheney*, 2009, pp. 214–221).

If Trump prevails in those lawsuits, free speech, transparency in government and democratic discourse will lose, I argue, because the foundation of our democratic republic is citizen engagement in civic discourse and government's accountability to the public. The impact of the Honest Ads bill, however, is likely to be mixed. On one hand, it appears to meet the conditions of constitutionality under the U.S. Supreme Court's interpretation of the Federal Election Campaign Act's "express advocacy"/ "issue advocacy" doctrine, particularly considering the Court's denial of certiorari in *Delaware Strong Families v. Denn* (2016). Some, however, predict it will miss the mark because, among other shortcomings, it targets commercial speech when much of online fake news is political speech penned by trolls.

@RealDonaldTrump: Is There State Action?

No one disputes that Trump started @RealDonaldTrump in 2009 as a private account to promote his book *Think Like a Champion* (Daily News, 2016). The key question in the lawsuit brought by the Knight First Amendment Institute is whether Trump's use of the account as a public official, in other words state action, transformed it into a government-sponsored forum for expression and, thus, subjects it to the constitutional constraints of the public forum doctrine. Simply put, if the courts find that the Trump Twitter account is a public forum, the president cannot block access to his account from critics solely because he dislikes their views.

The Justice Department also argued that Knight First Amendment Institute and its fellow plaintiffs lack standing to sue "most significantly because they cannot seek their requested relief against the President; it would flout the separation of powers for the Court to issue an order limiting the President's discretion in managing his account" (Memorandum of Law in Support of Motion for Summary Judgment, p. 9). Justice, however, provided no precedential authority to support such a sweeping claim of presidential immunity.

The Knight First Amendment Institute (*Brief for the Knight First Amendment Institute*, 2017, p. 2) argues that Trump's Twitter account has become a public forum for information and debate mostly because the president, press secretary and social media director have,

> promoted the President's Twitter account as a key channel for official communication. Defendants use the account to make formal announcements, defend the President's official actions, report on meetings with foreign leaders, and promote the administration's positions on health care, immigration, foreign affairs, and other matters. The President's advisors have stated that tweets from @realDonaldTrump are "official statements," and they have been treated as such by politicians, world leaders, the National Archive and Records Administration, and federal courts.

In its motion to dismiss the Knight First Amendment complaint, the U.S. Department of Justice (*Memoranda in Support of Defendant's Motion for Summary Judgment*, p. 13) argues that Trump's use of the @RealDonaldTrump account as president doesn't amount to state action:

> But the fact that the President may announce the "actions of the state" through his Twitter account does not mean that all actions related to that account are attributable to the state. Public officials may make statements about public

policy—and even announce a new policy initiative—in a variety of settings, such as on the campaign trail or in a meeting with leaders of a political party. The fact that an official chooses to make such an announcement in an unofficial setting does not retroactively convert into state action the decision about which members of the public to allow into the event. Similarly, the President's decision to block Twitter users on his personal account is not properly considered state action.

Justice also argues that even if a court were to find state action, blocking does not implicate the First Amendment public forum doctrine, but rather the government speech doctrine (*Memoranda in Support of Defendant's Motion for Summary Judgment*, pp. 13–14). As the U.S. Supreme Court recently explained in *Walker v. Sons of Confederate Veterans* (2015, p. 2245), "When government speaks, it is not barred by the Free Speech Clause from determining the content of what it says." In *Walker* (p. 2246), the Court ruled that Texas's right to government speech allowed it to reject a request by a local Sons of the Confederate group's request for a specialty design license plate featuring the Confederate flag, finding that "our precedents regarding government speech (and not our precedents regarding forums for private speech) provide the appropriate framework through which to approach the case." In the Trump case, the Justice Department contends that the interactivity of Twitter—the reply function allowing for conversation—was not created by Trump and that is a significant, if not controlling, distinction in determining whether the government speech doctrine controls:

> At bottom, it is a mistake to analyze the President's decision … to use the Twitter account he created as a private citizen to block individuals on a private social media platform—"in terms of a doctrine rooted in the government's historic regulation of speech, by private citizens on real, public property" … Instead of applying the "highly strained analogy" of the public forum … the better course is to treat the @realDonaldTrump account for what it most plainly is: the speech of the President participating in a privately run forum, not the government managing the participation of others in a public one. (*Memoranda in Support of Defendant's Motion for Summary Judgment*, 2017, p. 23)

Blocked Tweets: Legal Precedents

In their initial legal filings, the Justice Department and the Knight First Amendment Institute failed to address the only two rulings that directly address the issue of a government official's use of a privately owned social media site and the state action and public forum doctrines, *Davison v. Loudoun County Board of Supervisors* (2017) and *Davison v. Plowman* (2017). The rulings favor the Knight First Amendment Institute and the government speech doctrine was not raised. *Loudoun*, the more important of the two rulings, was handed down in late July 2017, which may explain the rulings' absence from the initial court filings. The significance of the rulings, however, did not escape the attention of media law observers:

> This is obviously a timely and relevant ruling, given the lawsuit against President Trump for blocking Twitter followers. While it's tempting to distinguish a Twitter stream from a Facebook page (where comments in a typical sense are the norm), Twitter's format has also changed, highlighting the importance of comments and "threads." In any event, I'm not sure this is a critical distinction. Much of the ruling's reasoning is equally applicable to the @POTUS Twitter account. What started off looking like a lark of a case could turn into consequential precedent for constraints on the ability of politicians, including President Trump, to block members of the public. (Balasubramani, 2017)[3]

By late 2017, in his second of two rulings on a free speech and due process action brought by Brian C. Davison against Loudoun County, Virginia, officials, federal trial Judge James C. Cacheris provided the sole judicial analytical template for answering the "novel legal question: when is a social media account maintained by a public official considered 'governmental' in nature, and thus subject to constitutional constraints" (*Davison v. Loudoun County Board of Supervisors*, 2017, p. 14)? In *Davison v. Loudoun*, the chair of the county board, Phyliss J. Randal, had banned Brian Davison for about 12 hours from leaving comments on her Facebook page, though he was able to post his comments on other Facebook pages during that same period. Randall argued that her page was privately owned and, consequently, Davison had no constitutional right to access it. (*Davison v. Loudoun County Board of Supervisors*, p. 14)

Cacheris's ruling suggests the following analytical steps:

1. Determine whether the government official/owner of the originally private social media page has operated the site under the color of the law or used state action analysis to maintain the site.
2. Determine whether the plaintiff had engaged in protected speech.
3. Determine whether the defendant opened a forum for speech on a social media site.
4. Identify the nature of that forum according to the public forum doctrine: Is it a public forum, non-public forum or limited (or designated) public forums?

The Court applies public forum doctrine analysis to determine when a government entity seeking to regulate its own property may place limitations on expressive activities, including information gathering, assembly and discussion. In *Cornelius v. NAACP* (1985, p. 820) the Court explained that government transforms its property that had been traditionally closed to assembly and debate into a public forum "only by intentionally opening a nontraditional forum for public discourse."

> Thus, the public forum, limited-public-forum, and nonpublic forum categories are but analytical shorthand for the principles that have guided the Court's decisions regarding claims to access to public property for expressive activity. The interests served by the expressive activity must be balanced against the interests served by the uses for which the property was intended and the interests of all citizens to enjoy the property. Where an examination of all the relevant interests indicates that certain expressive activity is not compatible with the normal uses of the property, the First Amendment does not require the government to allow that activity.

Public streets and parks are traditional public forums. In such places, government may ban speech such as demonstrations, leafleting and or soapbox speeches for the views that are expressed only subject to strict scrutiny analysis, its most speech-protective test (*Perry Education Association v. Perry Local Educators' Association*, 1983, p. 45). In other words, government must show that the ban advances a compelling government interest and must be the least restrictive means of achieving that end. A viewpoint- neutral regulation of expressive activity conducted in a traditional public forum, however, is subject to time, place, and manner limits and must be narrowly tailored to serve a significant government interest, and leave open ample alternative channels of communication (*Perry Education Association v. Perry Local Educators' Association*, 1983, p. 59).

In contrast, a non-public forum is government-owned property not traditionally open to the public for speech purposes such as a prison or a military base (See *Greer v. Spock*, 1976). Government may ban speakers from non-public forums "based on subject matter and speaker identity so long as the distinctions drawn are reasonable in light of the purpose served by the forum and are viewpoint neutral" (*Cornelius v. NAACP Legal Defense Fund*, 1985, p. 806).

In the third category, designated or limited public forums consist of public property not traditionally open to the public, but the government has "purposefully opened to the public, or some segment of the public, for expressive activity. Once a limited or designated public forum is established, the government can not exclude entities of a similar character to those generally allowed" (*ACLU v. Mote*, 2005, p. 443). Courts, however, require a finding of intent on the government's part, but "intent can be determined in part based on 'policy and practice' and whether the property is a type compatible with expressive activity" (Lidsky, 2011, p. 1984). Accordingly, a government created social media site could be properly categorized as a traditional or limited/designated public forum, even if it is not a physical property like a park or military base. If so, deleting or blocking access to the site based on a commenter's viewpoint could give an individual a First Amendment claim against the government for censoring constitutionally protected expression.

State Action or Under Color of Law

In *Davison v. Loudoun* (2017, p. 15) Judge Cacheris ruled that though the defendant's Facebook page was initially personal, she, nevertheless, operated under the color of law by blocking Davison from commenting on a county controversy because there was a sufficiently close nexus between the content of the page and her official duties. Cacheris cited *Rossignol v. Voorhaar* (2003) as precedent. In *Rossignol*, off-duty law enforcement officers attempted to censor a newspaper that had been critical of their boss by buying all copies of the newspaper on the night before the election (*Davison v. Loudoun*, p. 16). The newspaper sued on First Amendment grounds, but the district court ruled that because the officers' conduct occurred off-duty, they were not acting in an official capacity and, thus, not acting under color of state law (*Davison v. Loudoun*, 2017, p. 16). Reversing, the Fourth Circuit found sufficient connections between the officers' public duties and their off-duty actions (*Davison v. Loudoun*, 2017, p. 16).

"As in *Rossignol*, Defendant's actions here 'arose out of public, not personal, circumstances,'" the judge noted (*Davison v. Loudoun*, 2017, p. 17). Randall created her page site the day before she took office "for the purpose of addressing her new constituents" and later "used it as a tool for governance" to engage in conversations with her constituents (*Davison v. Loudoun*, 2017, p. 18). For example, the judge noted that Randall relied on county resources because her chief of staff helped to create the page and maintain it, and her newsletters, drafted by county employees, provided links promoting her Facebook page (*Davison v. Loudoun*, 2017, p. 19). Randall also tried to "swathe" her page with the "trappings of her office" by, among other efforts, asking her constituents to use the page (*Davison v. Loudoun*, 2017, p. 20).

The banning of Davison, the judge noted, resulted not from a private dispute between Randall and the plaintiff, but arose out criticisms he posted about a debate that had occurred in a town hall meeting. Randall banned Davison because he had criticized her colleagues at that earlier meeting. The judge said by banning Davison, Randall "acted out of a 'censorial motivation' to suppress criticism of county officials related to 'conduct of their official duties'" (*Davison v. Loudoun*, 2017, p. 22). Because Randall operated her Facebook page under color of state law, the First Amendment protected Davison's comments from censorship. Nevertheless, Davison's free speech claims against Randall in her official capacity failed because the page did not adhere to the county's social media policy nor did the county endorse or empower banning Davison, the judge ruled (*Davison v. Loudoun*, 2017, p. 23).

Determine Whether the Defendant Opened a Forum for Speech on a Social Media Site

To determine whether Davison could bring a speech claim against Randall in her individual capacity, the judge asked whether the content of Randall's message was constitutionally protected speech. It was protected, the judge said, because it ranked as criticism of official conduct, speech that "lies at the very 'heart' of the First Amendment" (*Davison v. Loudoun*, 2017, p. 25).

Cacheris ruled that Randall had created a public forum for speech with her Facebook page mostly based on three precedents—*Packingham v. North Carolina* (2017), *Page v. Lexington County School District One* (4th Cir. 2008) and *Cornelius v. NAACP* (1985) and the fact that she "allowed virtually unfettered discussion" and "solicited comments from her constituents" (*Davison v. Loudoun*, 2017, pp. 25–27).

He read *Page* as suggesting that government opens a public forum for speech when it includes chat rooms, bulletin boards in which private viewers are invited to comment. In *Page*, the Court of Appeals for the Fourth Circuit rejected a claim that a school board's website that had advocated opposition to a proposed law was a public forum that was required to allow oppositional voices. In non-controlling dicta, the court (*Davison v. Loudoun*, 2017, p. 25) said,

> Had a linked website somehow transformed the School District's website into a type of "chat room" or "bulletin board" in which private viewers could express opinions or post information, the issue would, of course, be different. But nothing on the School District's website as it existed invited or allowed private persons to publish information or their positions there so as to create a limited public forum.

Cacheris (*Davison v. Loudoun*, 2017, p. 26) said that generally Facebook pages are digital spaces "for the exchange of ideas and information," adding that Randall had "allowed virtually unfettered discussion on" her Facebook page. He invoked *Packingham v. North Carolina* in which the U.S. Supreme Court overturned North Carolina's ban on social media use by sex offenders. In Packingham (*Packingham*, 2017, pp. 1735–1736), the Court noted:

While in the past there may have been difficulty in identifying the most important places (in a spatial sense) for the exchange of views, today the answer is clear. It is cyberspace—the "vast democratic forums of the Internet" in general ... and social media in particular. Seven in ten American adults use at least one Internet social networking service. ... On Facebook, for example, users can debate religion and politics with their friends and neighbors or share vacation photos. On LinkedIn, users can look for work, advertise for employees, or review tips on entrepreneurship. And on Twitter, users can petition their elected representatives and otherwise engage with them in a direct manner. Indeed, Governors in all 50 States and almost every Member of Congress have set up accounts for this purpose.

Cacheris said it was unnecessary to determine whether Randall's social media page was a traditional, limited or non-public forum because the record demonstrated that Randall "engaged in viewpoint discrimination by banning plaintiff from her Facebook. Viewpoint discrimination is 'prohibited in all forums'" (*Davison v. Loudoun*, 2017, p. 27; *Byrne v. Rutledge*, 2010, p. 54, n. 8). Ultimately, Davison won only declaratory relief: "By prohibiting plaintiff from participating in her online forum because she took offense at his claim that her colleagues in the county government had acted unethically, defendant committed a cardinal sin under the First Amendment" (*Davison v. Loudoun*, pp. 29–30).

In contrast, in a related ruling, *Davison v. Plowman*, Davison lost his First Amendment claim against the Loudon County Commonwealth's Attorney Office because his comment did not comport with the county's social media comments policy. The county reserved the right to remove comments that were "clearly off topic" (*Davison v. Plowman*, 2017, p. 14). The terms of the policy, Cacheris ruled, created a limited public forum—"one created for a limited purpose such as use by certain groups ... or for the discussion of certain subjects" (*Davison v. Plowman*, 2017, p. 12). Under the public forum doctrine, when restricted speech "falls outside the bounds of the designated forum, the Court need determine only whether the speech restriction applied is viewpoint neutral and reasonable in light of the purpose of the forum" (*Davison v. Plowman*, 2017, p. 13). The court ruled that the county did not violate Davison's First Amendment rights by excising the comments because the comments "did not comport with the purpose of the forum, and the restriction justifying its removal was both viewpoint neutral and reasonably related to the purpose of the form" (*Davison v. Plowman*, 2017, p. 16).

Applying Davison to Knight First Amendment Institute at Columbia University v. Trump

Has Trump operated his privately owned account under the color of law? There is abundant evidence to show that he has. As in *Rossignol* and *Davison v. Loudoun*, Trump has used his Twitter account as "a tool of governance" (*Davison v. Loudoun*, 2017, p. 18). The Knight First Amendment Institute notes several actions, including the fact that the account is registered to (i) Donald J. Trump, "45th President of the United States of America, Washington, D.C."; (ii) "the header photograph has shown images of President Trump performing his official duties, such as making a speech to the Department of Energy, flanked by Vice President Mike Pence and Secretary of Energy Rick Perry" (*Brief for the Knight First Amendment Institute*, 2017, p. 13); (iii) "his aides have made clear that they consider statements published on @realDonaldTrump to be official statements of the President"; (iv) "The White House social media director, Dan Scavino, promotes @realDonaldTrump, @POTUS, and @WhiteHouse equally as channels through which "President Donald J. Trump … communicat[es] directly with you, the American people!" and (v) foreign leaders have responded publicly to challenge his tweeted policy announcements (*Brief for the Knight First Amendment Institute*, 2017, p. 15).

Moreover, the Ninth Circuit Court of Appeals, noted in a ruling about the president's power to control immigration, that Trump's tweets are composed of "official statements" when it relied on one tweet about the President's travel ban (*Hawai'i v. Trump*, pp. 48–49, n. 14). The Ninth Circuit ruling would appear to be an indirect rejoinder to the Justice Department's argument that "the fact that the President may announce the 'actions of the state' through his Twitter account does not mean that all actions related to that account are attributable to the state" (*Memorandum of Law in Support of Summary Judgment*, 2017, p. 21). *Hawai'i v. Trump* suggests that it is sufficient that some of the tweets can be reasonably understood to voice official positions and policy.

Have the plaintiffs engaged in protected speech? Undoubtedly, yes. Trump blocked the six plaintiffs because they commented on his policies. Their comments are speech deserving the strongest constitutional protection—political speech. For example, Brandon Neely, a Houston, Texas, police officer was blocked after he tweeted in response to Trump's touting, "Congratulations! First new Coal Mine of Trump Era Opens in Pennsylvania." Neely said, "Congrats and now black lung won't be covered under #TrumpCare" (*Brief for the Knight First Amendment Institute*, 2017, p. 21).

Did Trump open a forum for speech on his Twitter account? By the standard set by *Davison*, clearly he has. The account is interactive. Trump has invited anyone to post on his account even though Twitter provides privacy and safety settings to limit access ("How to protect and unprotect your tweets," 2017).

The Knight First Amendment Institute notes,

> The @realDonaldTrump account is accessible to the public at large without
> regard to political affiliation or any other limiting criteria. President Trump has
> not "protected" his tweets, and anyone who wants to follow the account can
> do so. He has not issued any rule or statement purporting to limit (by form or
> subject matter) the speech of those who reply to his tweets. The account has 33
> million followers—14 million more than @POTUS and 19 million more than @
> WhiteHouse. "The only users who cannot follow @realDonaldTrump are those
> whom the President and/or his aides have blocked." (*Brief for the Knight First
> Amendment Institute*, p. 13)

The Justice Department's response to that argument is meritless and
strains credibility. It blames the technology and policy of Twitter as though
we are to believe that Trump has no alternative but to use Twitter. "[Since
2009] his use of the account has been governed by Twitter's own structural
limitations; any features he may or may not use are created by Twitter and
shared by every other user" (*Memorandum of Law in Support of Motion for
Summary Judgment*, p. 20). As noted above, Twitter account owners can
limit access by using privacy settings.

Clearly, Twitter is property that is more than merely compatible with
expressive activity; its sole purpose for users is to share their thoughts with
others. Weighing Trump's Twitter content—statements about his policies
and views on public controversies and individuals—and how foreign heads
of states and the Ninth Circuit perceive the status of the president's tweets,
Trump has created a limited purpose forum for discussion of certain subjects
for anyone, except those he disagrees with, based on practice. The subject
matter would appear to be anything he tweets about.

Unlike the defendant in *Davison v. Plowman*, Trump cannot invoke a
viewpoint-neutral censorship policy. (*Davison v. Plowman*, 2017, p. 14).
There appears to be no such policy and Knight First Amendment plaintiffs
did not use profanity nor were there tweets clearly off target.

Accordingly, by excluding speakers who fall within the class to which
the limited purpose public forum has been created, a restriction "based on
the content of the speech must satisfy strict scrutiny, that is, the restriction
must be narrowly tailored to serve a compelling government interest" (*Pleasant
Grove City v. Summum*, 2009, p. 1132). The Justice Department has
not identified a narrowly tailored and compelling government interest that
justifies blocking the Knight First Amendment Institute plaintiffs. The government's response, as noted above, is that Trump's use of the account is
protected under the government speech doctrine (*Memorandum of Law in
Support of Motion for Summary Judgment*, p. 22).

Presidential Records Act

Trump also argues, among other points, that his personal ownership of his Twitter account exempts him from complying with the Presidential Records Act (PRA) Cushing, 2017). The PRA, passed in 1978, "changed the legal ownership of presidential records from private to public and established a new statutory structure under which Presidents [and Vice President] must manage their records" (National Archives, 2017). Consequently, the Twitter account's original personal ownership status is hardly dispositive on whether Trump can delete tweets that arguably should be property of the people.

The success of the plaintiffs' case, it seems, hinges on the question of presidential immunity. The Justice Department argued that the President's compliance with the PRA cannot be reviewed by the judicial branch because such review "would substantially upset Congress' carefully crafted balance of presidential control of records creation, management, and disposal during the President's term of office" (*Memorandum of Law in Support of Motion to Dismiss, Citizens for Responsibility and Ethics*, 2017, p. 12). The quote comes from *Armstrong v. Bush* (1991, p. 290), also known as *Armstrong* I, and Justice places a great deal of reliance on the precedential value of the ruling. It does acknowledge, however, that subsequent rulings on the PRA can be read to undercut claims of immunity from judicial review, but those rulings are "incorrectly decided, distinguishable, or both," Justice contends (*Memorandum of Law in Support of Motion to Dismiss, Citizens for Responsibility and Ethics*, p. 27).

Armstrong I concerned emails created by the Reagan and Bush White Houses. The plaintiffs argued that materials stored on the National Security Council computer system during the last two weeks of the Reagan Administration could not be erased under the PRA without the approval of the Archivist of the U.S. (*Armstrong*, 1991, p. 284). The court in *Armstrong* I said, "permitting judicial review of the President's compliance with the PRA would upset the intricate statutory scheme Congress carefully drafted to keep in equipoise important competing political and constitutional concerns. We therefore hold that the PRA is one of the rare statutes that does impliedly preclude judicial review" (*Armstrong*, 1991, p. 290).

In contrast, the same court in *Armstrong* II said the limited scope of judicial review under the PRA as decided in *Armstrong* I, "does not stand for the unequivocal proposition that all decisions made pursuant to the PRA are immune from judicial review" (*Armstrong v. Executive Office of the President*, 1993, p. 1293). In *Armstrong* II, the U.S. Court of Appeals for the D.C. Circuit noted, "We did not hold in *Armstrong* I that the President could designate any material he wishes as presidential records, and thereby exercise 'virtually complete control' over it, notwithstanding the fact that the material does not meet the definition of 'presidential records' in the PRA" (*Armstrong v. Executive Office of the President*, 1993, pp. 1293–1294).

Six years later in *Citizens for Ethical Responsibility and Ethics in Washington v. Cheney*, a U.S. District Court Judge said *Armstrong I* foreclosed "judicial review of creation, management, and disposal decisions" and not "the initial classification of existing materials" (*Cheney*, 2009, p. 214). Quoting *Armstrong I*, the judge in *Cheney* explained that "creation" "refers to the determination to *make* a record documenting presidential activities"; management "describes the day-to-day process by which presidential records are maintained"; and disposal was defined by statute. "*But guidelines describing which existing materials will be treated as presidential records in the first place are subject to judicial review* [emphasis added]" (*Cheney*, 2009, p. 214). That is precisely how the plaintiffs interpret the line of rulings starting with *Armstrong I*. CREW and the National Archive argue that by destroying tweets and electronic messaging apps, Trump is deciding which existing materials will be treated as presidential records.

Justice, however, argues that *CREW v Cheney* incorrectly applied *Armstrong II*, noting that the current action does not raise an issue of Freedom of Information Act authority.

> The exception recognized in *Armstrong II* was "limited," "narrow" and "clearly defined" ... In other words, the *Armstrong II* holding only applies when a FOIA plaintiff is contending that he did not obtain documents to which FOIA entitles him because the President wrongfully classified them as presidential records. As to materials that are presidential records, and that are not subject to FOIA during the President's time in office, both *Armstrong I* and *Armstrong II* make abundantly clear that Congress left it to the President to comply with the statute, absent judicial intervention. (*Memorandum of Law in Support of Motion to Dismiss, Citizens for Responsibility and Ethics*, pp. 27–28)

Perhaps Congress will resolve the matter. In June 2017, Rep. Mike Quigley (D-Ill.) introduced the COVFEFE Act to classify presidential social media posts and tweets as presidential records.

> President Trump's frequent, unfiltered use of his personal Twitter account as a means of official communication is unprecedented. If the President is going to take to social media to make sudden public policy proclamations, we must ensure that these statements are documented and preserved for future reference. Tweets are powerful, and the President must be held accountable for every post (Press Release, 2017).

Honest Ads Act

Though there had been a great deal of news coverage about Russian-linked fake news designed to sow dissension and misinformation during the 2016 election campaign (See Timberg, 2016), confirmation of the existence of Russian-paid political ads on the social media sites did not surface until September 2017. In a blog post, Facebook Chief Security Officer Alex Stamos (2017) announced, "we have found approximately $100,000 in ad spending from June of 2015 to May of 2017—associated with roughly 3,000 ads—that was connected to about 470 inauthentic accounts and Pages in violation of our policies" linked to Russians.

Though disturbing to many, no law prohibited foreigners from buying such ads. In general, the Bipartisan Campaign Reform Act of 2002 (BCRA) bars foreign nationals from donating money or expertise to election campaign groups, committees and candidates. BCRA, however, "does not restrain foreign nationals from speaking out about issues or spending money to advocate their views about issues. It restrains them only from a certain form of expressive activity closely tied to the voting process—providing money for a candidate or political party or spending money in order to expressly advocate for or against the election of a candidate" (*Bluman v. FEC*, 2012, p. 290). Consequently, the online Russian-finance ads and fake news, which take positions on political and social issues, are not banned under the BCRA.

The proposed Honest Ads Act ("H.R.4077-Honest Ads Act") is designed to shore up that gap and the absence of language covering online advertisements. It would mandate that Internet companies reveal the identities and content of advertisements related to elections or campaigns, require websites with at least 50 million monthly viewers to maintain a public list of any organization or individual who spends at least $500 in election-related ads during an election cycle, and political ads addressing issues of national importance.

The bill has its critics. Eric Wang (2017), a senior fellow with the Institute for Free Speech, argues,

> At a general but very pervasive level, [the proposed bill] would regulate online political speech, pure and simple. The scope of regulated content would include not only speech about elections and candidates, but also speech about legislative and policy issues. In other words, the bill would regulate speech that is at the core of the First Amendment's protections.

TechFreedom President Berin Szóka also voiced concerns about the constitutionality of requiring registration of ads addressing national issues of public importance, raised doubts that a law that regulates broadcasting can be constitutional when applied to the Internet because cyberspace enjoys full First

Amendment protection when broadcasting does not and argued that the $500 spending threshold "will obviously chill the use of the Internet as a cost-effective way to test potentially delicate messages" (TechFreedom, 2017). But any constitutional challenge to the Honest Ads Act would have to address the ruling in *Delaware Strong Families v. Atty. Gen. of Delaware* (2015) in which the U.S. Court of Appeals for the Third Circuit upheld the constitutionality of the Delaware Elections Disclosure Act (2013). The Delaware Elections Disclosure Act—which in many aspects is similar to the proposed Honest Ads Act and its precursor, the BCRA—requires disclosure of donors who spend *more than $500* for an election ad that refers to a candidate [emphasis added] and distributed to the relevant voters "30 days before a primary election ... or 60 days before a general election" (*Delaware Strong Families v. Atty. Gen. of Delaware*, 2015, p. 307). The court used the BCRA disclosure requirements as an analogue to the Delaware disclosure requirements. Similarly, it is reasonable to conclude that BCRA is analogous to the proposed Honest Ads Act with regards to determining the constitutionality of its disclosure requirements.

Delaware Strong Families, a Religious Right group, created a Voters Guide that it intended to distribute via the Internet, and argued that the state elections disclosure law was unconstitutional. Prior to the 2013 law, the group posted a voters guide without disclosing its donors and the guide mentioned candidates by name. A federal district court enjoined the statute. The federal trial court judge said that the relationship between the statute's purpose and the limitations it placed on free speech was "too tenuous" (*Delaware Strong Families v. Biden*, 2014, p. 395). The U.S. Court of Appeals for the Third Circuit reversed.

In its analysis, the Third Circuit reviewed the precedents on regulating election campaign communication. *Buckley v. Valeo* established the distinction between "express advocacy" and "issue advocacy" election communication, the court noted. "The former encompasses 'communications that expressly advocate the election or defeat of a clearly identified candidate,' while the latter are communications that seek to impact voter choice by focusing on specific issues (*Delaware Strong Families*, 2015, p. 308). Generally, issue advocacy would be constitutionally protected speech, while express advocacy would not. The distinction, however, is not rigid, the court said citing *McConnell v. FEC* (*Delaware Strong Families*, 2015, p. 308).

The court determined that the Delaware statute implicated *issue advocacy* yet it implied exacting scrutiny to test its constitutionality. Under exacting scrutiny analysis, government must show a substantial relationship between a government-imposed limitation on a constitutional right and a sufficiently important governmental interest (*Delaware Strong Families*, 2015, p. 309). The Delaware statute, the court said, served a sufficiently important government interest by aiding voters by identifying financial donors and helping voters to make informed decisions. "Providing information to the electorate is vital to the efficient functioning of the marketplace of ideas, and thus to advancing the democratic objectives underlying the First Amendment" (*Delaware Strong Families*, 2015, pp. 309–310).

Delaware Strong Families argued that no substantial relationship existed between the law's goal and the $500 threshold or the type of media covered. The court, however, disagreed citing *Buckley* in which the U.S. Supreme Court said, "that deciding where to locate a monetary threshold 'is necessarily a judgmental decision, best left … to congressional discretion' and determined that the thresholds presented were not 'wholly without rationality'" (*Delaware Strong Families*, 2015, pp. 309–310). The state law exceeded the scope of BCRA to include "television, radio, newspaper or other periodical, sign, Internet, mail or telephone."

The court, however, ruled that the state law was sufficiently tailored to meet the state's goal primarily because the inclusion of non-broadcast media reflected the media used by Delaware political candidates. "Had the legislature limited 'electioneering communication' to media not actually utilized in Delaware elections, the disclosure requirements would fail to serve the State's interest in a well-informed electorate thereby resulting in a weaker fit between the two" (Delaware Strong Families, 2015, p. 311).

The U.S. Supreme Court declined to review the ruling, with only Justice Clarence Thomas dissenting (*Delaware Strong Families v. Denn*, 2016). Thus, *Delaware Strong Families* suggests that controversial language in the Honest Ads legislation—the inclusion of "satellite, paid Internet" as "public communication" (S. 1989-Honest Ads Act, 2017–2018)—and targeting communications about "a national legislative issue of public importance" (S. 1989-Honest Ads Act, 2017–2018)—would survive exact scrutiny analysis.

Is the Act likely to be effective? Rutgers University Law Professor Ellen Goodman and third-year law student Lyndsey Wajert predict that,

> The Honest Ads Act represents a promising effort to address the lack of transparency surrounding political ads on the Internet. … The bill will have only marginal impact—the extent of which will depend heavily on the will of the online platforms themselves—but impact at the edges can begin to build a culture of disclosure. Questions remain about what specifically constitutes political advertisements, whether the types of communications Russian nationals apparently supported on social media sites will be captured by the bill, how online communications will change to avoid capture, and how social media companies will cooperate in a way that leads to more disclosure. (Goodman & Wajert 2017, p. 7)

Conclusion

This chapter examined the merits of two lawsuits and one proposed federal statute, all responses to the use of social media for political communication during the 2016 presidential election campaign and the first year of the Trump presidency. The lawsuits—*Knight First Amendment Institute at Columbia University v. Trump* and *Citizens for Responsibility and Ethics in Washington v. Trump*—challenge the president's deletion of tweets from his personal Twitter account, @realdonaldtrump, on constitutional and federal statutory grounds.

At stake in *Knight First Amendment Institute at Columbia University v. Trump* are the continued development of member-constituent communications and the expansion of democratic discourse on the Internet. A loss in the courtroom for Trump will be a victory for representative democracy as Trump and other elected officials will no longer be able to argue that the private online accounts that they use to communicate their thoughts about government policy issues are beyond the First Amendment's reach. Nor will elected officials be allowed to delete users' tweets merely because they disagree with users' views.

Likewise, if *Citizens for Responsibility and Ethics in Washington* prevails in its legal action against Trump, the public's ability to hold the president accountable will be bolstered by expanding the law's reach to social media. If Trump prevails, his deleted tweets, many of which shed light on issues and controversies of historic significance, are likely to be lost from the scrutiny of scholars, public commentators, legislators and public policymakers. There are, however, private efforts such as TrumpTwitterArchive.com attempting to fill in the gap.[4]

The proposed federal Honest Ads Act's purpose is to shine a light of transparency on election campaign ads buyers in an effort to thwart foreign influence in our elections. Yet, it is not clear whether the bill will promote free speech and democratic discourse on social media despite the strong possibility that it is likely to withstand judicial scrutiny. Arguably, the bill is paternalistic and anti-democratic because it represents Congress's mistrust of voters' abilities to intelligently sort out the truth in the online marketplace of ideas (See Mill, 1863, p. 36). Nevertheless the proposed law appears constitutionally sound as the U.S. Supreme Court has long considered "disclosure requirements—certainly in most applications" as "the least restrictive means of curbing the evils of campaign ignorance and corruption that Congress found to exist" (*Buckley v. Valeo*, 1976, p. 68).

Notes

1. On June 5, 2018, the White House said it planned to appeal a federal judge's ruling in the previous month that President Trump's practice of blocking critics from his Twitter account violated the First Amendment. Knight First Amendment Institute v. Trump, 1:17 Civ. 05205 (S.D.N.Y, 2018). Retrieved from https://knightcolumbia.org/sites/default/files/content/Cases/Wikimedia/2018.05.23%20Order%20on%20motions%20for%20summary%20judgment.pdf.
2. The acronym COVFEFE is a pun. It exploits the mistyping of the word "coverage" found in one of Trump's tweets (see Uchill, 2017).
3. See also *Brief of Amici Curiae First Amendment Legal* 5 (2017)
4. *Davison v. Loudoun County Board of Supervisors* (2017), provides precedent for the proposition that the existence of an alternative database such as Trump Twitter does not undercut the plaintiffs' First Amendment case: "The Court cannot treat a First Amendment violation in this vital, developing forum differently than it would elsewhere simply because technology has made it easier to find alternative channels through which to disseminate one's message."

References

ACLU v. Mote, 423 F. 3d 438, 443 (4th Cir. 2005).

American Historical Association v. National Archives and Records Administration, 516 F. Supp. 2d 90, 93 (2007). Retrieved from https://www.leagle.com/decision/2007606516fsupp2d901598

Armstrong v. Bush, 924 F.2d 282 (D.C. Cir. 1991).

Armstrong v. Executive Office of the President, 1 F.3d 1274, (D.C. Cir. 1993).

Balasubramani, V. (2017, July 27). Politicial can't ban constituent from her official Facebook page—*Davison v. Loudoun County Supervisors. Technology & Marketing Law Blog.* Retrieved from http://blog.ericgoldman.org/archives/2017/07/politician-cant-ban-constituent-from-her-official-facebook-page-davison-v-loudoun-county-supervisors.htm

Bernstein, L. (2017, August 11). First amendment suits pile up against governors who block Facebook, Twitter users. *WJL.com.* Retrieved from http://wjla.com/news/nation-world/lawsuits-pile-up-against-governors-who-block-facebook-Twitter-users

Bluman v. FEC, 2012, 800 F. Supp. 2d 281, 290 (D.D.C. 2011), *aff'd* 132 S. Ct. 1087 (2012).

Brief of Amici Curiae first amendment legal scholars in support of plaintiffs motion for summary judgment, Knight First Amendment Institute at Columbia University v. Trump, 17-cv-5205 (S.D.N.Y. November 6, 2017). Retrieved from http://www.law.georgetown.edu/academics/centers-institutes/constitutional-advocacy-protection/upload/knight-amicus-brief.pdf

Brief for the Knight First Amendment Institute at Columbia University v. Trump, 1:17-cv-05205 (S.D.N.Y. July 11, 2017). Retrieved from https://assets.documentcloud.org/documents/3892179/2017-07-11-Knight-Institute-Trump-Twitter.pdf

Buckley v. Valeo, 421 U.S. 1 (1976).

Byrne v. Rutledge, 623 F.3d 46 (2d Cir. 2010). Retrieved from https://scholar.google.com/scholar_case?case=13016790165176712402&q=Byrne+v.+Rutledge++623+f.3d+46+2010&hl=en&as_sdt=8006

Caplan, L. (2017, October 11). Should Facebook and Twitter be regulated under the first amendment. *Wired*. Retrieved from https://www.wired.com/story/should-facebook-and-Twitter-be-regulated-under-the-first-amendment/

Citizens for Responsibility and Ethics v. Trump, 1:17-cv-01228 (June 22, 2017 Retrieved from https://s3.amazonaws.com/storage.citizensforethics.org/wp-content/uploads/2017/06/22122345/Complaint.pdf

Cornelius v. NAACP, 473 U.S. 788, 802 (1985).

Crew v. Cheney, 593 F. Supp.2d 194 (2009). Retrieved from https://scholar.google.com/scholar_case?case=15992727367940037028q=CITIZENS+FOR+RESPONSIBILITY+AND+ETHICS+v.+Cheney,+593+F.+Supp.+2d+194+(D.C.+2009)&hl=en&as_sdt=8003&as_ylo=2008&as_yhi=2010

Cushing, T. (2017, October 11). DOJ says No One has the Right to Question the Administration's Handling of Records, Not Even the Courts. *Techdirt.com*. Retrieved from https://www.techdirt.com/articles/20171010/13005838382/doj-says-no-one-has-any-right-to-question-adminstrations-handling-records-not-even-courts.shtml

Daily News. (2016, May 31). He made the real Donald Trump into @realDonaldTrump on Twitter. *Los Angeles Daily News.* Retrieved from http://www.dailynews.com/2016/05/31/he-made-the-real-donald-trump-into-realdonaldtrump-on-Twitter/

Davison v. Loudoun County Board of Supervisors, 2017 WL 3158389 (E.D. Va. July 25, 2017), appeal docketed, No. 17 2002 (4th Cir. Aug. 29, 2017). Retrieved from https://cases.justia.com/federal/district-courts/virginia/vaedce/1:2016cv00932/348006/132/0.pdf?ts=1501081939

Davison v. Plowman, 1:16cv180 (JCC/IDD) (E.D. Va. March 28, 2017). Retrieved from https://docs.justia.com/cases/federal/district-courts/virginia/vaedce/1:2016cv00180/339125/42

Delaware Strong Families v. Atty. Gen. of Delaware, 793 F.3d 304 (2015).

Delaware Strong Families v. Biden, 34 F.Supp.3d 381 (Del. 2014).

Delaware Strong Families v. Denn, 136 S.Ct. 2376 (2016). Retrieved from https://scholar.google.com/scholar_case?case=16321964903621380919&q=buckley+v.+valeo+express+advocacy+issue+advocacy&hl=en&as_sdt=8003&as_ylo=2016

Goodman, E. P., & Wajert, L. (November 2, 2017). The Honest Ads Act won't end social media disinformation, but it's a start. Retrieved from SSRN: https://ssrn.com/abstract=3064451

Greer v. Spock, 424 U.S. 828 (1976).

Hawai'i v. Trump, 17–15589 (9th Cir. 2017). Retrieved from https://cdn.ca9.uscourts. gov/datastore/opinions/2017/06/12/17-15589.pdf

"How to protect and unprotect your tweets," (2017). *Twitter.com*. Retrieved from https:// help.twitter.com/en/safety-and-security/how-to-make-Twitter-private-and-public

H.R.4077-Honest Ads Act. Retrieved from https://www.congress.gov/bill/115th-congress/house-bill/4077/text

Lidsky, L. B. (2011) Public forum *2.0*. *Boston University Law Review*, (91). Retrieved from http://www.bu.edu/law/journals-archive/bulr/volume91n6/documents/lidsky. pdf

Memorandum of Law in Support of Motion for Summary Judgment, Citizens for Responsibility and Ethics in Washington v. Trump, 1:17-cv-01228-CRC (June 9, 2017). Retrieved from https://s3.amazonaws.com/storage.citizensforethics.org/wp-content/ uploads/2017/01/21142452/2017-06-09-34-MTD.pdf

Memorandum of Law in Support of Motion for Summary Judgment, Knight First Amendment Institute at Columbia University v. Trump, 17-cv-5205 (S.D.N.Y., October 13, 2017). Retrieved from http://www.sdnyblog.com/files/2017/10/2017.10.13-Trump-Brief-re-Twitter-Blocking.pdf

Mill, J. S. *On Liberty*. Boston: Ticknor and Fields (1863).

National Archives. (2017, July 5). Presidential Records Act of 1978. Retrieved from https://www.archives.gov/presidential-libraries/laws/1978-act.html

Packingham v. North Carolina, 137 S. Ct. 1730 (2017).

Perry Education Association v. Perry Local Educators' Association, 460 U.S. 37 (1983).

Pleasant Grove City v. Summum, 129 S.Ct. 1125 (2009).

Presidential Libraries. (2017, July 5). Presidential records act (PRA) of 1978. *National Archives*. Retrieved from https://www.archives.gov/presidential-libraries/laws/1978-act.html

Press Release. (June 12, 2017). Quigley Introduces the COVFEE Act. Retrieved from https://quigley.house.gov/media-center/press-releases/quigley-introduces-covfefe-act

Romm, T. (2017, October 31). Watch: Facebook, Google and Twitter testify to Congress about Russia and the 2016 election. *Recode.Net*. Retrieved from https://www. recode.net/2017/10/31/16570988/watch-live-stream-facebook-google-twitter-russia-trump-2016-presidential-election-senate

Rossignol v. Voorhaar, 316 F. 3d 516 (4th Cir. 2003).

S. 1989-Honest Ads Act-115 Congress. (2017–2018), https://www.congress.gov/ bill/115th-congress/senate-bill/1989/text

Sezzi, P. (2005) *Personal versus private: Presidential records in a legislative context—A bibliographical exploration*. Lanham, MD: Scarecrow Press. Retrieved from https:// books.google.com/books?id=OEy1jkPO-ckC&pg=PR11&dq=presidential+ records+act&hl=en&sa=X&ved=0ahUKEwjD_Mf6v53XAhWBQyYKHT-

nUCfAQ6AEIRTAG#v=onepage&q=presidential%20records%20
act&f=false

Stamos, A. (2017, September 6). An update on Information operations on Facebook. [Web log comment]. Retrieved from https://newsroom.fb.com/news/2017/09/information-operations-update/

Straus, J., & Glassman, M. (2016, May 26). Social media in Congress: The impact of electronic media on member communications. *Congressional Research Service*. Retrieved from https://fas.org/sgp/crs/misc/R44509.pdf

TechFreedom. (2017, October 19). Well-intentioned 'Honest Ads' bill raises serious free speech Concerns. Retrieved from http://techfreedom.org/well-intentioned-honest-ads-bill-raises-serious-free-speech-concerns/

Timberg, C. (2016, November 24). Russian propaganda effort helped spread "fake news" during election, experts say. *Washington Post*. Retrieved from https://www.washingtonpost.com/business/economy/russian-propaganda-effort-helped-spread-fake-news-during-election-experts-say/2016/11/24/793903b6-8a40-4ca9-b712-716af66098fe_story.html?utm_term=.313fd909b93e

Uchill, J. (2017, June 12). COVFEFE Act would make social media a public record. *TheHill.com* Retrieved from http://thehill.com/policy/cybersecurity/337416-covefe-act-would-make-social-media-a-presidential-record

Walker v. Sons of Confederate Veterans, 135 S. Ct. 2239 (2015). Retrieved from https://scholar.google.com/scholar_case?case=14885642386066449353&q=walker+v+texas+division+sons+of+confederate+veterans+inc&hl=en&as_sdt=8003&as_ylo=2013

Wang, E. (November 2017). Analysis of Klobuchar-Warner-McCain internet ads legislation (S. 1989, 115th Cong.). *Institute for Free Speech*. Retrieved from http://www.ifs.org/wp-content/uploads/2017/10/2017-11-01_Legislative-Brief_Federal_S-1989_Honest-Ads-Act.pdf

Contributors

William A. Babcock is Senior Ethics Professor at Southern Illinois University Carbondale's School of Journalism where he is editor of *Gateway Journalism Review*. He has a B.A. from Principia College (English & History), an M.A. from American University (International Communications & West Europe Affairs), and a Ph.D. from SIUC (Journalism and Natural & Environmental Sciences). He is the founding director of the Media Ethics Division of the Association of Education in Journalism and Mass Communication. During the 1990s, he directed the University of Minnesota's Silha Center for the Study of Media Ethics and Law. Formerly the Senior International News Editor (Asia & Latin America) and staff writer at the *Christian Science Monitor*, he is the editor of *Media Accountability: Who Will Watch the Watchdog in the Twitter Age?* (2012) and co-editor of *Controversies in Media Ethics* (2011) and author of several peer review articles.

Mitchell T. Bard is an Assistant Professor, teaching at Iona College's Department of Mass Communication in New Rochelle, New York. He studies how the atomization of the 20th century mass media system has affected news in the 21st century, especially on television and online. He holds a Ph.D. from the University of Wisconsin and a J.D. from the University of Miami School of Law and scholarly research has been published in *Journalism and Mass Communication Quarterly* and *The Journal of Appellate Practice and Process*. He has served as a featured blogger for the *Huffington Post* (2008–2018).

Christopher Benson is an Associate Professor at the Medill School of Journalism, Media, Integrated Marketing Communications at Northwestern University. He earned his B.S. and M.S. degrees in journalism at the University of Illinois and his J.D. at Georgetown University. Benson is co-author with Mamie Till-Mobley of *Death of Innocence: The Story of the Hate Crime That Changed America* (2003), the Robert F. Kennedy Book Award-winning account of the 1955 lynching of Mrs. Till-Mobley's son, Emmett Till. A lawyer, he worked as associate counsel at Johnson Publishing Company. A journalist, he worked at WBMX-FM in Chicago, *Ebony* magazine as it as Washington editor and contributed to *The New York Times*, *The Washington Post*, the *Chicago Tribune* and the *Chicago Sun-Times* and, most recently, written commentary for *The Chicago Reporter* and the *Huffington Post*.

William Brown is a Professor and Research Fellow in the School of Communication and the Arts at Regent University in Virginia Beach, Virginia. He received a Bachelor of Science Degree in Environmental Science from Purdue University, a Masters Degree in Communication Management from the Annenberg School for Communication at the University of Southern California in Los Angeles, and a M.A. Degree and Ph.D. in communication from the University of Southern California. His academic research interests include international media and development communication, celebrity influence, health communication, political communication, and the use of entertainment for social change. His scholarship includes articles published in *The Handbook of Global Health Communication and Development*, *Eastern Africa Journal of Humanities and Sciences*, *Health Communication*, *Journal of Communication and the Journal of Communication and Religion*.

Dianne Bystrom served as the Director of the Carrie Chapman Catt Center for Women and Politics at Iowa State University from July 1996 until her retirement in August 2018. She earned a Ph.D. in communication from the University of Oklahoma. She is the co-author or co-editor of seven books and has contributed chapters to twenty books, including *Gender and Elections: Shaping the Future of American Politics* (2018), *Cracking the Highest Glass Ceiling: A Global Comparison of Women's Campaigns for Executive Office* (2011) and *Anticipating Madame President* (2003). She is a frequent commentator about political and women's issues for state, national, and international media.

June Deery is a Professor of Media Studies at Rensselaer Polytechnic Institute and author of *Consuming Reality: the Commercialization of Factual Entertainment* (2012), *Reality TV* (2015) and co-editor (with Andrea Press) of *Media and Class: TV, Film, and Digital Culture* (2017). Her work examines commercialization, politics, representations of gender and class, and cultural understandings of fact, fiction, and reality. She holds a Ph.D. in literature and philosophy of science from Oxford University and a B.A. in literature from Trinity College, Dublin, Ireland.

Jeffrey Delbert, Assistant Professor of Communication at Lenoir-Rhyne University, Hickory, North Carolina, earned a B.S. in broadcast journalism from The College at Brockport, State College of New York, an M.A. in communication from the same institution, a Ph.D. in communication from the

University of Missouri and a postdoctoral fellowship in Media of the Future from *the* University of Missouri. His research focuses on the intersection of media, politics, and popular culture, exploring how rhetoric influences the public sphere. *His peer-reviewed articles have been published in Speaker & Gavel, Relevant Rhetoric, Argumentation and Advocacy, Human Communication and Presidential Studies Quarterly and he has contributed a chapter to the Praeger handbook of political campaigning in the United States (2016).*

Tao Fu is an Associate Professor of Communication Studies at the University of International Business and Economics, Beijing, China. Fu obtained her Ph.D. in Mass Communication and Media Arts from Southern Illinois University. She has published articles in journals such as the *Chinese Journal of Communication, Information, Communication & Society*, and *China Media Research*. Fu is a contributor to books including *Guide to Key Issues in Mass Media Ethics and Law* (2015), and *Music as a Platform for Political Communication* (2017). She is also a co-editor of the book *Online Courtship: Interpersonal Interactions across Borders* (2015). Fu's research interests include ICTs and social change, and media ethics focusing on artificial intelligence and big data.

Sara Steffes Hansen is Chair and Associate Professor in the Department of Journalism at the University of Wisconsin Oshkosh. She received her B.A. in journalism from the University of Wisconsin-Eau Claire, M.B.A. from the University of Colorado-Denver, and Ph.D. in mass communication from the University of Wisconsin (Madison). She has 15 years of professional experience, including work as a director, manager, and consultant in strategic communication, largely with high-tech and Fortune 500 companies. Her research focuses on brands and social media related to consumer marketing and political image-making, with published work in journals such as *Journal of Marketing Communications, Journal of Interactive Advertising, Journal of Marketing Management, Computer Communications, Journal of Electronic Commerce*, and *Howard Journal of Communications*.

Arthur S. Hayes is an Associate Professor in the Communications & Media Studies Department, Fordham University, in New York. His research focuses on journalism performance, media ethics and news media accountability, and the intersection of media technologies and free expression and privacy law. A former legal affairs journalist with the *American Lawyer*, the *National Law Journal* and the *Wall Street Journal*, he holds a B.A. and M.A. from Fordham University and a J.D. from Quinnipiac Law School. His publications include *Press Critics are the Fifth Estate: Media Watchdogs in America* (2008), *Mass Media Law: The Printing Press to the Internet* (2013) and *Sympathy for the Cyberbully: How the Crusade to Censor Hostile and Offensive Online Speech Abuses Freedom of Expression* (2017).

Melissa A. Johnson is a Professor in the Department of Communication at North Carolina State University. She holds a Ph.D. in mass communication research from the School of Journalism and Mass Communication at the University of North Carolina, Chapel Hill. Her research explores communication concepts in international news, international public relations, ethnic media, and ethnic public relations. She serves on the editorial boards of *The Journal of Public Relations Research, The Howard Journal of Communication,* and *The International Journal of Hispanic Media.* She has authored and co-authored articles published in *Journal of Communication, Public Relations Review, International Communication Gazette, Public Relations Inquiry, Howard Journal of Communications, Visual Communication, Mass Communication & Society and Critical Studies in Mass Communication.* She has contributed chapters to *Sage Cases in Methodology* (2014), *Ethical Issues in International Communication* (2011) and *Companion to Media Studies* (2003, 2006), to name a few. Along with academic experience, she has more than a dozen years of communication practitioner experience. This included positions as vice president of corporate relations for a California bank and director of public relations for a U.S. school of public health. She has also worked in radio broadcasting and agency public relations.

Flora Khoo is a Ph.D. candidate and doctoral fellow in the School of Communication and the Arts at Regent University in Virginia Beach, Virginia. She received a Bachelor of Arts Degree from the National University of Singapore and a Masters Degree in Journalism from Regent University, Virginia Beach, Virginia. Her academic research interests include communication and terrorism, the U.S. presidency and public opinion.

Beth Knobel, an Associate Professor in Fordham University's Department of Communication and Media Studies, won an Emmy Award for her coverage of the 2002 Moscow theater attack and an Edward R. Murrow and Sigma Delta Chi award for her coverage of the 2004 Beslan school siege in North Ossetia, both while working for CBS News. She is the co-author with her CBS News colleague Mike Wallace of *Heat and Light: Advice for the Next Generation of Journalists* (2010) and sole author of *The Watchdog Still Barks: How Accountability Journalism Evolved for the Digital Age* (2018). She earned a BA from Barnard College, and her MA and PhD, both in public policy, from Harvard University.

Shu-Yueh Lee is an Associate Professor in the Department of Journalism at the University of Wisconsin Oshkosh. She received her Ph.D. in communication and information from the University of Tennessee in 2009. Her research focuses on media effects, body image, and the use of new media. Her research articles have been published in journals such as *Communication,*

Culture, and Critique, Journalism & Mass Communication Quarterly, Atlantic Journal of Communication, Journal of Magazine & New Media Research, Computer Communications, and *Journal of Electronic Commerce.*

Laurel Leff is an Associate Professor of Journalism at Northeastern University. She was formerly a reporter for *The Wall Street Journal* and *The Miami Herald* and an editor with *American Lawyer Media Inc.* and *The Hartford Courant.* Leff also is the Stotsky Professor of Jewish Historical and Cultural Studies at Northeastern University, and the associate director of the university's Jewish Studies Program in the College of Social Sciences and Humanities. She is the author of *Buried by The Times: The Holocaust and America's Most Important Newspaper* (2005). Her other scholarly publications include: "Jewish Victims in a Wartime Frame: A Press Portrait of the Nuremberg Trial," a chapter in *From the Protocols of Zion to Holocaust Denial Trials: Challenging The Media, the Law and The Academy* (2006); "News of the Holocaust: Why FDR Didn't Tell and the Press Didn't Ask," *Hakirah: A Journal of Jewish and Ethnic Studies*; "'Liberated by the Yanks': The Holocaust as An American Story in Postwar News Articles," *Journal of Ecumenical Studies.* Leff holds a MA in the study of law from Yale University and a MA in communications from the University of Miami. She received an A.B. from Princeton University with a major in the Woodrow Wilson School of Public and International Affairs.

Kimberly Nelson is a master's degree student in journalism and mass communication at Iowa State University, where she also serves as a graduate research and teaching assistant in the Greenlee School of Journalism and Communication. Her research interests include science communication and media studies.

John H. Parmelee, a Professor and Chair in the Department of Communication at the University of North Florida, is the author of *Politics and the Twitter Revolution: How Tweets Influence the Relationship between Political Leaders and the Public (2012)* and *Meet the Candidate Videos* (2003). He has published research articles in *Political Communication, New Media & Society, Communication Studies, Communication Quarterly, Telematics and Informatics, Journal of Mixed Methods Research, Encyclopedia of Political Communication, Central European Journal of Communication, Atlantic Journal of Communication* and *Florida Communication Journal.* Parmelee holds an MS from Columbia University Graduate School of Journalism and a Ph.D. from the University of Florida, Gainesville.

Victor Pickard is an Associate Professor in the Annenberg School for Communication at the University of Pennsylvania. Previously he worked on media policy in Washington, D.C., as a Senior Research Fellow at the media reform organization Free Press and the public policy think tank the New America Foundation. His work has been published in a number of scholarly journals, including the *Journal of Communication*; *Global Media and Communication*; *International Journal of Communication*; *Media, Culture & Society*; *Communication, Culture & Critique*; *New Media and Society*; *Journal of Communication Inquiry*; *Newspaper Research Journal*; *Journal of Internet Law*; *International Journal of Communication Law and Policy*; and *Critical Studies in Media Communication*. With Robert McChesney, he is the co-editor of the book *Will the Last Reporter Please Turn out the Lights* (2011), and the author of *America's Battle for Media Democracy* (2014).

Héctor Rendón is a Research Scholar in the Laboratory for Analytic Sciences at North Carolina State University. His research focuses on the intersection of communication, media coverage of minorities, and data analytics. He mostly studies issues related to international communication, ethnic and inter-cultural communication, media reliability, social issues, and public policy. He holds a Ph.D. in communication, rhetoric, and digital media from NC State, an MA in digital media from the Hochschule für Künste Bremen in Germany and a BA in communication from the National Autonomous University of Mexico. In addition, he has studied issues related to U.S. Policy in Latin America, Data Journalism, and Public Opinion Analysis. His work has been published by several international journals and publishers.

Nataliya Roman is an Assistant Professor in the Communications Department of the University of Northern Florida. She earned her M.A. and Ph.D. in mass communications at the University of Florida and was a Fulbright Scholar (2009–2011). A former journalist and documentary filmmaker, Roman worked for Inter TV Channel, National Television News (NTN) and Voice of America.

Mira Sotirovic is an Associate Professor and Karin and Folke Dovring Scholar in Propaganda in the Department of Journalism at the University of Illinois, Urbana-Champaign. She received her Ph.D. in mass communications from the University of Wisconsin, Madison. Her research interests are in news media effects on how people think and perceive social issues, and how those perceptions may affect support for social policies. She has published chapters in books such as the *Handbook of Political Communication Research* and articles in scholarly journals such as *Journal of Communication, Mass Communication and Society* and others.

Jason Turcotte, an Assistant Professor in Communication at California State Polytechnic University, Pomona, holds a Ph.D. in media & public affairs from Louisiana State University, an M.A. in media, culture, and communication with an emphasis in political and persuasive communication from

New York University (2010) and a B.A. in communication and political science from Roger Williams University. His research broadly concerns news and democracy. He examines how the news media cover campaigns and elections, and explores the implications of news coverage and strategic political communication for knowledge, citizenship, and political engagement. His research agenda is also focused on news trust in the digital era and unpacking how news norms and processes shape key campaign events including electoral debates and polling. His work has appeared in *Journalism & Mass Communication Quarterly, Mass Communication & Society, Journalism Practice, PS: Political Science & Politics, Political Research Quarterly, Communication Research Reports, Social Science Quarterly,* and the *Journal of Computer-Mediated Communication.*

Index

POLITICAL COMMUNICATION

FRONTIERS IN

General Editors
Mitchell S. McKinney and Mary E. Stuckey

At the heart of how citizens, governments, and the media interact ⟨...⟩ communication process, a process that is undergoing tremendous ⟨...⟩ as we embrace a new millennium. Never has there been a tim⟨...⟩ confronting the complexity of these evolving relationships ⟨...⟩ important to the maintenance of civil society. This series seeks bo⟨...⟩ advance the understanding of this process from multiple perspectiv⟨...⟩ it occurs in both institutionalized and non-institutionalized ⟨...⟩ settings. While works that provide new perspectives on tradition⟨...⟩ communication questions are welcome, the series also encou⟨...⟩ submission of manuscripts that take an innovative approach t⟨...⟩ communication, which seek to broaden the frontiers of study to i⟨...⟩ critical and cultural dimensions of study as well as scientific and ⟨...⟩ frontiers.

For more information or to submit material for consideration, c⟨...⟩

> Mitchell S. McKinney: McKinneyM@missouri.edu
> Mary E. Stuckey: mes519@psu.edu

To order other books in this series, please contact our Cu⟨...⟩ Department:

> (800) 770-LANG (within the U.S.)
> (212) 647-7706 (outside the U.S.)
> (212) 647-7707 FAX

Or browse online by series:
> WWW.PETERLANG.COM